The New European Diasporas

The New European Diasporas

National Minorities and Conflict in Eastern Europe

Michael Mandelbaum, Editor

COUNCIL ON FOREIGN RELATIONS PRESS
NEW YORK

Library of Congress Cataloging-in-Publication Data

The New European Diasporas: National minorities and conflict
   in Eastern Europe / edited by Michael Mandelbaum.
        p.   cm.
      Three of the four chapters were originally presented as papers at a
        conference entitled The Diasporas of Eastern Europe, which was held
        May 18–19, 1998, Washington, D.C.
      Includes bibliographical references and index.
      Contents: Partitioned nation : Hungarian minorities in Central Europe /
        Bennett Kovrig—All quiet on the Russian front? : Russia, its neighbors,
        and the Russian diaspora / Aurel Braun—Diaspora, or, The dangers of
        disunification? : putting the "Serbian model" into perspective / Susan L.
        Woodward—The Albanian national question / Elez Biberaj.
      ISBN 0-87609-257-1 (alk. paper)
        1. Europe, Eastern—Ethnic relations—Congresses. 2. Minorities—
      Europe, Eastern—Congresses. 3. Nationalism—Europe, Eastern—
      Congresses. I. Mandelbaum, Michael.

DJK26.N48 2000
305.8'0094—dc21   00-021642

Contents

Foreword   vii

Acknowledgments   ix

Introduction   1
Michael Mandelbaum

1. Partitioned Nation: Hungarian Minorities in
   Central Europe   19
   Bennett Kovrig

2. All Quiet on the Russian Front? Russia, Its Neighbors,
   and the Russian Diaspora   81
   Aurel Braun

3. Diaspora, or the Dangers of Disunification? Putting
   the "Serbian Model" into Perspective   159
   Susan L. Woodward

4. The Albanian National Question: The Challenges of
   Autonomy, Independence, and Separatism   214
   Elez Biberaj

Conclusion   289
Michael Mandelbaum

About the Authors   310

Index   313

Foreword

THE MOST important international event of the last year of the twentieth century, NATO's war in Yugoslavia, had its origins in a dispute over borders between two national groups—Serbs and Albanians. They had lived together, if uneasily, for most of the twentieth century as part of a multinational state: Yugoslavia. When it collapsed and borders were redrawn, the Kosovar Albanians were dissatisfied at remaining part of the Serb-dominated lesser Yugoslavia. They rebelled, triggering a civil war into which NATO intervened in March 1999.

The circumstances that produced the initial fighting between Serbs and Albanians were not unique. The upheavals in Europe in the course of the century, beginning with the Balkan war that led to the establishment of an independent Albanian state and included Kosovo in Serbia in 1913, have left in their wake a series of national minorities in Eastern Europe.

These "new diasporas" have been created by the movement not of people but of borders. The interaction of these minorities, the new states in which they are located, and the homeland states where their conationals predominate and from which they have been separated is the leading cause of large-scale conflict in the wake of the collapse of communism. The politics of four of these European "national triads" is the subject of this book.

Hungary sided with Germany in World War II in an unsuccessful attempt to reincorporate Hungarians who had been assigned to other countries by the post–World War I settlement. The status of these Hungarian diasporas remains today, as Bennett Kovrig describes in chapter 1, a major issue for Hungary. The Russian diaspora is the largest and potentially the most explosive in Eastern Europe. An estimated 25 million ethnic Russians live outside the borders of the Russian Federation. How they have adapted to the status of national minorities thrust upon them by the dissolution of the Soviet Union is the subject of chapter 2 by Aurel Braun.

Post–Cold War violence on the largest scale has emerged from the politics of the Serb diasporas following the breakup of Yugoslavia, a politics recounted in chapter 3 by Susan L. Woodward. Albania is the least known of the region's divided nations. As the twentieth century's last decade ended, its diasporas in the Serb-dominated Yugoslav province of Kosovo and in independent Macedonia were involved in actual and potential violence, the causes and consequences of which are analyzed in chapter 4 by Elez Biberaj.

At the heart of the unrest occasioned by these national triads are the changing rules for determining borders, which are described by Michael Mandelbaum in his introduction. In his conclusion, he surveys the methods available for mitigating the conflict to which internal minorities all too often give rise.

Lawrence J. Korb
Maurice R. Greenberg Chair,
Director of Studies
Council on Foreign Relations
December 1999

Acknowledgments

THIS VOLUME is part of the Council on Foreign Relations Project on East-West Relations, which is supported by the Carnegie Corporation of New York. Three of the chapters in this volume were presented as papers at a symposium titled "The New Diasporas of Eastern Europe" held on May 18 and 19, 1998, in Washington, D.C. The views expressed are those of the authors alone.

The editor is grateful to all those who attended the conference as well as to those involved in the production of this volume, especially Tracy Dunn, Mark Patton, Miranda Kobritz, Patricia Dorff, and Shane Smith.

Introduction

MICHAEL MANDELBAUM

I N 1948, looking back 100 years, the distinguished historian Lewis
Namier wrote, "The year 1848 marks, for good or evil, the opening
of the era of linguistic nationalisms shaping mass personalities and
producing their inevitable conflicts." He went on to describe the nature
of those conflicts:

> a nation which bases its unity on language cannot easily renounce groups
> of co-nationals intermingled with those of the neighboring nation; and an
> alien minority within the State, or an intensely coveted *terra irredenta*, are
> both likely to distort the life of the nation. . . . The alien community within
> the disputed borderland, hostile to the State and possibly plotting against
> it, provokes repressions . . . while fellow-countrymen across the border
> awaiting liberation keep up international tensions. . . .[1]

Fifty years after Namier wrote, the conflicts he identified persisted
because the conditions that gave rise to them endured. These conditions
and the resulting conflicts are the subject of this book.

The national principle as the basis for statehood has triumphed. The
belief that national groups—generally defined by common language, or
religion, or ethnicity, or sense of political community, or some combination of them—should have their own states has embedded itself
in the thinking of peoples everywhere and to a great extent in international practice. But few countries consist entirely of one nation; not
every self-described nation has its own state; and not every nation is
gathered into a single state: Some are distributed among several.

The difficulties to which the mismatch between state and nation
has given rise are not minor. In the wake of the Cold War and of the

communist era in Europe, the major cause of deadly violence on a large scale was not, as it had been for most of the modern era, the drive for riches, territory, glory, or all three. Nor did the greatest threat to peace come from the ambitions of megalomaniacal dictators, as during the first half of the twentieth century, or from the conflict of political and economic systems that marked its second half. In the region of Eurasia once governed by the communist system and, indeed, all over the world, wars were triggered by the presence of one national group within the borders of a jurisdiction dominated by another.[2]

The problem is all the more complicated, and the chances of large-scale violence all the greater, under the circumstances to which Namier referred: when a national minority has ties to another jurisdiction where its conationals predominate. This is the defining characteristic of a feature of global society far older than nationalism: diasporas.

Diasporas—the term comes from the Greek for "dispersal"—are ancient features of human history. The first recorded diaspora was created in the eighth century B.C. when the kingdom of Judea was conquered by the Assyrians to its north and 27,000 Jews were forced to return with their conquerors to Mesopotamia, to live in what in Jewish history is known as the Babylonian captivity.

The experience of the prominent diasporas of modern times—the Chinese in Southeast Asia, the South Asians in East Africa, the Germans in Eastern Europe, as well as Jews, Mexicans, and many others in the United States—has not been a uniformly positive one. Most have been subject to discrimination, some to expulsion, the Jews to a serious attempt at complete elimination. The diasporas discussed in the four chapters that follow, however, have occasioned violence, or could produce it, on a different scale. The Hungarian, Russian, Serb, and Albanian cases differ from the others in a central, defining way. The older "classical" diasporas of the Jews, the Chinese, the Indians, and the Germans were created when *people* moved. The new diasporas, the subjects of this book, were created when *borders* moved.[3]

The difference invests the new diasporas with two features that classical diasporas lack and that can provoke violence on a large scale.[4] The creation of new diasporas has aroused feelings of injustice as the formation of the older, classical ones did not. The classical diasporas may be compared to a bride in some traditional societies. She moves voluntarily from the home in which she has been raised to that of her new husband. She retains ties with and obligations to her original family, which are well established in custom. But these are not supposed to conflict with her duties to her new family, to which she owes her primary obligations. The authority of the new family is voluntarily accepted and, therefore, to use the language of politics, legitimate. She is where she belongs.

While classical diasporas have also knowingly chosen their fate, the new diasporas have not. The creation of a new diaspora is thus more akin to a kidnapping. A national group is suddenly, unexpectedly, and against its will transferred, politically although not physically, from one jurisdiction, where it had long resided and where it constituted the majority, to another, where it is outnumbered, when borders are redrawn. Its reaction is anger, resentment, and the desire to escape.

Not only the kidnap victim but also the inhabitants of the home from which the victim has been "stolen" are resentful.[5] That is the second reason that new diasporas are more susceptible than classical ones to large-scale conflict. The national minority's home of origin, like its new jurisdiction, is a sovereign state, which means that what happens to the minority is not strictly a matter of the domestic politics of the host country in which it now resides. Its fate is, rather, an international issue. This difference between the violence involving classical diasporas and the conflict arising from the status of the new diasporas is the difference, in the worst case, between a pogrom and a war. Pogroms—the persecution of the minority by the majority—can be dreadful indeed; however, because their scope is broader, wars, measured by the toll of death and destruction, can be even worse. Moreover, classical diasporas all over the world have lived relatively peacefully for long periods of time;[6] new diasporas are standing causes of conflict. Adolf Hitler's drive to bring all Germans within one state was a cause of the greatest, and worst, conflict in all of European history: World War II.[7]

The conflict, actual or potential, arising from the creation of a new diaspora involves three participants: the national minority itself, the homeland state to which it feels attached and that reciprocates the sense of attachment, and the government of the new jurisdiction in which the movement of borders has placed the minority. The three are bound together in what the sociologist Rogers Brubaker has called a "triadic nexus"; that is, the actions of each one affect the conduct of the other two.[8] It is the combustible interrelationship among the three parts of four "national triads" in Eastern Europe that the chapters that follow describe and analyze.

The Chapters

Each of the four cases discussed in this volume fits the definition of a new diaspora. Hungarians, Russians, Serbs, and Albanians are all nations divided, their people dispersed among different sovereign states. In each case, they were divided among the several jurisdictions in which they reside and brought within the authority of the governments to which they are subject when borders were redrawn without their active participation and often against their will. In each case the politics of the divided nation involves the interaction of a national minority, a host state in which it has been placed, and a homeland nation from which it has been severed. Each case has three further distinguishing features: multiple diasporas, the presence of which complicates the politics of each individual diaspora; a recent history of communist rule, which can intensify nationalist feelings; and a political and strategic significance for the West that places the politics of its national triad on the agendas of Western and American foreign policy.[9]

By the terms of the post–World War I settlement, Hungarians found themselves not only in a shrunken, albeit a wholly independent, Hungary, but also in four other countries: Slovakia—then a part of the newly created Czechoslovakia and after 1992 an independent country; the Yugoslav province of Vojvodina; the territory west of the Carpathian Mountains that became part of Czechoslovakia after World War I, of the Soviet Union after World II, and of newly independent Ukraine after the Cold War; and, in the largest numbers and generating the greatest bitterness, in the Transylvanian region of the newly enlarged Romania.

As for the Russians, at the time of the breakup of the Soviet Union they were living in every one of the 15 republics that became independent countries. In political terms, the most significant Russian diasporas are those found in the three Baltic countries—Latvia, Estonia, and to a lesser extent Lithuania—and in Ukraine and Kazakhstan. Although not large, the most rebellious Russian minority was the one left in Moldova, a country dominated by ethnic Romanians.[10]

The disintegration of Yugoslavia left Serbs living outside Serbia (which, with Montenegro, retained the official name Yugoslavia) in Croatia and Bosnia, both former Yugoslav republics that declared themselves independent states. In the wake of the disintegration, the Serbs living in Kosovo bore some of the characteristics of a national minority—they were certainly a minority numerically, as well as an increasingly beleaguered one—although Kosovo remained, according to international law, a part of the Serb-dominated and now greatly reduced Yugoslavia.

Kosovo, in turn, harbored one of two sizable communities of Albanians living outside Albania: The other was in the former Yugoslav republic that became the independent state of Macedonia. Ethnic Albanians also lived in the Yugoslav province of Montenegro. All had been excluded from the Albanian state that was created in 1913.

For much of the twentieth century, all four nations—Hungarians, Russians, Serbs, and Albanians—lived under communist rule. Communism sought to erase or supersede national identity and replace or complement it with a different set of allegiances—to the party, to the working class, and to the international communist movement. Communist governments thus had the same aim as one often pursued by the host states in which national minorities suddenly and unwillingly found themselves: to dissolve or overcome a political and social identity that could subvert its own authority.

In this enterprise the communist regimes had some success. An appreciable number of Russians and others thought of themselves as Soviet citizens; the last Soviet leader, Mikhail Gorbachev, an ethnic Russian, was certainly one of them.[11] Similarly, a small but significant percentage of the citizens of communist Yugoslavia listed themselves, in the official census, as Yugoslavs rather than Serbs, Croats, Slovenes, or one of the other nationalities.[12]

Many of these people no doubt were those whose livelihoods depended on the existence of a communist multinational state: military officers, government bureaucrats, and teachers of Marxism-Leninism, as well as those involved in, or the offspring of, marriages between partners of different national groups. Whether or not they harbored a belief in orthodox communism, they did have important personal stakes in the perpetuation of the multinational states that communism had created. Such people were not, however, numerous or powerful enough to save those states. When communism collapsed, the political vacuum that followed was largely filled by nationalism. Far from extinguishing nationalist sentiment, moreover, the communist experience in Europe actually strengthened it, although in differing ways in the different nations that are the subjects of this book.

Under communism, Hungary was a sovereign country. While its citizens were not free to choose the political system under which they lived or the foreign policies their government pursued, Hungary was a state of and for Hungarians. But Budapest was prevented, until near the end of the communist period, from offering overt expressions of concern for Hungarians living outside Hungary. The status of Hungarians in Romanian Transylvania was particularly important to Hungarians in Hungary after the fall of communism because it had been impossible for Budapest to intercede on behalf of the Transylvanian Hungarians during most of the communist era.[13]

In the Soviet Union, communist rule unintentionally helped to *foster* nationalism. The expression of overt nationalist sentiment was strictly forbidden, and where signs of it appeared—briefly in the then-Soviet republic of Ukraine in the early 1970s, for example—it was hastily and ruthlessly suppressed. Yet the very structure of the Soviet Union had the effect of promoting national identity. "The regime went to remarkable lengths . . . to institutionalize both territorial nationhood and ethnic cultural nationality as basic cognitive and social categories."[14] The Soviet constitution divided the country into republics organized along national lines and thereby created local elites who were ethnic or national in origin and language, although nominally Soviet in ultimate allegiance.[15]

Yugoslavia offers yet another version of the unintended strengthening of nationalist sentiment under communism. National identity was constitutionally recognized from the reestablishment of the country after World War II: Yugoslavia was, until the end, a federation of constituent nations. The way the federation was operated, however, both before and after World War II, encouraged the belief among each individual national group that it was being short-changed politically and economically. The groups were being deprived, they came to believe, of the control over their collective destinies and the country's resources to which they were entitled. By the end of the 1980s, such attitudes were particularly strong among the Slovenes and Croats, who, in the early 1990s, seceded from Yugoslavia. These attitudes were also widely held by the Serbs and Albanians: The sense of historical grievance, to which the communist experience unintentionally contributed, weighs on the politics of both the Serb and the Albanian national triad.

The four nations discussed in this volume have a third distinctive feature. The actual and potential violence associated with the triad in which each is involved is of direct concern to the West. This is partly a matter of geography. Central and southern Europe are the neighbors of Western Europe. The countries in the two regions are seeking, with varying degrees of seriousness, to join the principal Western European international organizations. Hungary is negotiating for membership in the European Union and has joined the ranks of the North Atlantic Treaty Organization (NATO), which has itself intervened in the affairs of the Yugoslav successor states, stationing troops in Bosnia and waging the first actual war in its history in Kosovo and Serbia. As for postcommunist Russia, it remains what tsarist Russia and the Soviet Union were for three centuries: a great European power, although in weakened condition. Its foreign policy is bound to affect the rest of Europe and the world.[16] Despite these three basic similarities, the four cases differ from one another in important ways.

The Hungarian case is arguably the oldest, stretching, as Bennett Kovrig describes it in chapter 1, from 1867, when Hungary achieved autonomy under the Habsburg crown, to the present. Over the course of these decades the Hungarian national question has passed through a number of stages. From 1867 through World War I, Hungary was itself host to non-Hungarians whom it sought to assimilate. From 1920 to 1940 the smaller, post–World War I Hungary was a revisionist state, seeking to undo the work of the Paris Peace Conference and reacquire the territories that it had lost. As an ally of Germany in World War II, Hungary did—partly and momentarily—succeed in overturning the post–World War I settlement, only to be forced, with the German defeat, to return to the borders previously imposed on it. For most of the communist period, Budapest was unable to take an active interest in the fate of Hungarians outside Hungary, but this began to change in the 1980s. The restraints disappeared in 1989 with the fall of communism, leaving in place the triadic relationships characteristic of new diasporas.

Of the four cases, Hungary is the one in which the likelihood of large-scale conflict seems lowest. Hungarians are the most fully reconciled to the persistence of Hungarian communities outside the borders of Hungary itself. Budapest is committed to securing the rights of Hungarian minorities within the now-existing borders, and to doing so peacefully. But a decade after the end of communism, neither the government in Budapest nor the Hungarian minorities were entirely satisfied with the political conditions in which the minorities lived. The Hungarian triad was thus fluid, although not volatile.

The Russian case is numerically the largest one: An estimated 25 million Russians live outside Russia. It is also the most important of the four: Should the triadic politics of the Russian nation provoke armed conflict involving Russia itself, all of Europe would be affected. The frequently cited comparison between post-Soviet Russia and Weimar Germany is not entirely off the mark. Like Germany after World War I, Russia is a defeated great power, reduced in size, with many of its nationals living outside its new borders due to a process many Russians regard as arbitrary, unjust, and in need of reversal.[17] But almost a decade after the creation of a Russian national triad, the Russian case was, as Aurel Braun notes in chapter 2, tentatively and provisionally a hopeful one. While there had been all too much violence on the territory of the former Soviet Union, most of it in the Caucasus and Central Asia, virtually none had arisen from the status of ethnic Russians living outside Russia.[18]

Judged by the amount of violence generated, the case of the Serbs is the worst of the four. Serbs living outside the borders of Serbia were at the heart of three wars, in Croatia, Bosnia, and Kosovo. For this reason, in the West the post–World War I German precedent is widely thought to apply to the Serb national triad. Serbs have been seen as revisionist. Their leader, Slobodan Milošević, has been considered a Hitler-like figure, ready to wage war in the most brutal fashion to reunite the Serb nation. As Susan Woodward notes in chapter 3, however, this version of Serb history in the final decade of the twentieth century is incomplete in some respects and wrong in others. The violence, death, destruction, and suffering that have arisen from the mismatch between people and borders in the Serb case is even more tragic than is implied by the version of these events that has been current in the West. Contrary to the received wisdom, there were in fact more and better opportunities for resolving the conflict and preventing or limiting violence than is commonly believed.[19]

The final case in this book, that of the Albanians, was, at least until 1999, the least known of the four. Even with the war over Kosovo, Albanian national history, which Elez Biberaj summarizes in chapter 4, is virtually unknown to Westerners. The "new diaspora" of Albanians is in one sense the oldest of the four: The borders creating the Albanian state, which excluded large numbers of Albanians from it, were drawn before World War I, in 1913. The Albanian diaspora is proportionately the largest of the four: Fully 40 percent of all Albanians live outside Albania. For that and other reasons, the Albanian state plays a less central role in the politics of Albanian nationalism than Hungary does for the Hungarians, than Russia does for the Russians, or than Serbia does for the Serbs. As the events of 1998 and 1999 demonstrated, the Albanian triad is an explosive one. The NATO war in the former Yugoslavia was triggered by an insurgency against Serb rule in Kosovo by the Kosovo Liberation Army, a guerrilla movement committed to merging the Yugoslav province of Kosovo with Albania and the Albanian-dominated part of Macedonia to form a "greater Albania." Albania and Macedonia were drawn into the conflict when they were flooded with refugees from Kosovo who were put to flight by a Serb assault against them that coincided with the NATO bombing campaign. Thus the clash of the diasporic politics of the Serbs and the Albanians led to a war involving not only the southern Balkans but all of Europe.

The International Context

While the politics of divided nations in each of the four cases is the product of the interaction of the three parts of the national triad, another crucial influence exists in each case. None of the four can be understood in isolation from the international context in which triadic politics is played out. The international environment bears on the politics of Hungarian, Russian, Serb, and Albanian nationalism in two ways: through the policies of outside powers, in particular the Western Europeans and the United States; and through the international norms concerning borders and sovereignty.

The West plays a role in all four triads, but it is a different role in each. For Hungary, the West is a model. The goal of Hungarian foreign policy is to become part of the West by joining its principal international organizations. Budapest understands that a condition of the membership it seeks is adherence to Western norms of international behavior, which excludes efforts to change borders.

Russia's orientation toward the West is less pronounced. In the politics of the Russian triad, the West acts principally as a deterrent. It is clear, if not explicitly stated, that a Russian effort to alter the post-Soviet borders with its western neighbors, Ukraine and the Baltic countries, or even heavy-handed Russian tactics to secure the rights of Russian minorities would damage relations with Western Europe and the United States. It would raise, in fact, the specter of renewed Russian imperial aspirations.

In the Serb case, the West did intervene. It intervened indirectly by arming Croatia, which made possible, in 1995, the eviction of Serbs from the Krajina region where they had lived for centuries but that came under the jurisdiction of Croatia with the breakup of Yugoslavia and where the Serbs tried to establish a separate political entity. And the West intervened directly in Bosnia, designing and brokering the Dayton Accords that kept the country nominally united while conceding broad autonomy to the Serb sector and then dispatching troops to enforce the accords.

As for the Albanian case, in 1993 the United States sent a token force to Macedonia, the home of a large ethnic Albanian minority, to signal its commitment to the territorial integrity of that Yugoslav successor state. In 1998 NATO inserted itself into the fighting between Albanians and Serbs over the status of Kosovo, and in 1999 it went to war when the government in Belgrade refused to accept a Western plan granting Kosovo autonomy while keeping it formally a part of Yugoslavia.

Although the West has been a model or a military force in the politics of the Hungarian, Russian, Serb, and Albanian diasporas, the end of the Cold War has made outside powers less germane to the politics of Eastern Europe than they were for most of the second half of the twentieth century. With the end of the rivalry with the Soviet Union and the consequent eclipse, at least for the moment, of the traditional great-power politics of Europe, the stakes for the United States and its Western European allies in this region became more modest. The wars of the former Yugoslavia unfolded as they did partly because of the relative indifference of the most powerful members of the international community to the Balkans.[20]

Still, NATO did intervene in Bosnia and Kosovo, and did so nominally on behalf of, or at least not in opposition to, a norm that came to govern the issue at the heart of the politics of the new diasporas: how borders should be determined. The basic principle, which underlay both Western interventions, is the inviolability of internationally recognized frontiers. But in post–Cold War practice the application of this rule was not simple, nor had it held sway throughout the twentieth century, a period that saw three great bursts of state creation. These were occasioned by the demise of three sets of empires: the dynastic ones of Central and Eastern Europe after World War I, the overseas empires of Western Europe after World War II, and the communist empires of Europe after the Cold War. Each upheaval altered the international norm governing the determination of borders.

Until the twentieth century, borders were set by Europe's dynastic rulers largely on the basis of military might. The multinational states governed by the Habsburgs, the Hohenzollerns, the Romanovs, and the Ottoman Turks were as large as their rulers' military power could make them. Borders were decided by the wars waged by and among these rulers. The winners gained territory at the expense of the losers. The conquest of territory was the principal reason for going to war.

While the European wars of the early modern period invariably resulted in the movement of borders, the regimes involved remained in power. The French Revolution, however, introduced a major change. A dynastic regime was overthrown. Its overthrow led to the greatest European conflict to that time, the 20-year struggle to contain France that culminated in Napoleon's defeat in 1815. The victors followed the familiar postwar pattern of dividing the contested territory, but this time with an important variation. The redistribution of 1815 was tempered by considerations of equilibrium. The peace settlement they made at Vienna sought to establish a balance of power among them, one that included France, so that none would be so powerful, or so dissatisfied, as to launch a renewal of hostilities.[21]

The norm changed at the end of World War I, in the first of the major twentieth-century alterations. Whereas at Vienna borders were set according to the balance of power among dynastic regimes modified by considerations of prudence, at the Paris Peace Conference the dominant consideration was supposed to be justice, defined as the fulfillment of national aspirations. It was at this conference in 1919 that the national principle was formally introduced as the basis for sovereignty.

Thus the governments of Europe were changed, with nation-states succeeding multinational empires. Government of the people, by the people, and for the people theoretically replaced hereditary monarchies; territory was allocated according to the requirements of these new regimes, with borders drawn in order to place people of the same national group in the same sovereign political unit. But this formula was not faithfully followed. The national principle was not consistently applied in redrawing the map of Europe, nor could it have been. In some areas national populations were intermingled. It was not possible, to take one prominent example, to place all Hungarians in one jurisdiction without including a substantial number of Romanians; thus the new borders of the Romanian state included a large number of Hungarians. (The alternative arrangement, which had been in force until World War I, would have given Hungary a large Romanian minority.) Such mixed demographic patterns were common in imperial Europe and outlasted the dynasties that had presided over them. In the final decade of the twentieth century, the most notorious and tragic example was the former Ottoman province, then Yugoslav republic, and finally internationally recognized sovereign state of Bosnia, with its substantial populations of Serbs, Croats, and Muslims.

After World War I, the national principle was in some cases not applied even in instances in which it was demographically easy. It was not, for example, applied to the German nation. German populations contiguous to the post-1919 German state—the Weimar Republic—that wished to be part of that state were nonetheless assigned to other countries, notably Poland. The national principle was violated in the German case because Germany had lost the war and the victors thought it a matter of justice to make Germans pay for what they had done in the past and a matter of prudence to weaken them in view of what they might attempt to do in the future. Hungarian communities were similarly kept out of the new Hungarian state, even when they were contiguous to it.

For all the revolutionary implications of the introduction of the national principle as the basis for sovereignty, moreover, there were, at Paris, important elements of continuity with the imperial past. The great powers retained the prerogative of deciding where borders were to be drawn. That prerogative was still in force, although the changes of boundaries were more modest, after World War II. Joseph Stalin moved the borders of the Soviet Union westward, into what had been Poland, and simultaneously moved the Polish border westward as well, putting lands that had been German for centuries within the Polish state.[22] As after World War I, there were changes of regime as well. Communist governments were installed on territories the Red Army had conquered on its march to Berlin, democracies created in countries in which the Germans had been evicted by the Western powers. The boundary between the two parts of Europe became known as the Iron Curtain.

Thus it was not World War II but rather the second period of twentieth-century state-creation, the one triggered by the end of the Western European overseas empires in Africa and Asia in the three decades after World War II, that raised the inviolability of existing borders to the status of an international norm. This second episode of imperial dissolution multiplied the number of sovereign states. When the United Nations was founded, in 1945, it had 50 members. By 1999 its membership had grown to 185. As the peoples of Africa and Asia gained political independence, there was little effort to apply the national principle, to make political frontiers correspond to the boundaries between and among linguistically and ethnically similar groups, as there had been in formerly imperial Europe after World War I. One reason was that this principle was less appropriate in what came to be called the Third World. In Africa many of the relevant social units—the tribes, clans, and other groups—were not self-conscious nations.[23] Another, more important reason was that, in the Third World, the application of the national principle would have been even more difficult than in Europe; the European imperial powers had drawn borders in Africa and Asia even more arbitrarily than in Europe itself, routinely placing together peoples who had never before been part of the same political unit.

The European-imposed borders were deemed immutable precisely *because* so many were arbitrarily drawn. They included so many different groups, and at the same time divided so many, that if the norm of inviolability had not been established, all such borders would have been subject to challenge; once challenged, there was no widely shared concept, no legitimate principle, no viable formula on the basis of which they could be redrawn. Thus they would have been redrawn by force. The alternative to the preservation of all existing borders, no matter how capriciously or even mischievously established, seemed to be violence and bloodshed on a large scale.[24]

The Cold War reinforced the norm of inviolability. The United States and the Soviet Union were wary of trying to change existing borders because doing so held the potential for creating conflicts into which they could be drawn, with potentially disastrous consequences. For that reason, and because they competed for the allegiance of third countries around the world, both made available arms and money that helped weak Third World governments of dubious legitimacy, in many cases composed of one group dominating others against their will, remain in power.

The norm of inviolability was on vivid display in West Africa at the outset of the 1970s. The Ibos of eastern Nigeria, resentful of the domination of the country by the Muslim Hausas of the north and the Yoruba of the West, attempted to secede. The Nigerian federal government crushed the effort in a bloody civil war. The Ibo cause received almost no international support.

Just as the national principle of the post–World War I period was not faithfully applied in the postcolonial era, however, so the postcolonial commitment to the inviolability of borders was not sustained after communism in Europe collapsed. That norm gave way to yet a third twentieth-century rule for allocating sovereignty and defining borders, a rule that might be called "orderly promotion."

The communist multinational states, the Soviet Union and Yugoslavia, collapsed in part because, unlike the multinational states of the Third World, the western side in the Cold War would not, and the eastern side could not, support them.[25] Upon their collapse, the world recognized as sovereign the next-largest subordinate administrative units of both countries: the six constituent republics of Yugoslavia and the 15 constituent republics of the Soviet Union. When the Soviet Union disintegrated, the borders of what had been Soviet Ukraine became, unchanged, the borders of sovereign, independent Ukraine. When Yugoslavia dissolved, the international community insisted that borders of the former Yugoslav republic of Bosnia-Herzegovina remain, without alteration, the borders of the independent country of Bosnia-Herzegovina.

This new dispensation was never formally proclaimed, let alone systematically debated. It can be understood as an ad hoc compromise, fashioned almost instinctively by the international community in response to a sudden, unexpected challenge. It was a compromise between the impossibility, and from many points of view the undesirability, of retaining the communist multinational states, on one hand, and the need, on the other, for as consistent and readily applicable a principle of sovereignty as possible in order to minimize the disruption and violence that making legitimate the revision of borders would inevitably provoke. The post–Cold War norm for sovereignty, like other principles of political order, is thus a compromise between rigidity and flexibility.

It is perhaps the best possible compromise, the one allowing for the least dissatisfaction and therefore the least violence, that could have been struck in Eastern Europe in the wake of the communist era. But it has not satisfied all groups. It has some large imperfections.

One of them is the flaw that afflicts the principle of orderly promotion elsewhere. Just as an individual selected on the basis of competence in one position may not be suited to another, different, more trying post, so the lines of division established for one purpose—to organize internal administrative activities—may not be suitable for other, different, more consequential ones, in this case apportioning the far more formidable responsibilities of sovereignty. No serious army promotes all its colonels to the rank of general; but all former Soviet and Yugoslav republics became sovereign states.

Moreover, the post–Cold War practice of orderly promotion has proven historically perverse. For it has meant that everything Lenin, Stalin, and Tito did was discredited and discarded *except* the borders that they enforced, which were deemed sacrosanct. In addition, by the standards of the late twentieth century, these lines of division were unjust; the communist dictators and their imperial predecessors had sometimes drawn or retained internal borders in order to *separate* national groups, the better to control them, using the familiar imperial strategy of divide and rule. Finally, preserving preexisting lines of demarcation contradicted the norm of national self-determination. It meant that Russian communities in Ukraine and Kazakhstan, although previously part of a Russian-dominated state and although contiguous to post-Soviet Russia, could not choose to belong to it. The international community decreed that Bosnia-Herzegovina had to be an independent state within its Yugoslav borders despite the fact that the majority of the people living within those borders were opposed to this—indeed violently opposed—while Kosovo could not be sovereign despite the fact that the vast majority of its inhabitants desired independence and many were willing to fight to achieve it.

In post–Cold War Europe, the inviolability of borders has taken precedence, in theory and thus to a considerable extent in practice, over national self-determination. But the reverse priority would not have been a recipe for universal harmony. The fact that it is borders, not nations, that are internationally "privileged" has created a particular set of tensions and conflicts. Whether the problems with which Europe has to deal are more dangerous and more difficult to resolve than the problems that preferring nations to borders would have created is impossible to know. What is certain is that the post–Cold War norm governing borders, and the circumstances to which it gives rise, is the common context of the four chapters that follow. Relations among the three parts of the Hungarian, Russian, Serb, and Albanian national triads are played out against the backdrop of a widely held, if not consistently enforced, conviction that certain borders—those decided at Paris after World War I for

Hungary and the internal borders of the vanished communist multi-national states in the cases of the Russian, Serb, and Albanian nations—should not be changed. Where the misalignment between states and nations causes difficulties, the international community has decided that it is nations, not states, that must adjust. That process of adjustment, with all its difficulties and uncertainties, is the subject of this book.

Notes

I am grateful to Anne Mandelbaum for her customary peerless editing and to Bennett Kovrig and Susan Woodward for helpful suggestions.

1. Lewis Namier, "Nationality and Liberty," in Namier, *Vanished Suprema-cies: Essays on European History, 1812–1918* (New York: Harper Torch-books, 1958), p. 53.

2. It was a cause of the largest African conflict of the 1990s. The war that dis-lodged the Central African dictator Mobutu Sese Seko had its origins in his regime's pressure on the Banyamulenge Tutsi living in the eastern part of what was then called Zaire, pressure that a military force composed of Tutsis from neighboring Rwanda set out to relieve.

3. Borders often moved in twentieth-century Eastern Europe. In this region "a traveler can meet a man born in Poland, brought up in the Soviet Union, who now lives in Belarus—and he has never left his village." Anne Apple-baum, *Between East and West: Across the Borderlands of Europe* (New York: Pantheon, 1994), p. xx. Similarly, someone born near the Carpathian Mountains in 1918 could, if he or she had lived to the age of 73, have been a Habsburg, then a Czechoslovak, then a Soviet, and finally a Ukrainian citizen, all without ever leaving home.

4. In view of this difference it is reasonable to ask whether the Hungarian, Russian, Serb, and Albanian cases can rightly be termed diasporas, or whether they should instead simply be designated national minorities. For the case that it is analytically useful to group the two types together under a single rubric, see Charles King, "Introduction: Nationalism, Trans-nationalism, and Postcommunism," in King and Neil Melvin, eds., *Nations Abroad: Diaspora Politics and International Relations in the Former Soviet Union* (Boulder, Colo.: Westview Press, 1998). King implies a late-twentieth-century convergence of the politics of the two types of diaspora: While the homelands of the "classical" diasporas are taking a greater interest in the circumstances of their conationals living abroad, the homeland states of the "new" diasporas are abandoning the goal of incorporating them in favor of a similar ongoing concern for their welfare.

David Laitin refers to Russians who acquired diasporic status "because the borders of the Soviet Union receded, rather than because they dispersed from their homeland" as a "beached diaspora." Laitin, *Identity in Formation: The Russian-Speaking Populations in the Near Abroad* (Ithaca, N.Y.: Cornell University Press, 1998), p. 29.

5. Terms used in English to describe these circumstances connote the inherent tension. The new political unit in which the previously dominant group suddenly finds itself a minority is the "host state," implying that the minority is visiting for a short time, enjoying the temporary hospitality of the majority. (In biological terms, a host can also be a creature that unwittingly provides a home for a parasite.) The state where the minority's conationals form the majority, and from which it has been severed, is the "homeland state," implying that that is where the minority belongs, where it is truly at home. The terminology is from Rogers Brubaker, *Nationalism Reframed: Nationhood and the National Question in the New Europe* (New York: Cambridge University Press, 1996), especially chapter 3.

6. Thomas Sowell's comprehensive account of these diasporas, *Migrations and Cultures: A World View* (New York: Basic Books, 1996), although not omitting episodes of violence against them, emphasizes their economic roles.

7. This was not unforeseen. The status of the national minorities created in the wake of World War I was a central issue in the international politics of interwar Europe. Writing in 1934, C. A. Macartney, perhaps the leading English student of this issue, noted that it was "an abiding source of international unrest. For the minority in one state is usually nationally identical with the majority in another, which is often its neighbour, sympathizes with its sufferings and is prepared to go to great lengths, sometimes even to the length of war, in order to right them." Macartney, *National States and National Minorities* (New York: Russell and Russell, 1934; rpt. 1968), p. 18.

8. Brubaker, *Nationalism Reframed*, p. 4.

9. These three features distinguish the diasporas in the four chapters that follow from other cases of divided nations and actual or potential mass violence. The conflict between Armenians and Azeris over the predominantly Armenian enclave of Nagorno-Karabakh that falls within the official borders of Azerbaijan, for example, involves only one diaspora. The predominantly Muslim Indian state of Kashmir, the scene of an insurgency against the Indian government and the subject of a long and bitter dispute between the nuclear-armed governments of India and Pakistan, is untouched by communist rule. The status of ethnic Uzbeks in the other newly independent states of Central Asia has not attracted the active involvement of the West.

10. It was not so much a Russian as a Russian-*speaking* minority that asserted itself in Moldova. The prospects for the emergence of a Russian-speaking social and political identity outside Russia is an important theme of Laitin, *Identity in Formation*.

11. Gorbachev not only embraced a Soviet rather than a national identity, he also believed that most of the people he ruled embraced it, an error that

proved fatal to his own career and to the Soviet Union itself. He consistently underestimated the power of nationalist sentiment while overestimating the breadth and depth of the attachment to the Soviet Union and its kind of socialism.

12. This was true of 5.4 percent in 1981 and 3.0 percent in 1991. Cited in Susan Woodward, *Balkan Tragedy: Chaos and Dissolution after the Cold War* (Washington, D.C.: Brookings Institution, 1995), p. 32.

13. The fate of the Transylvanian Hungarians under communism is an irony of the Cold War. Among the non-Russian member states of the Warsaw Treaty Organization, Nicolae Ceauşescu's Romania was the diplomatic favorite of the West because its foreign policy was the most independent of Moscow. The Romanian leader could afford a degree of independence because he relied less heavily on the Soviet Union to remain in power than did his fellow East European dictators. His relative independence, in turn, was the result of two features of his rule that were emphatically not in keeping with Western values: a degree of repression unusual even for a European communist country and a measure of legitimacy among the Romanian majority earned by his harsh treatment of the country's Hungarian minority.

14. Brubaker, *Nationalism Reframed*, p. 8; see also pp. 17 and 29–34.

15. On the Soviet Union as the incubator of nations and nationalism, see Ronald Grigor Suny, *The Revenge of the Past: Nationalism, Revolution, and the Collapse of the Soviet Union* (Stanford, Calif.: Stanford University Press, 1993), especially chapter 3. The Soviet experience may also be seen as a particular instance of the general pattern proposed by Ernest Gellner, in which nations emerge as by-products of the efforts by states to create the conditions necessary for operating industrial economies, notably mass literacy in a common language. See Gellner, *Nations and Nationalism* (Oxford: Blackwell, 1993).

16. Russia's relations with its immediate neighbors, and with the rest of the world, are discussed in Michael Mandelbaum, ed., *The New Russian Foreign Policy* (New York: Council on Foreign Relations, 1998).

17. On this comparison see Brubaker, *Nationalism Reframed*, pp. 135ff. A good discussion of related issues is in Anatol Lieven, *Chechnya: Tombstone of Russian Power* (New Haven, Conn.: Yale University Press, 1998), especially chapters 5 and 7. The two cases differ in an important way. Russia was not defeated in battle. Unlike the Treaty of Versailles, which set Germany's post–World War I borders, the end of the Soviet Union was initiated voluntarily, by Russia. Germany's borders were defined by Germany's conquerors; post-Soviet Russia's borders, if not fully defined by Russians, at least were not imposed on them.

18. The exception is the Moldovan enclave of Transdniestria.

19. An analysis of the opportunities to avoid large-scale conflict in the collapse of Yugoslavia, and specificially in Bosnia, is in Steven L. Burg and

Paul S. Shoup, *Bosnia-Herzegovina: Ethnic Conflict and International Intervention* (Armonk, N.Y.: M. E. Sharpe, 1999), chapter 8.

20. Ibid., chapters 4–6.

21. This is a major theme of Paul Schroeder, *The Transformation of European Politics, 1763 to 1848* (New York: Oxford University Press, 1992).

22. The Germans of these lands, many of whose ancestors had lived there for centuries, were evicted. An estimated 12 million Germans were expelled from territories to the east of Germany that had been conquered, and were controlled, by communist forces between 1945 and 1947.

23. Even in Europe nationalism is, in historical terms, a relatively recent development, not an identity that has existed from time immemorial. A brief summary of some of the contemporary literature on nationalism, to which this point is central, may be found in Eric Hobsbawm, *Nations and Nationalism Since 1780: Programme, Myth, Reality* (Cambridge: Cambridge University Press, 1990), introduction.

24. "Julius Nyerere, the founding president of Tanzania, is reported to have mused that the borders of African states are so absurd, there is no choice but to consider them sancrosanct." Laitin, *Identity in Formation*, p. 336.

25. Western economic assistance to Yugoslavia was relatively generous during the Cold War, when such aid was seen as a way of strengthening a communist regime not controlled by, and sometimes opposed to, Moscow. The assistance dwindled as the East-West conflict ended. On the economic causes of the disintegration of Yugoslavia, see Woodward, *Balkan Tragedy*. Similarly, the United States was willing to provide generous economic aid to reform communist Josip Broz Tito in the 1960s and 1970s, but not to reform communist Mikhail Sergeyevich Gorbachev in the 1980s and 1990s.

1

Partitioned Nation: Hungarian Minorities in Central Europe

BENNETT KOVRIG

O F THE 13 million Hungarians in Central Europe, some 3 million are dispersed among the seven countries that ring Hungary proper. Official statistics, which often underestimate minorities, show 567,000 ethnic Magyars in Slovakia, 170,000 in Ukraine, 1,620,000 in Romania, 341,000 in Yugoslavia, 25,000 in Croatia, 12,000 in Slovenia, and 4,000 in Austria.[1] Today they represent collectively the largest ethnic minority in Europe west of the former Soviet Union. These Hungarians owe their minority status to the peacemakers who, after World War I, redrew the map of the region. They constitute consolidated national minorities that are as deeply rooted as their ethnic neighbors; it was not the population but the political boundaries that shifted, putting Hungarians under the jurisdiction of other sovereign states.

The fragmentation of the Hungarian nation had a profound and lasting impact on the political cultures of Hungary and the principal host states. By their very existence, the larger Magyar minorities—in Slovakia and Romania—hindered the formation of cohesive nation-states and complicated relations between the host countries and Hungary. Without ever pursuing their collective interests to the point of violence, the minorities exacerbated nationalistic tendencies in the host states as well as in Hungary; they suffered policies of assimilation and exclusion, served as a pretext for irredentism, and affected peacetime as well as wartime alignments in the region.

A succession of democratic and authoritarian regimes failed to resolve the national question by forging a stable modus vivendi with the larger Magyar minorities. During the 40 years of Soviet communist rule, nationalism was largely supplanted by the class-based principle of "socialist internationalism." In the postcommunist era, the international climate favors minority rights, but it remains to be seen whether the tension between cultural loyalties and civic obligations will be dissipated in the process of modernization and European integration.

The dynamics of the Hungarian problem are played out in what may be termed a triadic relational nexus, a complex pattern of interaction linking minorities, nationalizing host states, and the "mother state."[2] In addition to this triad, third parties—major powers as well as international institutions—have played from the start a significant and at times determining function.

This ongoing political drama is set in a part of Europe where the vagaries of history have produced an inextricable tangle of ethnic groups and where ethnically pure descent is probably more the exception than the rule. Yet ethnocultural identities were nurtured over centuries, giving rise to mutually antagonistic nationalisms that blended the civic approach to nationhood, exemplified by France, and the Germans' atavistic emphasis on blood (still evident in the patriation clause of the Federal Republic's constitution). Although ethnocultural pluralism had its champions, the nationalizing states proved more disposed to pursue inclusion by assimilation, exclusion by suppression and expulsion, or indeed a combination of these approaches.

All nation-states nurture founding myths and adapt them to changing circumstances, but such myths—which are marked more by ethnocentric bias than by outright fantasy—have played an exceptionally prominent part in the belated process of nation-building in Central and Eastern Europe.[3] The history of the region lends itself to the syndrome of mutual retrospective grievance. Each ethnocultural entity perceives itself as a sometime victim of one or several others, and the mirror image of victim and oppressor informs national ideology in many a dyad.

It is necessary, therefore, to adumbrate the historical matrix that gave rise to the competing nationalisms of the region and to the minority status of Magyars, before proceeding to an examination of the evolution of triadic relationships from the interwar period to the present day. If large-scale violence, defined in terms of loss of life, is set as the measure of the problem, then it can be noted at the outset that apart from a few isolated instances, the Magyar minorities have neither incurred nor displayed the kind of murderous passion that animates the Yugoslav civil wars of the 1990s. Nevertheless, the triadic nexus that encompasses these minorities has been characterized by threats to their cultural and economic survival.

The dilemmas inherent in modern liberal-democratic ideology are vividly displayed in the dynamic interdependence of the three political entities: minority, host state, and mother state. The tensions between statehood and nationhood, pluralism and majoritarianism, nationalism and multiculturalism, individual rights and collective rights are as difficult to eliminate in theory as in practice. These general problems are illuminated by the case study of the Magyar minorities, which provides not only a historical lesson but also a diagnosis of political problems yet to be resolved.

The case study can be divided into five distinct periods. In the nineteenth century, Hungary was a multinational state that, particularly after 1867, attempted to "nationalize" its own ethnic minorities. The territorial truncation imposed by the Treaty of Trianon (1920) gave rise to Magyar minorities in the successor states and to an irredentism that dominated Hungarian politics in the interwar period. Between 1938 and 1941, Hungary recovered those fragments of territory holding the largest concentration of Magyars. At the end of World War II the Trianon borders were restored, and when the Magyar minorities came under communist rule, they would variously benefit from the ethnically undifferentiated application of Stalinism and Titoism and suffer from a resurgence of majority nationalism. Finally, in the postcommunist era, the minorities, openly supported by Hungary, have tried to promote their separate interests in the new, more or less democratic polities.

The Road to Trianon

Hungarians and their ethnic neighbors are situated at the continent's crossroads, in a region long exposed to the imperial ambitions of Habsburgs and other Germans, Turks, and Russians. Foreign domination failed to suppress ethnic identity. On the contrary, it induced a resistance founded on each ethnic group's early history. Precedence with respect to settlement and statehood would nourish many a national myth and historical debate.

The Middle Danube Basin was occupied by Magyar tribes that arrived from the east at the end of the ninth century. The region, which had seen the flux and reflux of Romans, Goths, Slavs, and Huns, was momentarily free of any overarching sovereignty. By the early Middle Ages, the Magyars had consolidated a powerful feudal state encompassing a multitude of ethnicities. Political power rested with a social caste of freemen, composed predominantly of Magyars, which came to be known as the Hungarian "nation" (a term that had yet to acquire an ethnic connotation). As an English historian of the region observed, few of Europe's peoples have displayed the power of attraction that enabled the Magyars to absorb ethnically alien elements into their nation.[4] In the early sixteenth century, on the eve of the Ottoman conquest, the greater part of the population was Magyar by descent or natural assimilation. The status of non-Magyars depended more on social rank than on ethnic origin, although there were exceptions. The German Saxons of Transylvania had enjoyed a degree of autonomy ever since their settlement in the early Middle Ages; the native and immigrant Romanians in Transylvania were treated as less than equal, apart from those who joined the Magyar nobility; and Croatia was linked in quasi-federal vassalage to the Hungarian crown.

In the mid-sixteenth century, Hungary was divided into three parts. The central region, where Magyars predominated, was occupied by the Turks, who bled it of wealth and population; the northwestern fringe was ruled by the Habsburgs; and Transylvania, in the southeast, became a principality that tried to preserve its independence from both imperial powers. When Christian armies finally expelled the Turks in the late seventeenth century, the Habsburgs extended their dominion over the region. By imperial design as well as spontaneous migration, depopulated areas were colonized by Germans, Slavs, and Romanians.

In the nineteenth century, when the ideology of nationalism swept over Europe, little more than half of the country's population claimed Hungarian as its mother tongue. The Magyars were in the forefront of the process of national awakening, and their drive for independence from Austrian rule went hand in hand with cultural Magyarization. The spirit of nationalism stirred in other ethnic groups as well. When, in 1848, Hungarians rose in arms against the Habsburgs, the Croats and Serbs fought on the side of the latter; and most of the Saxons and Romanians—as well as some Slovaks—saw better prospects under Vienna's distant rule than under Hungarian administration.

In the Compromise of 1867 with Austria, Hungary obtained full autonomy in internal affairs. The following year, a notably liberal nationalities law granted broad linguistic and cultural rights to the non-Magyars, although the preamble underscored that Hungary's citizens formed an indivisible and unitary Hungarian nation. The latter principle came to dominate the application of the law, and Magyarization became the operative policy. Subsequent laws and regulations reduced the political weight of the minorities and their linguistic rights in the spheres of justice, administration, and education.

Voluntary assimilation into the Hungarian nation had proceeded for centuries, and many legendary figures, from King Matthias Corvinus (Mátyás Hunyadi) in the fifteenth century to the leader of the 1848 revolution, Lajos Kossuth, were of mixed ethnic descent. In some countries, notably France, uninterrupted sovereignty and policies of cultural homogenization had facilitated the forging of a cohesive nation-state. Hungary, long under foreign rule, tried to follow suit in the late nineteenth and early twentieth centuries. The active pursuit of Magyarization was far from ineffectual. Magyar became the language not only of the ruling elite, of administration and government, but also of the commercial and intellectual middle classes in the towns. Yet these signs of progressive assimilation and linguistic dominance were somewhat deceptive. In the 1910 census, only 54.5 percent of the population claimed Hungarian as its mother tongue.[5] The minorities may have been administratively integrated and linguistically marginalized, but they were far from immune to the ideology of nationalism.

Kossuth, in exile, tried to promote the idea of a Danubian federation to accommodate the multinational character of the region, but such alternatives were out of tune with the spreading popularity of nation-statehood. Politicized intellectuals from Hungary's minorities agitated overtly for collective rights and covertly for autonomy. Émigrés, along with the states of Romania and Serbia, offered encouragement to their ethnic cousins in Hungary; pan-Slav propaganda from Russia had an impact among Slovaks as well as Czechs. It is moot whether the Magyars, left undisturbed, might have prevailed over these challenges and preserved the integrity of the "Lands of the Holy Hungarian Crown." By the time Magyarization was adopted as official policy, minority nationalism was also in the ascendant, and neither Hungary's geographic location nor its ethnic mix favored the creation of a homogeneous state on the model of France. Whatever might have resulted, World War I brought defeat to Austria-Hungary, and the peacemakers effected a drastic political reconfiguration of the region.

The dismemberment of the Austro-Hungarian dual monarchy was motivated by both strategic and ideological considerations.[6] Britain and France had been intent on winning allies and imposing a new order that weakened Germany. Thus, as early as August 1915, they and Russia concluded a secret agreement with the Serbs, promising the latter not only Bosnia, Herzegovina, Dalmatia, Slavonia, and Croatia but also part of the Banat and other fragments of southern Hungary. Another secret accord, in August 1916, induced the Romanians to change sides with the promise of Transylvania and a further slice of Hungary, the Partium, lying to the west of that province.

Czech nationalists, led by Tomáš Masaryk, worked assiduously to persuade the Western allies of the justice of their cause. Evoking a Swiss, confederal model, Masaryk won the support of Slovak émigrés in the United States for the creation of a joint Czech-Slovak state. Shortly before the war's end, the Western powers formally recognized the Czechoslovaks as allies and promised them independence within their historical borders. That formula encompassed Bohemia and Moravia as well as Upper Hungary, home to the majority of Slovaks. The statehood and boundaries of the first two provinces were rooted in history, but there was no precedent for delineating a Slovak state; indeed, Germans and Magyars constituted a majority in the putative Slovak capital of Pozsony (to be renamed Bratislava), where several of Hungary's kings had been crowned.

Some of these commitments already had been made when the United States entered the war. To give Americans ideological purpose, President Woodrow Wilson proclaimed guidelines for a more peaceful international system; these included national self-determination and collective security in a League of Nations. The principle of self-determination bolstered the national aspirations of the dual monarchy's minorities; and while it did not augur well for historic Hungary, the Magyars nursed hopes that at least their nation would benefit equally from its application.

Every factor militated against Hungary. There were, to begin with, the secret treaties and commitments. At war's end, the Czechs and Slovaks, Romanians, and Serbs backed up their claims by military occupation of Hungarian territory, and France was particularly indulgent in endorsing provisional lines of demarcation that progressively reduced the area under Hungarian administration. In Budapest, on October 31, 1918, a peaceful revolution brought to power a government of liberal democrats and socialists led by Mihály Károlyi. His minister of nationalities, the liberal scholar Oszkár Jászi, tried to preserve Hungary's territorial integrity by offering its minorities full equality and autonomy on the Swiss model; failing that, he counted on plebiscites to keep most Magyars within the boundaries of their mother state.

Confronted with an Allied ultimatum to evacuate further Hungarian territory, Károlyi resigned in March 1919, thus opening the way for an impromptu coalition of communists and radical socialists to seize power. The de facto leader of this Soviet republic, a Leninist revolutionary named Béla Kun, alienated much of the population with his crude attempts to impose the Soviet model. Ironically, this ardent "internationalist" won more popularity by drawing on Hungarian nationalism to combat foreigners: his Red Army registered some successes in Upper Hungary against the Czechs and tried to hold back the

Romanians. But the Western statesmen who had assembled at Paris for the peace conference were even less sympathetic to the Bolshevik Kun than they had been to the liberal democrat Károlyi. When, at the end of July, Kun's dictatorial regime collapsed, Romanian forces occupied Budapest.

In late 1919 and early 1920, Hungary made some desperate attempts to forestall truncation or at least alleviate its impact. There were talks with Slovak anti-Czech nationalists concerning an autonomous Slovakia linked to Hungary, as well as with Romania on the option of an autonomous Transylvania. There was even an abortive rapprochement with France, where the foreign ministry's new secretary-general, Maurice Paléologue, contemplated drawing Hungary into an anti-Bolshevik cordon sanitaire and sought commercial concessions while making vague promises to reconsider the peace terms.[7]

Hungary, a defeated power, was not a participant in the peace conference. The delegation that was ultimately summoned to receive the peace terms submitted detailed briefs on the country's ethnic and economic interests, but these carried little weight in Paris. The Americans had earlier expressed reservations about the ethnic justification of some proposed frontier lines, and when Budapest initially rejected the peace terms, England and Italy favored some modification of those lines in favor of Hungary. France remained adamant, and the only concession was a separate note evoking the possibility of eventual rectification. The Treaty of Trianon, signed in June 1920, sealed Hungary's fate.

It was, by any standard, a harshly punitive diktat. Hungary was reduced to roughly a third of its former territory and population. The Wilsonian principle of national self-determination was applied exclusively to the benefit of nations represented by the successor states. In the new configuration of states, some 1.7 million persons of Magyar mother tongue found themselves in Romania, close to 900,000 in Czechoslovakia, around 550,000 in the southern Slav kingdom, and 26,000 in Austria. Hungarians would never forgive that, despite all the fine talk of democratic self-determination, their country was dismembered without recourse to plebiscites. Truncated Hungary, with a population of 8 million, became ethnically the most homogeneous state in the region, next to Austria. In contrast, all of the successor states encompassed large Magyar and other minorities, whose basic rights they were bound by minority treaties to respect.[8]

Thus history's balance shifted, assigning several million Hungarians to minority status. The fragmented region became divided between winners determined to preserve their gains and losers (Hungarians, Germans, Bulgarians, and even Italians) intent on rectifying what they perceived as injustice. In both camps, minorities became grist to the mill of nationalist passion.

The Minorities and Irredentism in the Interwar Period

A multiplicity of factors came to bear on the evolution of these newly minted Magyar minorities. The latter had to accommodate profound change in their political, social, and economic status and to recast their cultural and civic identity and allegiances. The nationalizing host states had to develop minority policies that would foster loyal or at least compliant citizenship. Hungary had to devise a viable relationship with both the minorities and the host states. Third parties, the principal European powers, had to take into account the fragmentation and cleavages of Central and Eastern Europe as they pursued their divergent foreign policy interests. In this complex web of interdependence, each actor influenced the behavior of the others, and while their basic roles were cast early in the interwar period, the relationships did not remain wholly static.

Before turning to a case-by-case survey of the several Magyar minorities, one must take note of the ultimately decisive role played by Hungary and third parties. Obviously, if Hungary had reconciled itself to the loss of territory and sizable Magyar populations, the minorities would have had a greater incentive to comply and assimilate. Conversely, if Hungarian minorities had shown a disposition to accept their new status and offer undivided loyalty to the host state, Hungary's revisionism would have lost much of its force. Neither was the case.

Hungary came to be ruled by a succession of conservative governments, with Miklós Horthy, a onetime admiral in the Austro-Hungarian navy, serving as regent and head of state. István Bethlen, the prime minister who guided Hungary's fortunes in the 1920s, declared that the nation's very survival depended on revision of the Treaty of Trianon.[9] That belief became axiomatic in Hungarian political culture between the wars and revisionism a national obsession and industry. The government and various semiofficial patriotic organizations engaged in a campaign of nationalistic and irredentist propaganda designed both to galvanize Hungarians and to impress the outside world with the justice of Hungary's grievances—much as France, on a lesser scale, had remained irreconciled to the loss of Alsace-Lorraine. Maps of mutilated Hungary and the pervasive slogan *"nem, nem, soha"* (no, no, never) symbolized the denial of Trianon's legitimacy.[10] The close to 400,000 Magyars, mainly public servants and professionals, who moved from the severed regions to Hungary no doubt reinforced the revisionist ethos.

There were, to be sure, differences of opinion regarding tactics and objectives. Some stressed the historical case—adorned with economic and geographic arguments—for reconstituting the domain of the Hungarian crown. Others were more concerned with the return of Magyar-inhabited areas and argued for partial revision of the Trianon borders. Yet it is fair to say that the nation was of one mind in its concern for the minorities, abhorrence of Trianon, and desire for rectification. The ample social and economic problems of postwar Hungary produced political cleavages that were partially represented in the limited democratic system of the era, but no political party or movement came anywhere near challenging the revisionist dogma, save the proscribed and inconsequential communists, who themselves were entangled in the ideological contradictions of internationalism and Lenin's nationality policy.

All this reinforced the determination of Czechoslovakia's foreign minister, Edvard Beneš, to raise a bulwark against Hungarian revisionism. By 1921 the system of alliances known as the Little Entente was in place; it linked Czechoslovakia, Romania, and Yugoslavia, and enjoyed the backing of France.

With his country diplomatically isolated and on the brink of economic collapse, Bethlen pragmatically toned down irredentism to secure League of Nations support for a financial stabilization program. Hungary, he believed, had to rebuild its strength and find powerful patrons before it could engage in meaningful discussions with its neighbors. In the meantime, Budapest addressed numerous petitions to the League of Nations concerning the status of the Magyar minorities. In 1927, new wind came into the sails of revisionism. In Britain that cause acquired influential champions in Lord Rothermere, publisher of the *Daily Mail*, and other members of the House of Lords; and Mussolini's Italy concluded a treaty of eternal friendship and arbitration with Hungary. But only with the rise of Adolf Hitler and German assertiveness did revision of the peace treaties appear on Europe's diplomatic agenda. Thereafter Hungary would take its part in the short-lived reconfiguration of the region.

States, and particularly young nation-states, are seldom inclined to compromise on their territorial integrity. Created or expanded by the fiat of the great powers, the successor states took on the task of nation-building with some confidence. The League of Nations, led by Britain and France, was dedicated to preserving the status quo. Hungary's obvious irredentism reinforced its neighbors' perception that it was a hostile power; but even without that irredentism, Hungary undoubtedly would have been depicted in their national ideologies as a historic oppressor. The Magyar minorities, in turn, were bound to be identi-fied—and to identify themselves—with their mother country. Thus nationalism, which feeds on enemies, exacerbated a multiplicity of mutual fears and grievances in the region. Overtly or covertly, each national myth conjured up the punishing hand of historical justice.

THE BURGENLAND

The Burgenland, a 4,000-square-kilometer district awarded by the peacemakers to Austria, held the smallest Magyar minority. Hungari-ans found it particularly galling that their former master, Austria, which bore much of the responsibility for the Great War, should share in the dismemberment of their country. Although the Burgenland had belonged historically to the Hungarian crown, the vast majority of its population was German-speaking, and the peacemakers made the ges-ture to bolster Austria against bolshevism at a time when Béla Kun ruled in Budapest. After much petty sword rattling and diplomatic dis-pute, Hungary managed to obtain the holding of a plebiscite in the town and neighborhood of Sopron (Ödenburg), which in December 1921 voted to stay Hungarian.[11] The Magyars, mostly farmers, in the annexed territory subsequently benefited from equitable treatment, and the Burgenland would not figure on the agenda of Hungarian revision-ism and grievances.[12]

SLOVAKIA

The case of Slovakia—the former Upper Hungary—was far more con-tentious. The original Magyar conqueror-settlers found some Slavonic people in the region, but no clear sovereignty, and Upper Hungary would form an integral part of the Magyar kingdom until 1920. Over the centuries, Magyars and Slovaks mingled in the region, the former being concentrated in the plains, the latter in the mountains and valleys lying to the north. Of the Slovaks who migrated southwards, many became Magyarized, both by natural assimilation and, later, under offi-cial inducement. In 1918 there were 1,686,700 people of Slovak and 893,600 of Magyar mother tongue in the region, accounting, respec-tively, for 57 and 30 percent of the population. The Czechoslovak cen-sus of 1921 registered (by nationality) 1,942,000 Slovaks and 635,000 Magyars. The drop in the latter's number was accounted for by the exo-dus to Hungary of some 100,000 Magyars, most of them state employ-ees, such as officials and teachers, and by the choice of Magyarized Slovaks to reclaim their ancestral identity.

In opposing the transfer of Upper Hungary, Hungarians argued that the notion of a Czecho-Slovak nation was a modern, and essentially Czech, fabrication, and that a plebiscite would show a Slovak preference for Hungary.[13] Indeed, the small Slovak intelligentsia divided over the question, but the Czechs were adamantly opposed to a plebiscite. It was in the comparatively democratic environment of the Czechoslovak state that the Slovaks, resentful of a Czech paternalism that allowed them little autonomy, came to acquire a full sense of separate nationhood.

The evolution of Czech-Slovak relations is a separate tale, but it would have an impact on the situation of the Magyar minority in Slovakia. The Czechs were intent on forging a democratic nation-state, and, at least in principle, the minorities enjoyed equal political rights. Thus the Magyars eventually were allowed to form a clearly nationalist party, and—despite some unfavorable gerrymandering—they managed to win representation both in the Prague parliament and in the Provincial Council of Slovakia. The minorities, and even Slovaks, enjoyed little autonomy at the local level, for power passed largely into the hands of appointed Czech administrators.

The Czechoslovak Republic's Language Law, enacted in 1920, allowed the use of other languages in administrative and judicial dealings wherever the minority accounted for at least 20 percent of the population. This liberal provision was then partially undermined by the reconfiguration of districts to bring the proportion of Magyars below that benchmark. The same law provided for education in the mother tongue wherever there were at least 40 minority children of school age, and minorities had the right to found separate schools and other cultural organizations. Although the Magyars lost many of their pre-Trianon schools, most of them could obtain elementary and secondary education in their own language; one of their major grievances was the absence of a Hungarian-language university. The Czechs' abhorrence of conservative, revisionist Hungary was reflected in the heavy censorship of publications from south of the border.

Land reform was on the agenda of all states of the region in the post-Trianon period. The successor states—unlike Hungary—enacted a sweeping redistribution, the consequences of which were unfavorable for their Magyar minorities. Thus, in Czechoslovakia, most of the expropriated landowners, whose compensation represented a small fraction of their property's value, were Magyars; and since Magyar claimants benefited less than equally from the redistribution, many laborers from the former estates found themselves jobless and landless. The Hungarians also drew grievance from the fact that new agricultural colonies of Czechs and Slovaks were implanted in areas that had been purely Magyar. In other respects, Magyar peasants prospered under the new regime, as did merchants and industrial workers. Apart from landowners, it was the middle class that suffered the most from the change of sovereignty. The region's Magyar middle classes traditionally had sought employment in state service, but mistrust of the minority and the pent-up demand among the majority now limited this option in Czechoslovakia as well as in the other successor states.[14]

In regional comparison, most Magyars in Slovakia fared well. Thanks to Prague's progressive social policies and agricultural protectionism, their material circumstances became better in some respects than those of their counterparts in Hungary. Yet even if there was little overt discrimination, the divisive forces of nationalism were at work. The Czechs imposed their program of nation-building with some impartiality, but younger generations of Slovaks became increasingly intolerant of the Magyars, a people that their new national myth was depicting as historic oppressors. The Magyars, for their part, tended to regard Slovaks as backward and deeply resented their own reduced status. The modernity of the Czechoslovak state had some appeal, particularly for those of more liberal or socialist persuasion, and there were strong moral and material inducements for supporting the Czechoslovak parties; yet, at the 1935 elections, the unified Magyar parties garnered over 230,000 votes.

The Magyars resented what they perceived to be majority chauvinism but generally abstained from revisionist provocation. There was little emigration after the initial wave, and the pressure to conform and assimilate to the preponderant nationality had some effect; the 1930 census showed that, despite a healthy natural increase, the number of people claiming Magyar nationality had fallen by 9.9 percent, to 572,000. Although they were comparatively well treated, most Magyars did not become truly loyal subjects of the new state. Hungary was too near, its revisionist clamor too loud, and history too recent to allow for the minority's full integration. The vast majority of Slovakia's Magyars was concentrated in a strip of land along the border with Hungary, and this patent contradiction of the principle of national self-determination stuck in the craw of Magyars on both sides of the line. The sense of historical injustice continued to fuel the flames of revisionism.

RUTHENIA

Ruthenia, Hungary's easternmost region, was also awarded to Czechoslovakia by the Treaty of Trianon. The largest autochthonous group in this sparsely populated, mountainous area consisted of Ruthenes (or

Rusyns), ethnic cousins to the Ukrainians across the Carpathian Mountains. For centuries, the poor and backward Ruthene peasants were considered among the most loyal subjects of the Hungarian crown, and Magyarization, notably of the Ruthenes' Uniate clergy, was far advanced. The 1910 census found (by mother tongue) 320,000 Ruthenes and 170,000 Magyars, representing, respectively, 56 and 30 percent of the population. As in Slovakia, the Slavs were concentrated in the mountains and the Magyars in the plain; the towns, notably Ungvár (Uzhgorod), Munkács (Mukacevo), Huszt (Chust), and Beregszász (Beregovo), were largely Magyarized.

During the war, Masaryk obtained the support of Ruthene émigrés in the United States for linking an autonomous Ruthenia to the new state of Czechoslovakia. The local population initially gave signs of preferring autonomy within Hungary, but when Czech and Romanian troops occupied parts of the region, it was persuaded by émigrés to support the other option. Czechs as well as peacemakers were motivated more by strategic than by ethnic factors. Ruthenia's annexation to Czechoslovakia would give the latter a common border with Romania, separate Poles and Hungarians, who had some historical affinities, and prevent Bolshevik Russia from expanding over the Carpathians.

Ruthenia thus became a nominally autonomous province under Czech administration. The situation of the Magyar minority, which, according to the Czechoslovak census, numbered 110,000 in 1930, was in most respects similar to that of the Magyars in Slovakia. Landless Magyar peasants received little of the estates expropriated from their mainly Hungarian owners, and Slavic colonists were settled in Magyar villages. As in the case of Slovakia, the existence of predominantly Magyar districts along the frontier lent some weight to the case for revision.

TRANSYLVANIA

For reasons of history as well as because of the size of the Magyar minority, Transylvania's transfer to Romania became the most contentious legacy of Trianon. In the second and third centuries, that mountainous region was the Roman Empire's province of Dacia, and, according to Romanian national myth, the local Geto-Dacian peoples (known as Vlachs) and Roman colonists were the ancestors of the Romanians. After the Romans withdrew, Goths and other peoples passed through the region, and there is scant evidence of the Romanians' presence when, in the tenth century, Hungarians settled in Transylvania. However, from the thirteenth century onward, large numbers of Romanians migrated from Moldavia and Wallachia to Transylvania.

Meanwhile, Hungary's kings had implanted Germanic settlers, known collectively as Saxons, in this border region. The population thus became a mix of Magyars, their Székely ethnic cousins, Saxons, and Romanians, as well as numerous smaller ethnic groups.

Transylvania enjoyed a varying degree of autonomy under the Hungarian crown, and the same applied to each of its three feudal nations, the Magyars, Székelys, and Saxons. The Romanians, initially shepherds who practiced seasonal migration, were excluded from this political partnership. The Reformation made deep inroads in Transylvania, which came to enjoy remarkable religious pluralism—except that the Romanians' Orthodox religion was merely tolerated and not granted full legal recognition. When much of Hungary fell under the occupation of Ottoman Turks in the sixteenth and seventeenth centuries, Transylvania—with some adjacent territories—became a quasi-independent principality, the last bastion of Hungary's political and cultural survival. Thereafter, Transylvania retained a separate status under Habsburg administration, and only in 1867 was the province fully reunited with Hungary.

Transylvania's multicultural character endured into modern times. The nobility, Magyar by descent or assimilation, served as the political elite in alliance with the Saxons, who jealously guarded their special privileges. The Romanians—apart from those who became Magyarized nobles—were traditionally regarded as backward folk unfit for political participation; yet, over the centuries, their clergy and small intellectual stratum nurtured a sense of collective identity and periodically appealed to Vienna or Budapest for equal recognition. When, in 1848–49, Hungarians challenged Habsburg rule, most Romanians and Saxons opposed the reunification of Transylvania with Hungary, and sided with the Austrians.[15]

All legal distinctions between ethnic groups were erased when Transylvania was reunited with Hungary in 1867, but, by then, the forces of Magyar and Romanian nationalism were set on collision course. The Magyars controlled administration and justice, promoted the Magyarization of education, and manipulated the electoral system to the disadvantage of Romanians. The latter's intelligentsia, meanwhile, continued to develop a national ideology based on the theory of Daco-Roman continuity—that Transylvania had been the home of their Romanized ancestors, and thus the cradle of Romanian nationhood.

Magyarization made gains, notably in towns, but the most resistant were the largely rural Romanians, whose national awakening received reinforcement from Romania proper. Some of Transylvania's Romanians pressed for genuine equality and collective autonomy within Hungary; others dreamed of union with their cousins over the Carpathians. They had, in any case, come to form the majority of Transylvania's population. The 1910 census showed that of the 2,678,000 inhabitants of Transylvania proper, 1,472,000 were Romanian, 918,000 Magyar, and 234,000 Saxon. The territory subsequently annexed to Romania, which also included the Crisana, Maramures, and part of the Banat, held 2,800,000 Romanians, 1,705,000 Magyars, and 560,000 Germans (Saxons and Swabians).

On December 1, 1918, an assembly of Romanians at Gyulafehérvár (Alba Iulia) called for the union of Transylvania with Romania, promising complete national liberty for all ethnic groups. That promise led the pragmatic Saxons to endorse the initiative; Transylvania's Magyars, on the other hand, were viscerally opposed. The Romanian army thereupon occupied the entire region that came to be awarded to Romania in the Treaty of Trianon. As in the case of the other annexations, the frontier line owed more to political and strategic factors than to ethnic distribution, for there remained large pockets of Magyars, Germans, and Serbs along Greater Romania's northwestern periphery. However, a significant part of the Magyar-Székely population lived far from the new border with Hungary, in east-central Transylvania, the historic Székelyföld (land of the Székelys).

The shoe was now on the other foot, for Romania's constitution declared it to be a unitary national state and ruled out collective recognition of minorities. The regime's explicit objective became to Romanianize Transylvania.[16] That goal was more sociopolitical than cultural, for the Romanians had little interest in or hope of fully absorbing the Magyars into their nation. They saw the task as primarily one of social revolution: to develop a national middle and upper class that would assume the reins of power in all fields.

Romania's legal structure was nominally democratic and liberal, while administrative practice was slack and corrupt, all of which often worked to the advantage of the Magyar and other minorities. The Magyar National Party, formed in 1922, won representation in parliament but found little scope to advance the minority's interests. Regional, municipal, and local administration became dominated by appointed, ethnic Romanian officials. The shortage of alternative candidates led to the retention of many Magyars in lower-level administration until the early 1930s, when they were systematically replaced by a new generation of educated Romanians. The Hungarian language was effectively expunged from official life, and all place-names were Romanianized.

The state education system included minority-language schools, with some compulsory instruction in Romanian, and the minorities were allowed to set up separate, church-affiliated schools (a stipulation of the Minority Treaty signed by Romania and the other successor states). The Magyars complained about the insufficiency of state schools in their language and the pressure—particularly in Székely districts— to send their children to Romanian schools. Higher education was wholly Romanianized, except for a chair of Hungarian Literature at the formerly Hungarian University of Cluj (Kolozsvár); and Romania, like the other successor states, retaliated against Hungarian revisionism by refusing to recognize degrees granted by universities in Hungary. On the other hand, the minority's cultural activities and publications met with little official hindrance.

The postwar land reform necessarily affected the Magyar landowner class as well as Magyar churches, but it was not applied in a particularly discriminatory fashion. The practical exclusion of the Magyar middle class from state employment was a more painful blow. The command-ing position of the Magyar, Saxon, and Jewish minorities in the private economy was somewhat eroded by preferential measures to promote ethnic Romanian enterprise. By the 1930s, nationalists were clamoring for tougher measures to improve the relative economic position of eth-nic Romanians; "a Romania free from Jews and Magyars" was one of the slogans of the Romanian fascist movement, the Iron Guard.

To be sure, the situation of the Magyar minority was far better than what it would become 40 years later under the rule of Nicolae Ceauşescu. It was also better than that of their ethnic cousins in next-door Yugoslavia. But the loss of status and, for many, of adequate employ-ment was painful, as was the severance from Hungary proper. By 1924 some 197,000 Magyars had fled, most of them to Hungary, and a further 169,000 emigrated over the remainder of the interwar period. There remained, in 1936, 1,483,000 Magyars in the annexed territories, where they accounted for 26.7 percent of the population; the figures for Tran-sylvania proper were 998,000 and 31 percent.[17] They voted massively for the Magyar party, which rather hopelessly invoked the Alba Iulia promises of devolution and ethnic self-government.

Historically, social stratification among the Magyars of Transylvania had been less pronounced than in Inner Hungary. Reduced to minority status, the Magyars displayed a remarkable cohesion that was rein-forced by their Catholic and Protestant churches—traditional defenders of cultural identity—and sundry organizations. Magyar minorities in other countries, as well as those in the territories beyond Transylvania proper that were awarded to Romania, simply felt detached from the motherland. The Transylvanian Magyars, on the other hand, inherited a history of dual allegiance, to Transylvania as well as to Hungary.

This sense of local nationalism was developed in the interwar period into a myth of Transylvanism, which highlighted—and idealized—the province's separate history, experience of multiculturalism, and religious tolerance. Looking to the future, Transylvanism evoked the prospect of an autonomous Transylvania where the different nationalities would coexist peacefully.[18] This romantic notion may have held appeal even for some Transylvanian Romanians, who felt culturally distinct from their cousins in Wallachia and Moldavia, but the cleavage between the political cultures of Magyars and Romanians was even greater. The former, partly thanks to the strength of Calvinism, were better prepared to draw a distinction between nation and state and to accept pluralism and the rule of law; the latter valued nationhood above other allegiances and displayed a comparatively passive acceptance—nurtured in part by Orthodoxy—of the temporal power.

In Hungary, the option of an independent Transylvania drew wide support, for even radical nationalists had to acknowledge that reannexation of the entire province was an ethnically unjustifiable goal. In an autonomous Transylvania, linked perhaps to Hungary, or Romania, or both, the ethnic balance would be less unfavorable to the Magyars. However, even if the scheme had some theoretical merit, it obviously conflicted with Romania's fiercely nationalistic ethos, in which Transylvania was regarded as the ancestral cradle of the nation, henceforth inalienable; nor did other European powers show interest in such radical revision of the map. Meanwhile, the Hungarian Revision League campaigned for a different solution to the problem of the Hungarian minority: the reannexation of the Székely lands, linked to Hungary by a corridor through Cluj, and of the Magyar-inhabited border districts. Until the late 1930s territorial revision remained a dream, but neither the Magyar minority nor Hungary became reconciled to Trianon.

YUGOSLAVIA

In the case of Yugoslavia, too, expediency on the part of the peacemakers worked in favor of Serb ambitions and to the detriment of Hungary. The new Kingdom of Serbs, Croats, and Slovenes (its original title) was a concatenation of regions divided by history and culture. Historically, Croatia had preserved a varying degree of autonomy under Austrian and Hungarian suzerainty, but few Croats wished to perpetuate this link. In 1910 Croatia had a population of 1,622,000, of whom 106,000 were Magyar.

The bulk of Yugoslavia's Magyar minority lived in Vojvodina, a 19,000-square-kilometer stretch of rich agricultural land that had been part of Hungary proper. It encompassed the southern end of Baranya County between the Drava and Danube Rivers; the Bácska (Backa) region between the Danube and the Tisza Rivers; and, east of the Tisza, a slice of the Banat. As late as the fourteenth century, the population was predominantly Magyar, but after the devastation of the Turkish conquest, the region was repopulated with Serbs and Germans. The Magyar population grew again in the late nineteenth century; Magyarization was, at least in political terms, successful among the German Swabians, but much less so among the Serbs, whose nationalism focused on Belgrade. In 1910 the region's population stood at 1,350,000, including 455,000 southern Slavs, 442,000 Magyars, and 311,000 Germans. By 1921 the number of Magyars had fallen to 382,000. The greatest concentration of Magyars was found near the new frontier, in the Baranya triangle, in northern Bácska, and in northwestern Banat.

With the assent of the Allied (French) command, Serbian troops occupied the region (as well as an additional slice of Hungary) in November 1918. By some estimates, a plebiscite would have favored Hungary, but a local assembly of Serbs called for union with Yugoslavia.[19] In drawing the eventual frontier line, the peacemakers accommodated the Serbs' strategic claim even to areas where they were in a minority.

The main priority of Yugoslavia's Serbs was to consolidate a state founded on their association with Croats and Slovenes, and the smaller ethnic groups became in some respects the incidental victims of the Serbs' hegemonic bent. The Magyars were mainly peasants lower on the socioeconomic scale than local Serbs and Germans; they were left with little leadership after the repatriation of Hungarian officials and the expropriation of the few major landowners. The Serbs, for their part, regarded the Magyars as archenemies, and thus the latter were hit particularly hard by Belgrade's illiberal nationality policies.

The minority's early attempts at political organization were brutally repressed, and the situation scarcely improved with the advent of royal dictatorship in 1929. At the local level, the election of Magyars (and Germans) was routinely annulled, and Serbs were appointed to official posts; minority languages were excluded from public life; all placenames were Serbized; and the minorities were progressively expunged from the civil service. Yugoslavia, unlike the other successor states, limited minority-language education to the elementary level and severely restricted the Magyars' cultural and economic activities. The large class of Magyar agricultural laborers and subsistence farmers was virtually excluded from the redistribution of land, and it was not even allowed to buy land within 50 kilometers of the Hungarian frontier. Serb colonists, meanwhile, were settled in all parts of the Vojvodina.

Economic discrimination contributed to the alienation of the minority from the new state, as did the revisionist stance of their early leadership and of Hungary, although the latter tended to concentrate its fire on Czechoslovakia and Romania. In the early 1930s, a new Magyar political leader in Vojvodina adopted a more conciliatory approach and obtained minor concessions. But the vast majority of Yugoslavia's Magyars, as well as Germans, remained decidedly uncomfortable under the Serbs' iron rule and harbored a wish to rejoin Hungary.

In summary, the interwar period was marked by a persistent and fierce resentment in Hungary as well as among the Magyar minorities at the terms of the Trianon settlement. Irredentism, which helped to legitimate Hungary's conservative regime, poisoned regional relations. The Magyars in Czechoslovakia fared the best, followed by those in Romania, but none of them accepted the finality of their severance from the mother country. The host states, engaged in a process of nation-building, treated the minorities as subversive aliens. Thus none of the actors was disposed to seek a peaceful compromise.

Frontiers Revised and Restored

When Hitler's pursuit of territorial and hegemonic objectives met with Western appeasement, the prospects of Hungarian revisionism began to improve. Hungary's leaders correctly anticipated that they would find more sympathy in a Berlin and Rome eager to buy influence than in Paris or London. When Britain and France acquiesced in March 1938 to the Austrian *Anschluss* and, in September, at Munich, to Germany's annexation of the Czech Sudetenland, Hungary felt encouraged to seek similar support for its own revisionist claims, first with regard to Czechoslovakia.[20]

However, if Hitler's aggressiveness, backed by German might, induced the West to compromise, Hungary earned no such accommodation. Slovak separatism was on the rise, but it did not favor reattachment to Hungary. For its part, the Magyar minority in Slovakia solidly supported its political party and was more than ever revisionist in sentiment, although it did not follow the Sudeten Germans' resort to agitation and terrorism. Following inconclusive negotiations between Prague and Budapest, the dispute was settled by Italo-German arbitration, which, in November 1938, produced the first Vienna Award.[21] The settlement restored to Hungary a 12,000-square-kilometer strip of Slovakia and part of Ruthenia; the territory encompassed 869,000 people, including 752,000 Magyars. When, in March 1939, the Germans extended their rule to the remaining Czech lands, Hungary proceeded to occupy the rest of Ruthenia. Thus reduced, Slovakia became a separate state under German tutelage.

Germany, the Soviet Union, and the Western powers vied for influence in what remained of independent East-Central Europe. London urged Budapest to settle its territorial dispute directly with Bucharest, but the talks reached an impasse. In August 1940, by the second Vienna Award, Hungary regained some 40 percent of the area granted to Romania at Trianon, covering a swath of northern Transylvania that encompassed the most heavily Magyar-inhabited districts. The reannexed segment held 1,343,000 Magyars and 1,069,000 Romanians. Romania's leaders proceeded to align themselves with Germany, hoping thereby to obtain an eventual restitution of Transylvania as well as of the territories they had been forced earlier to cede to the Soviet Union.

In December 1940 Hungary signed a pact of eternal friendship with Yugoslavia. When, the following April, Germany moved its troops across Hungary to invade Yugoslavia, Prime Minister Pál Teleki took his own life in protest, but Hungary could not resist the temptation to share in the spoils and reannexed the larger part of Vojvodina. That completed the cycle of territorial revision. The reannexations expanded Hungary's area from 29 to 53 percent of its extent before Trianon, and its population from 8.7 to 14.7 million. Once again, the bulk of the region's Magyars were united in a single state, but the proportion of ethnic minorities in that state had risen from 10 to 22 percent.

In the process, what many Hungarians had feared all along, their subjection to German influence, came to pass. Irredentism and anti-bolshevism had led Hungary into the Axis camp. In 1939, the country joined the Anti-Comintern Pact and left the League of Nations; and, in 1941, it became an active belligerent against the Soviet Union. Budapest tried to pursue a delicate balancing act to salvage Hungary's autonomy and succeeded to the point that Hitler was provoked to impose military occupation on the country in March 1944. But even if the Western powers had originally endorsed some of the border changes in favor of Hungary, they were not likely to show the same sympathy for a nominally enemy state.

There was great patriotic rejoicing at the reannexations and national reunification. To be sure, in the case of Upper Hungary, 20 years of separation had brought about some sociopolitical differentiation between the Magyars of Slovakia and of Hungary. The minority had benefited from a more equitable distribution of land, more progressive social policies, and greater tolerance of left-wing movements than obtained in Hungary, and the return to Hungarian administration led to some regression at least in the latter two respects. On the other hand, the reannexed Magyars escaped the more oppressive and nationalistic, quasi-Nazi regime that came to dominate rump Slovakia and, of course, regained full cultural rights.[22]

The restoration of Hungarian administration in the reannexed part of Transylvania similarly satisfied the local Magyars' nationalistic sentiments and cultural needs, notably in the reestablishment of the Hungarian university at Kolozsvár (Cluj). The non-Magyar minorities in the reannexed territories suffered little active discrimination, and it has to be recorded that, until 1944, the situation of Jews remained better in Hungary's central and reclaimed parts than in Slovakia or Romania. The partition of Transylvania did produce a two-way migration of Magyars and Romanians; in one of the larger population shifts of the times, some 200,000 of the Magyars left on the Romanian side of the border moved to northern Transylvania or central Hungary.

For much of the war, conditions remained comparatively stable and peaceful in Upper Hungary and Transylvania. The Vojvodina, on the other hand, was touched by the partisan campaign waged by several Yugoslav factions against the Germans and their Hungarian allies. When, in reprisal against partisan attacks, Hungarian troops massacred 3,300 civilians at Újvidék (Novi Sad), relations between Serbs and Magyars hit a new low.

At war's end, the successor states promptly reimposed their rule over the disputed territories. Both Yugoslavia and Czechoslovakia benefited from Allied status, which in the case of the latter led the Big Three to overlook Slovakia's pro-Nazi autonomy. To win the sympathy of the Allies, Romania changed sides at the last moment. Meanwhile, Hungary's attempts to seek a separate peace with the Western Allies fell victim to the reality of Soviet military predominance in the region and to German occupation. Thus the interests of Hungary and of the prewar Magyar minorities were not destined to weigh heavily in the next round of peacemaking, and all the less because of the preponderant influence of the Soviet Union.

In their planning for peace, the Allies had agreed that the territorial revision effected since the Austrian *Anschluss* was null and void. American planners nevertheless devoted some attention to Hungary's claims and recommended minor frontier modifications to fit the criteria of self-determination and ethnic homogeneity; these involved a few Magyar-inhabited districts just beyond the Trianon borders with Slovakia, Romania, and Yugoslavia.[23] Soviet support for the successor states carried the day. Although Moscow advised Budapest to seek accommodation with its neighbors, Stalin had no sympathy for the Hungarians, nor any interest in favoring their freely elected government, in which the majority was anticommunist. As a result, after 1945 the Magyar minorities would face conditions far harsher than in the interwar period.

CZECHOSLOVAKIA

In the case of Czechoslovakia, Edvard Beneš, head of the government-in-exile, was intent on consolidating his country by eliminating disloyal ethnic minorities. At Potsdam, the Allies agreed to the expulsion of ethnic German minorities but not of Magyars. Nevertheless, the Magyars of Slovakia were branded with collective guilt. In the spring and summer of 1945, a series of decrees stripped them of property and all civil rights.

In response to Budapest's protests, the Allies recommended bilateral negotiation. The Czechs envisaged a combination of population exchange, expulsion, and re-Slovakization; the Hungarians argued for reannexation of solidly Magyar districts and for a balanced exchange involving the remaining Magyars. Agreement was reached on a limited exchange, and the Paris Peace Conference instructed the protagonists to persevere in this approach. In addition, the peacemakers partially satisfied Czechoslovakia's demand for a further fragment of Hungarian territory, across the Danube from Bratislava (Pozsony), which was claimed to be necessary for that city's economic expansion.

Ultimately, over 70,000 of Slovakia's Magyars were exchanged—mostly against their will—for a somewhat smaller number of Slovaks from Hungary. Another 32,000 Magyars had been branded war criminals and summarily expelled to Hungary, and over 40,000 were deported to the Czech territories recently cleared of Sudeten Germans. Those remaining were deprived of property and citizenship, and of all educational and cultural facilities; they also were subjected to re-Slovakization.[24]

RUTHENIA

An even grimmer fate awaited the Magyars in Ruthenia, a region that Beneš accommodatingly handed over to the Soviet Union and that became the Transcarpathian district of the Ukraine. At war's end, much of the adult male population was deported eastward; for many, it was a one-way voyage. The minority's schools, cultural facilities, and churches were shut down, and the region was sealed off from Hungary.

TRANSYLVANIA

Stalin had promised Transylvania to the Romanians, partly as an inducement to change sides and partly as compensation for the reannexation of Bessarabia and northern Bukovina to the Soviet Union. When the region came under Soviet-Romanian occupation in the fall of 1944, the Magyar minority was subjected to a reign of terror at the hand of vengeful Romanians, known as the Maniu guards, who had the tacit encouragement of the government in Bucharest. Over 100,000 Magyars left Transylvania in this chaotic period, some voluntarily, others under pressure from the retreating German and Hungarian forces or the Romanians.

A momentarily favorable circumstance was that Romania's small and hitherto proscribed communist movement included a dispropor-tionate number of Magyars (including Jews). The latter condemned Bucharest's anti-Hungarian incitement, and the Soviets temporarily shunted aside Romanian officials to put northern Transylvania under military administration.

In February 1945, the Bucharest government enacted a liberal nation-alities statute that granted minorities certain collective rights with regard to language and education. The next, communist-dominated government, headed by the comparatively pro-Magyar Petru Groza, enjoyed the backing of the minority's sole political organization, the leftist-led Hungarian People's Federation. The latter drew the support of most Magyars—for practical rather than ideological reasons, as the traditional Romanian parties were violently nationalistic.

Groza obtained the return of northern Transylvania to Romanian administration by promising equitable treatment of the minorities, but few of his promises came to be implemented. Magyars who had tem-porarily left Transylvania were stripped of their citizenship; they, and those who had opted for Hungarian citizenship in the wake of the Vienna Award, were branded traitors and had their property seized. The Magyars were allowed to retain most of their schools, and the Hun-garian university at Cluj was reopened, although most of its facilities and equipment were taken over by a Romanian-language institution. Economic reforms were applied in discriminatory fashion, notably with regard to the redistribution of land and the producers' and consumers' cooperatives that had been founded by Magyars. The minority's access to newspapers and other cultural products from Hungary was severely constrained.[25]

Although the Hungarian People's Federation failed to obtain the codification of broader minority rights, it declared itself satisfied with the minority's prospects in a "democratic" Romania and opposed to any territorial partition in favor of Hungary. That optimistic opinion was not shared by many Magyars, either in Romania or in Hungary. In March 1946, when relations between Washington and Moscow were turning frosty, the American envoy to Budapest observed that it might be fruitful to bolster Hungary's pro-Western government with an ethnically justified boundary adjustment, particularly at a time when Romania was fast slipping into the Soviet sphere.[26] Moscow advised Budapest to negotiate with Groza, but the Hungarians' various proposals for modifying the boundary were rejected both by the latter and in the Council of Foreign Ministers. As an American diplomat observed, "east of the dividing line the United States showed little inclination to tilt at windmills by pressing for 'ethnic lines' and 'fair solutions.'"[27] The Trianon order was restored, this time under the patronage of the Soviet Union. The Magyar minorities' future circumstances would be determined by the interests of the Kremlin and its several client regimes.

VOJVODINA

The restoration of Yugoslav rule in Vojvodina occurred amid systematic reprisals that took the lives of over 20,000 Magyars, including much of the intelligentsia (along with 200,000 indigenous Germans).[28] Although a few Magyars had joined Tito's partisans, initially the minority as a whole was treated as a defeated enemy. Some 30,000 Magyars fled to Hungary, the majority of the surviving German population was expelled, and over 40,000 Serbs were settled along with their families in Vojvodina under the terms of a new land reform.

The communist internationalism of Tito's movement received practical application when, in 1946, the Yugoslav Federal Constitution entrenched the principle of national equality. In a party-state that was initially closely modeled on the Soviet Union, Vojvodina became a province of the Serbian Republic. Its Magyar minority was allowed a (communist-led) Cultural Association, and Hungarian-language schools at the primary and secondary level were reopened. At the same time, the Magyars suffered disproportionately from the party's iron rule and persecution of anticommunists. But Tito's Yugoslavia was both a member of the United Nations and closely linked, until 1948, to the Soviet Union. Budapest was reduced to pleading for lenient treatment of the minority and to negotiating a voluntary population exchange that never was implemented.

In sum, revision of the Trianon borders may have satisfied Hungarian nationalists and brought momentary relief to the Magyar minorities, but it scarcely dispelled national antagonisms in the region. After the war, the successor states reacted violently to their minorities' disloyalty and to what they regarded as Hungary's predatory acts. The mutual stereotypes remained essentially negative and the mutual grievances greater than ever. For the common Magyar who once again found himself under foreign rule, peacemaking was equated with injustice.

Magyar Minorities under Communism

With Europe divided by an Iron Curtain that was all too palpable, the issue of ethnic minorities in the East acquired a wholly new complexion. The dynamic interaction of Magyar minorities, host state, mother country, and third parties that had characterized the interwar period was superseded by the sweeping social revolution conducted under Soviet auspices. Once it had consolidated its hold over the region, the Soviet Union no longer needed to exploit the minority issue to advance its interests. Stalinism imposed institutional uniformity and a commonality of revolutionary purpose. National particularism was proscribed for ethnic majorities and minorities alike, in domestic affairs as well as in bilateral and interparty relations.

Thus, for the first time since 1918, Hungary fell silent on the issue of Magyar minorities, and the silence would remain unbroken until the 1970s. The minorities, in turn, were sealed off from contact with the mother country and came to be regarded by their communist masters, at least officially, as the undifferentiated subjects of a historic experiment in social engineering. According to the legitimizing propaganda of the totalitarian communist states, nationalism and interethnic antagonism were aberrations of the bourgeois past, to be superseded by socialist internationalism, by loyalty to the Soviet Union, and by united support of the ruling party. Over time nationalism would resurface, both in popular revolts and in the practices of certain regimes; but at the outset ethnic discrimination and interests were laid to rest. Ironically, the principal Magyar minorities drew some marginal benefit from the imposition of Stalinism.

CZECHOSLOVAKIA

In Czechoslovakia, the Magyars began to emerge from a four-year-long nightmare of persecution. In 1948 their citizenship and civil rights—communist version—were restored, and most of those deported to the Sudetenland were allowed to return to Slovakia. It is a measure of their lingering fear that no more than 350,000 people claimed to be Magyar in the 1950 census; ten years later, after the annulment of the re-Slovakization decree, the number rose to 518,000.

The Magyars' property losses were never compensated, but they shared more or less equally in the economic vicissitudes that accompanied the building of socialism. Once again, their intelligentsia had been severely depleted as a consequence of the expulsions, population exchange, and, at least potentially, the hiatus in education. Hungarian-language instruction was reintroduced in elementary schools in 1949 and soon afterward in secondary schools as well. The 1960 constitution spelled out the minorities' right to cultural development and education in their mother tongue.

The Magyars' nemesis, Slovak nationalism, was far from a spent force, but in the 1950s it was kept in check by the strongly centralist Prague regime. Meanwhile, the minority's sole official spokesman, the Cultural Association of Hungarian Workers of Czechoslovakia (CSEMADOK by its Hungarian acronym), acted as a dutiful servant of the state. CSEMADOK came to life as a Magyar interest group only in 1968, during the Prague Spring, when it submitted a proposal for limited self-government by the national minorities. The principle that the latter had collective rights was enshrined in the Action Program of the Czech party reformers.

The reformist spirit lingered for a while after the restoration of pro-Soviet rule. A new constitution carried over, in watered-down form, the notion of collective minority rights, but it also federalized the country, thereby giving greater scope to Slovak nationalism. In October 1968 the Slovak National Council adopted a nationalities law that made no provision for cultural autonomy, although it did establish an advisory Council of Nationalities. The following year a Magyar, László Dobos, became a minister in the first Slovak government, and under his leadership, CSEMADOK styled itself a sociopolitical association representing the minority's interests. In the same period the Magyars earned some cultural concessions, including a publishing house, a youth organization, and a regional theater in Kosice (Kassa).

In the early 1970s, concessions gave way to a process of Slovakization. The notion of collective minority interests and cultural autonomy was denounced as anti-Leninist, and CSEMADOK was reduced to its earlier bureaucratic functions. Dobos and other Magyar officials lost their posts, state investment in Magyar districts was sharply reduced, and more Slovak-language courses were introduced in Magyar schools. In 1976 the Bratislava authorities drew up plans to cut by half the number of pupils in Magyar schools, to be accomplished by a combination of dissuasion and preferential development of Slovak schools. Between 1970 and 1980, enrollment in Magyar primary schools fell by 30 percent.

Official pressure was probably more significant than voluntary assimilation and intermarriage in reducing the number of people declaring Magyar nationality; the 1980 census showed 560,000 Magyars, which, taking into account natural growth rates, represented a relative decline in their number.

The progressive Slovakization of education contravened the minorities' constitutionally guaranteed rights, argued a group of Magyar intellectuals who, under the leadership of the geologist Miklós Duray, formed themselves in 1978 into a Committee for the Defense of the Rights of the Hungarian Minority in Czechoslovakia. Drawing encouragement from the recent Helsinki agreements, the committee relayed its protests to the Czech civil rights group, Charter 77, the Conference on Security and Cooperation in Europe (CSCE) follow-up meeting in Madrid, and the London-based Minority Rights Group.[29]

In 1982, Duray was arrested and charged with bourgeois nationalist activities. By then the promotion of human rights in the Helsinki process had made a palpable impact in the Soviet sphere of dominance. The trial was attended by foreign observers as well as by representatives of the Hungarian Writers' Union, and Budapest reportedly conveyed its misgivings to Bratislava. Duray was freed without a verdict. The scenario was replayed in 1984, when the Magyars mounted public protests against a draft bill aiming at further reduction of their educational facilities; once again Duray was arrested and, after a year's detention without trial, freed under a general amnesty. In 1986, when Hungarian cultural institutions in Bratislava were vandalized, Charter 77 joined in condemning anti-Magyar violence.

Thus, as the state-socialist system was nearing its end in the East, both majority and minority nationalism became more manifest in Slovakia, although the former was obviously the superior force. Discrimination in the educational and economic spheres had served to depress the Magyars' socioeconomic status and cultural levels. Hungarian place-names were eliminated from signs; Magyars were forbidden to use their mother tongue in administrative dealings and in institutions and workplaces, and were pressured to Slovakize their given names. The power of the party-state made policies of assimilation far more oppressive than had been the case in the interwar period. Access to Hungarian radio and television programs no doubt reinforced the Magyars' cultural consciousness, but they had particular reason to cheer the advent of democracy in 1989.

The issue of the Magyar minority did not figure, at least openly, in interstate or interparty relations. The Hungarian troops that participated in the Warsaw Pact intervention of 1968 earned little welcome among the Magyars, let alone the Slovaks, and Budapest's cordial relations with Prague reflected the former's close emulation of Soviet foreign policy. Hungary's official indifference to the minority's grievances does not seem to have mitigated the Slovak nationalist tendency to see cultural Slovakization as the necessary remedy to a dangerous alien presence. In the late 1980s a Hungarian-Czechoslovak project for dams on the Danube drew much unofficial criticism in Hungary because of its ecological impact, notably on the most compact area of Magyar settlement on the Slovak side of the border. But independent pressure groups and ecological considerations, like ethnic minorities, carried little weight in the party-states.

THE TRANSCARPATHIAN DISTRICT

Given the Hungarian regime's subservience to Moscow, it is scarcely surprising that the fate of the Magyar minority in the Transcarpathian district (oblast) of Soviet Ukraine remained unmentionable in communist Hungary. According to the Soviet census of 1979, there were some 164,000 Magyars in the former Ruthenia; most of them lived in compact ethnic enclaves, notably in the Beregovo (Beregszász) district.

The postwar sanctions on the minority were eased in the mid-1950s, when some Hungarian secondary schools were reestablished. In the late 1960s the number of purely Magyar schools began to decline and the number of mixed-language schools to grow, reflecting official pressure on parents to favor Ukrainian- and Russian-language education; technical education was available only in the latter languages, and a mere handful of candidates were admitted to Hungarian studies at Uzhgorod State University.

Meanwhile, the Magyars' limited cultural facilities served mainly to propagate the official ideology and national perspectives of the Russians and Ukrainians; Hungarian radio and television was the minority's only contact with the mother country. The scope for ethnic self-assertion in the Soviet Union was even more limited than in the other host states. In 1971, in a rare display of protest, a group of young Magyar poets and writers issued an appeal against the Ukrainianization of the minority's schools; their association was promptly banned, and some of the authors eventually were allowed to resettle in Hungary—a method of dealing with dissidents that the Soviet regime came to adopt in the late 1970s.[30] If the majority of Magyars managed to retain their cultural identity, it was partly thanks to their rural existence in clusters isolated from other ethnic groups.

TRANSYLVANIA

The Magyar minority in Transylvania had drawn some marginal benefit from the calculated tolerance of the pro-communist National Democratic Front during Romania's transition to single-party rule, but the respite was short-lived. With the imposition of integral Stalinism, the Magyar intelligentsia incurred charges of being not only class enemies but also nationalist, and, along with non-Orthodox churchmen, it suffered disproportionately from official persecution. Meanwhile, the anti-Titoist purges served as an opportunity to eliminate the strong Magyar (and Jewish) contingent from the Romanian Communist Party's higher echelons. The Hungarian Federation was similarly purged, then stripped of all practical functions.

The 1952 constitution emulated the Soviet model in creating a Hungarian Autonomous Region to cover the main Székely districts, home to a third of Transylvania's Magyars. Official use of Hungarian was gradually restricted to this ethnic enclave, and some Magyar cultural institutions were transferred from Cluj to the region's principal town, Tirgu-Mures (Marosvásárhely).[31] Regional autonomy turned out to be largely illusory in the centralized party-state. In 1960 the boundaries were redrawn to reduce the proportion of Magyars from 75 to 62 percent, and the name was changed to Mures-Maghiar Autonomous Region. Six years later, administrative regions were abolished and supplanted by the county system. Two counties, Harghita (Hargita) and Covasna (Kovászna), had a predominantly Magyar population but no more autonomy than the defunct region.

The constitutional status of Magyars was that of a coinhabiting nationality in a Romanian national state. Successive constitutions and amendments reaffirmed the minorities' language rights in education, culture, and local administration and proscribed ethnic or other discrimination as well as "nationalistic-chauvinistic propaganda and incitement to racial or national hatred." In practice, party rule supplanted the rule of law, notably by the application of confidential internal regulations and by the activity of the ubiquitous secret police, the Securitate.

Respect for the Magyar minority's educational and cultural rights was greater in the early 1950s, at the height of Stalinism, than in the later period, when Romanian nationalism became a key legitimizing tool of the Ceauşescu dictatorship.[32] Church-affiliated schools, 80 percent of which had been Hungarian, were nationalized; on the other hand, education in the Hungarian language was offered not only in primary and secondary schools but also at several postsecondary institutions, notably the Bolyai University at Cluj and a medical faculty and drama school at Tirgu-Mures. Even the Csángós, a community of some 70,000 Catholic Magyars who had survived in isolation around Bacau (Bákó), in Moldavia, obtained Hungarian-language schools.

The short-lived revolution of 1956 in Hungary drew some open displays of sympathy from Transylvania's Magyars. There followed mass arrests and trials of Magyars and a succession of Romanizing measures punctuated by minor concessions. Thus, after the abolition of the autonomous region, a Council of Workers of Hungarian Nationality was created, and the Magyars got a publishing house as well as a television program in their language.

The state exercised its exclusive control over the economy and allocation of labor to progressively alter the ethnic mix in Transylvania. The government's strategy was to boost the proportion of ethnic Romanians, particularly in the towns, and to disperse Magyar professionals and other workers to predominantly Romanian parts of the country. Thus Magyars were reduced to a minority in such towns as Cluj, Oradea (Nagyvárad), and Satu-Mare (Szatmárnémeti), and their proportion of Transylvania's population fell from 25.7 percent in 1948 to 22 percent in 1977. In the same period the officially reported number of Magyars rose from 1,500,000 to 1,700,000, while Romania's total population grew from under 16 million to over 21 million—a disparity in growth rates that many suspected was not fully attributable to voluntary assimilation. At the same time, growing discrimination in admission to higher education reduced the proportion of Magyar professionals. In 1959, the Magyar university in Cluj was merged with the Romanian one to become an almost exclusively Romanian-language institution; the event was marked by the suicide of several Magyar professors.

The Romanianization of education had begun earlier, when Magyar primary schools were merged with Romanian ones. The Csángós, for their part, lost their last Magyar school in 1958. The merging of Magyar and Romanian secondary schools began in 1959 and was completed by the mid-1980s. In the wake of this consolidation, the teaching staff and language of instruction in nominally Magyar school sections were progressively Romanianized. The result was a steady decline in the proportion of Magyar children educated in the mother tongue; and they, like others, were taught a history of Transylvania that largely ignored the predominant role played by Hungarians.

Magyars were progressively excluded from the administrative apparatus of the party-state, the officer corps, and economic management, in a process of Romanianization that culminated in the 1980s, when many Magyar educational and cultural institutions also came to be headed by ethnic Romanians. The few Magyars who reached higher office in the party were not regarded as representatives of the minority either by their superiors or by their conationals, and neither were those in the rubber-stamp Grand National Assembly. The Council of Workers of Hungarian Nationality, officially designed to represent the Magyars' interests, consisted of party-state appointees and never acquired its own statutes or organization. At first, the council included some notable members of the Magyar intelligentsia and tried to address issues of interest to the minority, but in 1971 the leadership was purged, and there were no further meetings for three years. Later the council was occasionally reconvened to serve as an obedient mouthpiece of the regime. Thus the minority had no legitimate outlet for promoting its interests.

Beginning in the late 1970s, the rising pressure of Romanianization and the Helsinki human rights campaign prompted sporadic protests by the Magyars. A few prominent figures, including Lajos Takáts, a former rector of the Magyar university, and the former Central Committee member Károly Király, addressed petitions of grievances to the authorities. Magyar intellectuals who launched an underground information bulletin were soon arrested and expelled from the country. Far from turning conciliatory, the regime denounced the dissidents and the minority in general as harboring chauvinistic and revisionist sentiments and intensified repressive measures.

To be sure, all Romanians suffered from the oppressive nature of the system, which came to be ruled in tyrannical fashion by Nicolae Ceauşescu and his family. But Romania was distinguished from its socialist allies by the regime's effort to win legitimacy through the promotion of nationalism. In the foreign policy arena, Ceauşescu's independent posturing irritated the Kremlin and earned some scarcely deserved plaudits in the West.

The official nationalist ideology revived and accentuated the nation-building myths of the prewar period. Thus the ethnic Romanian nation and its state were represented as an organic unity; the Magyars were depicted as historical interlopers in the process of Daco-Roman continuity, as the fundamentally alien oppressors of Romanian Transylvania in the past, and as an unassimilable, crypto-revisionist threat to the integrity and cohesion of contemporary Romania. The Magyars' claim to cultural autonomy implied that a distinction could be drawn between cultural and civic allegiance, but Romania's rulers emphatically rejected the civic form of nationalism in favor of the essentially xenophobic dogma of organic Romanian nationhood.[33] By the early 1980s, the regime's favored authors were publishing virulent diatribes against the Magyars.[34]

Thus ethnic Romanians were encouraged to believe that all their troubles, past and present, owed to the presence of Magyars. The latter, on the other hand, were too conscious of their history and too rooted a community to accept the status of unwanted, second-class citizens. To be sure, cordiality was not wholly absent in daily contact between Transylvania's Magyars and ethnic Romanians; and the autochthonous Romanians were generally less hostile than those transplanted from Moldavia and Wallachia. But the fact is that the nationalistic propaganda struck a responsive chord among the mass of Romanians. The few active Magyar dissidents soon lost hope of conciliating the latter or the rulers; their efforts were aimed more to raise minority spirits and alert world public opinion.

Official nationalism may have appealed to ethnic Romanians, but its discriminatory and exclusionary character weighed heavily on the Magyar and other minorities. Bucharest plainly wished to be rid of all minorities, and West Germany as well as Israel obliged by paying a per capita ransom; the country's German and Jewish communities were rapidly depleted by emigration. Hungary had neither the financial means nor the political will to follow suit, and the Magyars, by far the largest minority, were less disposed to leave their ancestral home. Still, by the 1980s a growing number became sufficiently desperate to seek emigration to Hungary and the West. The regime welcomed the departure of Magyar intellectuals and professionals who might have given leadership to the minority but, perversely, made the process of obtaining an exit permit arduous and humiliating.[35] Meanwhile, at Romania's initiative, cultural relations with Hungary were kept to a minimum; there was virtually no tourist traffic, and the Magyars of Transylvania had little access to Hungarian media other than the radio.

It is a common tactic of regimes facing difficulty in satisfying socioeconomic needs to seek legitimacy by demonizing an internal or external enemy, and the Magyars as well as Hungary fulfilled this function for Romania's rulers. The minority was scarcely in a position to put up active resistance, and since it could be neither assimilated nor expelled en masse, it remained a hostage to majority nationalism.

Hungary's communist regime readily excoriated its predecessors' irredentism and nationalism, but it abstained from criticizing the rise of intolerant nationalism in Romania. The difference between the two countries' approach to nationalism owed to hegemonic as well as domestic factors. Hungarian nationalism had precipitated the 1956 revolution, which momentarily swept away the communist system; both the Kremlin and its client regime in Budapest were intent on preventing a recurrence, and subsequent attempts at political legitimation were restricted to economic reform and a more permissive cultural policy. In the case of Romania, insofar as its leaders promoted nationalism to consolidate an oppressive party-state, they served Soviet interests. Given Romania's marginal strategic importance, the Kremlin could afford to overlook Ceauşescu's occasional deviation from Soviet foreign policy, and all the more so because such deviation gave substance to the myth that the satellite states were truly sovereign.

When the Hungarian party leader János Kádár visited Romania in 1958, he dutifully reiterated that his country had no territorial claims and made no reference to the local Magyars. The minority remained a taboo topic until the 1960s, when some literary and scholarly interest was allowed to develop. In the next decade, Budapest's policy evolved to the extent of allowing publication of ostensibly apolitical reports on the minority; the change probably was facilitated by Ceauşescu's relative unpopularity in Moscow. When Kádár and Ceauşescu met in 1977, they allowed that ethnic minorities could form a bridge between neighboring countries and agreed to expand cultural relations as well as to open consulates in Cluj and Debrecen (Hungary). The thaw proved to be illusory. Tourist traffic increased, but Romania procrastinated on the consulate and further curtailed cultural contacts; even the tiny flow of Transylvanian Magyar students to Hungary was stopped. Relations between Budapest and Bucharest reached a nadir in the 1980s, when the Ceauşescu regime tried to defuse domestic tensions by actively promoting anti-Magyar sentiments among ethnic Romanians.[36]

Only in the mid-1980s, when the international climate turned more favorable to human rights advocacy, did Hungary begin to raise the minority issue at CSCE meetings. Finally, in early 1988, the Hungarian party formally addressed the question, referring to the region's Magyar minorities as part of the Hungarian nation and affirming Hungary's interest in their welfare. By then the regime was floundering, and two clusters of political dissidents campaigned openly not only for democratic reform but also for a vigorous advocacy of the rights of Magyar minorities. The more nationalist of these movements, Hungarian Democratic Forum, produced detailed reports and organized debates on the Magyar minorities. That same year the megalomaniacal Ceauşescu launched a systematization program to increase agricultural production by razing thousands of villages and concentrating farmers in newly built centers; Magyars saw in the scheme a covert design to destroy their communities and cultural legacy, and there was a public protest in Budapest. Ceauşescu's days were numbered, and the Democratic Forum was heading to be Hungary's first democratically elected government since 1945.

There is little reason to believe that the behavior of either the Transylvanian Magyars or Hungary had much of an impact on Romanian minority policy in the communist era. Although that policy occasionally was influenced by external factors, such as the Hungarian revolution and the invasion of Czechoslovakia, it was essentially driven by the Bucharest regime's strategy of legitimation by nationalism. The strategy succeeded in heightening nationalism among ethnic Romanians and alienating the minority, thus leaving a twin legacy that would burden both the new democratic order and relations between postcommunist Romania and Hungary.

YUGOSLAVIA

Of the Magyar minorities in communist states, the one in Yugoslavia fared best, at least once Tito had rejected Soviet tutelage. The first federal constitution affirmed the right of nationalities to self-determination and even to secession, but when, in 1948, the Soviet bloc launched a virulent campaign to topple Josip Tito, the priority shifted to national unity. Communist Hungary was an active participant in the campaign, charging that the Magyar minority suffered from "chauvinist pan-Serbian" oppression.[37] Unsettled by the Soviet threat, Tito shifted to a centralist policy based on the notion of Yugoslavism. The resulting constraints on regional autonomy had the side effect of sheltering Magyars from the arbitrariness of local officials.

When Stalin's successors made their peace with Tito, the latter momentarily entertained hope that other communist countries might emulate his nonalignment. Since Hungary's Stalinist leaders had been exceptionally vicious in their anti-Titoism, he looked sympathetically on the revolution that broke out in October 1956. Only when events took a decidedly anticommunist turn did he endorse, with some reluctance, the forceful restoration of Soviet suzerainty. Yugoslavia's Magyars, for their part, had been happy enough to avoid the Stalinist oppression that prevailed in Hungary and remained loyal to the host state during this turbulent period.

The principle of national equality was reaffirmed by the ruling party in 1958, and minority rights, including official use of mother tongue, were entrenched in the 1963 statute of the Autonomous Province of Vojvodina. The 1960s ushered in a progressive decentralization of the federation. The 1974 constitution drew a distinction between "nations" (the Serbs, Croats, and Slovenes) and "nationalities" (the Magyar and other lesser minorities), reserving to the former the right of self-determination and secession. Thus devolution did not extend to the Magyars. Their practical grievances involved comparatively minor issues, such as insufficient bilingualism in public services. The minority had a far higher proportion of blue-collar workers than the Slavs, and while it shared in the province's agriculture-based prosperity, social mobility was largely contingent on assimilation to the Serbs.[38] This, promoted in some measure by intermarriage, explains why, between 1950 and 1980, the number of self-professed Magyars in Yugoslavia declined from 450,000 to 427,000 and enrollment in Hungarian schools fell by a third. There was, in the same period, a heavy influx of mainly Serb settlers.

By the region's yardsticks, the Magyar minority was well served in educational and cultural facilities, and interethnic relations in Vojvodina became comparatively harmonious. Under Tito, Serbian nationalism was muted, although appearances were somewhat deceptive. On the rare occasion when Magyar intellectuals would protest at what they construed to be discrimination, they were promptly punished for unseemly nationalism. As late as 1983, the Magyar literary journal *Új Symposion* was shut down for spreading alien views and for oppositionism.

Official Yugoslavia took pride in its nonalignment and ethnic pluralism, and, from the 1960s onward, its citizens were no longer cut off from the outside world. In the same period, Hungary took a reformist course, and the two countries resumed normal relations; visa requirements were abolished in 1966, and cultural as well as economic contacts were intensified, all of which served the interests of Vojvodina's Magyars. The Kádár regime chose to gloss over the latter's subordinate status, but national sensibilities were easily provoked. As the Magyar minority was being eroded by more or less induced assimilation, its intellectuals and some in Hungary were emboldened to sound the alarm. When, in 1982, the Hungarian writer Gyula Illyés complained in a Western interview about the situation of Magyar minorities and mentioned Yugoslavia as a case in point, he was roundly denounced in the Yugoslav press for interference and implicit revisionism.[39]

To recapitulate, the political and cultural situation of the Magyar minorities in the Soviet sphere, specifically in Czechoslovakia and Romania, had been better in some respects during the early 1950s than when their host states began to show signs of nationalism. In the former period, nationalism was proscribed, ethnicity was subordinated to class, and national minorities were expected to preserve their folkloric features while blending harmoniously into a classless socialist society. The difficulties of legitimating state socialism in the satellites derived partly from the lack of participatory democracy and economic dynamism and partly from the suppression of nationalism, which was not only un-Marxist but also a latent anti-Soviet force. The subsequent exploitation, for purposes of legitimation, of majority nationalism was socially divisive in that it excluded the minorities. The latter's attempts to defend their cultural rights and separate identity tended only to reinforce majority nationalism and invite reminders of Hungary's irredentist past. Yugoslavia was unique in its independence and state ideology of multinationalism; although ethnocultural prejudice lurked below the surface, outward manifestations remained largely suppressed in Tito's lifetime.

In Hungary, nationalism was constrained both by the dominant ideology and by the burden of history. The party's propaganda condemned the revisionist nationalism of the old bourgeois order, and the Magyar minorities in the surrounding states became a taboo topic. For the first three decades of communist rule, Hungarians were deprived of information about the minorities and had little opportunity of direct contact with them, even though many Hungarians had family ties across the frontiers. When, in the 1960s, the Kádár regime began to court popular legitimacy with economic reform and cultural tolerance, it initially tried to keep the lid on public debate of the minority issue. Only Hungarian émigrés were free to champion the cause.

The situation began to change in the late 1960s. The liberalization of foreign travel (with Transcarpathian Ukraine a notable exception) allowed many Hungarians to learn firsthand about the vicissitudes of the Magyar minorities. Scholars and writers began to exploit the regime's cultural permissiveness and investigate the past and present of Magyars beyond the borders. In an article published in 1977, the doyen of Hungarian letters, Gyula Illyés, could only allude to the persecution of Transylvanian Magyars, but that was enough to provoke a violent official reaction in Romania. In the years that followed, he and other literati would address the issue with growing openness. In the 1982 interview noted earlier, Illyés gave vent to the Magyars' chronic fear about the survival of their nation. He evoked the pressures suffered by Magyar minorities in the region, Yugoslavia included, deploring in particular the "de-Magyarization" of towns; alluded to the injustice of the Trianon diktat; and speculated about a confederal solution to the problem. The decompression of Hungary's political system allowed for an awakening of national consciousness that inevitably encompassed all fragments of the Magyar nation.

By the early 1980s the Helsinki process had emboldened not only Hungarian intellectuals but also Magyar spokesmen in Slovakia and Romania, and the Budapest regime put its official weight behind the campaign for minority rights. At CSCE meetings Hungary pressed for international codes that went beyond the generalities of the 1975 Final Act, impelling the host states to defend their practices. The campaign failed to reverse assimilative policies in Slovakia and Romania, but it raised international awareness of the problem and contributed to the fall from diplomatic grace of the Ceauşescu regime.

In bilateral diplomacy, Budapest remained constrained by Warsaw Pact solidarity. It promoted the positive role of minorities as cultural bridges, and behind-the-scenes intercession may have alleviated some particular problems, notably in the Duray affair. The Kádár-Ceauşescu meeting brought no positive change in Romanian policy. Budapest's more activist stance only prompted semiofficial charges in Romania that Hungary was eternally revisionist and the minority a Trojan horse of that revisionism. A massive history of Transylvania by Hungarian scholars, commissioned in 1976 and published in 1986 in Budapest, received good reviews in the West but drew virulent criticism from Romania for challenging some cherished elements of the national myth.[40]

Thus the Kádár regime could show few tangible results. It had belatedly acknowledged that Hungary's national interest encompassed the welfare of Magyar minorities. It also came to treat Hungary's own, small ethnic minorities with notable liberality in the hope of inducing reciprocity. The host states, where the minority problem was of an altogether different scale, remained impervious.

The only external power that counted in East European affairs was the Soviet Union, itself home to a small Magyar minority. As long as the satellite parties maintained order and followed the Soviet lead, their national minorities must have counted for little in the Kremlin's calculations. To be sure, whenever Bucharest ventured to mention Bessarabia (today's independent Moldova), Moscow would retaliate by evoking Transylvania, or vice versa. Notwithstanding such diplomatic skirmishes, the Kremlin had no interest in altering the territorial status quo in its sphere and was as indifferent to minority rights as to political and civil rights in general.

Dissidents of all colors in East Central Europe drew encouragement from the more permissive climate induced by Mikhail Gorbachev's perestroika, but, by coincidence, the regimes in the host states with the largest Magyar minorities, Czechoslovakia and Romania, resisted the winds of liberalization to the bitter end. Hungary's ruling party showed greater readiness to adapt and thus facilitated a smooth transition to democracy. Among its legacies was the most intractable issue of national interest, one which 40 years of socialist internationalism had failed to eliminate or resolve: the Magyar minorities.

The Minority Question since 1990

When, in 1989 and early 1990, the regimes of the Soviet satellites gave way in quick succession to governments ostensibly committed to pluralism, hopes ran high that liberal democracy, the free market, and a welcoming Europe would remedy the accumulated ills of the past. The euphoria soon subsided, and it became clear that the national interests unleashed by democracy remained least reconcilable on the very issue of ethnic minorities.

The relational context, on the other hand, underwent radical change. The minorities became active participants in pluralistic political systems; governments became dependent on electoral support; and the states became sovereign actors in a European order marked by a multiplicity of integrative institutions. The assimilation of Western modernity was bound to be arduous, and, with regard to minority rights, the West offered no certain model.

In Hungary, the center-right government of József Antall lost no time in putting the minority issue near the top of its foreign policy priorities. In May 1990, all parties represented in Hungary's freshly elected parliament endorsed a statement that termed the Trianon partition a tragedy but affirmed the permanence of the country's borders and invited guarantees for the collective rights of Magyar minorities. In Hungary's official view, since these minorities were as indigenous as the majorities in the host countries, they ought to be full participants in the building of the democratic state and be granted local and territorial autonomy as well.

The political climate had never seemed so propitious. The passage of time had largely erased the opprobrium of Hungary's prewar irredentism and fateful alliance with the Axis. Revisionism was no longer a significant element in the political culture, and the government, like its communist predecessors, unambiguously excluded territorial revision from its agenda. The Hungarian revolution of 1956, the "goulash communism" of the later Kádár era, and the orderly transition to democracy all contributed to the country's unprecedentedly positive image in the West. Hungary's foreign orientation had been tilted westward even before the fall of communism; its last communist regime had helped to precipitate that fall by allowing masses of East Germans to transit to the West. The desire to integrate in a democratic Europe was shared by its neighbors, where new governments initially showed a conciliatory disposition with respect to the Magyar minorities.

To be sure, a small cloud lurked on this sunny horizon: The restoration of sovereignty liberated nationalism from the shackles imposed by most of Moscow's client regimes, although not by that of Romania. But opposition to Soviet and communist dominance had produced a sense of solidarity, and there was reasonable hope that the demands of modernization and the lure of Europe would focus patriotic energies on positive and integrative tasks.

Antall's government approached the minority problem from several directions. In the CSCE (soon rebaptised the Organization for Security and Cooperation in Europe, or OSCE) and the Council of Europe (CE), it intensified Hungary's diplomatic quest for international conventions that went beyond individual rights and recognized the collective rights of national minorities. Minority rights were also promoted in Budapest's regional diplomacy, notably in the Visegrad Group and the Central European Initiative, and bilaterally, in framework treaties that would include appropriate guarantees. On the home front, the government counted on the demonstration effect of the new and exceptionally liberal Minorities Statute (1993) that entrenched collective rights.[41]

This activism on behalf of the Magyar minorities initially enjoyed broad popular support, but the difficulties that it encountered, together with the considerable social stress generated by economic transition, gradually reduced its salience for the average Hungarian. As will be seen, the Antall government's activism would induce growing irritation in the host states, most of which proved reluctant to acknowledge collective minority rights and Hungary's *droit de regard*. The prime minister's emotional remark, made in May 1990, that in his heart, he carried a brief for all 15 million Magyars, at home and abroad, would earn him sharp rebukes from Bratislava and Bucharest. In fact, the constitution, as revised in November 1989, affirms that Hungary "feels responsible for the fate of the Hungarians living beyond its borders and promotes the cultivation of contacts with Hungarians."

Antall's successors, a coalition of socialists (ex-communists) and liberals led by the former communist Gyula Horn, chose, partly in response to pressure from the European Union (EU) and NATO, to mute their advocacy of minority rights. The more conservative coalition, headed by Viktor Orbán, that took office in July 1998 promised to address the issue with greater vigor. It cited Canada, Belgium, Italy, Finland, and Spain as models for the protection of minority rights.

SLOVAKIA

With regard to Slovakia, the 1991 census reported the presence of 567,000 Magyars, accounting for 10.8 percent of the population.[42] Some 440,000 of them live in towns and villages where they constitute an ethnic majority, and these localities are concentrated in pockets along the Slovak-Hungarian frontier.

Early consultations between Budapest and Prague produced agreement on cultural cooperation and, at least in principle, on the collective rights of minorities. President Václav Havel went so far as to endorse the proposal for a Hungarian university in Slovakia. It was apparent, however, that the Slovak political elite was far less sympathetic than the former Czech dissidents who had risen to power. The first legal provisions brought little comfort to the Magyar minority. Restitution of property and compensation covered only the communist era, thus excluding the losses suffered by Magyars during the immediate postwar period. A language law, adopted by the Slovak National Council in October 1990, limited official use of other languages to communities where the minority represented at least 20 percent of the population; it was subsequently invoked to eliminate minority-language place-names and signs in many ethnically mixed localities.

Three Magyar political parties emerged in the new political system: Coexistence, which initially aimed to represent all ethnic minorities, the Hungarian Christian Democratic Movement, and the Hungarian People's Party. In the June 1990 elections, a coalition of the first two parties garnered 8.66 percent of the vote in Slovakia, while candidates of the Independent Hungarian Initiative ran on the list of the Slovak Public Against Violence movement. Two years later, in a second round, the Magyar coalition obtained 7.42 percent of the votes and 14 seats in the Slovak National Council. However, the winner of that election was the Movement for a Democratic Slovakia, led by Vladimír Mečiar, who championed independence and was clearly antagonistic to minority rights.

Fearful of Slovak nationalism, the Magyars opposed the new ruling elite's bid to make Slovakia independent. When the divorce was consummated in 1992, the Magyar coalition abstained in the parliamentary votes on the declaration of sovereignty and the new constitution. One of their objections was to the revision of the latter's draft preamble from "We, the citizens of the Slovak Republic" to "We, the Slovak nation." The constitution designated Slovak as the state language and made no reference to the minorities' language and education rights. It did offer the minorities a guarantee of universal progress, while stipulating that the exercise of this right "must not endanger the sovereignty and territorial integrity of the Slovak Republic or cause discrimination against the rest of the population." On the other hand, the constitution gave legal precedence to international human rights commitments.

The Magyars feared that the ambiguity in Slovakian legislation would be exploited by nationalists to facilitate restrictive and assimilative practices, but Mečiar refused to discuss their complaints. The estrangement was aggravated by the Magyar coalition's briefs to the CSCE and CE in late 1992 and early 1993. The submission to the Council of Europe restated problems that already had been identified by that organization's rapporteur: two regressive steps, the removal of Hungarian-language signs and the ban on registration of Magyar baptismal names; a proposed redrawing of boundaries that would alter the ethnic composition of administrative and electoral districts; and the exclusion of compensation for material losses pursuant to postwar decrees based on the presumption of collective guilt. The Magyar politicians also made a case for greater devolution of administrative authority, notably in the sphere of education, along with the requisite resources.

Hungary had been the first ex-communist state to be admitted to the Council of Europe, and when Slovakia's candidacy came up for consideration, it lobbied for stiff preconditions concerning the Magyar minority. Concurrently, in February 1993, the CE Assembly, in its Recommendation 1201, called for guarantees of minority rights to be added to the European Convention on Human Rights; the recommendation included a politically charged but nonbinding reference (Clause 12) to collective rights. When Bratislava procrastinated in applying the CE's recommendations, Hungary first tried to block Slovakia's accession, then abstained in the final vote. The CE did endorse two Hungarian amendments to the terms of accession, one calling for the repeal of the postwar discriminatory decrees and the other for a periodic monitoring of compliance with CE recommendations.

In the course of 1993, the Slovak parliament removed the restrictions on personal names and surnames (the Slovak suffix "ova" had been mandatory for women's surnames) and on the translation of Slovak place-names and street signs (without, however, permitting the use of earlier Hungarian toponyms). Ominously, there was much wrangling between nationalist and liberal Slovaks on the merits of these concessions, and Magyars in the border town of Komarno (Komárom) staged a mass protest when the transportation minister ordered the removal of Hungarian-language signs.

The nationalistic and generally authoritarian tendencies of the Mečiar government continued to give rise to apprehensions on the part of the Magyar minority and of Hungary. In 1995, a law was adopted declaring Slovak to be the sole official language and leaving the status of minority languages to be determined at a later date. At a meeting with Antall in September 1992, Mečiar insisted that minority rights were an internal affair and could not be addressed in bilateral accords.[43] It took considerable Western pressure, in the context of a Stability Pact conceived by the French prime minister, Edouard Balladur, before Budapest and Bratislava signed a framework treaty in 1995.

That treaty included a rather vague clause on minority protection (Article 15). Having failed to obtain a promise of territorial autonomy for the Magyars, Budapest had to content itself with an anodyne reference in the accord to the CE's Recommendation 1201, which it chose to interpret as sanctioning such autonomy. Bratislava rejected that interpretation, and the OSCE's high commissioner for national minorities helpfully opined that the recommendation did not impose any change on states that had not recognized collective rights. The treaty eventually was ratified by both sides, but the Hungarians were far from satisfied. Meanwhile, the dispute over the Gabcikovo-Nagymaros dam project continued to cast a shadow over Slovak-Hungarian relations and the minority issue. When Budapest halted work on the project on ecological and financial grounds, the matter was referred to the International Court of Justice, and only in 1998 did Hungary agree to proceed with a modified version.

With regard to the Magyars, Bratislava's position remained that their educational and cultural needs were served; that Slovakia's international commitments and the bilateral treaty offered sufficient guarantees; that the Magyars' generally lower socioeconomic status did not owe to any discrimination; and that further concessions, such as a university or territorial autonomy, would produce an unacceptable ethnic division of the country. That last argument lacked some credibility, at least for the Magyars, in light of the Mečiar government's own ultranationalistic and therefore divisive stance. Behind the official line lay the prejudicial sentiment, shared by many Slovaks, that the Magyars' objections signified disloyalty to the state or even covert revisionism and that the presence of the minority hindered the long-delayed consolidation of an independent Slovakia.[44]

The Magyar parties and Budapest failed to make Bratislava fully apply the letter and spirit of the basic treaty and other conventions regarding minorities. No law was enacted to allow the use of Hungarian in official transactions. Indeed, the minority was subjected to rather petty measures of Slovakization, such as the education ministry's ban on school reports in Hungarian; the responsible minister belonged to the ultranationalist Slovak National Party. A law, passed in July 1996, redrew the boundaries of regions and districts in such a way as to reduce the proportion of Magyars, and thus their capacity to influence the administration of education and other local services. A meeting in August 1997 between Mečiar and his Hungarian counterpart, Gyula Horn, brought no breakthrough on the disputed matters. Worse, Mečiar subsequently gloated in public that when he proposed a "voluntary exchange" of Slovakia's Magyars and Hungary's Slovaks, Horn looked appalled.[45]

The political pendulum swung in the Slovak elections of late September 1998, giving a majority to four opposition parties, including 15 deputies from the Hungarian Coalition. Another coalition member, the ex-communist Party of the Democratic Left, was particularly hostile to the Hungarian Coalition, and the latter had to undertake not to raise the most contentious issues—local autonomy, a Hungarian university, the dam project, and restitution—before being invited to participate in the government led by the Christian Democrat Mikulas Dzurinda. One of the Hungarian Coalition leaders, the former dissident Miklós Duray, acknowledged that a majority of Slovaks were hostile to his party's presence in the government. Thus the Magyars in the new cabinet, notably Pál Csáky, a deputy prime minister in charge of minorities and regional development, were constrained in the promotion of minority interests.

Intent on winning membership for Slovakia in the European Union and NATO, the Dzurinda government has shown some disposition to accommodate minority demands and forge cooperative relations with Hungary. In July 1999, the Bratislava parliament passed a government bill allowing official use of a minority language in localities where that minority constitutes at least 20 percent of the population; the Hungarian Coalition, which wanted the minimum level set at 10 percent, abstained in the vote. Opposition politicians, notably Mečiar and the Slovak National Party's Ján Slota, continued to denounce all concessions and to indulge in rabidly antiminority and anti-Budapest rhetoric; they demanded that the language bill be submitted to a referendum. Earlier, the government had revealed that, under Mečiar, the secret service engaged in provocative operations designed to retard Hungary's accession to NATO, and it issued a formal apology to Budapest.

UKRAINE

Motivated mainly by its interest in the Magyars of the Transcarpathian region, Hungary became the first country to recognize Ukraine's independence. Hungary's president, Árpád Göncz, was invited to visit the region, and a joint declaration, followed in December 1991 by a state treaty, acknowledged that the Magyar minority had collective as well as individual rights. The treaty provided for preservation of the minority's ethnic, cultural, linguistic, and religious identities; education at all levels in the mother tongue; and the Magyars' participation in local authorities charged with minority affairs. Minority rights had been codified by the Ukrainian parliament the previous November.

The amenability of the Kiev government owed to its quest for international respectability as well as to the relatively inconsequential size of the Magyar minority, numbering upward of 170,000. Budapest thereafter would cite the treaty as a model of its kind. Some Hungarian legislators had objected, however, to including in the treaty a renunciation of any eventual border adjustment.

Transcarpathia's Magyars made rapid progress in the political and cultural spheres. The Hungarian Cultural Association of Subcarpathia (HCAS), founded in February 1989, served as an effective advocate of the minority's interests and participated successfully in elections to the Council of the Transcarpathian District. The number of Hungarian schools multiplied, Hungarian history was added to the curriculum (a first in the history of Magyar minorities), and bilingual signs were sanctioned along with other symbolic affirmations of Magyar identity. More recently, the HCAS has campaigned against a new education bill that, in its view, did not adequately guarantee the minority's access to native-language instruction.

The HCAS and its offshoot, the Hungarian Democratic Alliance of Ukraine, had proposed creation of an autonomous Magyar region in the subdistrict of Beregovo (Beregszász), which adjoins the border with Hungary, and where some 100,000 Magyars constitute a majority of the population. Concurrently, the Ruthenians called for conversion of Transcarpathia into a self-governing administrative territory. These questions were included in the referendum, held in December 1991, on Ukraine's independence. A majority of Transcarpathia's voters favored autonomy, while the Magyar proposal won majority support in the Beregovo area. There was no follow-up to these initiatives, for the Ruthenes' demand antagonized Ukrainian nationalists, who persist in denying that the former are a distinct nationality. The Magyars' display of sympathy for Ruthenian aspirations thus backfired.

The generally favorable turn in the Magyar minority's political and cultural circumstances was not matched in the economic sphere, where Ukraine has shown a lamentable decline affecting the entire population. Thus the major threat to the minority's survival has become emigration to Hungary.

ROMANIA

The 1992 census in Romania indicated the presence of 1,620,000 Magyars, who accounted for 7.1 percent of the country's population, and

20.7 percent in Transylvania. (The Magyars complained about irregularities in the census and, drawing on denominational data, estimate their number to be closer to 2 million.) Some 60 percent of the Magyars live in localities where they form the majority, including the counties of Harghita (85 percent) and Covasna (75 percent). As a result of resettlement policies in the communist era, the Magyars have been reduced to a bare majority in the largest city of the Székely region, Tirgu-Mures (Marosvásárhely); only the region's smaller cities, notably Odorhei (Székelyudvarhely) and Miercurea Ciuc (Csikszereda), remain predominantly Magyar.[46]

The collapse of the Ceauşescu dictatorship was sparked off in the Banat city of Timisoara (Temesvár), where, in December 1989, Magyars were joined by ethnic Romanians in protest at the police harassment of a Magyar human rights activist, the Calvinist pastor László Tőkés. Despite the murderous intervention of security forces, the spirit of revolt spread across the country. In many localities, Magyars played an active part in the clashes with defenders of the old order.

Magyars and ethnic Romanians were momentarily united in the effort to overthrow tyranny, and the initial statements of the National Salvation Front (NSF), an interim regime of former communists, reflected this newfound solidarity. A Declaration on the Rights of National Minorities, issued in January 1990, condemned Ceauşescu's policies and pledged individual and collective rights. The NSF decreed that the minorities would enjoy proportional representation in parliament, and it even promised to reopen the Magyars' university in Cluj. The foreign minister of Hungary's interim government, Gyula Horn, paid a visit and reaffirmed his country's respect for Romania's territorial integrity as well as its interest in the codification of the Magyar minority's rights.

The signs of interethnic harmony proved to be deceptive. Although Ceauşescu was gone, his demonization of the minorities had left its mark on Romanian consciousness.[47] The regime's early promises found only partial fulfillment in law and administrative practice, for a powerful ultranationalistic backlash materialized in the form of the Vatra Romaneasca (Romanian Hearth) movement. When, in February 1990, Magyars at Tirgu-Mures requested the restoration of mother-tongue educational facilities, the Vatra mounted public protests. The Magyars responded with a massive silent demonstration. A few weeks later, the Vatra set off a series of violent attacks that left eight dead and over 300 injured. The government initially blamed the clash on Magyar provocation.

The absence of a significant Romanian dissident movement in the communist era goes a long way toward explaining why the May 1990 elections were dominated by former communist apparatchiks. The NSF, which won by a wide margin, had monopolized the media; and the election was marred by irregularities, notably the disqualification of two Magyar human rights activists. Nevertheless, the runner-up turned out to be the newly founded Hungarian Democratic Federation of Romania (HDFR), which campaigned for democratic reforms as well as for minority rights; with over 7 percent of the votes (including 77 percent in Covasna County and 85 percent in Harghita County), it evidently secured the support of most Magyars and of some ethnic Romanians as well. The HDFR thus obtained 29 out of 387 seats in the lower chamber and 12 out of 118 in the Senate. The Vatra's political arm, the Party of Romanian National Unity (PRNU), emerged as the most radical opponent of concessions to the minorities.

The NSF government made some gestures to win foreign approval, notably in a parliamentary report that largely exonerated Magyars in the Tirgu-Mures confrontation. However, it progressively trimmed its domestic policies to accommodate Romanian ultranationalists. In December 1991 the HDFR's deputies and senators voted against the new constitution, partly on the grounds that its guarantees of minority rights were potentially undermined by a clause stating that "protective measures taken by the state in order to maintain, develop, and express the identity of persons belonging to national minorities have to be in accord with the principle of equality and non-differentiation related to other citizens of Romania," for it could then be argued that concessions to the minorities discriminated against ethnic Romanians. The constitution and subsequent laws offered little guarantee of official use of minority languages even at the local level, and local autonomy was limited by the central appointment of prefects. Meanwhile, as in the case of Slovakia, Budapest tried without success to block Romania's admission to the CE.

The municipal and local elections of February 1992 reflected a further polarization of Romanian politics between, on one hand, the HDFR and the more liberal groups in the Democratic Convention, and the NSF and PRNU, both of which adopted a nationalistic and anti-Magyar tone. Radical Romanian nationalists were elected in many Transylvanian localities. In Cluj (Kolozsvár), where Magyars account for a quarter of the population, the new mayor was the chairman of the PRNU, Gheorghe Funar; he mounted a lasting campaign to eliminate Magyar symbols, such as street names, signs, and even the inscription on a statue in the central square identifying the medieval monarch Matthias as king of Hungary. At one point, the government was impelled by rising tensions to dispatch troops to the city, but its political dependence on the nationalist vote made it reluctant to challenge local measures even when these obviously contravened the new constitution.

The 1992 parliamentary elections confirmed the spread of popular Romanian nationalism. There were now two ultranationalist and anti-Magyar parties, the PRNU and the Greater Romania Party, and both the Democratic National Salvation Front and the rump NSF adopted a more nationalistic tone. Between them, these parties won a majority; the HDFR held on to its 7.5 percent share. The new minister of education was a member of the Vatra, as was one of the two ethnic Romanian pre-fects appointed to head Covasna and Harghita Counties.

In response to the growing evidence of ethnic Romanian intolerance, some members of the HDFR raised demands for territorial autonomy along ethnic lines. The Bucharest government was adamantly opposed, and the HDFR compromised by joining the Romanian opposition parties in calling for broad decentralization and devolution. Even the latter parties had rejected the notion of ethnic territorial autonomy, and they condemned the HDFR's decision, in August 1993, to submit a petition to the Council of Europe.

The HDFR's brief charged that radical nationalism had once again become the prime legitimizing factor in Romanian political life and that the government not only tolerated neofascist movements but colluded with them. Education, including the government's refusal to reestablish a Hungarian university, figured prominently among their grievances; it may be noted that in this and some other respects the Magyars were inviting the restoration of rights that they had enjoyed in the early post-war period. Meanwhile, in the economic sphere, Magyar farmers shared in the return of collectivized land, but the new government evidently was intent on favoring ethnic Romanians in the process of privatizing state enterprises.[48]

To domestic and foreign critics, the government would respond that the minority already received a proportionate share of the education budget. Its other response, designed partly to ease Romania's admission to the Council of Europe, was the establishment of a consultative Council for National Minorities. In September 1994 the HDFR walked out of this council in protest against the lack of progress in meeting its demands, and it developed a proposal for a minorities law in which such groups would be treated as "autonomous communities" entitled to self-government and collective rights.

Education remained the most contentious issue. Although Magyars make up at least 7.1 percent of the population, only 4.9 percent of students have been receiving their education in Hungarian. A law, adopted in 1995, required that civics as well as the country's history and geography be taught exclusively in Romanian and abolished Hungarian-language education in a wide range of technical and professional fields.[49] The HDFR gathered some 500,000 signatures for a petition in support of its own education proposals and lobbied the Council of Europe, the European Parliament, and the OSCE. The Strasbourg parliament addressed a rebuke to Bucharest, and, on a visit to Romania, Hungary's foreign minister, Géza Jeszenszky, criticized the law. The government, for its part, drew some encouragement from a modestly qualified endorsement of the law by the OSCE high commissioner for minorities and stood firm.

The impasse was reflected in the slow progress on a bilateral accord. Both Hungary and Romania were keen on joining NATO as well as the European Union, and Western powers applied diplomatic leverage in favor of a compromise. The framework treaty, concluded in 1996, included the usual renunciation of territorial revision and confirmed the applicability of international conventions on minorities. As in the Slovakian accord, the reference to "persons belonging to the Magyar minority" was designed to highlight individual rights at the expense of collective rights.[50] Bucharest obtained a footnote to the annex of the treaty stating that the CE's Recommendation 1201 did not refer to collective rights or require ethnic territorial autonomy. The Magyar minority and opposition parties in Budapest regarded the accord as a defeat. The treaty was roundly criticized by the HDFR and, for contrary reasons, by the more radical Romanian nationalist parties; all of them voted against ratification in the Romanian Chamber of Deputies and abstained in the Senate.

In the November 1996 elections, the political pendulum swung sharply in favor of the Romanian democratic opposition. The HDFR won 25 seats in the lower house and 11 in the Senate (with 6.6 and 6.8 percent of the votes, respectively) as well as the mayor's office in most municipalities with a Magyar majority. In the second round of the presidential election, the Magyars voted massively for the more liberal candidate, Emil Constantinescu, tilting the balance in his favor.

The HDFR thereupon joined the Democratic Convention and Social Democratic parties to form a coalition government and obtained some portfolios, notably that of a newly constituted Office of Minority Affairs. The Magyars also were promised a few prefectorial posts and more liberal policies regarding education and language. On the other hand, participation in the government compelled the HDFR to suspend its advocacy of territorial autonomy.

There followed a number of conciliatory measures. A decree issued in May 1997 stipulated that in towns where Magyars made up at least

20 percent of the population, they were entitled to bilingual signs and to use their mother tongue in official transactions. In July, another decree guaranteed schooling in Hungarian wherever a minimum of 15 children required it. However, not all members of the coalition favored concessions to the minorities. Nationalists in the Senate retaliated with legislation that once again restricted the Magyars' education rights and ruled out the creation of Hungarian university faculties. Meanwhile, at the local level, Romanian nationalists protested the restoration of Magyar signs and the appointment of the first Magyar prefect, in Harghita County; and Cluj's Mayor Funar persevered with petty anti-Magyar measures, staging a mock burial of the Hungarian-Romanian treaty and doing his best to obstruct the belated opening, in 1997, of a Hungarian consulate.

The Magyar minister for minority affairs, Péter Eckstein-Kovács, indicated in March 1999 that his office's priorities were a bill banning all forms of discrimination, ratification of the European Charter on Regional and Minority Languages, and restitution of minority and church assets. In September 1998 the government had decreed the establishment of a joint Magyar-German university in Cluj, prompting an unsuccessful attempt by Romanian nationalist parties to challenge the constitutionality of the measure. The issue was overshadowed by the passage in July 1999 of a new education law that went a long way toward satisfying Magyar demands. It guaranteed minorities the right to education in their mother tongue from kindergarten all the way to university (the exception being the teaching of Romanian history and geography beyond grade five) as well as to establish private postsecondary institutions.

Bilateral relations improved after the advent of the new government in Bucharest. Whereas Hungary was invited, in 1997, to negotiate adherence to NATO and the EU, Romania's slower transition to democracy and a market economy kept it out of the first cut. Budapest actively supports Bucharest's bid for membership, partly on the premise that this will favorably influence Romanian minority policies and partly out of concern that Transylvania's Magyars will become more isolated if the enlarged European Union's borders divide them from Hungary. Bucharest, for its part, has courted international respectability, in particular by signing the CE's Charter on Regional and Minority Languages and Framework Convention on the Protection of Minorities.

At the same time, Romanian political life remains marked by a pervasive mistrust and dislike of the Magyars. The postcommunist governments have shown little capacity to manage economic transition and thereby to foster the prosperity that would win them popular support. Thus, as in the communist era, the temptation remains great to exploit majority nationalism as a legitimizing device. Transylvania's Magyars expected democratization to quickly produce a legal order that would eliminate discrimination and satisfy their needs and demands. They were bound to be disappointed, for institutions are easier to change than ingrained political cultures, and pluralism can unleash negative as well as positive tendencies; in June 1999, the Council of National Minorities deplored the proliferation of publications that propagated "xenophobia, personal and collective aggression against members of ethnic minorities."[51] Only recently has a Romanian scholar ventured to question some aspects of his nation's historical myth.[52] In Romania, as in Slovakia and rump Yugoslavia, the Magyar minority suffers from the host state's difficulty in assimilating the conventions of a truly democratic polity.

YUGOSLAVIA

Although the eclipse of communism did not resolve the hoary problem of minority rights, it nevertheless allowed the latter to be addressed in a democratic institutional context and with reference to international codes as well as to European practice. The glaring exception turned out to be Yugoslavia, a country that once prided itself on having enshrined multinational harmony. The resurgence of both hegemonic and particularistic nationalism can be traced back to the late Tito era, and the sudden collapse of communist regimes in the Soviet sphere only accelerated the functional disintegration of Yugoslavia. In the process, and almost incidentally, the Magyar minority fell victim to the major groups' confrontation and to civil war. That war caused irreparable damage to the comparative harmony and ethnic equilibrium that had prevailed in Vojvodina.

In 1989, Yugoslavia's Serbian Republic responded to the autonomist pressures of ethnic Albanians by a constitutional amendment that essentially nullified the self-governing status not only of Kosovo but also of Vojvodina. Serbian nationalism was further inflamed by secessionist movements in the other constituent republics. The minorities' right to education in their mother tongue was progressively restricted, and the number of Magyars in the public service and economic management was drastically reduced.

The minority's prospects became even bleaker when the federation broke up. Hungary's foreign policy scarcely mollified the Serbs, for Budapest was among the first to recognize the independence of Croatia and Slovenia, and it even approved some covert arms sales to the former. It subsequently joined in the international sanctions against rump

Yugoslavia and agreed to the establishment in Hungary of a U.S. military base designed to serve U.N. and NATO peacekeeping operations. In June 1991, Prime Minister Antall went so far as to suggest that the Trianon boundary might have lost its legal validity with the creation of a rump Yugoslavia under Serb rule.

As the civil war intensified, so did measures of intimidation and discrimination against Vojvodina's Magyars. Although the latter had no wish to be drawn into the fighting, a disproportionate number were marshalled to serve in the Serb-dominated army. Meanwhile, Serb refugees flooded into the region. In 1991–92, over 250,000 Serbs arrived from Bosnia, and in 1995, some 150,000 more came from Croatian Krajina. The Belgrade government encouraged their resettlement in minority communities, where the unruly newcomers readily resorted to armed violence to displace Magyars and other non-Serbs from their homes. Protests from abroad, including Hungary, led the justice minister at one point to concede that there had been serious violations of minority rights, but the resettlement program was sustained.

The Democratic Community of Vojvodina Hungarians (DCVH), formed in 1989 to promote the minority's interests, protested that the Serbs were pursuing a calculated policy of ethnic cleansing and aimed to drive Magyars out of the province. Indeed, tens of thousands sought refuge in Hungary to escape military service and harassment. Whereas in 1981, 385,000 Magyars had been counted in Vojvodina, by 1991 their number had fallen to 341,000, and it continued to decline; the Magyars' share of Vojvodina's population, once 20 percent, was thus considerably reduced by emigration and Serb resettlement.

The DCVH had favored the preservation of Yugoslavia and its transformation into a liberal democratic confederation that allowed for greater cultural and financial autonomy at the local level. In the December 1990 elections to the Serbian parliament, the great majority of Magyars backed DCVH candidates, eight of whom were elected (along with another Magyar). They found no political allies in their protests against measures such as the rationalization of the school system, which led to the termination of many Hungarian-language classes and the Serbianization of the state-funded media.[53]

Minority languages lost their official status in 1992, when a new constitution declared Serb (in its Cyrillic form) to be the sole official language. Concurrently, the DCVH adopted a program based on the collective right to self-government. Budapest had endorsed, indeed helped to inspire, the initiative, which encompassed the creation of an autonomous district in the area where 56 percent of the Magyars are concentrated, and form a majority; local self-government in the more scattered communes with a Magyar majority; and minority councils to oversee educational, cultural, and social affairs in localities where the Magyars are in a minority. The Magyars' proposals, along with their antiwar stance, brought down charges of disloyalty and secessionist intent. Two years later a splinter group founded a competing organization, the Alliance of Hungarians in Vojvodina (AHV), but their overall objectives did not change.[54]

In December 1998, as the storm clouds were gathering over Kosovo, the Milošević government rejected the AHV's call for a restoration of Vojvodina's autonomy on terms similar to those offered to the Albanian-inhabited province. The situation of the Magyar minority—and relations between Budapest and Belgrade—became even more tense when in March 1999, less than two weeks after Hungary had been inducted into NATO, the alliance launched a bombing campaign against Yugoslavia. In Hungary, government and public opinion backed the operation but hoped that the minority would be sheltered from its consequences. As in the Bosnian phase of the civil war, Vojvodina Magyars did not wish to be conscripted for Milošević's ethnic cleansing campaigns (all men aged 18–60 were barred from leaving the country) and feared the backlash of Serb nationalism.

In May 1999, the congress of the principal member of Hungary's governing coalition, the Young Democrats–Hungarian Civic Party, adopted a resolution calling for the restoration of Vojvodina's autonomy as part of a settlement of the Kosovo crisis. When, a few weeks later, Milošević capitulated, Prime Minister Orbán declared that any stabilization plan for the Balkans should include formal guarantees of the Magyar minority's rights. Presumably more than a few Hungarians, on both sides of the border, privately shared the view of an opposition politician, István Csurka, that if Yugoslavia disintegrated, the main Magyar-inhabited district should be reannexed to Hungary.

CROATIA AND SLOVENIA

The Magyars in independent Croatia and Slovenia, numbering around 25,000 and 10,000–12,000, respectively, fared much better. As in the case of Ukraine, these small and quiescent minorities were not regarded as a hindrance to nation-building, and both of the newly founded host states had an interest in establishing cordial relations with neighboring Hungary. The bilateral accords with Budapest were broadly similar to the Hungarian-Ukrainian model; the Slovenian treaty guaranteed collective rights and the Croatian one cultural autonomy for the minorities. Croatia's Magyars could not shelter themselves from the damage wrought by the Serb-Croat conflict, but they have access to instruction in their language and promote their interests through the Federation of Hungarians in Croatia as well as the Hungarian People's Party. Slovenia has materially supported Hungarian-language instruction and cultural facilities for the so-called Magyar Community of the Mura Region.

The region's Magyar minorities thus became the focus of intensive triadic relationships in the postcommunist era, and the actors in those triads have displayed varying tendencies with regard to the problem. Although their circumstances improved in all host states except Yugoslavia, the Magyars continued to air grievances—at inadequate educational facilities, cultural and economic discrimination, and outright violence—as well as demands focusing on collective rights and local autonomy. The problems and proposed remedies (leaving aside the unrealistic option of peaceful reunification with Hungary) had changed little since Trianon.

Free to participate in the new democratic systems, they generally chose to form and back their own parties, thus confirming the ethnic cleavages. This, of course, runs counter to the theoretical model of a mature civil society, in which ethnicity is submerged in a party system marked by cross-cutting cleavages. But that model is far from a reality even in such solid democracies as Belgium or Canada; and none of the host states can be said to have a well-developed civil society. Unlike Hungary, the host states are still engaged in a process of nation-building in which majority nationalism figures as a key legitimizing force. To be sure, minority parties run the risk of self-encapsulation if they become marginalized and fail to give their constituents a sense of political efficacy. On the other hand, as Magyar parties in both Slovakia and Romania are discovering, they may have to give up some of the minority's essential demands in order to participate in government. Such compromises, in turn, provoke divisions among activists and electors alike.[55]

As long as the minorities feel compelled to seek separate representation, they cannot escape these political dilemmas. At the same time, their parties help to preserve the minority's identity and political clout by defining priorities and interacting with domestic and external agencies. Moreover, the Magyar parties have displayed a greater commitment to authentic democratization than many of their counterparts, and few of the latter have taken any pains to win the allegiance of Magyars. The Magyar parties expect pluralistic democracy to facilitate entrenchment of their cultural rights; the parties of the ethnic majorities regard democratic institutions as a tool for consolidating the nation-state.

These divergent perspectives reinforce mutual distrust, which lies at the heart of the problem. Despite wide variations in size, the Magyar minorities have been remarkably resilient in preserving their cultural identity through the vicissitudes of the prewar and postwar eras. Size, on the other hand, appears to have been a critical factor in the responses of the host states. It is hardly coincidental that the smallest Magyar minorities—those in Austria, Transcarpathian Ukraine, Croatia, and Slovenia—have earned the most liberal treatment, as have Hungary's own minorities. Romania, too, is readier to pamper its small, less assertive non-Magyar minorities. The Magyar communities in Slovakia, Transylvania, and Vojvodina are of a size that allows for greater self-assertion and that, in the eyes of majority nationalists, represents a potential threat to national unity. An alliance of Magyars with majority reformers—the current experiment in Romania and Slovakia—may reduce polarization and encourage the perception that minority rights are not a zero-sum game but a necessary dimension of political modernity.

The factor of scale also influences the attitude of the mother country. More populous nations can better afford to be neglectful of their extraterritorial fragments than, in this instance, the Magyars, a quarter of whom live in neighboring states. The small nations of the region have developed an acute sense of vulnerability, and the linguistically isolated Hungarians are peculiarly given to fears of cultural extinction. This sensitivity extends to the Magyar minorities; hence their dogged attachment to both the fundamental guardians of identity, such as mother-language schools, cultural institutions, and historical relics, and to the more symbolic recognition offered by, say, bilingual street signs.

Officially, and notably in the bilateral treaties with its neighbors, Hungary has renounced territorial revision and accepted the finality of the borders set at Trianon and confirmed in the Paris Peace Treaty of 1946. This renunciation is somewhat deceptive, although not deceitful. It is deceptive because most Magyars, in Hungary and in the surrounding countries, remain convinced that Trianon was punitive and unjust and that, ideally, borders should be more congruent with ethnic distribution. At the same time, it is not deceitful, for Hungarians recognize that the brief triumph of revisionism between 1938 and 1945 owed to exceptional circumstances that are not likely to recur; that the international community is viscerally opposed to opening the Pandora's box of border revision in Europe; and that, given the territorial distribution of Magyar minorities, only a fraction of the latter could be reattached to Hungary without incorporating substantial numbers of other nationalities. To be sure, some Hungarian nationalists have deplored this renunciation and even advanced the artful claim that territorial concessions to states that no longer exist—that is, Czechoslovakia and Yugoslavia—have lost their legal standing. But few would dispute the fact that neither the host states nor the international community is ready for a renegotiation of borders.

Post-Trianon Hungary never had the strength to change borders by force. The revisions effected between 1938 and 1941 owed entirely to German-Italian preponderance in the region. Today, even if Hungary had the political will, it could scarcely develop a military capability sufficient to impose a revision of frontiers on its neighbors, and certainly not on Romania or rump Yugoslavia, unless these countries suffered a total collapse. It is possible to conjure up radical scenarios, for example, one in which an ultranationalist regime launches a pogrom against its Magyar minority, whereupon a similarly nationalist regime in Budapest intervenes militarily to protect the latter. But, for the foreseeable future, such scenarios belong to the realm of idle speculation and academic war games. The threat of Hungarian revisionism survives mainly in the minds of ultranationalists in the host states, and it may be suspected that even they evoke it merely for domestic political purposes. With revisionism laid to rest, first by the communist regimes, then by their freely elected successors, there is little likelihood that the problem of Magyar minorities will give rise to interstate violence.

However, much as Hungary's prewar governments could not concede the finality of Trianon, so the popular legitimacy of today's elected governments is partly contingent on an active pursuit of minority rights. That advocacy, although buttressed in part by international conventions and guidelines, has proven a rather thankless task. The host states are, as ever, inclined to qualify Hungary's self-arrogated *droit de regard* as interference in their internal affairs and to minimize the minority problem. The minorities, for their part, welcome Budapest's concern for their welfare but, as in the case of the Hungarian-Romanian treaty, are quick to construe diplomatic compromise as betrayal by the mother country. And third parties soon grow weary of being reminded of the injustice of Trianon or of the grievances of minorities that, in the main, suffer no spectacular violence.

The overriding interest of these third parties—essentially the members of NATO and the EU, with Russia playing an ambiguous role—is in regional stability, which, as they recognize, depends in part on interethnic peace. Both the EU and NATO have made it clear that the settlement of minority disputes is a precondition of membership, and this has served as a powerful incentive not only for the conclusion of bilateral treaties between Hungary and its neighbors but also for a more conciliatory approach to the Magyar minorities in the host states. Third-party pressure has had some positive impact on domestic politics in Romania and, more recently, in Slovakia, but very little so far in Yugoslavia.

The more diffuse authority of the CSCE/OSCE also has been brought into play, notably in a series of conferences on the definition and protection of minority rights. CSCE fact finders tried to assess the plight of Magyar and other minorities in Yugoslavia before being expelled by the Milošević government. The OSCE's high commissioner for national minorities, former Dutch Foreign Minister Max van der Stoel, tried to mediate some disputes, and, exercising his early-warning mandate, appointed a team to investigate minority rights in Slovakia and Hungary; despite the absence of any request from Hungary's Slovaks, Mečiar had insisted on a balanced exercise. The Council of Europe played a key role in the assessment and authentication of democratic reform in the former communist states, and its conventions and recommendations have served in regional diplomacy as a benchmark for minority rights. In 1998–99, Senator György Frunda, a member of the HDFR and of Romania's delegation to the CE, was instrumental in the establishment of committees to monitor minority rights and the activity of secret service agencies with regard to ethnic minorities.

In theory, there is no incompatibility between ethnicity and citizenship, which are essentially complementary forms of identity and allegiance. However, when the state is explicitly and officially identified with the ethnic majority, as is the case in Slovakia, Romania, and Serbian Yugoslavia, this dual allegiance becomes a source of psychological stress and political tension. The unifying ideology of such nation-states logically leads to policies of assimilation, or, alternatively, to the political exclusion—by expulsion or denial of civil rights—of the minority. The Magyar minorities have shown little disposition to assimilate, and contemporary democratic orthodoxy does not condone forced assimilation, let alone exclusion or ethnic cleansing. Thus the majority's imposition of national uniformity, a practice common in the nineteenth century, is no longer politically viable.

Again, in theory, there are two basic models of democratic integration for ethnic minorities desirous of preserving their cultural identity: a consociational system in which majority rule is qualified by recognition of collective minority rights, and which is confederal or otherwise devolutionary in structure, and a unitary system in which the minority's cultural rights are codified in the context of individual rights.[56] Variations on the former model are found in numerous Western countries: confederal in Switzerland, federal in Canada and Belgium, broadly devolutionary in Spain, more modestly devolutionary in Italy (Alto Adige) and, now, Britain. In Central and Eastern Europe, the trend has been in the other direction, away from federalism and consociationalism and toward a consolidated nation-state identified with the ethnic majority.

Thus collective rights remain a bone of contention. Faced with majority nationalism, and sharing in the legacy of mutual mistrust, the Magyar minorities have little faith in the efficacy of individual rights to protect their cultural identity. Historically, statism has prevailed in the region. The propertied churches once played an important role, but the funding of educational and cultural institutions has long been considered the responsibility of the state. In these economically underdeveloped societies, ethnic minorities lack the material means to equip themselves with the full panoply of supplementary educational and cultural institutions. What they seek, in effect, is positive discrimination, which necessarily entails recognition of their collective entitlement and thus transcends the egalitarian thrust of individual rights. Burdened by the same scarcity of resources, as well as by nationalist ideology, the majorities are reluctant to accept the principle of the minorities' collective entitlement.

Many Western democracies are ambivalent about codification of collective rights. They may pursue policies of positive discrimination to serve historically disadvantaged groups ranging from Afro-Americans to women and subsidize socioeconomic groups such as farmers, but they prefer to preach the virtues of individual rights as the nondiscriminatory remedy to the discontent of ethnic minorities in Central and Eastern Europe. The consensus rule in international organizations such as the OSCE and the Council of Europe means that their guidelines on minority rights will be similarly fudged.[57]

The mother country's proximity and interest clearly stiffen the resolve of Magyar minorities to defend their cultural identity. Their demands for collective rights and territorial or local autonomy have been encouraged and in part inspired by Budapest. As noted, it is moot whether Hungary's diplomatic advocacy of minority interests is counterproductive with regard to the host states; the communist era, at least, offered little evidence that minorities benefit from the absence of such advocacy. In February 1999, the Budapest government convened a conference, attended by representatives of the seven principal Magyar organizations in the neighboring countries, and designed to foster dialogue between the minorities and Hungary. The participants decided to institutionalize these political consultations by way of an annual "Hungarian Standing Conference."

In contrast to the Balkans, the Central European sphere faces little danger of civil or interstate war over its national minorities. The issue of Magyar minorities has inspired more heated rhetoric than outright violence. To be sure, ultranationalists in Romania, Slovakia, and rump Yugoslavia are ever ready to victimize the minorities, and the prolonged pain of economic transition may induce an accentuation of chauvinism as well as a certain nostalgia for authoritarianism. In Hungary, on the other hand, ultranationalists enjoy little popular support, and democracy has taken root in the political culture. Foreign Minister János Martonyi has observed that he would be happy if the militant nationalists in the neighboring countries were as few in number as their counterparts in Hungary.[58]

The avoidance of violence is reinforced by the ongoing process of continental integration. Western democracies have a moral as well as strategic interest in inducing host states to respect minority rights. The enlargement of NATO should serve to enhance perceptions of security in the region; that of the European Union should promote the economic and social modernization that underpins democracy. To be sure, democracy offers no guarantee of peaceable interethnic relations (see Ulster and the Basque country) or of genuine harmony (see Belgium and Canada), but more porous borders and greater prosperity may help to attenuate a xenophobia based on insecurity, ignorance, and envy. The Magyar minorities, host states, and the mother country have a long way to go before their respective interests are fully reconciled, but, in most of the triads, there is at least a reasonable prospect of peaceful accommodation.

Notes

1. In their native tongue, the Hungarians call themselves Magyars, and their homeland, Magyarország, "country of the Magyars." To distinguish ethnicity from citizenship, the term "Magyar" is applied here to the minorities.

2. Rogers Brubaker, *Nationalism Reframed: Nationhood and the National Question in the New Europe* (Cambridge: Cambridge University Press, 1996), p. 55; cf. Robert Hamerton-Kelly, "National Minorities and the Integration of Europe: A Theoretical Perspective," in László Póti, ed., *Integration, Regionalism, Minorities: What Is the Link?* (Budapest: Hungarian Institute of International Affairs, 1997), pp. 122–29.

3. See Geoffrey Hosking and George Schöpflin, eds., *Myths and Nationhood* (London: Hurst, 1997).

4. C. A. Macartney, *Hungary and Her Successors: The Treaty of Trianon and Its Consequences, 1919–1937* (London: Oxford University Press, 1937), p. 14.

5. Ibid., pp. 32–34.

6. For a summary, see Zsuzsa L. Nagy, "Peacemaking after World War I: The Western Democracies and the Hungarian Question," in Stephen Borsody, ed., *The Hungarians: A Divided Nation* (New Haven, Conn.: Yale Center for International and Area Studies, 1988), pp. 32–48.

7. See Mihály Fülöp and Péter Sipos, *Magyarország külpolitikája a XX. században* (Budapest: Aula, 1998), pp. 86–90.

8. On the minority treaties and their application, see József Galántai, *Trianon and the Protection of Minorities* (Budapest: Corvina, 1992).

9. Eva S. Balogh, "Hungarian Foreign Policy, 1918–1945," in Borsody, ed., *The Hungarians*, p. 52.

10. George Barany, "Hungary: From Aristocratic to Proletarian Nationalism," in Peter F. Sugar and Ivo John Lederer, eds., *Nationalism in Eastern Europe* (Seattle: University of Washington Press, 1994), pp. 287–89.

11. For the sake of historical authenticity, place-names are given in the official language of the day, with the alternative-language version in parentheses.

12. According to official census figures, the Burgenland's Hungarian-speaking population fell from 15,000 in 1923 to 4,000 in 1981; however, a microcensus conducted in 1991 found that over 14,000 people had a knowledge of Hungarian.

13. See Macartney, *Hungary and Her Successors*, pp. 87–94, 103.

14. Joseph F. Zacek, "Nationalism in Czechoslovakia," in Sugar and Lederer, eds., *Nationalism in Eastern Europe*, p. 195.

15. See Sándor Vogel, "Transylvania: Myth and Reality, Changing Awareness of Transylvanian Identity," in André Gerrits and Nanci Adler, eds., *Vampires Unstaked: National Images, Stereotypes and Myths in East Central Europe* (Amsterdam: North Holland, 1995), pp. 78–80 and passim.

16. Macartney, *Hungary and Her Successors*, p. 285.

17. Ibid., p. 253 n. 3.

18. Vogel, "Transylvania: Myth and Reality," pp. 81–82.

19. Macartney, *Hungary and Her Successors*, p. 435.

20. For a balanced account of Hungary's diplomacy in this period, see Thomas L. Sakmyster, *Hungary, the Great Powers, and the Danubian Crisis, 1936–1939* (Athens: University of Georgia Press, 1980).

21. See ibid., pp. 208ff.

22. One of the Magyar minority's political leaders, János Eszterházy, chose to remain in rump Slovakia to represent the interests of the remaining 69,000 Magyars. He was the sole member of that country's parliament to protest at a measure to deport Jews to Germany. Subsequently convicted of purported "war crimes," he died in prison in 1957.

23. See Bennett Kovrig, "Peacemaking after World War II: The End of the Myth of National Self-Determination," in Borsody, ed., *The Hungarians*, pp. 71ff.; and Ignác Romsics, ed., *Wartime American Plans for a New Hungary: Documents from the U.S. Department of State, 1942–1944* (Boulder, Colo.: Social Science Monographs, 1992), passim.

24. See Kálmán Janics, *Czechoslovak Policy and the Hungarian Minority, 1945–1948* (New York: Social Science Monographs, 1982).

25. See Mihály Fülöp and Gábor Vincze, *Revizió vagy autonómia? Iratok a magyar-román kapcsolatok történetéről (1945–1947)* (Budapest: Teleki László Alapitvány, 1998), pp. 360–65 and passim.

26. Kovrig, "Peacemaking," p. 76.

27. John C. Campbell, "The European Territorial Settlement," *Foreign Affairs* 26, no. 1 (October 1947): 201.

28. Lajos Arday, "Hungarians in Serb-Yugoslav Vojvodina since 1944," *Nationalities Papers* 24, no. 3 (1966): 469.

29. Borsody, ed., *The Hungarians*, pp. 177–90.

30. See Steven Bela Vardy, "The Hungarians of the Carpatho-Ukraine: From Czechoslovak to Soviet Rule," in Borsody, ed., *The Hungarians*, pp. 213–18, 223–25.

31. Rudolf Joó, ed., *Report on the Situation of the Hungarian Minority in Transylvania* (Budapest: Hungarian Democratic Forum, 1988), pp. 51–52.

32. Changes in the education system up to the 1970s are analyzed in Elemér Illyés, *National Minorities in Romania: Change in Transylvania* (Boulder, Colo.: East European Monographs, 1982), pp. 167–211.

33. See George Schöpflin, "Transylvania: Hungarians under Romanian Rule," in Borsody, ed., *The Hungarians*, pp. 124–29.

34. The most notorious of these works was Ion Lancranjan's *Cuvînt despre Transilvania* (Bucharest, 1982); see Louis J. Elteto, "Anti-Magyar Propaganda in Rumania and the Hungarian Minority in Transylvania," *Hungarian Studies Review* 16, nos. 1–2 (Spring–Fall 1989): 121–33.

35. On this and other aspects of official harassment, see the diary of one of Transylvania's leading Magyar writers: András Sütő, *Napló* (Budapest: Helikon, 1998). Sütő was partially blinded during the Romanian nationalist attacks on Magyars at Tirgu-Mures (Marosvásárhely) in 1990.

36. Fülöp and Sipos, *Magyarország külpolitikája*, p. 447.

37. Andrew Ludanyi, "The Hungarians of Vojvodina under Yugoslav Rule," in Borsody, ed., *The Hungarians*, p. 195.

38. Arday, "Hungarians in Serb-Yugoslav Vojvodina," pp. 470–72.

39. Ludányi, "The Hungarians of Vojvodina," pp. 206–7.

40. Béla Köpeczi, ed., *Erdély története I–III* (Budapest: Akadémiai kiadó, 1986). See Thomas Szendrey, "A History of Transylvania: Its Impact and Reception," *Hungarian Studies Review* 16, nos. 1–2 (Spring–Fall 1989): 137–49; and Norman Stone, "History of a Troubled Region," *Hungarian Quarterly* 36, no. 146 (Summer 1997): 118–20.

41. Hungary's population of 10.4 million includes some 100,000 Slovaks, 80,000 Croats, 25,000 Romanians, 5,000 Serbs, 5,000 Slovenes, 1,500 Ruthenes and Ukrainians, and a large but elusive number of Roma (Gypsies).

42. Parts of this section are based on the author's *Hungarian Minorities in East-Central Europe* (Washington, D.C.: Atlantic Council, 1994).

43. For a critical analysis, see Minority Protection Association, *The Slovak State Language Law and the Minorities* (Budapest, 1996).

44. Cf. Alexander Duleba, "Transfrontier Cooperation, Ethnic Minorities and Slovak Foreign Policy," in Póti, ed., *Integration*, pp. 95–103.

45. *Economist*, September 13, 1997, p. 35.

46. Sándor Vogel, *A magyar kisebbség Romániában* (Budapest: Hungarian Institute of International Affairs, 1997), pp. 4–7.

47. See the interviews with Transylvanian Magyars in István Schlett, *Kisebbségnézőben: Beszélgetések és dokumentumok* (Budapest: Kossuth, 1993), pp. 37–41.

48. Vogel, *Magyar kisebbség*, pp. 7–8.

49. For the text and an analysis, see Minority Protection Association, *The Romanian Law on Education: A Critical Approach from the Viewpoint of Minorities* (Budapest, 1996).

50. For a comparative analysis of the several framework treaties concluded between Hungary and the host states, see Sándor Vogel, "The Old-New Problems of the Hungarian Minorities in Central Europe," in Póti, ed., *Integration*, pp. 143–62. See also Vogel, "A Comparison of the Hungarian-Slovak and the Hungarian-Romanian Basic Treaty," and Géza Jeszenszky, "Hungary's Bilateral Treaties with the Neighbours and the Issue of Minorities," in *Ethnos-Nation* 4, nos. 1–2 (1996): 113–28.

51. RFE/RL Newsline, June 24, 1999. A survey conducted in Transylvania in autumn 1997 revealed a wide disparity between the civic allegiance of ethnic Romanians and that of Magyars. Among the former, 76 percent agreed with the proposition that they would "much rather be a citizen of Romania than a citizen of any other country"; only 47 percent of Magyars shared that opinion. See György Csepeli and Antal Örkény, "Nemzetek a lelkekben: Az identitás a világ 22. országában," *Népszabadság*, August 1, 1998, p. 21.

52. Lucian Boia, *Istorie si mit în constiinta româneasca* (Bucharest: Humanitas, 1997); see Sándor Vogel's review article in *Külpolitika* 4, no. 1 (Spring 1998): 125–38.

53. Arday, "Hungarians in Serb-Yugoslav Vojvodina," p. 479.

54. Norbert Spannenberger, "Die Ungarn in der Vojvodina: Interessenverbände und Autonomiepläne," *Ethnos-Nation* 4, nos. 1–2 (1996): 140–47.

55. József Somai, "Gondolatok as RMDSZ struktúrájával és müködésével kapcsolatosan," *Romániai Magyar Szó* (Cluj/Kolozsvár), December 3, 1997, p. 3.

56. See André Liebich, *Les Minorités nationales en Europe centrale et orientale* (Geneva: Georg, 1997), pp. 170–74.

57. Cf. Georg Brunner, *Nationality Problems and Minority Conflicts in Eastern Europe* (Gütersloh: Bertelsmann, 1996), pp. 107–9.

58. *Népszabadság,* July 8, 1999, p. 6.

2

All Quiet on the Russian Front? Russia, Its Neighbors, and the Russian Diaspora

AUREL BRAUN

THE COLLAPSE of the Soviet Union is surely one of the signal events of the twentieth century. Sudden and largely unexpected, it not only led to the creation of 15 sovereign states but also produced the world's largest diaspora. Approximately 25 million ethnic Russians (see Table 2.1) found themselves in 14 Newly Independent States (NIS) while the Russian Federation, which remains the world's largest territorial state, was left with a similar number of non-Russian citizens.[1] Furthermore, the end of the Soviet Union was not only the collapse of an empire, it was also the implosion of an ideology. Radical change was possible for the successor states. They have committed themselves, or at least have so claimed, not only to building new states but also to fundamental political and economic restructuring. But despite Western hopes and expectations, the processes of transformation in these states have not been marked by uninterrupted progress toward stable democracies and successful market economies.

In Russia, President Boris Yeltsin's sudden policy shifts, including his December 1999 surprise resignation, were so unpredictable that deciphering them at times made the dreary Kremlinology of the Soviet era look almost like a science. The shaping of a Russian national identity has been no less uncertain than the course of Russian politics. Shortly after winning the 1996 presidential elections, Yeltsin ordered his aides to develop a "national ideology" (or "national idea") that would unite the citizens of Russia,[2] despite having argued previously that, in

Table 2.1   **Ethnic Russians in the Near Abroad and the Baltic States (1996)**

	Total Population	Titular Group as a % of Total	Ethnic Russians as a % of Total
Armenia	3,816,000	93	2
Azerbaijan	7,507,000	83	5
Belarus	10,320,000	79	12
Estonia	1,572,000	64	29
Georgia	5,478,000	70	6
Kazakhstan[a]	14,950,000	53	31
Kyrgyzstan	4,754,000	57	19
Latvia	2,643,000	54	33
Lithuania	3,782,000	81	9
Moldova	4,350,000	65	13
Tajikistan	6,155,000	62	8
Turkmenistan	4,260,000	72	10
Ukraine	52,498,000	73	22
Uzbekistan	23,308,000	71	8

[a]1999 figures.
Sources: The World Bank Group, *Europe and Central Asia,* 1997; *World Book Encyclopedia,* 1997; Kazakhstan Statistics Agency, cited by *Russia Today,* May 14, 1999; *The Economist,* April 13, 1999, p. 36.

the past, ideologies had caused horrendous damage to Russia. The government's commission set up to develop a "national idea" came up empty-handed. More than that, the commission became something of a national joke. Russia's politicians have not even been able to choose appropriate words for its new national anthem, which is based on Mikhail Glinka's nineteenth-century operatic music. All this is emblematic of the frustration, pain, and disorientation that post-Soviet Russia has experienced. It has had to endure not only the postimperial trauma of losing both its external (East European) and internal empires but also the transition pain of political and economic restructuring as it seeks to establish democracy and markets.

Little wonder that, given the turmoil and uncertainty in Russia and in the other successor states, there has been a constant fear of violence. The tragic conflicts in what was once federal Yugoslavia have raised fears and indeed expectations of violence on the territory of the former Soviet Union. The worst-case scenarios envision Yugoslavia writ large.

In fact, there has been loss of life and violence in Russia. More than 60,000 people have been killed or are missing, and there have been over 1 million refugees on the territory of the former Soviet Union.[3] Most of the conflicts involved, however, occurred among non-Russians; the ones in which Russians were involved did not arise from the creation of

Russian diasporas in the new bordering states.[4] Given the uncertainties in Russia and the region, it would be foolish not to be anxious about the present or concerned about the future. But thus far, there has been no Yugoslavia-like violence. In that sense, Russia is a success story.

The collapse of the Soviet Union has unleashed a whole wave of ethnonational forces. Moreover, like the former Yugoslavia, there are national minorities, nationalizing states, and an external national "homeland" engaged in a triadic relational nexus that has the potential to produce large-scale violence. Russia as an external national "homeland," the Russian diasporas, and the NIS interact in a triadic relationship.[5] This chapter examines how these triads in the former Soviet Union were created, why large-scale violence has been absent, and prospects for such violence in the future.

Large-scale violence must be differentiated from competition, pressure, discontent, resentment, discord, or distress. All of these may, of course, contribute to eventual large-scale violence but do not necessarily cause it and should not be equated with it. Large-scale violence is qualitatively different and involves a violent, fundamental breakdown of relations within the triad. Because there are three fields of differentiated and competing positions—the national minority, the nationalizing state, and the external national "homeland"—the triadic relationship represents a dynamic intertwining, a relational and interactive perspective that should and does allow for a better explanatory and perhaps even predictive analysis of actual or potential large-scale violence involving the diasporas than earlier studies. Each part of the triad is likely to be insufficient in explaining violence; the interaction within the triad can better explain the creation at times of a particularly toxic mix, which in turn can result in violence.

Yet despite its great strengths, this relational and interactive perspective does have its own limitations. It speaks (rightly) of contingent outcomes and acknowledges that violence is not foreordained.[6] There is, moreover, a tendency at times to look at the manifestations of confrontation and conflict rather than the causes. It should therefore be useful to supplement the triadic approach. The field of international relations has provided some helpful insights. Positive contributions have also come from the studies of transitions. True, in "transitology," the tension between comparative and area studies (with the occasional infusion of strategy studies) has produced mixed results. Critics have rightly pointed out the problems of selecting the wrong analogies and the need for asking the relevant questions.[7] Yet even some of the harshest critics of transitology, such as Guy Hermet, who in highlighting the epistemological contradictions and tensions between the macro and micro levels of analysis demonstrated convincingly the general unpredictability of the future of postcommunist states, do not suggest that there cannot be any predictability or that the communist past does not in any way influence the postcommunist present and future.[8]

International relations theory and transitology then can supplement the triadic approach and clarify the problems and prospects for the non-Soviet space. This chapter thus has three parts: first, the past as influence; second, national identity, nationalism, and the national interest; and third, exogenous factors, that is, elements that are not inherent in the triad but could affect it. These include the role of democracy as a source of political legitimacy and influence on questions of war and peace, the security environment as shaped by the enlargement of the North Atlantic Treaty Organization (NATO), and the determinations of at least a significant part of the Russian elite, epitomized by Yevgeny Primakov, to cling to a Russian version of "manifest destiny"—a dangerously unrealistic ideal of a powerful but undemocratic Russia competing with and effectively challenging the West for world influence—that inevitably involves the Near Abroad, the 14 successor states around the Russian Federation, the only place where Russia has any reasonable hope of exercising preponderant influence.

The Past as Influence

The Marxist-Leninist past of the post-Soviet space is relevant to its future. This is not to dismiss older legacies but rather to focus on that which is most pertinent to the present and the future. In focusing on the recent past, I will concentrate on three areas: the national question, intent and expectations, and priorities.

THE "NATIONAL QUESTION"

The framework for dealing with internal imperialism and nationalism in the Soviet Union was formulated by Vladimir Lenin. Subsequent superstructures were constructed on his foundation. To Lenin, imperialism was an inherent characteristic of advanced capitalism, and nationalism was a manifestation of that doomed system. What he perceived to be ethnic Russian hegemony within what became the Soviet Union represented for him a form of internal colonialism, which could divert the attention of the proletariat from developing the requisite revolutionary consciousness. The risk of diversion applied both to the "oppressor" nation and to the national minorities, and could imperil the legitimacy of the political order. Lenin, however, was a "strategic

Marxist,"[9] devoted to Marxist theories but also thoroughly familiar with Karl von Clausewitz. There would be no change in the revolutionary strategy of destroying capitalism and building socialism, but there could be considerable flexibility in tactics. Lenin believed that such flexibility would not endanger his "scientific" strategy of revolutionary transformation. Internationally, therefore, he felt perfectly comfortable and justified in supporting movements of national liberation in order to break the power of the imperialist states, which in his view had been able to sustain their elites in power by using some of the profits of colonialism to bribe, at least temporarily, their working classes. To Lenin, one immediate danger in the Soviet Union was great-Russian chauvinism. He therefore concluded that it made good *tactical* sense to support the right of "nations" within the union to self-determination in order to overcome non-Russian concerns about that chauvinism.[10]

But Lenin distinguished between the right of national self-determination and the right to secede. A brilliant propagandist, Lenin believed there was a need to effect a safe tactical reconciliation between the two. Since he was a vanguardist (the people were to be led by a revolutionary elite) and his geopolitical approach was metrocentric (focused on the urban proletariat and the need to support a revolutionary center),[11] he could not allow tactical concessions to imperil his strategy. His solution was typically vanguardist and reflected his unshakable faith in the infinite manipulability and malleability of the people. Concessions to nationalism would be temporary and limited, and intended to foster the longer-range development of class consciousness, which in his view would inevitably replace national consciousness.

He developed, therefore, what amounted to a system of "double sovereignty": the sovereignty of the Union of Soviet Socialist Republics (USSR), i.e., the federation; and that of its member republics. In the 1960s the prominent Soviet jurist B. L. Manelis attempted to reconcile the two concepts.[12] In his view, and in line with Lenin's goals, the federation was deemed to be sovereign because the attributes of sovereignty were attached to it at its provenance in 1922 rather than delegated to it by the member republics. The republics, in turn, Manelis reasoned, did not lose their sovereignty by entering the federation; they retained their full sovereign rights. Yet this retention of sovereignty did not exclude the existence of a *superior* sovereignty, that of the federation. He explained this apparent paradox by stating, first, that the sovereignty of the federation and that of its members were in organic unity, as envisioned by Lenin, and, second, again by referring to Lenin's declaration that the republics preserved their independence on entering the union. Territorial nationalism (which Soviet national policies enhanced), moreover, provided preferential treatment for members of the nation living in their homelands (*korenizatsiya*).[13] In reality, the vanguard party developed this creative tactical concession to retain control and to continue its vast experiment in social engineering. At least that was the Leninist view. Lenin's intentions matter, not only because the modus operandi of his regime set the parameters for successive Soviet leaderships but also because his supreme confidence in the "strategic" success of the revolution emboldened him and subsequent Soviet leaders to make tactical concessions that not only resulted in an arbitrary redefinition of terms and concepts but were pregnant with unintended consequences.

When Joseph Stalin suggested that "local nationalism" had overtaken great-Russian chauvinism as the USSR's most significant problem,[14] and even when after World War II his regime started to eliminate "the non-Russian nationalism that had been intensified by the militant patriotism of the war period,"[15] this did not represent a change in strategy. It was a new tactic deemed to be most appropriate for the preservation of the control over the population and the continuation of the social experiment. "Sovereignty" again was used cynically. The attempt to create a new "Soviet man," an individual whose interests and loyalty transcended national identity and nationalism, continued unabated and remained central to the Sovietization myth.

Mikhail Gorbachev accepted the Leninist construct and firmly believed in the Sovietization myth of a new Soviet man and socialist loyalty. Indeed, this belief gave him the confidence to pursue perestroika and glasnost. In his view, the internationalist legacy of the revolution foreclosed any major risk of nationalism, which was, in his view, no longer a significant danger.[16] Using Lenin's vanguardist, that is, top-down approach, Gorbachev felt confident in trying to restructure the psychology—in essence, alter fundamentally the mind-set—of the people as part of the grand social experiment that began in 1917.[17]

At first Gorbachev's faith in the Leninist experiment extended to Eastern Europe. Following World War II, when the Soviet Union acquired an empire there, the principles of "double sovereignty" were extended to that region. Although the Soviet leadership in the postwar period proclaimed its respect for the sovereignty of the East European states and expressed a general commitment to the validity of the concept, in essence, it imposed severe limits on the sovereignty of those states.[18] This was most starkly illustrated by the Brezhnev Doctrine, according to which Moscow set the parameters for East European sovereignty and placed the interests of the international proletariat, as interpreted by Moscow, above those of any East European regime. This was the justification for the invasion of Czechoslovakia in 1968. The contradictions between a formal commitment to sovereignty and its obvious violation in Eastern Europe were to be resolved, at least in theory, by the principles of proletarian internationalism. The latter was used to redefine in essence sovereignty, emphasizing the interest of the whole socialist community as pivotal to the preservation of the interests of its parts.

This was then a modified, external version of the Leninist concept of double sovereignty. The Brezhnev Doctrine remained in force until the late 1980s, when Gorbachev finally proclaimed that the Soviet Union had no moral or political right to intervene in the East European states.[19] Although eventually Gorbachev was willing to abandon proletarian internationalism in those states, he did not seem willing to abandon the concept of double sovereignty within the Soviet Union itself. He wanted to draw the line at the Soviet borders because, despite the disintegration of Marxism-Leninism in Eastern Europe, which he could not now stop, he retained an unshakable faith in its ultimate success in the Soviet Union.

But the great social engineering experiment that Lenin began—the creation of a new "socialist man" and Soviet loyalty—did not yield the results that Gorbachev had expected. The Soviet people had not been inoculated against nationalism. Despite the fact that Lenin had intended his policies on ethnicity to be limited tactical concessions, they became instead part of the larger process of modernization that included not only industrialization and urbanization but also the development of national consciousness among ethnic groups. And as many writers on nationalism have argued, the nationalization of ethnic groups and the creation of nations as forward-looking politicized and territorialized communities are essentially modern phenomena.[20] Granting concessions to and even encouraging ethnic groups to retain their language and culture, and especially endowing them with their own territorial polities, created in the Soviet Union expectations and reinforced the consciousness of minorities as ethnocultural nations. *Inadvertently*, Lenin created structures that actually fostered the development of the ethnic or national consciousness that he opposed.

The contradictions created by Lenin on ethnic and national matters were not entirely resolved with the collapse of the Soviet Union. The national revival of the ethnic majority and attempts to incorporate or assimilate minorities or induce them to leave now became issues in a new triadic relational nexus involving national minorities, nationalizing states, and the external "homeland." The political minefields inherited by the postcommunist successor states and the lingering belief that some clever political arrangement or interpretation can overcome fundamental problems perhaps may be called Lenin's Revenge.

Although Boris Yeltsin's government clearly rejected Leninism, traces remain, in particular, the current approaches and attitudes to sovereignty. At the very least, the concept of sovereignty has been muddled. In contrast to post–World War I Hungary or Germany, which were consciously prepared to violate the sovereignty of neighboring states in order to try to protect Hungarian and German minorities, provocative or harsh Russian responses or policies regarding the Russian diasporas may be due in part to an inadequate appreciation of the legal barriers posed by sovereignty, barriers long established by key principles of international law. This was evident in Yeltsin's loose employment of the term "sovereignty," which he applied to ethnic minorities in the Russian Federation and in certain respects to Russian policies toward the other successor states. Although Russia formally recognizes the sovereignty of the other 14 states that emerged from the Soviet Union, much of its rhetoric and some of its policies suggest a reluctance to accept the sovereignty of the host government as stipulated by international law when it comes to the rights of ethnic Russians (and even Russian-speaking populations) in what Russians call the Near Abroad.

It is true that Yeltsin originally insisted only that the rights of ethnic Russians and Russian-speaking "compatriots" be protected through "legal" and "political" means.[21] Further, after independence, he appealed repeatedly to international organizations and even Western governments for help in protecting the rights of the Russian diasporas. Yet this does not mean that Russia has abjured the right to intervene on behalf of the Russian diasporas. The weight of evidence, in fact, suggests that since late 1992, Russia has asserted that it has the right to intervene in states of the Near Abroad to punish violations of the rights of ethnic Russians or even Russian speakers.[22] This is not the policy preferred by Yeltsin or the democratic forces represented by those who may be called Atlanticists (Western-oriented democrats supporting transatlantic ties). But they clearly have had to make concessions to the Eurasianists—advocates of stronger links to Asia and the former Soviet republics—and the neo-Slavophiles—anti-Western pan-Slavic nationalists. At the very least, there is confusion in Russia regarding the rights and the barriers of sovereignty on the territory of what was the Soviet Union. Consequently, even such Atlanticists as the former Russian Foreign Minister Andrey V. Kozyrev advocated harsh measures, including coercive economic pressures, against states in the Near Abroad that did not honor the human and citizenship rights of ethnic Russians or refused to grant them dual citizenship.

Still, this was not outright imperialism. Especially in the case of the democrats, this was not an attempt to reestablish the Soviet Union or to create a new kind of internal empire in the geographic space that the Soviet Union had occupied.[23] But Moscow's concern about the Russian diasporas has pushed it toward seeking a significant say in the Near Abroad that is bound to create tension. Moreover, Russian attitudes (as expressed by ultranationalists, by the communists, and specifically by likely presidential candidates Moscow Mayor Yury Luzhkov and General Aleksandr Lebed), which hold sovereignty permeable and claim the right to intervene not in order to save the proletariat threatened by counterrevolutionary forces as in the Soviet era but to protect ethnic Russians persecuted by the titular nations, may have been and might continue to be reinforced by a number of factors: the manner in which the Soviet Union broke up, the intentions and expectations of the elites in the successor states, and the perceptions of the various populations.

INTENTIONS AND EXPECTATIONS

Gorbachev and Yeltsin differed in August 1991 in their expectations of the attempt to transform the Soviet Union into a union of sovereign states, when a treaty for such a conversion was ready. It would have created a country with powerful republics and a weak center. Gorbachev was reluctant to support the treaty and did so only as a tactical concession to save his larger strategy—the preservation of the Soviet Union. Thus he supported it only as an alternative to the disintegration of the Soviet Union. Yeltsin was more flexible, but he also originally did not envision the breakup of the Soviet Union. Rather, he sought to strengthen the status of Russia in order to ensure that it had dominant membership within the union of sovereign states.[24] But Yeltsin also wanted to rid the country of Gorbachev and supplant him. Thus Yeltsin had two motives: to strengthen the Russian Federation and to remove Gorbachev so that he could begin a fundamental political and economic transformation within the Russian Federation. In November 1991, though, only seven republics, including Russia, agreed to sign the treaty, and it became clear that the union of sovereign states was a dead letter. In December 1991, the Soviet Union was legally dissolved by the leaders of Russia, Ukraine, and Belarus in favor of a Commonwealth of Independent States (CIS), comprising 11 republics, including Russia.

Yeltsin's ambivalence was evident throughout 1991. He did not set out to destroy the Soviet Union. He used the term "sovereignty" (*suverenitet*) to mean not "independence" but "autonomy." Despite the fact that Yeltsin in November 1991 had encouraged some regions to seize sovereignty, when the government of the Chechen-Ingush Republic proclaimed its formal independence from the Russian Federation, he ordered that armed forces put down the secession. The order was coun-termanded by his own parliament, and a stalemate ensued.[25] Nonethe-less, in certain respects Yeltsin did see the union (of 15 republics) as a burden on the Russian Federation, just as Gorbachev had come to per-ceive the outer empire (Eastern Europe) as a burden to the Soviet Union.

Still, there is no indication that Yeltsin believed that the dissolution of the union would result in an irreversible separation of the other republics from the Russian Federation, or that the 25 million ethnic Rus-sians living beyond the borders of the federation might be put into jeop-ardy. After all, Stalinism had created an extraordinarily high level of economic interdependence among the constituent republics; therefore there would be, at the very least, a strong incentive for reintegration. At a minimum, Russia, it seemed, would continue to exercise preponder-ant influence. Most important, Yeltsin was intent on ridding the coun-try of Gorbachev. Given how tenaciously Gorbachev clung to power, that meant destroying his edifice of power—that is, the Soviet Union—quickly and stealthily. Thus, Yeltsin did not prepare the Russian people for the consequences of the breakup of the Soviet Union, and his govern-ment did not make contingency plans to protect the Russian diasporas.

This stealthy breakup at the end of 1991 represented only a tempo-rary congruence of interests between Yeltsin and the Ukrainian leader-ship. For Ukraine, the central concern was independence, not the Gorbachev leadership. Different intentions among the three leaders, however, meant that there would be different expectations. And these differences in intentions and expectations, not only among the leaders of the three aforementioned states but throughout the CIS and the Baltic states, continue to have an influence on national goals and perceptions, and particularly on the triadic relational nexus and its potential for large-scale violence.

Although the Yeltsin leadership may have viewed the dissolution of the union as largely a tactical move, the Ukrainian leadership, which participated fully in that dismantlement, had a substantially different vision. To most Russians, Belarussians and Ukrainians were people of one blood (*edinokrovnye*).[26] The Ukrainians, however, did not see them-selves as "Little Russians." The Ukrainian leader, Leonid Kravchuk, who had Ukrainian independence as his primary goal, received partic-ularly strong support for this from western Ukraine, the west bank of the Dnipro (or Dnieper) River, where Rukh, the Ukrainian movement for democracy and eventually national independence, was strong. There was less enthusiasm for independence in the East, although there was some support based on the expectation that economic indepen-dence would bring economic improvement.

Still, more than 11 million Russians live in Ukraine. They constitute about 22 percent of the country's population, and in some parts of the country, such as the Donbas, on the eastern border with Russia, ethnic Ukrainians are more fluent in Russian than in Ukrainian.[27] There is also the matter of Crimea, in southern Ukraine on the Black Sea, with its predominantly Russian population. In 1954 Nikita Khrushchev, in a grandiose but at the time meaningless gesture, transferred Crimea to Ukraine as a kind of "anniversary present" celebrating 300 years of Russian and Ukrainian unity.

Russian leaders even in 1991 and 1992 were not entirely unaware of the potential problems. For instance, Foreign Minister Andrey Kozyrev spoke out in support of Russian minorities in the Near Abroad, and St. Petersburg Mayor Anatoly Sobchak warned of "forced Ukrainianization" of the Russian minority and a potential territorial conflict.[28] It was believed, however, that all of these potentially explosive problems could be worked out during the next few years of transition.

For the leaders of the Baltic states, Estonia, Latvia, and Lithuania, which had been forcibly incorporated into the Soviet Union in 1940, independence was imperative. The Baltic republics were at the forefront of the antiunion struggle in the late 1980s. Baltic independence movements, such as *Sajudis* in Lithuania, at first even sought Russian-minority support for independence and drew on Lithuania's tradition as a multiethnic regional power.[29] Russians constituted just over 9 percent of the population at the time of independence, and over 80 percent had been residents for 21 or more years.[30] The Baltic states in essence achieved independence after the 1991 coup, months before the other republics. They did not join the CIS; they moved quickly toward a reintegration with the West by shifting their trade westward and establishing links with Western institutions, and they refused to consider themselves part of Russia's Near Abroad.

Yet all three states have substantial ethnic minorities. In Latvia and Estonia, ethnic Russians represent a significant portion of their population: about a third in Latvia and almost a third in Estonia.[31] Moreover, these ethnic populations are concentrated in particular parts of Latvia and Estonia. It was not difficult to predict friction. The heavy in-migration of Russian and to a lesser degree Ukrainian populations during the post-1945 period was viewed by two of the titular (the ethnic group after whom the state is named) nations as a threat to national survival. Yet Russia assumed that ethnic Russians in those states would receive fair treatment. Moscow also expected to be able to maintain its military position in the Baltic region. This, too, was a potential cause of conflict.

Moldova presented a somewhat different problem. A large part of the republic had been Romanian territory in the interwar period. The majority of the population is ethnically Romanian and has resisted attempts at Russification. There are also important minorities in Moldova: Russians, Ukrainians, and Gagauz (a Turkic people). The Dniester River is an important dividing line: east-bank Russians, for example, from the beginning sought a separate republic, the Transdniestrian Moldovan Republic, which was supported by the Russian Fourteenth Army later led by General Lebed. The Gagauz on the west bank also sought independence.[32] Although Moldova is not contiguous with the Russian Federation, from the very early days of independence, Russia asserted the right to protect its diaspora there through Russian military power.

In Central Asia, the situation was still different. There the local elites were quite unprepared for independence and spent much of the first year of independence seeking to persuade Russia to create an effective commonwealth that would include them.[33] Of the five Central Asian states, Kazakhstan, Turkmenistan, Uzbekistan, Kyrgyzstan, and Tajikistan, only the first borders directly on the Russian Federation. Kazakhstan is vast, as large as all of Western Europe. Historically, its border with Russia was not a barrier to the movement of people.[34] This has long influenced Russian attitudes. The vagueness of the border facilitated settlement in Kazakhstan by ethnic Russians, particularly in Soviet times, as industrialization and urbanization increased. More than 6 million Russians out of a total population of about 17 million live in Kazakhstan, most of them concentrated near the border with Russia.[35] The titular population represents less than half the total,[36] so that the dissolution of the Soviet Union would have put considerable pressure on the Kazakh leadership to assign a high priority to its relations with its gigantic northern neighbor.

In Tajikistan, unlike Uzbekistan, Kazakhstan, and Kyrgyzstan, which share Turkic historical roots, most of the 5.7 million people are ethnically close to Iranians. One of Russia's primary concerns after independence was the threat from Islamist forces against the Tajik government. Beginning in the spring of 1992, a bloody civil war was fought in Tajikistan, with as many as 60,000 people killed and at least four times that number forced to flee. The primary threat was not to the ethnic Russian minority, a small portion of the total population, but rather the general danger of radical Islam, which could destabilize the region and create problems for Russia itself, with its sizable Muslim minorities. Russia sent in over 10,000 troops who turned the tide in favor of the government, which therefore favored the continued Russian presence. Russians, in fact, have argued that their forces in Tajikistan are "peacekeeping" troops together with those from other CIS states.[37] With the success of the Islamic fundamentalist Taliban in neighboring Afghanistan, Russia in 1998 increased its forces in Tajikistan as a protective measure.

In Transcaucasia, none of the three states, Georgia, Azerbaijan, and Armenia, has a large Russian population. By virtue of minorities in Abkhazia and South Ossetia, in Georgia there is a direct Russian concern because of Abkhaz and Ossetian minorities within the Russian Federation. There are also Russian military bases and pipelines in Georgia. Under the leadership of President Eduard Shevardnadze, Gorbachev's onetime foreign minister, Georgia was compelled to seek Russian military support in fighting Abkhazian separatists. Yet relations have remained uneasy because of difficult negotiations over Russian military bases and accusations that Russian hard-liners, outside of the control of President Yeltsin, were behind a March 1998 assassination attempt against President Shevardnadze.[38]

Armenia has had no problems with Russia, and certainly not with its tiny Russian ethnic minority. It has been far more preoccupied with the conflict in Nagorno-Karabakh. Azerbaijan's first concern appeared to be the conflict with Armenia, as both states engaged in their version of ethnic cleansing. The Azeri government resented Russian support for Armenia, but when Haidar Aliyev, a former top party official in the Soviet Union, took over the leadership in Baku, he launched a successful policy of accommodation with Russia, which included a series of concessions in the oil industry. As Azeri wealth may increase exponentially with the gigantic oil discoveries in the Caspian Sea, disputes with Russia also may grow, but these are not likely to be ethnically based. Russian military interventions in Tajikistan and Georgia, which were not driven by concerns over the status of ethnic Russians, demonstrate that there are other motives for dispatching Russian troops to the Near Abroad.

PRIORITIES

Given the heterogeneity of the Near Abroad and the Baltic states, the multiplicity of Russian interests, and limited Russian resources, Moscow has had to develop an order of priorities to monitor the situation of ethnic Russians and Russian speakers in the other successor states and in its commitment to protect their rights and interests. Several factors have helped determine these priorities. First, the notion of *edinokrovnye* has placed a special focus on Ukraine and Belarus, even though the latter has not only not posed significant ethnic problems for

Russia but has enthusiastically sought reunification. Second, the size of the Russian ethnic minority and the percentage that it represents of the total population of a successor state has mattered. This criterion covers Ukraine, and especially Crimea, but also Kazakhstan, Latvia, and Estonia. Moldova qualifies because of the heavy concentration of Russians in Transdniestria. Third, Russian security and economic interests also have been linked with concerns over the fate of ethnic Russians. Ukraine, Kazakhstan, Belarus, Moldova, and the Baltic states again are pertinent. Last, because the triadic nexus involves a dynamic, interactive relationship, the order of priority does shift periodically, based in part on how the titular nation deals with the Russian minority.

Elite views do not necessarily coincide with those of the population at large. According to the *New Russian Barometer* survey, although most Russians are somewhat concerned about their conationals living in the CIS countries and the Baltic states, they are reluctant to intervene militarily on behalf of the Russians outside Russia.[39] Nevertheless, ethnicity and blood ties do seem to create a desire for closeness. More than three-quarters of the respondents want closer ties with Belarus and Ukraine.[40] Furthermore, Russian public opinion would likely shift quickly and radically if the Russian minority were to be subject to violent persecution in a neighboring state.

There has also been a gradual shift in the relative importance of relations with the new states of Central Asia. While not based primarily on issues concerning national minorities, nationalizing states, and external national "homelands," the results may nevertheless affect how the triadic relationship will develop in this part of the former Soviet Union. As frustration with the shortcomings of the CIS have increased—illustrated by Kazakhstan President Nursultan Nazarbayev's angry criticism, at the April 1998 CIS summit in Moscow, of the failure to implement the 1994 agreement to create a free-trade zone—these states have looked for alternate solutions to regional problems.[41] Uzbekistan, Kazakhstan, and Kyrgyzstan formed the Central Asian Union (CAU), an alliance that was enlarged with the admission of Tajikistan in March 1998. The CAU has been concerned not only with economic matters but also with what the governments perceive as an Islamist threat and particularly the support for Islamist groups by Iran and Pakistan.[42] This is not to suggest that the CAU states do not continue to assign a great deal of importance to their relations with Russia but that their increased CAU interaction may influence both regional and individual national identity. This in turn may affect the triadic relationship, particularly in states such as Kazakhstan, with its huge Russian population.

National Identity, Nationalism, and National Interest

The assessment of the current status of the three parts of the triad involves an examination of Russia's self-image as an external national "homeland" for ethnic Russians, surveying the policies of the governments of the non-Russian successor states toward the Russian minorities and evaluating the status of the Russian diasporas: Have they become alienated national minorities? Have they reached a level of alienation at which they demand cultural territorial autonomy or seek external help?

There is a tendency to depict nations as primordial (especially in the case of Russia), but primordialist definitions ultimately are static and, therefore, would be particularly inadequate in any analysis where interaction is employed, as it is here. Modernist definitions, though, which largely tend to ignore the vital importance of a shared belief in a common ancestry, ignore the interplay among the past, present, and future. Consequently, in looking at national identity, it may be best to try to integrate elements of primordialism and modernism, as suggested for instance by Anthony D. Smith.[43] Nationalism could be viewed as the ideology and the political action of the nation, with some elaboration. Generally, nationalism may be seen as combining three ideals: collective self-determination, the expression of national character and individuality, and the division of the world into separate nations.[44]

Occasionally the desire to have a state can generate an overbearing attitude toward other nations or national minorities. Nationalism, though, is not the same thing as chauvinism.[45] But there are different types of nationalism, and two in particular are important for the discussion that follows: "civic" nationalism, encompassing notions of citizenship in a territorial unit, shared membership in a political community, and political culture informed by key shared values; and "ethnic" nationalism, based on membership in a more narrow exclusionist community of common religion, descent, or customs, one where these sources of identity correlate with interests that take top priority in political activity. Civic nationalism is inclusive: All share the same obligations and privileges of membership in a political community. In ethnic nationalism, groups are sharply divided along cultural, linguistic, or religious lines. In an ethnically homogeneous or largely homogeneous state, ethnic nationalism is not necessarily a threat since a tiny minority might be assimilated peacefully and such nationalism would remain a domestic matter. In a multiethnic or religious state, ethnic nationalism tends to become divisive and threatening to ethnic or religious minorities. Ethnic nationalism also can become aggressive nationalism both domestically and externally, either leading the titular nationality to worry about the "corruption" of the polity (by ethnic minorities) in their own state or inducing the titulars to aggressively seek to protect conationals beyond the national frontiers. The more aggressive forms of ethnic nationalism perhaps can be best referred to as ultranationalism.

RUSSIA AS EXTERNAL NATIONAL "HOMELAND"?

National identity is the foundation for nationalism. Russian national identity is weak, which may be fortunate in that it diminishes the risk of confrontation in the triadic relationship. This is not entirely new. Historically, there was no clear ethnic Russian identity.[46] Indeed, claims to be the Third Rome, the true center of Christianity and civilization, and Russia's absorption of innumerable ethnic groups in all strata of society, including the nobility, made it difficult to create an ethnically based national identity and nationalism. A swing to a more narrowly based version of Russian nationalism in the late nineteenth century was largely an act of desperation to deflect growing revolutionary threats. Moreover, it was ineffective.[47] In fact, it has been argued that since the early seventeenth century, Russia consistently has sacrificed the construction of a Russian nation to the creation and maintenance of an empire, undercutting the basis for a Russian national identity.[48]

The Soviet Union was itself an internal empire in which the development of a Russian national identity was stifled. This was true even during the period when Joseph Stalin, for tactical purposes, encouraged Russian nationalism. This is not to deny that, during Soviet rule, there were some periods of intense Russification, an attempt to impose the Russian language, culture, and even some notions of Russian ethnicity throughout the state, but this was used primarily as a means to control rather than to create a narrow, ethnically based state with a clearly defined ethnic Russian identity. However, since Marxism-Leninism did not create civic nationalism either, ethnic tensions developed despite the absence of a clear Russian national identity.

With the collapse of the Soviet Union, it would have been difficult for Russia to create a narrow, ethnically based national identity and pursue a policy of ethnic nationalism. After all, Russians make up barely 82 percent of the population, with Tatars, Ukrainians, Belarussians, Chuvash, Bashkir, Mordovians, Chechens, Jews, and others constituting almost one-fifth.[49] Moreover, given the low birthrate of the Russian population, it is entirely possible that the percentage of ethnic Russians will diminish in the future. In certain respects then, by not pursuing a narrow nationalist agenda, Boris Yeltsin's government simply accommodated demographic reality.

Yeltsin strove to eschew ethnic nationalism by emphasizing the primacy of human and civil rights—a kind of liberal-secular nationalism. He referred to Russia as *Rossiya* (the country of Russia, thus including all the ethnic groups), not the narrow nationalistic *Rus* (the lands of the Russians).[50] This is in contrast to the national bolshevism of the leader of the Communist Party, Gennadi Zyuganov, who combines his advocacy for the restoration of vanguardist party rule and a command economy with calls for strengthening ethnic Russian rule in the face of alleged encroachments and conspiracies by non-Russians, or the ultranationalist statements of Vladimir Zhirinovsky, who speaks of the need to re-create a new Russian empire and rants against the internal "enemies" of the Russian people.

Moreover, there has been considerable decentralization of power to the Russian Federation's 89 territorial units, with some, such as Tatarstan and Yakutia, gaining a considerable measure of autonomy that comes close to some of the attributes of statehood.[51] Tatarstan's prime minister, in fact, has spoken of the Republic of Tatarstan as "a state associated with the Russian Federation" with rights entrenched in international law.[52] Its treaty with Russia is one of creative vagueness.[53] It speaks of Tatarstan "participating in international relations" without clarifying the precise parameters. At the same time, Moscow retains jurisdiction over defense and foreign policy. Tatarstan, an oil-rich republic of some 4 million people, where Tatars number fewer than half the population, has gained the symbols of independence while Russia can claim that it has preserved its territorial integrity. And regional leaders may have a greater input in Russian politics as they use local power bases, such as Tatarstan. In August 1999, for instance, Mintimer Shaimiyev, the president of Tatarstan and one of the key leaders of All Russia, a predominantly centrist movement of local leaders, helped forge an alliance with the Otechestvo (Fatherland) Party of Moscow Mayor Yury Luzhkov[54] that could become a powerful if not predominant force in the December 1999 Duma elections.

In general, Russia has turned inward, which lends to a more modest, less imperial role. This is evidenced by the national security "concept," which Yeltsin signed in December 1997.[55] It is meant to be an expression of the national view of security. This inward-looking document acknowledges a whole range of problems, including attempts of criminal infiltration of the government, prospects that Russia may not hold together as a single federation, and concern about many unguarded or poorly guarded sections of Russia's borders. The state of the economy is also mentioned as a security threat to the Russian Federation. The emphasis thus is on domestic matters that can endanger the state's well-being.

Yet there are also different tendencies in the three areas of nationalism, decentralization, and national security. First, Yeltsin's push for a "national ideology" (or "idea"), following his reelection as president, was a concession to a collectivist approach and a sign of a nationalism that is more ethnic than civic. This approach certainly can lead to a much more hard-line emphasis on Russian ethnocultural uniqueness and an exclusionary type of nationalism.

Second, since 1997 there have been efforts at recentralization in Russia, and the leadership in Moscow continues to be concerned about the centrifugal forces throughout the vast territory of the federation. In fairness, it is worth noting that these efforts have been directed more at enforcing better tax collection and at setting somewhat more clearly the parameters for autonomy than at a recentralization that would create the kind of confrontations between the territorial units and the center that Moscow could ill afford. Even Mayor Luzhkov, a man with strong Russian nationalistic credentials, has been very careful to maintain good relations with regional governments. Still, even relatively modest attempts at recentralization can carry certain risks because almost inevitably they tend to emphasize what are perceived primarily as Russian rather than minority interests and thus reinforce ethnic Russian nationalism.

And third, there have been greater efforts by Russia to play a controlling role in the CIS. So far these efforts have been much less successful than Russia had hoped. The CIS is not a completely hollow organization. It performs a number of functions, such as coordinating civil aviation within the territories of the member states. But Moscow's attempts to force Russian policy on the CIS have proven to be largely unsuccessful, as demonstrated at summits in the fall of 1997 and in April 1998, where Russian demands for closer economic and foreign policy cooperation under Moscow's leadership were rebuffed and Moscow was severely criticized.[56] Yevgeny Primakov expressed his frustration at the problems in the CIS (and basically with dealing with the Near Abroad) in his year-end foreign policy review in December 1997.[57] After citing as a main success that "nowhere have we slipped into a confrontation," he basically blamed others for the problems of dealing with the CIS on a whole range of issues from pipelines to military cooperation. Thus even Primakov, an ambitious though patient booster of Russian power, seemed to have been forced for the time being to console himself with some of Russia's more modest achievements and to appreciate Russia's limitations in the region.

Surveys of popular sentiments in Russia, such as the *New Russia Barometer,* show not just that only a small percentage perceives a threat from the ex-republics of the Soviet Union (22 percent) but that the people are far from willing to make an open commitment to protect the Russian diasporas.[58] Although most Russians are concerned about the diasporas, the overwhelming majority favors negotiation to resolve problems (92 percent), and only 16 percent would be prepared to advocate military action.[59] If Russia is to play the role of an external national "homeland," popular will at least would wish certain constraints on that role.

The definition of a Russian national identity is an ongoing *process* that continues to be influenced by myriad domestic and external factors and thus continues to respond to contradictory domestic impulses and a variety of external signals. Russian nationalism, moreover, will be shaped not only by national identity; it also will depend on and affect how Russia defines its national interests. Samuel Huntington, for instance, has contended that "a national interest is a public good of concern; a vital national interest is one which they are willing to expend blood and treasure to defend."[60] Thus the major question here is: Do the Russians perceive a vital national interest in defending their diasporas?

It is one thing for a homeland to monitor, to protest, even to use economic tools to pressure a nationalizing state to respect the rights of its diaspora; it is quite another to risk lives and national treasure to protect that diaspora or safeguard its interests. There is little predilection in Russia, even if viewed as an external national "homeland," for military action on behalf of the diasporas. Of course, continuing external and internal factors could radically change Russian nationalism and Moscow's definition of what constitutes a vital national interest. And among these, perhaps the most important is the treatment of the diasporas in the surrounding states.

NATIONALISM IN THE "NATIONALIZING STATES"

All the successor states in the former Soviet Union are ethnically heterogeneous. But the policies of their governments and the attitudes of the dominant elites and the titular groups toward minorities have varied considerably. In several, there has been no large-scale violence relating to the Russian diaspora; the possibility of violence, however, has by no means been eliminated. Three-quarters of the Russian diaspora lives in Ukraine, Belarus, and Kazakhstan. Moldova and two of the Baltic states, Latvia and Estonia, have experienced serious ethnic tensions.[61]

Ukraine

No other newly independent state is home to as many of the Russian diaspora and no other state is as important to the Russian Federation as Ukraine (see Map 2.1). Russians constitute slightly more than a fifth of Ukraine's 52 million people. They are concentrated in eastern Ukraine, on Russia's boundary, as well as in Crimea. Independent Ukraine has had to deal with difficult questions of national identity and cope with the enormous problems of transition. How it handles the minority question will have a profound impact on its stability. There has been friction with Russia over Crimea, the Black Sea Fleet, and the supply of natural gas and oil by Moscow. But there has been no descent into large-scale violence.

Identity and nationalism. Several factors have shaped Ukrainian identity and nationalism. First, like Russia, Ukraine is a multiethnic state with the titular group representing less than three-quarters of the total population. Not only are there a large number of Russians as well as other minorities, but many ethnic Ukrainians are in fact Russophones, that is, Russian speakers. Even President Leonid Kuchma is much more comfortable speaking Russian than Ukrainian. It is a country that is deeply divided ethnically and culturally. The Dnipro (or Dnieper) River divides Ukraine culturally, politically, and geographically: the west bank looks more toward Europe and independence; the east bank more toward Russia and Russophone culture.[62] There are important linguistic, ethnic, and religious differences in Ukraine. Therefore, it is difficult to find a majority, a nationwide consensus, on many issues. Andrew Wilson, for instance, has gone so far as to call Ukrainian nationalism a "minority faith," favored by only a minority of the ethnic Ukrainian population.[63] Wilson aside, an ethnically based nationalism would have difficulty in gaining the support of the majority of such a diverse population.[64] True, Ukrainians do have historical grievances that provide the potential for mobilizing ethnic nationalism: An estimated 5 to 7 million Ukrainians died during Stalin's forced collectivization and the ensuing famine. However, such an attempt at ethnic nationalism would be very risky and electorally unwise given the dangers of polarization and the large numbers of Russian and Russophone voters. This was illustrated during the March 1998 parliamentary elections. The Communist Party of Ukraine, which has strong support among the Russian minority in the eastern part of the country, won the largest number of seats, although not a majority.[65] Ukraine's moder-

Map 2.1   Belarus and Ukraine: Areas of Russian Concentration

Source: Jeff Chinn and Robert Kaiser, *Russians as the New Minority* (Boulder, Colo.: Westview Press, 1996), p. 130.

ately nationalist Rukh Party, by contrast, fared rather badly, winning only a total of 46 seats out of 450.[66] And hard-line nationalist parties did even worse.[67]

Ukrainian nationalism is also affected by the fact that Ukraine and Russia do not have the same kind of hostile relationship that existed, for instance, between Serbia and Croatia. It is not that there was no Russian pressure on Ukraine on a variety of issues, but rather the limits on such pressure created a far less confrontational relationship than that between Serbia and Croatia. Russian pressure began quite early on. Weeks after Ukrainian independence Vladimir P. Lukin, chairman of the Russian Parliament Foreign Relations Committee, presented a series of proposals (which came to be known as the Lukin Doctrine) that included the return of Crimea and the Black Sea Fleet to Russia.[68] The Russian Duma, moreover, passed a resolution declaring Nikita Khrushchev's 1954 gift of Crimea to Ukraine unconstitutional. Fully aware of Ukraine's economic weakness and dependence on fuel imports, Russia also has used economic pressure, including the manipulation of vital natural gas sales to Ukraine, to try to attain certain political goals, such as Ukrainian concessions on the Black Sea Fleet[69] and bases in Crimea and better Ukrainian cooperation in the CIS.[70]

The Yeltsin government, however, kept such pressures within limits. It did not threaten the independence of Ukraine. Russian Communist Party leader Gennadi Zyuganov's contention during the March 1998 parliamentary elections in Ukraine that the reunification of Russia and Ukraine was inevitable[71] was not the policy of the Yeltsin government. And in May 1997 Yeltsin and Kuchma signed a wide-ranging ten-year Treaty of Friendship, Cooperation, and Partnership.[72] In addition to arrangements for the Russian fleet to lease bases in Sevastopol, Crimea, the agreement basically recognized Crimea as Ukrainian territory. This did not end all possible Russian claims, but these efforts by Yeltsin's government at least helped calm relations and should help alleviate Ukrainian concerns about Russian irredentism. In June 1999 the Russian Duma ratified three accords on sharing the Black Sea Fleet with Ukraine.[73] Russia retains 83 percent of the fleet, and will continue to, based in Ukraine under clearly defined conditions. The accords should pave the way for the 1997 Russia-Ukraine friendship treaty to enter into force. There is therefore less of a risk that Russian threats would stampede Ukraine into *a narrow, ethnically based identity and nationalism.*

The peaceful breakup of the Soviet Union aided the development of a more civic-based nationalism in Ukraine; armed conflict would have greatly encouraged nationalist extremism both in Russia and in Ukraine. Not only was the breakup peaceful, but it also enjoyed widespread support across all ethnic and linguistic groups. In the Ukrainian referendum and election in December 1991, over 90 percent voted for independence and 62 percent for Kravchuk's election as president.[74] Significantly, there was support for independence in the heavily Russified, that is, predominantly ethnic Russian and Russian-speaking, oblasts, such as Donetsk. Even in Crimea, 54.1 percent voted in favor.[75]

Still, there is reason for caution. Russians and Ukrainians approached the issue of independence with different motivations and expectations. Russians in Ukraine hoped for improved economic conditions, whereas Ukrainians on the west bank of the Dnipro emphasized independence from Russia. Moreover, the Leninist legacy has created some confusion about what sovereignty or independence means. There has been also a gradual reevaluation by Ukrainians and ethnic Russians of their status within the country as Kiev's linguistic policies have become harsher and economic problems have remained unresolved. The tacit bargain between the Russian ethnic minority and the titulars in Ukraine over establishing a multiethnic state that is also multicultural (in the sense that differing ethnicity and culture are not only tolerated but that diversity is recognized as contributing to the well-being of the country), which has been so important to the maintenance of ethnic peace, is not free of stress. Great resentment and radicalization could develop, particularly if the minority should begin to feel gravely threatened, physically or culturally. As the Ukrainian economy, already in dire straits, is hurt further by the political and economic chaos in Russia, as its currency depreciates,[76] the economic pain is bound to increase and with it divisive suspicions of ethnic economic favoritism.

In general, the Ukrainian leadership has helped restrain nationalist pressures for the creation of an exclusivist national identity and restrictive ethnic nationalism. While he looked westward to Europe, Leonid Kravchuk, who started as a moderate nationalist president, was careful to maintain a dialogue with Russia, to sustain important economic relations, and to pay at least lip service to the goal of making the CIS effective although not supranational. In time he gradually became more nationalistic in dealing with Russia. In 1994 he lost the presidential election to Kuchma, who promised better relations with Russia. But Kuchma could not have been elected without strong support from the titular population. Although he, like other Russophones, may indeed believe that a natural integration within what he referred to euphemistically as "Eurasia"—which connotes the historical, cultural, and economic unity of the three eastern Slavic peoples—can be obtained while preserving independence,[77] this belief has not been translated into policies that endanger the rights or well-being of the titular population. Despite a generally favorable view of Russia, Kuchma has been serious about defending Ukraine's territorial integrity, as his tough stance during negotiations both on the Black Sea Fleet and bases in the Crimea demonstrated. And in July 1999 Kuchma strongly rejected the idea of creating a union of Russia, Belarus, and Ukraine. He declared, "I am not going to run for the presidency for a second term to become somebody's vassal."[78] His actions should not only help reassure the titular population but act as an antidote to the more extreme nationalist tendencies in Ukraine.

Economic relations alone do not alter the characteristics of nationalism in Ukraine or other states, but they do play a role. In Ukraine, continuing heavy dependency on Russia has meant not only pressure from Moscow but also a greater Ukrainian moderation on issues involving Russia and Russians. In an economically depressed country, one undergoing a painful transition, when many segments of society are suffering a loss of status and with corruption rampant, there will be a reluctance to risk the economic dislocation that would result from a confrontation with Russia over national and ethnic issues.

The sorry state of Ukraine's economy makes Russia's look positively enviable. Ukraine not only depends on Russia for natural gas and other resources, its trade with Russia accounts for 43 percent of its total foreign trade.[79] Furthermore, Yeltsin and Kuchma signed in February 1998 a landmark economic cooperation deal designed to more than double trade between the two states to $35 billion within the next ten years.[80] Russia's August 1998 currency and debt crisis put enormous pressure on Ukraine's largely unrestructured economy. The hryvnia fell sharply, wage and pension arrears piled up, and the Kiev government was forced to restructure billions of hryvnias of debt.[81] These stabilization attempts have restored some calm, but the Russian crisis highlighted the continuing interdependence of the two states.

These factors have helped restrain the nationalists in Ukraine, some of whom have advocated restrictive language policies and an anti-Russian foreign policy. Since Ukrainian identity, like its Russian counterpart, continues to evolve, these factors have the potential for continuing to induce moderation in the future, provided that the existing tacit bargains—for instance, on language—continue. Sudden shifts and gravely disappointed expectations, however, could give a boost to those who seek to develop an exclusionary form of nationalism in Ukraine.

Policies toward minorities. Language, symbols, jobs, and status can be important tools of any nationalizing agenda. Ukrainian nationalism in general has been moderate, as noted, and the titular leadership certainly did not demonstrate the kind of vindictiveness that the Croatian government of Franjo Tudjman showed toward the Serb minority. Still, after independence the Kiev government moved quickly on the language issue by encouraging education in Ukrainian and its use in the workplace.[82] In Ukraine not only did the vast majority of the Russian minority not speak Ukrainian, but a great many Ukrainians themselves, as noted previously, are Russophones who are more comfortable in the Russian language and culture. From the Ukrainian perspective, language policy was meant to counter the linguistic assimilation of ethnic Ukrainians that had occurred during the Soviet period. But language policies are also language politics and can lead to polarization. Despite the risks, the Ukrainian government pushed forcefully on the language issues, from mandatory and exclusive use of the Ukrainian language in state administration and higher education, to restrictions on broadcasting by Russian television networks and on controlling the flow of Russian-language information into Ukraine.[83]

When Ukrainian is required on the job, Russophones are at a disadvantage, which can mean a loss of position and of status. Although there are similarities between Ukrainian and Russian, the differences are great enough so that a "passive" understanding of Ukrainian is far from sufficient to be able to work in the language. In many regions in Ukraine, there has been skepticism about and resistance to attempts at Ukrainianization (which includes language and culture). Significantly, resistance comes not only from ethnic Russian minorities but also from Ukrainian Russophones, particularly in the eastern parts of the country, thereby demonstrating that language politics affects not only language but also "national consciousness" and territorial cohesion in indepen-dent Ukraine.[84] Resistance in places like Donetsk and Crimea has been fierce. Here the population strongly opposed any attempts to introduce, for instance, Ukrainian language requirements in the workplace. Although there has been some progress on Ukrainianization in Kiev and on the west bank, it is of considerable importance that the resis-tance in the predominantly Russophone areas *has been effective.*[85] These areas have maintained their cultural and linguistic autonomy, which indicates that both the Kravchuk and the Kuchma governments lacked the willpower or the ability to enforce linguistic Ukrainianization. It also demonstrates the continuing power and resilience of ethnic Rus-sians and Russophones. As long as this kind of standoff is maintained, the chances for violent confrontation are greatly diminished.

A change in the balance, however, might lead to a confrontation and possible violence. But the government's policy on Ukrainianization has been limited not only by resistance but also by a degree of self-restraint. This is most evident in the moderate policies on changing place-names in Ukraine, a change that, given centuries of Russification, is symboli-cally very important. In parts of Eastern Europe and the Balkans, the systematic replacement of place-names reflected the politics of ethnic nationalism. A study on toponymity in Ukraine shows that there has been a considerable reluctance to de-Sovietize and de-Russify place-names, in part explained by governmental self-restraint.[86]

Crimea. Of all the areas in the former Soviet Union where the triadic nexus could lead to large-scale violence, Crimea is perhaps the most worrisome. It is of great historic and considerable strategic significance to Russia. Russia wrested the territory from the Ottoman Empire in the eighteenth century; in 1942 Russian forces put up an epic 250-day defense against the Nazi invasion. Although symbolically not as impor-tant as Kosovo is to the Serbs, Crimea has been used as a symbol by all nationalistic forces in Russia. Furthermore, it is the only Ukrainian oblast with a Russian majority, which has expressed strong support for independence from Ukraine, in local parliamentary and presidential elections. Large-scale violent confrontation seemed possible on number of occasions, particularly following the election of Yuri Meshkov, a

Russian nationalist, as president of Crimea in January 1994.[87] Some violence has indeed occurred. But in Crimea, which has earned the sobriquet "Ukraine's Sicily" because of its rampant corruption and crime, the violence—gangland killings and the shooting of politicians—comes largely from criminal corruption rather than from Ukrainian-Russian interethnic hatred.

The reasons for the absence of large-scale interethnic violence here may give some indication of why things in the former Soviet Union have turned out so differently from Yugoslavia. Russian nationalists have supported secession. Yuri Luzhkov is particularly fond of staking Russia's claim to Crimea on his visits to Sevastopol, Crimea. The controversies over the division of the Black Sea Fleet also have persuaded many members of the Russian military to support the "recapture" of Crimea. Yet in 1994 Russia chose not to intervene and help President Meshkov in his standoff against Ukraine.

While the decision was perhaps colored by Moscow's unwillingness to become tied to someone as monumentally inept as Meshkov, it had other motives. First, Crimea is not ethnically homogeneous. Russians comprise 1.6 million of the 2.4 million people. There are more than 600,000 Ukrainians, many of whom are Russified; but most important, there are also large numbers of Crimean Tatars,[88] Muslim, Turkic-speaking people, many of whom were deported from Crimea by Stalin during World War II. Significantly, since 1991 over a quarter million Tatars have returned to the Crimea from places like Uzbekistan.[89] If Crimea were to separate from Ukraine, it runs the risk of Tatar separatism. Second, the separation of Crimea could set a precedent for the separation of regions within Russia itself. Finally, Russian restraint may be both a positive and a negative indicator. The danger of escalating and contagious secessionism may be deterring Russia. However, Russia also could be holding back in the hope of reintegrating all of Ukraine and may be willing to wait for this to occur rather than take risks to acquire just Crimea.

One other element is relevant: the ineffectiveness of the Russian diaspora in Crimea to push for independence, its inability to mobilize, and its unwillingness to risk serious bloodshed.[90] Here too the role of the Ukrainian government in the triadic relationship has been an important factor in shaping the attitudes of the Crimean Russians. While Kiev has annuled the Crimean parliament's moves for independence, removed Meshkov, appointed a pro-Ukrainian government led by a relative of President Kuchma, passed a law abolishing the Crimean presidency, and severely curtailed Crimean sovereignty, it also has been willing to compromise with the Russian minority. In 1992, for instance, a joint Ukrainian-Crimean declaration defined the peninsula to be an integral part of Ukraine but one that would enjoy a special economic status and the right to "enter into social, economic, and cultural relations with other states."[91] This arrangement is similar to Russia's with Tatarstan. And although the Ukrainian government has kept Crimea's separatist parliament on a tight leash when it comes to matters of independence, otherwise it has allowed considerable political activity.[92] Furthermore, the Kiev government also may have outmaneuvered Crimean (Russian) nationalists on the volatile issue of Sevastopol when it signed the Ukrainian-Russian treaty on May 30, 1997. By largely defusing the Sevastopol problem, Kiev deprived the nationalists of one of their rallying issues, one on which they had received considerable support from Moscow. Thus here the triadic interaction has not triggered large-scale violence. In particular, Ukrainian creativity and flexibility and the absence of a virulent Ukrainian ethnic nationalism have contributed to the avoidance of large-scale interethnic violence.

Belarus

The relations of Belarus (see Map 2.1 on page 101) with Russia may be categorized perhaps as "unrequited love." The triadic relational nexus is operating differently than in the Ukrainian case, for in Belarus the titular group is not in any way building a nationalizing state. With the exception of a small minority, in fact, Belarussian national identity is rather weak.[93] The titulars essentially seem to be quite content to reunify with Russia. The Russian national minority is not alienated, all have been given citizenship, and in 1995 Russian was raised to a "state" language status. It is Russia, the external national "homeland," that is playing the reluctant bride despite the promise of a union. There has been no large-scale violence and there seems to be little prospect of it.

In Belarus, even though the Russian population numbers less than one-seventh of the total, the titular nation is largely Russophone and is quite similar in its outlook to east-bank Ukraine and the Russophone parts of Kazakhstan, which border the Russian Federation. Despite the existence of some nationalistic feelings in Belarus, the movement for integration gained momentum after independence; after the 1994 presidential elections, won by Aleksandr Lukashenko, a former state farm director, reintegration became the government's primary goal. In 1993, a monetary union was signed with Russia, but after Lukashenko's election he sought to pursue full union. In preparing for what he believes is inevitable reintegration with Russia, Lukashenko has gone so far as to squeeze Belarus's language and history out of the school curriculum.[94]

Reform in Belarus, however, had been so ineffective that Russian democrats have opposed the treaty, and its ratification contributed to the resignation of Yegor Gaidar as economics minister in January 1994. So little economic progress has been made in Belarus that the World Bank and the International Monetary Fund froze loans in 1995.[95] Lukashenko, however, has repeatedly expressed his faith in the state management of the economy and has claimed impressive growth rates.[96] Furthermore, he has pursued an authoritarian political agenda, which has led to condemnation from a number of international organizations, such as the Organization for Security and Cooperation in Europe (OSCE).

Belarus is eager to unify with Russia for two main reasons. First, despite its faux stability (including highly questionable government-issued growth statistics), its economy is in deep trouble and desperately needs help. Belarus hopes that with unification such help will come from Moscow. Second, Lukashenko has political ambitions beyond Belarus and expects that unification will give him an entree into Russian politics.[97]

Russia did sign a union treaty with Belarus in April 1997, which created a Supreme Council of Belarus and Russia and provided for a whole range of integrative measures. The union, however, was watered down considerably by liberals in Yeltsin's government, who were worried not only that Belarus would be an economic burden and thus hamper Russian market reforms but that Lukashenko would become a force in Russian politics. Indeed, many in Russia increasingly view Belarus as a burden and Lukashenko as a danger.[98]

As long as Russia pursues a democratic, market-oriented path, it will have disincentives to integrating regions or states that are politically authoritarian and economically unreformed. But what if Belarus changes political leadership and at long last begins sustained democratization and a market-oriented transformation? Integration under such a set of circumstances may be both natural, that is, driven by economic and political rationality, and desirable. If such an integration were successful, this course might prove attractive in other CIS states, especially in areas inhabited by Russian minorities and Russophones in Ukraine and Kazakhstan. It could stimulate pressure for fundamental internal reforms in these states; in the absence of such reforms, or if they fail, it also could stimulate movement for secession.

There is yet another possibility. A Russia that begins to turn away from the democratic path, that is less restrained by market-oriented rationality, may find a union with an unreformed Belarus more desirable. On December 25, 1998, Boris Yeltsin and Lukashenko announced plans for a common policy on economic, foreign, and military matters.[99] Vadim Gustov, one of Russia's first deputy prime ministers, predicted that the two states would have a common currency and a single budget by the year 2000.[100]

Some of the impetus for pushing forward with integration may have come from Yeltsin and his supporters, who conceivably believed that the Russian president would be a realistic candidate to head an eventually unified Russian-Belarussian state and thus circumvent a constitutional prohibition against running for a new term in the 2000 presidential elections. The greatest support, though, came during the tenure of Prime Minister Yevgeny Primakov. Primakov, hardly an admirer of democracy or markets, had long been a strong advocate of union with Belarus. His first foreign trip as prime minister was to Belarus. Under Primakov's management, Russia's political and economic direction became a little less divergent from that of Belarus. And Lukashenko did declare that the future Belarussian-Russian union state could possibly be headed by Primakov.[101]

Primakov's replacement in May 1999 by Sergei Stepashin, a man considerably more sympathetic to democracy and markets, did not appear to cool the Russian government's support for reintegration. Stepashin's first trip outside Russia was to Belarus to discuss plans for a confederation treaty, possibly the Union of Sovereign Republics.[102] This occurred within the shadow of NATO's attack on Yugoslavia as both countries felt threatened. The armies of the two countries conducted joint military exercises in June 1999 against a simulated Western attack like the bombing campaign against Yugoslavia.[103] With a largely reintegrated air defense, intelligence, and arms production,[104] the goal now was to create an even higher level of military integration. That in essence would put Belarussian forces completely under Russian command. A confederation would be the framework for managing the process of reintegration.

Unification, however, is far from certain. Democratic forces in Russia, although weakened, still adamantly oppose unification with an unreformed Belarus. Despite retrenchment on market reforms, the Russian economy remains largely incompatible with Belarus's command economy, as shown by Lukashenko's numerous complaints about Russia's foot-dragging on reducing custom barriers or dropping certain cargo transit fees.[105] Furthermore, it is also noteworthy that the December 1998 agreements stipulate that both countries retain full sovereignty.[106] And Russian Deputy Prime Minister Nikolai Aksyonenko conceded in June 1999 that it will take "several years" to create a confederation.[107] Still, there is a real risk that a Russia that loses faith in democracy and markets may opt for unification with Belarus as part of an authoritarian pan-Slavic vision that would undoubtedly gravely concern several of Russia's neighbors.

Kazakhstan

The breakup of the Soviet Union brought about an enormous change in the status of the Russian minority in the huge state of Kazakhstan (see Map 2.2). Russians had emigrated confidently into the "virgin" lands of Kazakhstan, especially from the mid-1920s to the late 1950s, fully expecting that they would maintain their language, culture, and status. They had reason to be confident. For decades, although not a clear majority, the Russians significantly outnumbered the native Kazakhs. By 1989, though, for the first time since the 1920s, Kazakhs outnumbered Russians.[108] Moreover, since independence, the demographic trends have turned increasingly against the Russian minority, owing to higher Kazakh birthrates, the return of large numbers of Kazakhs from places like Mongolia, China, or Afghanistan, and the emigration of significant numbers of Russians.[109] President Nursultan Nazarbayev also has taken active steps to help strengthen the position of ethnic Kazakhs. His government has changed Russified place-names everywhere. It also moved the national capital to an obscure northern city, Akmola, located in a heavily Russian area (renamed in mid-1998 Astana, which simply means "capital"), in part to be able to channel more Kazakh-speaking officials to the Russified regions.[110]

Russia, though, has strong strategic and economic interests in Kazakhstan, and it is unlikely to ignore entirely the interests of more than 6 million Russians there who form a majority in nearly all bordering areas. Yet there has been no large-scale violence since the breakup of the Soviet Union, despite tensions and frustrations.

Kazakhstan is still in the process of developing a national identity. Despite nationalistic rhetoric, it remains, in certain respects, a multicultural state. Cultural and linguistic diversity is not only demanded by the Russian minority but is also strongly encouraged by the Russophone Kazakhs. Nearly two-thirds of urban Kazakhs speak Russian as their daily language. The Kazakhstan constitution has, in fact, elevated Russian to an official language of the country (although Kazakh remains the sole "state language"). Kazakhstan has not imposed a language requirement on Russians. Since 1995 Kazakhstan has made the acquisition of citizenship easier, although it firmly rejected Moscow's suggestions for dual citizenship for ethnic Russians.[111] Many Kazakhs, in fact, take great pride in the tolerance and inclusiveness of the Kazakh culture.

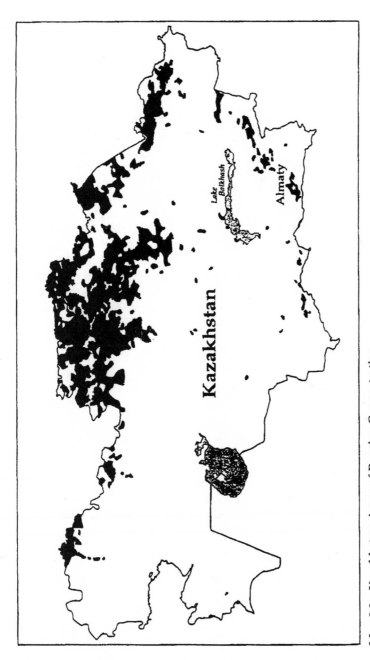

Map 2.2   Kazakhstan: Areas of Russian Concentration

Source: Jeff Chinn and Robert Kaiser, *Russians as the New Minority* (Boulder, Colo.: Westview Press, 1996), p. 186.

Kazakh nationalists, and they are still relatively few, therefore, must confront not only a huge Russian minority but also resistance from much of the Kazakh population, especially those in urban areas. Consequently, there have been but limited efforts, and even more limited successes, in what David Laitin has called minority incorporation or assimilation, where ethnic minorities integrate themselves linguistically and culturally into the "revived" nations in nationalizing states.[112] Kazakh nationalism also has been tempered by the belief that given demographic trends, Kazakhs will become a clear majority by the year 2010.[113] In fact, the Kazakh Statistics Agency claims that the 1999 national census shows that although the total population of the country declined to 14.95 million, in part owing to the emigration of Russians, the ethnic Kazakhs' share of the population has risen to 53.4 percent of the total.[114] Therefore, it seems worthwhile to be patient. The president of the republic, Nursultan Nazarbayev, also has played a moderating role, being careful not to aggravate relations among the ethnic groups or with Russia. Moreover, Nazarbayev has been creative in his approach, as evidenced by his answer to questions regarding problems of language and Russian emigration. He blithely turned the question around, asking: "How could there be a separate problem of the Russian-speaking population, when all Kazakhs are Russian speakers?"[115] His clever evasion does not necessarily rule out future Kazakh nationalist ambitions.

Russia also has been careful in its relations with Kazakhstan. Although the political and economic transformation in Kazakhstan leaves much to be desired, Moscow has found President Nazarbayev a useful, if not entirely trustworthy, partner. Russia has been able to reach agreements with him on a whole range of important issues, from space launch sites to dividing the Caspian Sea for oil exploration.[116] These issues, although important, are not as divisive as Crimea. And Russia does not have the same emotional ties to Kazakhstan as to Ukraine; there is no feeling of *edinokrovnye*. As long as there are no violent clashes involving Russian minorities, there are good reasons for Russia to avoid intervening into domestic Kazakh matters.

Despite attempts at indigenization—according preferential treatment to Kazakh speakers, usually ethnic Kazakhs—of the economy and the polity, the Russian minority in Kazakhstan, for the time being, remains relatively comfortable. In large part, this is because such indigenization has been limited. The economic payoff for speaking Kazakh remains low, and there has not been much movement to try to assimilate even Russophone Kazakhs.[117] Ethnic Russians, therefore, feel little compulsion to learn Kazakh and no immediate risk to their position.

Yet all is not well. Continued emigration to Russia suggests that Russians may not be sanguine about their future. Urban Russians appear to be greatly frustrated with the slow pace of economic and political reform and with continuing government efforts at indigenization, even if so far relatively unsuccessful, and afraid to undermine the urban, cosmopolitan culture in which they feel comfortable.[118] And as the demographic shift in favor of the Kazakhs accelerates, as the huge oil wealth provides increasing benefits to Kazakh speakers, and with the likely growth in the indigenization of the economy, the position of the Russian minorities may become much more tenuous. Kazakhstan may become less inclusivist and switch to ethnic nationalism, which a diminishing Russian minority could view as increasingly threatening.

The January 10, 1999, presidential election in Kazakhstan, which Nazarbayev won overwhelmingly,[119] also raises some questions. At one level his reelection may seem reassuring as it promises continuity. Moreover, during the electoral campaign he portrayed himself as the man who had saved Kazakhstan from falling victim to the simmering rivalry between Kazakhs and ethnic Russians. The message was clear—he intended to maintain ethnic peace.

Yet the election also may be cause for some concern. Nazarbayev brought the election forward by more than a year, in large part because worsening economic conditions for the next few years would make winning later more difficult. The way the election was conducted indicates a troubling tendency to authoritarianism. Nazarbayev's most credible opponent, former Prime Minister Akezhan Kazhegeldin, was barred from competing on the basis of a legal technicality.[120] Nazarbayev virtually monopolized access to the media and used control of local leaders not only to get the vote out but to intimidate the opposition. The OSCE declared that it would not recognize the results,[121] and Germany, which holds the European Union (EU) rotating presidency, termed the elections "a setback for democratization" and the rule of law.[122]

An increase in authoritarianism leaves ethnic minorities more vulnerable. When civil liberties are denied in general, ethnic minorities lose not only their basic rights, as do other citizens, but often find that their communal rights relating to language and culture are at risk since the government evinces little concern about or sensitivity to *any* rights. Further, although Nazarbayev is currently a popular leader, as Kazakhstan confronts difficult economic problems in at least the next few years, with oil, metal, and grain prices declining and financial problems in Russia reverberating throughout the region, his popularity may decline precipitously. It remains to be seen whether he will resist using the "ethnic card"—playing on ethnic prejudices and divisions—in order to restore political support and try to ensure his government's political legitimacy. If he does not, ethnic tensions could well spill over into ethnic violence.

Moldova

Moldova (see Map 2.3) merits inclusion here for two key reasons: There was large-scale violence involving the ethnic Russian minority and other minorities and Moscow gave far greater help and encouragement to this diaspora than to any other. Furthermore, in terms of the triadic nexus, violence occurred despite what would seem to be only modest provocation.

The large-scale violence occurred in 1992, with the attempt to create a separate state of Transdniestria, a thin strip of land on the east bank of the Dnieper (Dnipro) River, home to just over a sixth of Moldova's 4.3 million people. Throughout Moldova, Russians comprise only about 13 percent of the population, but in Transdniestria, together with Russophone Ukrainians (who in fact are slightly more numerous), they form a majority.[123] Transdniestria is important to Russia not only because of the Russian minority but for strategic reasons. This thin sliver of land borders Ukraine; thus Russian troops stationed there conceivably could be used to put pressure on Kiev.

Two of the parts of the triad—the Russian national minority and Russia acting as an external national "homeland"—clearly contributed to the conflict. The Russian and Russophone minorities feared Romanianization but were most concerned about possible union with Romania. Such a union would have provided little prospect for economic improvement. Romania's disastrous economic policies during the regime of Ion Iliescu, which succeeded that of Nicolae Ceauşescu, and the current political and economic turmoil there demonstrate that Moldovan concerns were not unfounded. Significantly, Russians and Russophones also had a very low opinion of Romanian culture. Further, Transdniestria has long been settled by Slavic people and was not part of Romania between 1918 and 1940 but rather was attached to the Ukrainian Soviet republic. Last, the ethnic Russians have had an aggressive leadership, notably Igor Smirnov, a hard-line "president" of Transdniestria, who began pushing relentlessly for independence even before the collapse of the Soviet Union.

Early mobilization was important for two reasons. First, preindependence mobilization not only gave Russian separatists in Moldova momentum but afforded them the protection of the Soviet state and prevented effective retaliation from the republican government. Second,

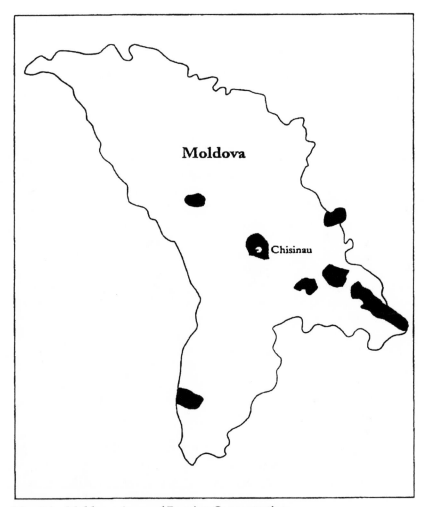

Map 2.3   Moldova: Areas of Russian Concentration

Source: Jeff Chinn and Robert Kaiser, *Russians as the New Minority* (Boulder, Colo.: Westview Press, 1996), p. 164.

hard-liners in Moscow, including the plotters against Gorbachev, became involved early on, providing encouragement and support. Following independence, however, it was a decision by the Russian Federation itself (some disclaimers to the contrary) that provided the ultimate protection for the separatists. The Russian Fourteenth Army, stationed in Transdniestria, gave overt support to the separatists from early 1992.

When General Aleksandr Lebed took over command in the summer of 1992, he called Transdniestria "part of Russia" and the west-bank city of Bendery, which the Russian forces captured, "an inalienable part of the Dniester Republic."[124]

The third part of the triad, the nationalizing state, did not provoke conflict. The Moldovan leadership clearly wanted to reestablish the Romanian identity of the republic, but not through ethnic nationalism. Its approach was one of civic nationalism. In February 1992 President Mircea Snegur announced that all residents of Moldova would be offered citizenship, including military personnel, party officials, and recent immigrants.[125] The Chisinau government, moreover, promised to respect local languages and customs, and the Moldovan constitution allows parents to choose the language of education of their children,[126] although it did change the Moldovan alphabet from Cyrillic to Latin, as it is written in Romania. Further, the Snegur government was at first reluctant to clamp down hard on the separatists and only declared a state of emergency on March 29, 1992, when it called on them to acknowledge Chisinau's authority.[127] Last, it has been suggested that as early as January 1991, the Moldovan government had offered the Transdniestrian leaders the option to decide the territory's own fate if Moldova chose to unite with Romania.[128]

Since the fighting, which ended in July 1992, there have been agreements for the separation of forces, but Transdniestria and the city of Bendery remain in the hands of separatist leaders, watched over by Russian troops acting as self-proclaimed peacekeepers. The Yeltsin government ignored requests by the OSCE in 1998 for Moscow to withdraw its troops from Transdniestria. The Moldovan government has been willing to grant the breakaway region broad autonomy and in 1997 signed a Russian-mediated accord with the Transdniester leaders, which, however, had not been implemented in 1998.[129] Meetings in July 1999 between Moldovan President Petru Lucinschi and Smirnov failed to resolve the key question about the separatist region's status.[130] Smirnov's proposal for a federation of two independent states is not acceptable to Moldova. And Russia continues to find it useful to keep some 2,600 troops in Transdniestria (and a huge arms stockpile)[131] close to Romania and on the western side of Ukraine at a time when NATO is expanding eastward. But there is no military confrontation. The ethnic disputes have not been resolved, but at least there has been a kind of "stand-down."

The events of 1992, though, show that even without the pressure from a nationalizing state, conflict can erupt. And the conflict was not exclusively the product of minority ethnocultural goals or fears. The Transdniestrian leadership exhibited a good deal of economic opportunism; in fact, it became so corrupt and criminalized that even General Lebed denounced it as "thieves and protectors of thieves."[132] The most important cause of the conflict was likely Russian encouragement, first by the hard-liners in Moscow and after the dissolution of the Soviet Union by hard-line elements in the Yeltsin government and by the commanders of the Russian Fourteenth Army.

For the Russians in 1992, the case of Moldova was in some ways unique. First, intervention offered little risk. Russian military power was overwhelming; Moldovan forces were disorganized and demoralized. Second, Russian intervention carried little danger of international sanctions. Unlike the Baltic states or Ukraine, there was scant Western interest in Moldova, and the authoritarian Romanian government of Ion Iliescu could generate little Western support for protests against Moscow's actions or for Moldovan-Romanian unification.

With the electoral success of the relegalized (1994) Communists in the March 1998 Moldovan elections, where they won the largest number of votes (with over 30 percent),[133] Russians and Russophone Slavs could feel reassured that there was little prospect, at least in the near future, for union with Romania. Besides, Romania with its current economic problems can ill afford to integrate a wretchedly poor and heavily indebted Moldova. Yet in the longer term, as a democratic Romania pursues fundamental political and economic reforms, Moldova could fall further behind Romania, especially economically. Despite its own economic problems Romania began to supply electricity to Moldova in November 1998 in response to Chisinau's request for aid. Cash-strapped Moldova's electrical supplies had been cut by Ukraine and its imports of natural gas were reduced by half by the Russian gas monopoly, Gazprom.[134] Romanian aid is a small step, but unification may become far more economically attractive to Moldova's Romanian majority if in the future Romanian fundamental reforms prove to be successful. Pressure for integration from Chisinau could increase to the point where a more economically successful Romania would feel obligated to help by unifying with Moldova.

Greater increase in support for unification in Moldova would cause more friction with the Russian minority. Further, if Romanian NATO membership ever becomes imminent, Russia might be tempted to use its military power to encourage Transdniestrian independence preemptively—once the alliance had been extended to Romania, Russia would find it difficult to engage in any military action so close to NATO's new borders in Romania. And it may be difficult to have a clean separation even if Chisinau accepted it in principle. Thus there remain some possibilities for violence in Moldova.

Latvia and Estonia

Of the three Baltic states, ethnic disputes in Lithuania are minimal. In fact, the Russian government often favorably contrasts the treatment of the Russian minority in Lithuania with that in Latvia and Estonia (see Map 2.4). Both of the latter two have large Russian populations and both have acted as nationalizing states, imposing a whole series of restrictions on the minorities. Russia has stridently protested the treatment of ethnic Russians. The Russian minority itself has expressed its unhappiness through a variety of threats and demonstrations. Yet despite protests and some incidents, there has been no large-scale violence in these two Baltic states.

The Nationalizing States. There was little doubt that, with independence, there would be strong movement for national revival in the Baltic states and that the titular nationalities would support a variety of nationalizing projects. All three states had been independent in the interwar period and had harsh experiences under Soviet rule. But whereas Lithuania developed an inclusivist approach, a type of civic nationalism, Estonia and Latvia chose ethnic nationalism. This can be explained in part by the historic and demographic circumstances of the two states. In the decades following their forced incorporation, in the 1940s, into the Soviet Union, they were flooded with Slavic and especially Russian immigrants. At independence, in Estonia the titular nationality numbered fewer than two-thirds and in Latvia barely more than half. (In Lithuania they numbered slightly over four-fifths.)[135] Estonians and Latvians were, therefore, angry about the past and anxious about the future. In both, but especially in Latvia, there was a belief that the ethnic survival of the majority itself was at risk. The titulars believed that the national interest itself had to be expressed in terms of guaranteeing such survival. Driven by such fears, linguistic and citizenship policies were harsh on the minorities, especially the largest group, the Russians. Some nationalist manifestations, particularly in Latvia, were especially insensitive and vindictive, such as public celebrations in March 1998 in Riga by survivors of Latvia's Waffen-SS Legion. More than 500 were allowed to parade through the capital.[136] In September of that year, the remains of 53 Latvian SS troops were reburied with an official military honor guard present.[137]

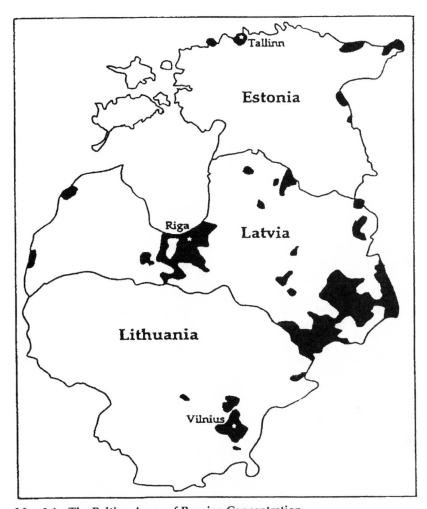

Map 2.4   The Baltics: Areas of Russian Concentration
Source: Jeff Chinn and Robert Kaiser, *Russians as the New Minority* (Boulder, Colo.: Westview Press, 1996), p. 94.

Estonian and Latvian language and citizenship policies have had a very negative impact on the Russian minority. Estonia established relatively quickly the rules by which ethnic minorities, including Russians, could gain citizenship and participate fully in political processes. Language requirements for citizenship, though, have been difficult and controversial. In 1999 about 220,000 residents, 17 percent of the population, remained "stateless."[138] And in 1999 Estonia tightened its language legislation with amendments that stipulate that businesspeople, public servants, and local government workers must speak Estonian to continue in their jobs.[139] This is bound to put great pressure on Russians in areas such as Narva where they comprise the vast majority of the population and where professionals had been able to work unhindered without a knowledge of Estonian. In Latvia, the situation has been worse. Its rules for citizenship have involved not only language but also quotas, with the result that the vast majority of Latvia's 700,000 Russian-speaking minority is yet to gain citizenship.[140] These policies have been the greatest source of controversy and of protest within these states and in Russia.

In some ways, the approach used in both states may be viewed as an attempt at minority incorporation or assimilation,[141] although, especially in Latvia, the preferred solution would be for the Russian minority to leave. Thus in Latvia, in particular, there appears to be a dual-track approach to the Russian minority: assimilate a relatively small number while holding out hope that most, or at least many, will leave, thus shifting the demographic balance radically in favor of ethnic Latvians. Not surprisingly, the Russian minorities in Estonia and Latvia have viewed these policies as part of an exclusionary political agenda, which at the same time seeks to impose cultural hegemony; that is, the minorities who choose to stay need to subordinate their culture and language to that of the titulars within each state. Yet even in Latvia, where police on occasion have treated Russian protesters harshly, there has been no mass violence. As hard as these language and citizenship measures were on the Russian minority in each state, they fell far short of what some nationalizing states elsewhere pursued against their minorities, the most extreme manifestation of which has been ethnic cleansing.

In both Estonia and Latvia, there were internal and external restraints on the governments. Internally, a variety of factors were at work. Both states have made significant progress toward democracy, the development of civil society, and the encouragement of markets. Part of the restraint derived from having achieved at least some success in assimilating the Russian minorities. In both Estonia and Latvia, considerable progress has been made toward the governments' goal of having a single national language, and both states have managed to effect a demographic shift in favor of the titular nationalities.[142]

Externally, restraints come from a number of sources. Both Estonia and Latvia wished to join NATO and the European Union. Although Latvia has been more resistant to external pressure, even its government has understood that it cannot cross the line between discrimination and persecution without risking confrontation with Russia and condemnation by the West. Even though Latvia has not allowed most Russians to become citizens, it has, for instance, provided governmental support for schools in Russian (and other minority languages). Moreover, even though the OSCE has been encouraging Latvia to change its citizenship laws and occasionally has been critical of its treatment of its minorities, the commissioner for national minorities, Max van der Stoel, stated in April 1998, "I cannot say that there is a consistent pattern of human rights violations in Latvia."[143] But Western pressure has its limits. Responding in part to Western concerns, in June 1998 Latvia's parliament passed amendments to the country's strict citizenship laws to make it easier for the Russian minority to gain citizenship.[144] Prime Minister Guntars Krasts's coruling Fatherland and Freedom Party spearheaded a signature campaign for a public referendum on the issue and thus blocked the amendments. In late August 1998, the party was successful in gathering almost twice the required 131,000 signatures.[145] President Guntis Ulmanis, a supporter of the amendments, blamed the West for the popular reaction. He contended that "recommendations from the West were perceived by society as pressure," and Latvians were rejecting Western meddling.[146]

Still, on October 3, 1998, Latvian voters rejected by a vote of 53 percent to 45 percent the attempt to block the amendments to the citizenship law that eliminated a number of restrictions on naturalization procedures for noncitizens living in Latvia.[147] The "naturalization windows" in the amendments allow the granting of citizenship to all children born after Latvian independence from the Soviet Union, if their parents request it. Moreover, in the simultaneous elections for the Saeima (parliament), the voters elected a minority government led by Vilis Kristopans of Latvia's Way; former Prime Minister Krasts was relegated to the post of deputy prime minister for European integration.[148]

Yet the seesaw over language issues continues. In July 1999 four major Latvian political parties agreed to support a Draconian language law that, among other things, requires all signs, posters, and advertisements to be written only in Latvian and demands that public speeches only be in Latvian.[149] The European Union criticized part of the legislation and the new Latvian president, Vaira Vike-Freiberga, who only returned to Latvia in the fall of 1998 after living in Canada for 44 years, sent the law back to the parliament for review. She defended the substance of the law but wanted parliament to review some "imprecise and improper" clauses.[150] Despite her good intentions, Vike-Freiberga embodies the contradictory political impulses in Latvia. She declared that Russians are welcome members of the state and that she will enroll in Russian language classes. But she also contended that Russians must learn the "state language," Latvian, and that Russians are colonizers who should have returned to their homeland after the collapse of their empire. She also declared that she will never give a speech in Russian while president.[151] The greatest external restraint, though, comes from Russian pressure. Russia's size, economic resources, and military forces, although greatly diminished from Soviet days, are much greater than those of any other former Soviet state, and the tremendous asymmetry acts as a powerful deterrent to more extreme acts or policies against the Russian diaspora.

The External National "Homeland." As an external national "homeland," Russia, despite its tough rhetoric on the treatment of the Russian minority, especially in Latvia, is also operating under some constraints. Four are particularly relevant. First, Russia has been able to gain concessions from both Latvia and Estonia on matters including the status of its military bases (before 1994), language, and certain aspects of citizenship and trade. Moscow was particularly effective in using its troop withdrawals as a bargaining chip. These successes, although limited, generally have had a moderating effect on Russian policies on the diaspora issues. Second, in addition to political and military leverage, Russia has been able to exert economic pressure. Russia remains Latvia's largest trading partner. Twenty-five percent of the latter's gross national product is derived from revenue from the transit of Russian oil and other goods.[152] In April 1998, for example, Russian President Boris Yeltsin, in retaliation for what Moscow claimed was police brutality in Latvia against ethnic Russian demonstrators, called on Russian oil companies to divert shipments to routes outside Latvia and hinted at further retaliatory measures.[153] The Latvian economy is weak, the country runs a large fiscal deficit, and its currency, the lat, was under pressure in the first half of 1999.[154] Thus, Latvia is economically vulnerable. Russian economic leverage occasionally can substitute for the use of military force. Third, military action by Russia would be constrained both by the sorry state of the Russian military and by the deterrent effect in Russia of the disastrous campaign in Chechnya. Fourth, there is considerable sympathy for the Baltic states in the West, stemming in part from guilt over their abandonment in 1940 but also due in part to their progress toward democracy and markets. Further, there are significant pro-Baltic lobbies in the major Western democracies, and thus any Russian military action would at the very least evoke strong Western condemnation.

The National Minority. Despite occasional mass protests and encouragement from Moscow, the Russian minorities in the Baltic states have not been willing to risk violent confrontation. Their ethnic identity is not as strong as that of, for example, the Serbs in Bosnia or Croatia. There has been no existential threat to them, no fear of physical extinction. Despite their loss of status, moreover, the Russian minorities in Estonia and Latvia still believe that they are better off than if they were in Russia. Responses cited in the *New Baltic Barometer* survey, for instance, indicate that 68 percent of Russians living in Estonia thought that they had a better chance for a rising living standard there than in Russia; 55 percent of the ethnic Russians in Latvia thought so.[155] In both states, ethnic Russians are developing competence in the titular language, with Russians in Latvia showing a much higher propensity to assimilate than in Estonia, Kazakhstan, or Ukraine.[156] And having seen and read what happened to Russians who were being "rescued" in Grozny, Chechnya, a majority of Russians in Estonia and Latvia view offers by Russian nationalists to use force on their behalf as threatening rather than reassuring.[157] In the case of the Baltics, it is probable that linguistic, and perhaps even ethnic, assimilation will continue. This is positive at least in the sense that it is likely to help avoid violence, as long as the titular nationalities do not overplay their hand.

National identities throughout the former Soviet Union continue to evolve. Russia appears to be developing a nationalism that is more civic than ethnic and an identity that is more European than Eurasian. The same may be said of Ukraine. But in neither case is the direction yet entirely clear. In Russia, the tumultuous events of August and September 1998—the collapse of the ruble, the default, in effect, on loans, and the dismissal of the Kiriyenko cabinet—have created more uncertainty. Prime Minister Yevgeny Primakov acquired increasing power and pushed for a more nationalistic policy and more state intervention in the economy. But his efforts created only the semblance of stability. In May 1999 Yeltsin dismissed Primakov and replaced him with Sergey Stepashin. Fundamental problems, however, remain unresolved. Stepashin was the only high-profile politician, with the exception of Yeltsin, still openly devoted to the politics of liberalism. A bare three months later, on August 9, 1999, Yeltsin replaced Stepashin with Vladimir Putin (his preferred successor as president), a tough technocrat who had headed the Federal Security Service (the domestic successor of the KGB) and was the secretary of the Security Council.[158] Putin, an avid pupil of the liberal former mayor of St. Petersburg, Anatoly Sobchak, and a man with extensive experience in dealing with regional leaders, has a commitment to Yeltsin's policies that should be encouraging to democrats. A continuation of Yeltsin's revolving-door policy on prime ministers, though, can only damage the credibility of democrats. And if Putin does not bring some high-profile democrats into his government, he may have the same difficulties in pushing for democratic change and markets as his immediate predecessor.

There are other disturbing signs. In November 1998 prominent liberal politician Galina Starovoitova was murdered in St. Petersburg.[159] Viciously anti-Semitic statements have been made openly not only by such well-known anti-Semites as Communist Duma deputies Albert Makashov and Viktor Ilyukin but also under the guise of attacking Zionism by Communist Party leader Gennadi Zyuganov.[160] The Communist-led Duma did not censure Makashov or Ilyukin. Primakov, who had been quick to blast liberal critics,[161] was remarkably slow in moving to stem these anti-Semitic outbreaks. Economic conditions continue to worsen, and Primakov's budget[162] for 1999 was unconvincing. In December 1998 Michel Camdessus, head of the International Monetary Fund, left Moscow without reaching an agreement on the release of further funds for Russia.[163] In July 1999, the IMF did approve a $4.5 billion loan to Russia but this was done more to help Russia repay old debts and to reward its cooperation in bringing Slobodan Milošević to the negotiating table rather than as a vote of confidence in Russia's economic plans.[164] Stanley Fischer, the IMF's first deputy managing director, stated the day after the approval of the loan that Russia has misrepresented crucial reserve data in the past.[165] The respected French daily *Le Monde* in August 1999 alleged that an international audit showed that in the past, Russia had diverted part of loans by the IMF to offshore companies connected to organized crime.[166] And Russia itself in a memorandum to the IMF acknowledged in 1999 that "the program for 1999 contains many elements of previous economic programs of the Russian government that were not always implemented on a sustained basis."[167]

There is a continuing debate in Russia among members of the government, intellectuals, and church leaders[168] over national identity and also over the interpretation of the national interest, especially of what constitutes a vital national interest. The outcome of that debate will be important for several triadic relationships and the possibility of violence. Together with civic nationalism, there is also evidence of other trends, of Latvia's strong ethnic nationalism, for instance. In the Baltics, there has been no violence in part because the Russian diaspora is poorly organized, demoralized, and/or relatively satisfied with economic conditions. Moreover, ethnic nationalism in places like Latvia has been moderated both by the internal constraints of democracy and by external pressures.

Just as the historic weakness of Russian nationalism and its adoption of civic nationalism have helped prevent large-scale conflict in the triadic relationship, so the weakness of nationalism in Ukraine and Kazakhstan, the two states that are home to more than two-thirds of the Russian diaspora, helps "calm" the relationship. Nationalism in Kazakhstan may become increasingly exclusivist as a government that may be less than sincere in fostering civic nationalism feels emboldened both by Russian weakness and new Kazakh economic strength. In the short term, though, Russia's size and ability to exert economic and military pressure still deters its neighbors from a systematic policy of persecuting ethnic Russians. This deterrence is a factor in the case of Kazakhstan and Ukraine and is particularly potent in Moldova and in the Baltic states, specifically in Latvia and Estonia, where tendencies toward ethnic nationalism are pronounced. In most other respects, though, Latvia and Estonia are very different from Moldova. In Moldova, little progress toward democracy and a demoralized titular nation, plus the presence of Russian troops, contribute to a hands-off policy, for now, toward the Russian minority. Latvia and Estonia continue to try to find a balance among their desire to build democracy, ensure national survival, integrate with the West, and avoid provoking Russia. The fate of the Russian diaspora is bound to be deeply affected by how that balance is struck. Last, Belarus, in its eagerness to unify with Russia, has forgone the "attractions" of nationalism and thus does not really qualify as a "nationalizing" state. Minsk's decision not to use Belarussian nationalism has ensured that the Russian minority does not feel threatened or excluded. But here too changes in government could create a triadic relationship that could prove to be troubling.

The Exogenous Factors

Three factors external to the triad are likely to have a significant impact: democracy; the security environment; and the determination of the nationalist Russian elite, epitomized by Yevgeny Primakov, that their country should play an indispensable international role. The progress of democracy in Russia and the neighboring states speaks to the treatment of minorities and also may significantly affect the peacefulness of these states in the triadic relationship. Changes in the security environment, in particular those that may be generated by NATO expansion, have the potential to alter the international context within which the triadic politics involving the Russian diasporas are played out. Primakov's and the nationalist Russian elite's determination that Russia play or at least be capable of playing an indispensable international role inevitably involves the Near Abroad since this is where Russia has the best hope of exercising preponderant influence and, in the nationalist elite's view, rebuilding its international status.

DEMOCRACY AND THE RESTRAINT OF LARGE-SCALE VIOLENCE

Democracy is not only the best means of ensuring the sustainable long-term legitimacy of the political order in these states; it is also likely to function as a necessary, although not a sufficient, condition for preventing the development, in the "nationalizing" states and in the external "national" homeland, of the kind of extreme ethnic nationalism that is not only exclusivist but also tends to violence. Successful democracies that "constitutionally" limit power do not systematically mistreat their minorities. Moreover, democracies are much less likely to engage in violent conflict with other democracies, which is relevant here because in the triadic relationship, violence involving ethnic minorities includes a vital international relations dimension. Therefore, the successful development of democracy in the successor states should play an important role in restraining large-scale violence.

Democratic Legitimacy as Internal Restraint

The sources of political legitimacy are understood differently in the various traditions of political philosophy. Some political theorists define a government as legitimate if it upholds the rule of law, governs in a procedurally correct manner, and ensures the personal rights of citizens. Others link legitimacy with the substantive of the "good life," defined with reference either to traditional values or to a consent-determined social purpose. A legitimate system is viewed as binding or as exemplary, and overall a political order is thought to be legitimate if in the minds' of its citizens it *ought* to go on. Nationalism, as noted, can play a role in creating political legitimacy. It becomes a problem when it is assigned too large a role in sustaining overall political legitimacy, then almost invariably becomes ethnic rather than civic nationalism. Absent all other supporting structures, nationalism becomes subject to its own "laws of diminishing returns." That is, when it is used by governments to avoid dealing with important political and economic issues, and employed as a substitute for all the other sources of legitimation, nationalism has to be ratcheted up constantly and ethnic nationalism becomes increasingly exclusivist, dangerous, and violent.

By the 1980s, the Soviet Union and the East European states suffered from increasing crises of political legitimacy.[169] In several of the post-communist states, the ruling elites continued to use nationalism, almost invariably ethnic nationalism, as a primary source of political legitimation and the means of establishing themselves as leaders of the new political order. Examples include the Iliescu regime in Romania, as noted, and those of Milošević in Serbia and Tudjman in Croatia. Such regimes have manipulated popular prejudices against minorities and used scapegoating to divert attention away from a variety of political and economic problems. Ethnic nationalism does not necessarily lead to violence, but there is a strong tendency in that direction. The antidote, therefore, would appear to be the creation of political legitimacy based on a variety of sustainable sources, which would certainly include the rule of law and the protection of the personal rights of citizens. Further, political legitimation should include an opportunity for participation from all strata and segments of society in order to create the consensus that is necessary to sustain the legitimacy of the political order. The opportunity for participation is particularly important.[170] In essence this would mean limitations of power and involve formal or informal checks and balances. Participation also requires political pluralism, which would need to involve both the titular nation and the ethnic minorities and would limit the exclusionary instincts of a nationalizing state as well as reduce the alienation of the national minorities. In a period of transition, such values and institutions cannot be created instantly. In fact, the struggle for pluralism continues even in long-established democracies.

Even in countries where political legitimation has been based on a democratic political order there can be ethnically based violence, discrimination, dissent, and controversy. The violence in Northern Ireland, the mistreatment of the Japanese in the United States during World War II, and the endless constitutional wranglings and threats of separation in Canada over Quebec demonstrate that democracies do not solve all such problems once and for all. Rather, democracy is a necessary but not a sufficient condition for resolving ethnic issues, for the avoidance of the kind of triadically induced explosions that occurred in Bosnia.

In developed democracies, there are strong restraints on the spread of violence and important incentives for resolving interethnic disputes peacefully. Even in emerging democracies, such as Estonia and Latvia (as badly flawed as they are in having excluded from citizenship long-time residents who had held full citizenship under Soviet rule), there are important internal restraints, as noted, against the outbreak of large-scale interethnic violence.

In countries in transition to democracy, much depends on the direction of the transition and the clarity with which the goals are laid out. Emerging democracies can develop into what Fareed Zakaria called "liberal democracies," which are characterized by the rule of law, a separation of powers, checks and balances, and the protection of basic liberties.[171] However, they also may become what he calls "illiberal democracies," which provide for majority rule but not limits on power. The treatment of minorities is one of the key distinctions between the liberal democracies and the "illiberal" ones.

Power, then, needs to be limited if minorities are to be protected. It is to be limited not only by the formal separation of powers, but in order to have well-functioning checks and balances there is also a need for a thriving civil society, one that has to include ethnic minorities. Juan Linz and Alfred Stepan define civil society as the arena "where self-organizing groups, movements, and individuals, relatively autonomous from the state, attempt to articulate values, create associations and solidarities and advance their interests."[172] Others, including myself, would add to this definition a second arena, "a relatively autonomous political society."[173] Civil society allows for, indeed fosters, a variety of inputs into all types of societal activities and thereby creates conditions in which self-organized groups, movements, and individuals can shape and make effective a variety of checks and balances. Moreover, ethnic minorities have a far better opportunity to express and protect their interests in a country that has a thriving civil society, which is likely to encourage the development of civic nationalism. Civil society is especially important during the transition and the consolidation of "liberal" democracy.

Consolidation is not the end of the process. The Jeffersonian axiom that democracy is a process that needs perennial tending and encouragement remains valid. Andrew Arato, though, has added that the consolidation of democracy is a process through which "democracy becomes the only game in town."[174] Within that context the checks and balances function well and power is limited structurally and through interactive processes. "Consolidated" democracy is basically Zakaria's "liberal" democracy. Thus in these transitions there is a concern with the consolidation of democracy, the movement toward "liberal" democracy.

When it comes to developing liberal democracy, Russia is by no means the postcommunist state with the worst problems. In fact, there are reasonable possibilities for its successful development in Russia. The Russian political tradition, contrary to what Isaiah Berlin has contended,[175] is not one that exclusively emphasized all-embracing ideologies. As Leonard Schapiro pointed out, there were also significant liberal traditions in Russian political thought, although their influence was limited.[176] Will Russia become a liberal democracy? There are five areas of concern.

First, too much power is vested in the presidency. An authoritarian ultranationalistic president with the current powers could steer Russia into an aggressive external policy that includes matters relating to the diaspora. He would be restrained only by the country's current—and probably temporary—military weakness. Moreover, transparency and predictability in decision-making have been lacking.

Second, despite certain positive developments in the Russian judicial system, Russia is far from having a well-established legal system and a competent, honest, and independent judiciary. The rule of law is also largely unknown in Russia.

Third, although there has been considerable development of civil society in Russia, as evidenced in part by the astonishing resourcefulness of the average Russian in coping, despite little or no help from the government, during crises such as the one that began in August 1998,[177] it is far behind countries like Hungary. There is, therefore, considerably less "input" by Russian society as a whole than in the liberal democratic West or in East European states where the transition to democracy has been most successful.

Fourth, Russia also falls short in sustaining momentum for democratization and creating societal consensus. Political and economic detours and zigzags have sapped popular support and patience and wasted opportunities for consolidating democratic institutions, entrenching democratic processes, and stabilizing the economy. This is not to disparage the progress that has been made or to understate the political achievements in Russia. The 1996 presidential elections, "the last referendum on communism,"[178] represented a transition to a more complex, multifaceted politics.[179] It was a rejection of the traditional communist solution to societal problems. Former Prime Minister Sergey Stepashin was probably right when he asserted in July 1999 that "Communists in Russia will never win. They will never get back,"[180] especially if he meant that there would be no restoration of the old Marxist-Leninist order. Yet it is also important to appreciate that the rejection of the ancien régime is not the same thing as the development of a consensus on the direction that Russian society should take. In a sense, as Richard Rose stated, Yeltsin won a *negative* mandate in 1996.[181] The election did not consolidate liberal democracy. The danger is not that Russia will revert to communism but rather that it will fail to become a liberal democracy. Interethnic conflict in Russia and external threats to Russian security, including widespread violence on its borders, and especially involving the Russian diasporas, therefore, also could have a significant impact on the fate of democracy.

Fifth, economic progress is likely to have an increasingly important effect on political stability. Here are major problems. In 1997 the Russian economy grew for the first time since the breakup of the Soviet Union, albeit by a modest 0.5 percent.[182] Despite a sharp contraction in 1998,[183] it shows that the Russian economy can grow. In fact, in the summer of 1999 Russian industrial production began to rise, inflation declined, and the Russian government claimed that in July 1999 it achieved a budget surplus of $51 million.[184] Russia, in fact, has enormous potential. It is limited in capitalizing on that potential by the absence of dependable commercial law and the criminalization of the Russian economy, evidence of which is the widespread corruption of privatization of government property, which allowed insiders to gain vast wealth and organized crime's infiltration of so many businesses. Although such criminalization may be overstated at times, in a society that had been imbued for more than 70 years with the idea that wealth equated theft, the perception of widespread criminalization and anger over increasingly visible inequality has the potential to play a key role in derailing the transition to democracy.[185] Studies of the 1995 parliamentary elections showed that economic voting (i.e., people voting primarily on the basis of economic considerations) has a strong potential to play a key role in political developments.[186] Although not the primary determinant of how people voted in 1995, pocketbook issues are likely to play an increasingly weighty role in future elections. If the economy begins to grow significantly, this will likely have salutary political consequences. On the other hand, given the fragility of the transformation, an economic downturn also has the potential to strengthen the antidemocratic forces, particularly those of ultranationalism, which could readily blame Russia's problems on "cosmopolitan," that is, Western-oriented, non-Russian elements, within Russia as well as Western conspiracies without. The plight of the Russian diaspora could be a rallying point for these forces. Downturns in Russia's economy like that in August 1998, therefore, are particularly worrisome.

Democracy and International Peace

Since in the triadic relational nexus large-scale violence also has the potential to lead to interstate war between the nationalizing state and the external national "homeland," it is relevant to examine the possibility of large-scale violence involving the Russian diasporas from two perspectives: first, the "war behavior" of liberal democracies; second, the war proneness of states in transition to democracy.

Unfortunately, parts of the debate on "war behavior" have been colored by simplistic interpretations of Immanuel Kant's work *Perpetual Peace* and the suggestion that democracies are not prone to war. First, one needs to be careful about the interpretation of democracy, for Kant, in fact, referred to liberal republics whose behavior was constrained by their liberal and constitutional character rather than by unfettered democratic majoritarianism.[187] Second, Kant only suggested that these liberal republics, which would be like today's liberal (consolidated) democracies, would not go to war with each other, rather than claiming that they would not go to war at all. In fact, Kant held that liberal republics at times would feel compelled to go to war with nonliberal states.

Consolidated liberal democracies do not fight each other. Of this there is considerable evidence. There has been criticism in the international relations literature of an approach that assumes a democratic peace,[188] but works by Michael Doyle, Jack S. Levy, and Zeev Maoz and Bruce Russett among others provide persuasive arguments that democracies have not gone to war with each other.[189] Even if that argument is not accepted as an ironclad law of history, the evidence supports the point that *democracies are significantly less prone to go to war with each other.* Thus, if all of the successor states in the former Soviet Union *do* become liberal democracies, the possibility of large-scale violence would diminish significantly. If the external national homeland— Russia—and the nationalizing states—the hosts to the new Russian diasporas—all were democracies, they would be far less prone to make war with each other.

If, however, Russia does become a liberal democracy but surrounding states do not, the assumption of peaceful democratic behavior would not necessarily predict a lesser possibility of conflict. It is not clear that democracies have constraints in going to war *against nondemocracies.* Indeed, a democratic Russia might even feel *compelled* to use force if a nondemocratic neighbor were to persecute an ethnic Russian minority.

In a liberal democracy, limits on the power of the government place limits in turn on antiminority measures. Further, in such a political order the need to tolerate a plurality of values and to allow wide-ranging input gives a minority a say in public decisions. Thus, such a political order is likely to diminish the alienation of the minorities and so lessen the chances for large-scale violence between the titular group and the minorities. Liberal democracy, therefore, provides a *layer of protection* against the outbreak of violence. If all the states become democracies, there would then be *an additional* protective layer, because of the unlikelihood of democracies going to war with each other. In the ideal outcome, a *double layer of protection* would guard against large-scale violence in the triadic relationship, combining internal and external restraints.

Does the *transition* from one political order to another make a difference in terms of war proneness? All the successor states in the former Soviet Union are in transition, although not necessarily in transition to democracy. Transition to democracy or from any one system to another can be disruptive and disorienting. Edward Mansfield and Jack Snyder have found that states in transition to democracy are two-thirds more likely, over the course of a ten-year period, to engage in conflict than those undergoing no regime change.[190] This is so because states in transition are not yet liberal democracies. In the effort to mobilize popular support, governments often stimulate or give in to strong nationalist sentiments directed against alleged enemies.

The former Soviet Union must move quickly and decisively to liberal democracy and be particularly alert to the possibilities of conflict. Each of the parties in a triadic relationship during transition must emphasize confidence-building measures, including the deliberate avoidance of inflammatory rhetoric and the encouragement of transnational contacts, to restrain those elements that stimulate large-scale violence.

In many ways, Europe has been fortunate in the post–Cold War period to see the development of a common security order.[191] Russia has been central to the creation of this common security order. Its particular role has been determined to a significant degree by the end of communism and the surge of democratization in Russia and across formerly communist Europe.[192] Any indication that democratization in Russia is in trouble would be an early warning sign of potential problems both for the common security order and for the triangular relationship under discussion in this chapter.

THE SECURITY ENVIRONMENT

This section assesses the possible impact on the security environment, within which the triad operates, of one of the most crucial decisions by the West in the postcommunist era: the enlargement of NATO.

The Russian Reaction

Democrats in Russia have consistently opposed NATO enlargement not so much because they envisioned a military threat from the West but because they feared the impact on Russian domestic politics. They argued that the enlargement of NATO, the movement of the alliance's military strength closer to the Russian frontier, would strengthen authoritarian and ultranationalistic forces. Russia, they contended, would feel diminished and betrayed. Nationalist forces would blame democracy and democrats for this humiliation and would use the opportunity to strengthen their position domestically and then pursue more aggressive policies externally, particularly toward the surrounding states and on such issues as the Russian diaspora.

In July 1997 in Madrid, NATO invited Hungary, Poland, and the Czech Republic to begin accession talks to join the alliance. On March 12, 1999, the three former members of the Warsaw Pact became NATO members. Yet reaction from Russia has been relatively muted. Communist and nationalist forces denounced NATO enlargement, but the Russian government has seemed cooperative or at least resigned and the Russian population uninterested. Does this mean that the feared reaction is not going to occur?

At first glance, it would seem that the fears of Russian (and Western) democrats have been largely unfounded. A whole series of developments appear to be reassuring. In May 1997 Russia and the alliance signed the NATO-Russian Founding Act,[193] which appeared to provide for a creative solution through a politically but not legally binding document. It created a NATO-Russia Permanent Joint Council (PJC) that would give Russia a consultative role but not a veto. Via the Founding Act, the Western alliance declared that it had no intention, no plan, and no reason to deploy nuclear weapons or establish nuclear storage sites on the territory of the new member states and had no plans to station additional substantive combat forces there.[194] Still, as Zbigniew Brzezinski and Anthony Lake rightly pointed out, NATO is not *bound* to consult first with Russia in a time of crisis or legally prevented from deploying nuclear forces or substantial conventional combat forces on the territory of the new member states.[195]

But Russia was given an opportunity for significant input through the PJC. The Russian foreign minister, Yevgeny Primakov, expressed some satisfaction in his 1997 year-end foreign policy review that the principle postulated in the Founding Act "banning" the permanent deployment of substantial "NATO armed forces" on new members' territory was now being clarified; moreover, the new figures for national and territorial parameters under the Treaty on Conventional Armed Forces in Europe (CFE) would further diminish the threat to Russia.[196] Writing later in 1998, NATO's assistant secretary-general for political affairs lent some credence to Primakov's assertions on NATO deployment.[197] Reassuringly declaring that "NATO [is not] moving a military machine eastward . . . the Alliance will carry out its collective defense and other missions by ensuring the interoperability, integration capability for reinforcement rather than by additional permanent stationing of substantial combat forces. . . . Moreover NATO allies have also reiterated that they have no intention, no plan and no reason to deploy nuclear weapons on the territory of new members."[198] (If Primakov is right, Henry Kissinger might have been closer to the mark in his criticism of the Founding Act when he suggested that there may now be a kind of antechamber for Russia and its participation may well dilute the alliance.[199]) Differences in interpretation, though, and particularly in Russian expectations, as expressed by Primakov, seem to be a recipe for misunderstanding and dispute between Russia and the alliance over the long term.

The difference between expectations and reality was starkly illustrated during eleven weeks of the NATO air campaign against Yugoslavia. Despite its vociferous opposition to military action against Yugoslavia, Russia found the PJC useless in blocking or even moderating NATO action. With three new East European members in tow, NATO launched its attack on March 24, 1999. Primakov melodramatically had his plane turned around in midair on his way to the United States, the day before the attack even though, as Grigory Yavlinsky, the leader of the Yabloko democratic group alleged, the Russian prime minister knew of the decision to attack before his plane took off from Moscow.[200] Besides verbal condemnation of the attack, Russia had no other way to manifest its opposition to the Alliance action than to freeze its ties with NATO and pull out of the Alliance's Partnership for Peace.[201] Russia did not participate in the April 1999 Fiftieth Anniversary celebrations of NATO's founding in Washington. With Russia absent and the three former Warsaw Pact states basking in the limelight of new membership, the summit communiqué ironically praised the PJC as "an important venue to consult, to promote transparency and confidence-building, and to foster communication."[202] There is little doubt that with the combination of NATO enlargement and the attack on Yugoslavia, Russians felt that some of their worst fears about NATO arrogance were justified. The enlargement of NATO, therefore, is potentially dangerous both for the democratization of Russia and for the triadic relationship involving the various Russian diasporas. Much of the evidence suggests that the Russian concerns about further enlargement have not been dealt with. For instance, the Baltic states continue to push for membership despite vociferous Russian opposition. These states declared in May 1997 that they also intended to become fully integrated politically and militarily into NATO[203] and have remained steadfast in their quest. After the end of NATO's campaign against Yugoslavia, which had elicited virtual universal condemnation in Russia,[204] Madeleine Albright, the U.S. secretary of state, and her deputy secretary, Strobe Talbott, both assured the Baltic states that they would not be excluded from the Alliance because of their geography or history.

Talbott, who usually showed considerable sensitivity toward Russian fears, nevertheless told the Baltic states at the meeting of the U.S.-Baltic Charter of Partnership Commission that there were considerable grounds for optimism that their goal of Alliance membership would be realized.[205] Yet Yeltsin held to his negative view that the enlargement of NATO is a grave and historic mistake, and his foreign minister, Igor Ivanov, called the March 12 accession of the Czech Republic, Poland, and Hungary a "movement in the wrong direction."[206]

The Near Abroad and the Baltics

As in the case of Russia, extraregional influences also will have an impact on the behavior of the states in the Near Abroad and the Baltics regarding the triadic relationship. Since NATO enlargement will most significantly affect the Baltic states, Ukraine, and (with possible Romanian membership) Moldova, I will focus only on these states.

NATO enlargement will not have only deleterious effects on issues relating to minorities in the aforementioned states. Prospective membership in NATO, for instance, helped to induce Hungary and Romania in 1996 to sign a treaty that was meant to settle outstanding problems, including those relating to the Magyar minority in Romania.[207] Hungary, which had by far the best prospects for joining the alliance, made the greater concessions on the ethnic minority issue.[208]

Is prospective membership for the Baltic states likely to have the same salutary effect? It does not seem likely, especially in the case of Latvia, which has pursued the most restrictive nationalities citizenship policy in the Baltics. Despite the fact that Latvia is seeking NATO membership, it has been reluctant to budge on the main pillars of its exclusionary citizenship policies, the 1998 amendments to its citizenship law notwithstanding. Furthermore, the belief among the Balts that they will gain NATO membership has been a factor in their prompt and cavalier rejection of the October 1997 Russian offer to guarantee their security.[209] While these states should not necessarily have accepted this offer, their confidence in gaining NATO membership has made them less flexible in dealing with Russia on security matters. Yet if NATO membership for the Baltic states should become imminent, Moscow is likely to increase pressure and may even encourage separatist agitation by Russian minorities. Russia is not likely to consider it a *casus belli*, as some of the past rhetoric suggests. Stirring up trouble over the diaspora would be an effective way for Moscow to block NATO membership for the Baltic states since, as noted, the settlement of all ethnic disputes is a precondition for alliance membership. The Baltic states may turn out to have exaggerated expectations of Western support, which already may have made them more intransigent on resolving issues of the Russian diaspora.

The situation is hardly less risky in Ukraine. Kiev signed a charter on a distinctive partnership with NATO in Madrid on July 9, 1997, and has not opposed the alliance's plans to admit new members. The charter in part was meant to help lock in the reform process in Ukraine.[210] While strengthening of democracy would surely improve the conditions of the Russian minority in Ukraine, these potential benefits may be far off-set by the risks to the area.

As NATO moves closer to Russia's borders and at least contemplates Baltic membership, even a moderate Russian leadership is likely to increase pressure on the surrounding states to provide Moscow with security assurances. Ukraine, which is by far Russia's most important NIS neighbor, would come under extraordinary pressure. And Moscow might use the ethnic Russian minorities in Crimea and eastern Ukraine to pressure Kiev or even encourage separatism.

Could Ukraine reach satisfactory security arrangements with Russia before such enlargements occur? Although Ukraine has not formally ruled out NATO membership, it has not applied for entry. According to reports in February 1998, President Kuchma told President Yeltsin that Ukraine did not intend to seek NATO membership.[211] This might help reassure Russia.[212] Further, as noted, Kuchma appears to believe that a natural integration with Russia (within "Eurasia") could occur without destroying Ukrainian independence.[213] What independence would mean in such circumstances is unclear. NATO's campaign against Yugoslavia brought Ukrainian and Russian perspectives on the West closer. Almost as high a percentage of Ukrainians (89 percent) as Russians (94 percent) opposed NATO's decision to bomb Yugoslavia.[214] The bombing strongly influenced threat perceptions in Ukraine. A survey found that 39 percent of Ukrainians thought that the United States was the greatest threat to their country compared to only 15 percent who feared Russia. Even in western Ukraine, where negative views of Russia are the strongest, 48 percent of respondents thought that the United States was the greatest threat to peace compared to only 29 percent who indicated Russia.[215] Possibly there could be an organic integration of the kind that has occurred in Western Europe to form the European Union.[216] Should democracy succeed in Russia, Ukraine, and Belarus, in the longer term it is conceivable these three Slavic states would be subject to the same centripetal forces that brought about European integration. A natural, normal, voluntary integration would not represent the re-creation of a Russian empire. Integration would be driven by genuine political and economic need and rationality in contrast to the imperial ambitions of the Gorchakov/Primakov type of "single economic area" (as will be discussed later). A true federation or confederation could be created that would, at the very least, mitigate the nationalities problem. And such a democratic organization need not pose a threat to neighbors or to the international system.

With democracy and economic progress under threat in both Russia and Ukraine, satisfactory security arrangements between the two are more difficult to attain. In January 1999 the Federation Council in Russia, in part at the urging of Moscow Mayor Yury Luzhkov, postponed the ratification of the 1997 Friendship Treaty, the "big treaty" with Ukraine.[217] Luzhkov and other nationalist regional leaders opposed the treaty, contending that it confirmed Ukraine's right to Sevastopol and Crimea.[218] The June 1999 accords on the Black Sea Fleet helped calm matters somewhat, but Russian nationalist leaders have not given up on many of their goals. These leaders are likely to use fears of Western "encirclement," fears fueled by NATO enlargement and compounded by the Alliance's attack on Yugoslavia, either to pressure Ukraine into an eventual union with Russia or to detach from Ukraine key strategic and predominantly ethnic Russian areas.

Nevertheless, given Russia's imperial history, it is not surprising that there is concern in the West that *any* Russian-Ukrainian integration would be a step toward the re-creation of an empire.[219] But even if this were the case—and the voluntary integration of two liberal democracies would not mark such a step—would blocking Russian-Ukrainian integration or tentative moves toward a union be the best way to prevent the reemergence of a Russian empire? There are dangers if the West cynically or recklessly attempts to use Ukraine to contain Russia. Ukraine is ill equipped to block Russian imperial ambitions. Just as exaggerating its importance in the European balance of power did not serve Poland well in the interwar period, so Western encouragement for Ukraine to perform a role that it is incapable of fulfilling could produce harmful results. NATO enlargement, especially combined with the election of a nationalistic leader to succeed Kuchma, could make Ukraine far bolder and more intransigent on the Crimea dispute, for instance, and greatly diminish prospects for continuing the current peaceful relations between Russia and Ukraine. And despite the charter on a distinctive partnership between NATO and Ukraine, and Western flattery, it is doubtful that, should a major crisis arise between Russia and Ukraine, the West would take the grave risks that would be necessary to defend Ukraine.

Last, NATO enlargement would severely complicate matters for Moldova. Romanian membership would raise new fears in Transdniestria, and Russian troops stationed there might again find themselves asked to support the Slavic side in outbreaks of large-scale violence. Thus NATO enlargement carries more risks than benefits. Enlargement is complicating the triadic relationship under discussion, and it may be encouraging exaggerated expectations and new illusions.

PRIMAKOV AND THE RUSSIAN QUEST FOR SPECIAL STATUS

The magnitude of the dilemmas the enlargement of NATO poses to Russia and the implications for the triadic relationship perhaps may be best understood by looking more closely at the views and policy inputs of former Russian Prime Minister Yevgeny Primakov. Primakov remains pivotal for several reasons. He is the most trusted politician in Russia.[220] He is extremely adept at enhancing his image as he demonstrated in March 1999. En route to the United States to arrange crucial IMF loans for Russia the day before the start of NATO's air campaign against Yugoslavia, he not only had his plane turned around when he claimed that he became aware of the impending attack, but to the approval of most Russians, grandly declared upon landing in Moscow that "Russia is not trading its principles" for economic benefits.[221] A few days before Yeltsin fired Stepashin, both Yury Luzhkov and the All Russian bloc coordinator, Oleg Morozov, expressed their hope that Primakov would head their list of candidates for the December 1999 elections to the Duma.[222] Primakov, healthy after successful surgery in Switzerland, on August 13, 1999, apparently accepted the eagerly proffered leadership position of "secretary-general" of the unified Fatherland–All Russia bloc,[223] thereby putting himself in a strong position for the presidency in 2000. He is most important, though, because his views and actions reflect deep tendencies in Russian politics that could have a significant impact on the course of Russian democratization and on the fate of the Russian diasporas. Primakov has continued to deplore the enlargement of NATO, although he played a key role in negotiating the NATO-Russia Founding Act. More than just opposing enlargement, though, Primakov, as noted, epitomizes a belief by some of the elites in Russia that the country should be an indispensable power in the world. Primakov's insistence on such an important role for Russia in world politics presupposes at the very least exercising preponderant influence in the Near Abroad.

Primakov first outlined the top-priority tasks for Soviet foreign policy in 1987, advocating a new approach that would make the Soviet Union turn more inward and successfully modernize.[224] Moscow needed to avoid confrontation with the West not because of the hope of convergence but because it needed the time to rebuild itself so it could if not confront, then at least compete with the West. With peace, the then Soviet Union also could strengthen its internal cohesion. Two elements exist: the avoidance of external confrontation and the strengthening of internal cohesion and power. Upon assuming the post of Russian foreign minister, Primakov outlined the top-priority tasks for Russia's foreign policy in a way that demonstrated a clear link to the ideas he expressed in 1987.[225] External security was essential in order to preserve territorial integrity and to "[strengthen] centripetal tendencies in the territory of the former U.S.S.R. The sovereignty obtained by the republics is irreversible but this does not negate the need for reintegration processes, first of all in the economic field."[226]

In the summer of 1998, Primakov came back to his favorite themes on Russian foreign policy by citing the policies of a nineteenth-century Russian foreign minister, Aleksandr Gorchakov, as a model for Moscow's approach to the world.[227] In most respects, Primakov argued, Gorchakov's policies remain valid and should be a model for future Russian actions. Gorchakov had assumed office in the wake of the disastrous Russian defeat in the Crimean War in 1856 and was able to rebuild Russia's power and influence. He was a passionate defender of the Russian Empire at a time when it seemed close to collapse. Primakov suggested that Russia should draw several lessons from Gorchakov. Among these he cited Gorchakov's belief that Russia, even when weakened by defeat, can pursue an active foreign policy and always has the strength to play an important role in world politics. According to Primakov, Gorchakov rightly believed that a "vigorous foreign policy" was essential for creating the conditions that would allow Russia *to renew itself at home* and regain influence abroad.[228] Russia's weakness, according to Primakov, thus is temporary; one of the principal goals of foreign policy is to rebuild Russian domestic strength. Russia's setbacks are grave but not irreversible, and it should be active in all areas of foreign policy and exploit the resentment of smaller powers to turn them against Russia's opponents or at least to neutralize them, as Gorchakov had done.[229] Although Primakov again expressed his disinterest in restoring the Soviet empire, he did write that Moscow must do everything it could to create a "single economic area" on the territory of the former Soviet Union.[230] Such a single economic area, created on a Gorchakov model, would very likely be a vehicle for protecting and enhancing Russia's imperial interests.

Given the consistency of Primakov's views over so many years, it is doubtful that he is now engaging in mere rhetoric. His suggestion that

Gorchakov's policies should serve as a model has profound implications for the West and for the triadic nexus involving the Russian diaspora. Primakov is not just a nationalist wishing to strengthen Russia. He represents a school of thought in Russia that continues to believe in a kind of manifest destiny: Russia needs to play a special role in the world and to control its hinterland. At the very least, Russia would need a free hand in the Near Abroad. Since Primakov blames the democrats for most of Russia's current problems, *the new Russia would certainly not be a liberal democracy.* While Russia is rebuilding its domestic strength, it needs to avoid confrontation with powerful adversaries, according to Primakov. But an active foreign policy should be used to gradually increase domestic and international strength. And, as noted, Primakov praised Gorchakov's ability to exploit the fears and resentments of many smaller powers to rebuild, and then expand, Russia's own influence. Great patience, though, would be crucial as Russia pursues policies to strengthen itself and undermine possible opponents.

When faced with overwhelming power (or political or economic setbacks), Primakov would likely favor tactical concessions while seeking the maximum long-term benefits. While some may view this tactic as just a pragmatic attempt to protect Russia's national interest, the latter must be interpreted in terms of both interests and values. What, more precisely, was Primakov seeking? Although Primakov was not harking back to the communist past, he appears to dislike democracy and the West in equal measure. His vision, it seems, is one of a nondemocratic Russia capable of challenging the West rather than seeking to integrate with it. In terms of NATO, he appears to have sought three (not mutually exclusive) main goals: (1) weaken NATO by diluting it and diminishing America's role; (2) limit the new members' participation in and protection by NATO by restricting the extension of Western conventional and nuclear forces eastward; (3) use the enlargement of NATO as evidence of the West's taking advantage of Russia's weakness to help domestic authoritarian forces and, at the same time, seek to convince the West that Russia should be compensated for its concessions on enlargement by allowing it to operate without Western interference within the geographic space of the former Soviet Union.

Primakov has made progress on the first two goals. The third is much more complex and requires a great deal of patience and finesse. A wall behind which Russia can operate freely has to be constructed very carefully *without provoking an early adverse Western reaction.* In relations with the CIS, therefore, Primakov has taken a subtle, gradualist approach combining patience with confidence in the ultimate outcome. He has stated that supporting the centripetal trends that actually exist in the post-Soviet space is a top diplomatic priority.[231] But significantly, he also argued that the chief obstacles to bringing these trends to fruition come not only from opponents of integration but from the communists who have been calling for the restoration of the USSR.[232] His message seemed to be: "Don't alarm the potential targets." Patience will pay off. Further, by reiterating that Russia, with his help, had made the best of a bad deal,[233] Primakov not only enhanced his own reputation but continued to encourage nationalistic feelings and put the blame for Russia's weakness squarely on the democrats.

NATO's attack on Yugoslavia greatly strengthened Primakov's image as a defender of the national interest—in contrast to that of Yeltsin and the democrats. The accommodating Viktor Chernomyrdin, Yeltsin's envoy to the Balkans who helped arrange the June 1999 agreement to end the Kosovo conflict, and indeed the whole Russian government were widely blamed for selling out Russian interests and betraying a historic ally, Serbia. That overall judgment was not altered by the temporary euphoria in Moscow generated by the news that 200 Russian troops (in an almost quixotic move) had dashed to the Pristina, Kosovo, airport on June 12, ahead of NATO forces. Primakov by contrast used the West's cavalier treatment of Russia to reinforce Cold War attitudes while trying to exploit fissures in the Alliance, in particular, by paying special attention to a wavering Germany.[234] His approach to dealing with the West was consistent. He wanted to make NATO's actions in Yugoslavia as difficult as possible in order to diminish at the very least the Alliance's appetite to intervene elsewhere. Thus, Primakov, as prime minister (and foreign minister), in cunningly seeking more concessions from the West and in weakening or trying to weaken the West's ability to move forces East, steadfastly attempted to create conditions where the West would be both less able and less inclined to intervene within the territory of the former Soviet Union.

Primakov thus worked unrelentingly for the creation of a *permissive space*, encompassing the territory of the former Soviet Union, within which Russia could operate unfettered. In exchange for expanding NATO to parts of Eastern Europe (or any concessions on Kosovo), the Western alliance should accept (in Primakov's view) a hands-off policy on matters involving Russian relations with neighbors within the territory of the former Soviet Union.

Even with a permissive space, initially Russia is likely to be constrained by the disastrous condition of its military (or the dire condition of its economy). But this does not guarantee peaceful behavior in the long term. With anything resembling a permissive space, there could be far fewer constraints on Russia as it transforms itself, particularly an illiberal Russia that is increasingly alienated from the post–Cold War settlement because of NATO's expansion eastward. Even if the leaders of such a Russia conclude mistakenly that the West had accepted a permissive space around Russia, they might act more recklessly in the triadic relationship. This could include a greater proneness to intervene militarily on behalf of the Russian diasporas or to stir up trouble, for instance, in the Baltic states, using the Russian diasporas to gain additional leverage in order to guarantee that these states are left out of NATO.

A permissive space also would magnify the possibilities for *inadvertent large-scale conflict* involving Russia.[235] Such conflicts arise out of misperception and miscalculation, the possibilities for which could be magnified in a triadic relationship that operated in a permissive space without significant extraregional constraints on Russia. Unfortunately, the triadic relation already contains factors that add to the likelihood of miscalculation and misperception. These include (1) reckless rhetoric (verbal imperialism, including statements by politicians that reject the sovereignty of neighboring states)[236] in Russia regarding the diaspora; (2) insensitivity in the nationalizing states toward minorities in the postcommunist states that fails to understand the need to respect the "collective rights" of the minorities (to preserve their language, culture, etc.) and thus causes needless friction that can, in turn, generate alarm in the external national "homeland"; (3) a tendency of the ethnic majorities in the postcommunist states to view themselves as victims (of past deprivation of political rights and of Soviet imperialism) and thus feel that they are absolved from having to make concessions to minorities since they themselves are the *primary* victims—a new majority victimology[237]; and (4) the decentralization of decision-making in Russia that creates opportunities for regional leaders or large corporations with interests in neighboring states to stir up trouble using the Russian diaspora to pressure those states into concessions.

Thus the potential creation of a permissive space (that the enlargement of NATO may well facilitate), a goal for which Primakov seemed to be working so avidly, would greatly increase the *possibility* for Russian assertiveness on the issue of its diasporas. It may foster Russian imperial overreach in the CIS. Combined with the probability that NATO enlargement (and the Alliance attack on Yugoslavia) in the longer term will significantly encourage and strengthen nationalistic forces in Russia and enhance the risk of inadvertent conflict, then Russia is indeed *likely* to play a much more aggressive role as part of a triadic relationship.

Conclusions

There is a tendency, if not a tradition, in the West of expecting the worst of Russia. A frustrated, humiliated Russia with a seemingly erratic leadership, engaged in a potentially volatile triadic relationship, where 25 million ethnic Russians remain outside its borders in what had been the internal empire, is bound to raise fears and perhaps even create expectations of large-scale violence. With limited exceptions, however, there has been relative calm in the region since the collapse of the Soviet Union.

Questions remain that cannot be answered conclusively, and many developments lend themselves to sharply differing interpretations. For instance, has Russian restraint on diaspora issues been due to internal democratic inhibitions and military exhaustion (leaving aside for the moment the interactive influences in the triadic relationship)? Is Russia giving up its imperial ambitions and perhaps settling for a more modest hegemony? Or does a currently weak Russia nevertheless remain confident that in the long term, despite serious setbacks, it will be able to restore its imperial position and that therefore it is not worth risking that attainable long-term goal for some limited, short-term gains? In the case of Ukraine and Kazakhstan, the relatively tolerant attitude and policies toward the Russian minorities also can be interpreted in different ways. Are these states persuaded of the benefits of civic nationalism, or are they confident that demographic trends (shaped in part by ethnic Russian emigration) and/or linguistic assimilation will in the long term resolve matters entirely in favor of the titular nationality?

Additional motivating factors may be at work. The general absence of large-scale violence may mean not that the most important issues involving the diasporas have been resolved but rather that concerns and tensions over key domestic and international issues have not yet reached the most difficult and confrontational stages.

There are negative indicators. In Russia, Leninist attitudes toward sovereignty have yet to be overcome entirely. Russia and most states in the Near Abroad continue to face enormous economic difficulties and political crises that could undermine political stability. An overconcentration of power in the presidency also means that there could be a sudden shift in Russia's policies on the diasporas, if a strong nationalist succeeds Yeltsin. There is inadequate transparency or predictability in Russian decision-making and a tendency toward provocative rhetoric on the issues of ethnic minorities. In the other states too, fragile or inadequate progress on democratization and seemingly intractable economic problems have the potential to fuel exclusionary ethnic nationalism. By bringing the alliance to the Russian border, NATO expansion, despite some concessions to Russia, creates a psychological wall. It alienates Moscow from the post–Cold War settlement in Europe, undermines Russian democrats and democracy, and encourages ultranationalist claims of betrayal. And in changing the Russian perception of the security environment within which Russia operates, it encourages policies that are likely to have deleterious effects on relations with the other states on the territory of the former Soviet Union, particularly on matters involving the Russian diasporas. Moreover, the intrinsic risks in interstate relations—the "nationalizing" state versus the external national "homeland"—of violent conflict over diaspora issues through inadvertence are magnified by ultranationalistic rhetoric throughout the region, the persistence of a new majority victimology, and the consequent insensitivity toward ethnic minorities.

Yet just as it is important to appreciate the problems, it would be a mistake to fail to recognize the positive factors, developments, and achievements. The breakup of the Soviet Union was largely peaceful, which greatly diminished the dangerous rancor and vindictiveness that usually follows the violent dissolution of an empire. Despite its difficulties, Russia has made significant progress in democratizing and in developing a market economy. The struggles for democracy in Russia, moreover, need to be understood in the context of the enormous difficulties that it is facing in the wake of the collapse both of its empire and of its ideology. It is heartening that in the dark days following the murder of Galina Starovoitova, in November 1998, and under attack from the communists and Primakov, 14 prominent democrats, including two former prime ministers, Sergey Kiriyenko and Yegor Gaidar, formed a new political bloc to fight a communist resurgence.[238] Vladimir Putin, despite a background in the KGB, demonstrated a capacity to push for democratic change and for a market economy as a key aide to Anatoly Sobchak, the liberal mayor of St. Petersburg. Moreover, he has committed himself to continue to pursue Yeltsin's goals of democracy and markets.[239] And it is an encouraging sign for democracy in Russia that Russian democrats continue to oppose strenuously the eager embrace of Lukashenko's unreconstructed, authoritarian Belarus, not only because of the potential economic burden but largely because of an aversion to antidemocratic contamination. Russia's size, as discomforting as it may be to its neighbors, usually functions as a deterrent to the systematic persecution of the Russian diasporas; thus, in a way, it helps "calm" the triadic relationship. Inchoate or unresolved national identities in Russia, Ukraine, and Kazakhstan do have the potential to at least buy time for the development of a vibrant civil society and sustainable civic nationalism in these countries. The absence of radical leadership in the Russian diasporas (except in Transdniestria) and the reluctance of the Russian minority in general to engage in confrontation with the titular group help discourage irredentism in Russia itself. Linguistic assimilation in the Baltics has the potential to resolve peacefully the minority issues, as long as Latvia, in particular, becomes more flexible on the granting of citizenship. In Ukraine and Kazakhstan, a more multiethnic approach with linguistic revival among the titular nation rather than linguistic assimilation of the Russian minority opens the potential for reaching a form of "consociation."[240] If these two states become stable, liberal democracies, they could provide and institutionalize a high degree of internal autonomy for the Russian minority, which would allow for peaceful coexistence between the titulars and the minority.

It has been less than a decade since the dissolution of the Soviet Union and the collapse of its organizing ideology—a very short period in historical terms. It is possible to learn some lessons, discover some clues to the future, and discern some tendencies. But perhaps we are too impatient and optimistic in looking for quick and definitive answers. Where the triadic relationships involving the Russian diasporas are concerned, it is premature to be alarmed by the prospects for large-scale violence, but it is equally dangerous to be complacent. The political landscape seems remarkably calm, almost flat. Yet it is surprising how quickly threatening funnel clouds can form on such a landscape.

Notes

1. The ethnic composition of the Russian Federation is as follows: Russian 81.5%, Tatar 3.8%, Ukrainian 3%, Chuvash 1.2%, Bashkir 0.9%, Belarussian 0.8%, Moldovian 0.7%, other 8.1%. Total 148,178,000. Radio Free Europe/Radio Liberty, *Russia: Facts and Figures,* www.rferl.org/bd/ru/info/ru-ciafacts.html, September 8, 1998.

2. Itar-Tass, July 12, 1996. This despite Article 13 of the Constitution of the Russian Federation, which explicitly forbids the adoption of a "state ideology." *Konstitutsiia,* 1993; see also George Breslauer and Catherine Dale, "Boris Yeltsin and the Invention of the Russian Nation State," *Post-Soviet Affairs* 13, no. 4 (1997): 303–32.

3. Lea Kadia Drobizheva, "Power Sharing and the Experience of the Russian Federation," ms., 1996, quoted by Gail W. Lapidus, "A Comment on 'Russia and the Russian Diasporas,'" *Post-Soviet Affairs* 12, no. 3 (1996): 285.

4. Igor Zevelev, "Russia and the Russian Diasporas," *Post-Soviet Affairs* 12, no. 3 (1996): 265–84. In Chechnya, though, the actions of the Russian

government, despite primary political motivations, did have an ethnic dimension that heightened tensions among ethnic groups, especially in the Caucasus.

5. Rogers Brubaker, for instance, has shown that it is possible to gain considerable insight into the causes of large-scale violence in such a triadic relationship through the emphasis on the interdependent relational nexus that exists in continuously contested political fields. Rogers Brubaker, *Nationalism Reframed: Nationhood and the National Question in the New Europe* (New York: Cambridge University Press, 1996), esp. chap. 3, pp. 55–76. Others have used such a triadic relationship to develop a concept of interactive nationalism. See Jeff Chinn and Robert Kaiser, *Russians as the New Minority: Ethnicity and Nationalism in the Soviet Successor States* (Boulder, Colo.: Westview Press, 1996).

6. Brubaker, *Nationalism Reformed*, p. 76.

7. Valerie Bunce, "Should Transitologists Be Grounded?" *Slavic Review* 53, no. 1 (Spring 1995): 122–25.

8. Guy Hermet, "Rethinking Transitology," in Aurel Braun and Zoltan Barany, eds., *Dilemmas of Transition: The Hungarian Experience* (Lanham, Md.: Rowman and Littlefield, 1999), pp. 31–46.

9. Walker Connor, *The National Question in Marxist-Leninist Theory and Strategy* (Princeton, N.J.: Princeton University Press, 1984), p. 30.

10. V. I. Lenin, "The Right of Nations to Self-Determination," in *National Liberation, Socialism and Imperialism: Selected Writings by V.I. Lenin* (New York: International Publishers, 1968), pp. 12–44. Also see pp. 46–109, 659–60.

11. Ariel Cohen, *Russian Imperialism: Development and Crisis* (Westport, Conn.: Praeger, 1996).

12. B. Manelis, *7 Sovetskoe gosudarstvo i pravo 17* (1964).

13. Chinn and Kaiser, *Russians as the New Minority*, p. 66.

14. Joseph Stalin, "Deviations Towards Nationalism," in *Marxism and the National and Colonial Questions* (New York: International Publishers, 1934), pp. 267–68.

15. Lowell Tillett, *The Great Friendship: Soviet Historians on the Non-Soviet Nationalities* (Chapel Hill: University of North Carolina Press, 1969), pp. 86–90.

16. Mikhail Gorbachev, *O natsionalnoy politike partiy v sovremennykh usloviyakh. Doklad i zaklyuchitelnoye slovo na Plenume TsK KPSS 19, 20 Sentyabrya 1989 goda* (Moscow: Politizdat, 1989), p. 13.

17. Aurel Braun and Richard Day, "Gorbachevian Contradictions," *Problems of Communism* (May–June 1990): 36–50.

18. Max Beloff, "Crises of the European Nation State," *Government and Opposition* 1 (Winter 1974): 25.

19. Gennadi Gerasimov, the spokesman for the Soviet Foreign Ministry, face-tiously called this the "Sinatra Doctrine," which he explained meant that the East European states could do things "their way." *New York Times,* October 26, 1989.

20. Eric Hobsbawm, *Nations and Nationalism Since 1780* (Cambridge: Cambridge University Press, 1990); Ernest Gellner, *Nations and Nationalism* (Ithaca, N.Y.: Cornell University Press, 1983); Walker Connor, "When Is a Nation?" *Ethnic and Racial Studies* 13 (January 1990): 92–103.

21. *Izvestiya,* December 29, 1990; *Krasnaya Zvezda,* June 11, 1992.

22. See Dieter Rauschning and Alfred Eisfeld, *Vom Sowjetimperium zum eura-sischen Staatensystem: Die russische Aussenpolitik im Wandel und in der Wech-selbeziehung zur Innenpolitik. Ausgewaehlte Beitraege von Boris Meissner* (Berlin: Duncker and Humblot, 1995).

23. Mette Skak, *From Empire to Anarchy: Post-Communist Foreign Policy and International Relations* (New York: St. Martin's Press, 1996).

24. For an excellent discussion see Breslauer and Dale, "Boris Yeltsin and the Invention of the Russian Nation State," pp. 303–32.

25. Ibid., p. 305.

26. Peter J. S. Duncan, "Ukrainians," in Graham Smith, ed., *The Nationalities Question in the Soviet Union* (London: Longman, 1990), pp. 96–100.

27. Andrew Wilson, "The Going Challenge to Kiev from the Donbas," *RFE/RL Research Report,* August 20, 1993, pp. 8–9.

28. Roman Solchanyk, "Ukraine: From Sovereignty to Independence," *RFE/RL Research Report,* January 3, 1992, p. 38.

29. Russians were far more integrated into Lithuanian society than else-where in the Baltics. Lithuania also has a rich, multiethnic society. As a large regional power, it had within its territory at various times huge numbers of Poles, Ukrainians, and other nationalities.

30. Baltic News Service, February 22, 1994; Richard Rose and William Maley, "Nationalities in the Baltic States: A Survey Study," no. 222, Centre for the Study of Public Policy, Glasgow (1994): 53.

31. Chinn and Kaiser, *Russians as the New Minority,* pp. 95, 109. There is also some controversy about the precise numbers, but in general reasonable estimates are 32 percent for Latvia and 29 percent for Estonia.

32. Chinn and Kaiser, *Russians as the New Minority,* pp. 173–75.

33. Karen Dawisha, "Russia, Democracy and the Imperial Temptation," in *U.S. Relations with Russia and Ukraine,* Aspen Institute Congressional Pro-gram 11, no. 3, August 18–24, 1996, p. 16.

34. Martha Brill Olcott, "Ceremony and Substance: The Illusion of Unity in Central Asia," in Michael Mandelbaum, ed., *Central Asia and the World*

(New York: Council on Foreign Relations, 1994), p. 20. The boundary, as Brill Olcott aptly described it, was an "endless hypothetical."

35. The World Bank, *Statistical Handbook 1994: States of the Former U.S.S.R.* (Washington, D.C.: World Bank Studies of Economics in Transformation, no.14, 1994).

36. Ibid. In 1993 the figure for the Kazakh population was 43.2 percent, but with steady emigration of Russians from Kazakhstan, the proportion of the titular population has been increasing. See also Bhavna Dave, "National Revival in Kazakhstan: Language Shift and Identity Change," *Post-Soviet Affairs* 12, no. 1 (1996): 51–72.

37. Viktor Zotin, "Diplomatic Efforts in Tajikistan," *International Affairs* (Moscow) 43, no. 1 (1997): 90–94.

38. *Russia Today*, European Internet Network, March 20, 1998, p. 3. Supporters of Shevardnadze believe that at least some in the Russian leadership would like to see the Georgian leader replaced by someone more amenable to Russian interests and also a less well-known or sympathetic leader who would not generate such ready Western support against Russian pressure on Georgia.

39. See the *New Russia Barometer VI* (Glasgow: Centre for the Study of Public Policy, University of Strathclyde, 1996), pp. 5–56, esp. p. 36. Whereas 92 percent of the respondents suggested negotiations, only 16 advocated military action.

40. Ibid.

41. *Izvestiya*, April 30, 1998.

42. *Russia Today*, March 27, 1998.

43. Anthony D. Smith suggests an approach based on what he calls "prenationalism." See Smith, *The Ethnic Origins of Nations* (Oxford: Basil Blackwell, 1986); see also Chinn and Kaiser, *Russians as the New Minority.*

44. Anthony D. Smith, "The Problem of Definition: Nationalism, Nations and Nation States in East Central Europe," in Paul Latawski, ed., *Contemporary Nationalism in East-Central Europe* (New York: St. Martin's Press, 1995), p. 4.

45. See Alexander J. Motyl, *Sovietology, Rationality, Nationality* (New York: Columbia University Press, 1990), pp. 161–65, for a discussion of Russian nationalism before the disintegration of the Soviet Union.

46. Breslauer and Dale, "Boris Yeltsin and the Invention of the Russian Nation State," pp. 303–32; Iver B. Neumann, *Russia and the Idea of Europe: A Study in Identity and International Relations* (London: Routledge, 1996); Yaroslav Bilinsky, "Russian Foreign Policy in Search of a Nation," *Orbis* (Fall 1997): 642–46; and Jack F. Matlock, "Dealing with a Russia in Turmoil," *Foreign Affairs* (May–June 1996): 38–51.

47. Anatol Lieven, *Chechnya: Tombstone of Russian Power* (New Haven, Conn.: Yale University Press, 1998), pp. 378–79.

48. Geoffrey Hosking, *Russia: People and Empire* (Cambridge, Mass.: Harvard University Press, 1997).

49. The ethnic composition of non-Russians in the Russian Federation is as follows: Tatar 3.8 percent; Ukrainian 3 percent; Chuvash 1.2 percent; Bashkir 0.9 percent; Belarussian 0.8 percent; Moldavian 0.7 percent; other 8.1 percent. Source: RFE/RL, *Russia: Facts and Figures*, www.rferl.org/bd/ru/info/ru-ciafacts.html, September 8, 1998.

50. *Rossiyskaya gazeta*, February 3, 1992; see also George Breslauer, "Leadership and Nation Building," in Timothy Colton et al., "Five Years after the Collapse of the U.S.S.R.," *Post-Soviet Affairs* 13, no. 1 (1997): 9–10.

51. The status and experience of Tatarstan, in fact, stands in sharp contrast with those of Chechnya (which was basically a political rather than an ethnic issue, though it clearly had ethnic overtones). Perhaps it is a reflection of the flexibility in the construction of Russian ethnic identity that Tatarstan has been given such an enormous amount of autonomy.

52. Farrid Mukhametshin, "Tatarstan in the Outside World," *International Affairs* (Moscow) 43, no. 4 (1997): 197–202.

53. Ibid., p. 197.

54. *Russia Today*, August 4, 1999.

55. David Hoffman, "Russia Draws Bleak Picture of Its Security," *Washington Post*, December 25, 1997.

56. *Izvestiya*, April 30, 1998.

57. *Nezavisimaya gazeta*, December 24, 1997.

58. *New Russia Barometer VI*, pp. 35–37.

59. Ibid., p. 36

60. Samuel P. Huntington, "The Erosion of American National Interests," *Foreign Affairs* (September/October 1997): 28–49.

61. I am leaving out the remaining Central Asian and Caucasian states not only for the sake of brevity but also because it seems that much of the remaining Russian diaspora in these states is likely to emigrate and there is a low prospect for large-scale violence.

62. Huntington (somewhat stretching his definition of civilizations) has contended that there is a fault line dividing civilizations within Ukraine itself, which separates Catholic western Ukraine from Orthodox eastern Ukraine. Samuel P. Huntington, "The Clash of Civilizations," *Foreign Affairs* (Summer 1993): 22–48.

63. Andrew Wilson, *Ukrainian Nationalism in the 1990's: A Minority Faith* (New York: Cambridge University Press, 1997).

64. Wilson argues quite persuasively that the relative drop in President Leonid Kravchuk's percentage of the popular vote, from 61.6 percent in December 1991 to 45 percent in July 1994, was due to the fact that he changed from running in the first instance as a moderate Ukrainian national communist to running as a Ukrainian nationalist, and thus lost to Leonid Kuchma, who ran on a pro-Russian, antinationalist ticket. Ibid.

65. The Communists gained 123 seats; their potential allies, the Socialist and the Progressive Socialist Parties, together gained 48 seats. *Russia Today*, April 2, 1998.

66. Ibid.

67. Ibid.

68. See also Yaroslav Bilinsky, "Ukraine, Russia and the West: An Insecure Security Triangle," *Problems of Post-Communism* (January/February 1997): 29–30. Russia sought to keep most if not all of the Black Sea Fleet. A settlement on its division, though, has now been reached by Russia and Ukraine. See Thomas A. Dine, "Europe Moves Eastward Slowly: What's Next in Ukraine and the Role of RFE/RL," July 15, 1998, *RFE/RL Research Report*, www.rferl.org/dine980715.html.

69. The Black Sea Fleet was one of the Soviet Union's three principal fleets. Moscow argued that Russia was entitled to the entire fleet following the breakup of the Soviet Union; Kiev sought an even split. An eventual compromise saw Russia hold on to the most important warships.

70. See Paul D'Anieri, "Dilemmas of Interdependence: Autonomy, Prosperity and Sovereignty in Ukraine's Russia Policy," *Problems of Post-Communism* (January/February 1997): 16–25.

71. *Russia Today*, March 26–27, 1998.

72. In January 1998 the treaty was ratified by Ukraine's Supreme Council. *Kommersant Daily*, January 16, 1998.

73. *Russia Today*, June 21, 1999.

74. Bogdan Nahaylo, "The Birth of an Independent Ukraine," RFE/RL Research Institute, *Report on the U.S.S.R.*, December 13, 1991, p. 2.

75. Ibid.

76. "Ukraine Welcomes Chernomyrdin's Return as PM," *Russia Today*, August 25, 1998.

77. Dominique Arel, "A Lurking Cascade of Assimilation in Kiev?" *Post-Soviet Affairs* 12, no. 1 (1996): 74.

78. *RFE/RL Research Report*, July 27, 1999, p. 5.

79. RTR News in Moscow, 11 A.M. (MT), February 27, 1998.

80. *Russia Today*, February 27, 1998.

81. *Russia Today*, November 21, 1998.

82. Dominique Arel, "Language Politics in Independent Ukraine: Towards One or Two State Languages?" *Nationalities Papers* 23, no. 3 (September 1995): 597–622.

83. Viktor Zamyatin and Yury Chubchenko, "Treaty with Russia Unites Kuchma and Parliament," *Kommersant Daily*, January 16, 1998.

84. Arel, "A Lurking Cascade of Assimilation in Kiev?" pp. 75–76.

85. Ibid., pp. 76–89; see also David Laitin, "Language and Nationalism in the Post-Soviet Republics," *Post-Soviet Affairs* 12, no. 1 (1996): 21–23.

86. Ihor Stebelsky, "The Toponymy of Ukraine," *Post-Soviet Geography and Economics* 38, no. 5 (1997): 276–87.

87. Lieven, *Chechnya*, pp. 258–59.

88. Chinn and Kaiser, *Russians as the New Minority*, pp. 148–49.

89. *Russia Today*, March 27, 1998.

90. Lieven, *Chechnya*, p. 260.

91. *RFE/RL Research Report*, June 12, 1992, p. 57; Chinn and Kaiser, *Russians as the New Minority*, p. 150.

92. There is a safety valve. There have been relatively freewheeling political debates.

93. Belarussians are a Slavic people. In 1990 Belarussian became the official language of the country. Because the use of Belarussian was discouraged by previous Soviet governments, the majority of the population, especially in the larger cities, continues to speak Russian. Belarussian, which is written in the Cyrillic alphabet, resembles Russian and Ukrainian but is a distinct language. *Russia Today*, November 21, 1998.

94. *Economist*, July 24, 1999, p. 46.

95. *Russia Today*, March 20, 1998.

96. Lukashenko claimed that in 1997 Belarus had an economic growth of 10 percent. Given the miserable state of the economy, this claim failed to impress Western governments or observers. *Russia Today*, January 23, 1998.

97. See "Alexander Lukashenko, Europe's Odd Man Out," *Economist*, July 25, 1998, p. 51.

98. *Izvestiya*, April 3, 1998.

99. *Economist*, January 9, 1999, p. 47.

100. Ibid.

101. RFE/RL *Newsline*, January 22, 1999, www.rferl.org/newsline, p. 2.

102. *Globe and Mail*, June 29, 1999.

103. Ibid.

104. *Economist*, July 24, 1999, p. 45.

105. RFE/RL *Newsline*, January 22, 1999, www.rferl.org/newsline, p. 2.

106. "Belarus Seeks Slav Unity to Counter US Influence," *Russia Today*, January 24, 1999.

107. *Globe and Mail*, June 29, 1999.

108. Chinn and Kaiser, *Russians as the New Minority*, Table 8.1, p. 189.

109. Ibid., Table 8.2, pp. 191–93; migration flows are stabilizing in Central Asia according to Justin Burke, "Language Policy and Citizenship in the Former Soviet Union," *Kennan Institute Meeting Report* 15, no. 8 (1998).

110. Dave, "National Revival in Kazakhstan," pp. 57–72.

111. Zevelev, "Russia and the Russian Diasporas," pp. 270–71.

112. Laitin, "Language and Nationalism in Post-Soviet Republics," pp. 4–24.

113. Makash Tatimov, cited in Dave, "National Revival in Kazakhstan," p. 54.

114. *Russia Today*, May 14, 1999.

115. Cited by Dave, "National Revival in Kazakhstan," p. 62.

116. *Russia Today*, April 10, 1998.

117. Laitin, "Language and Nationalism in Post-Soviet Republics," Table 1, pp. 6–7, 22.

118. Dave, "National Revival in Kazakhstan," pp. 56–57.

119. Nazarbayev won 78.3 percent of the vote. His main opponent, Serikbolsyn Abdildin, garnered only 13.5 percent of the total. *Russia Today*, January 11, 1999.

120. *Russia Today*, November 29, 1998.

121. *Russia Today*, January 11, 1999.

122. RFE/RL *Newsline*, January 24, 1999.

123. Chinn and Kaiser, *Russians as the New Minority*, pp. 165–74.

124. *RFE/RL Research Report*, July 17, 1992, p. 73.

125. Valeriu Matei interview. Cited in Chinn and Kaiser, *Russians as the New Minority*, p. 172 and n. 38.

126. Julie Moffett, "Moldova: Rights Respected, but Problems with Legal System Remain," Radio Free Europe/Radio Liberty, November 30, 1998.

127. *RFE/RL Research Report*, April 10, 1992, p. 63.

128. Chinn and Kaiser, *Russians as the New Minority*, p. 174.

129. *Russia Today*, March 20, 1998.

130. *Russia Today*, July 15, 1999.

131. *Economist,* June 26, 1999, p. 61.

132. Interview with Lebed by Anatol Lieven, cited in Lieven, *Chechnya,* p. 250.

133. *Russia Today,* March 26, 1998.

134. *Russia Today,* November 24 and 25, 1998.

135. One illustration of this demographic transformation is the rise of the Russian population, which increased from only 23,000 in 1945 to 475,000 by 1991. Raivo Vetik, "Ethnic Conflict and Accommodation in Post-Communist Estonia," *Journal of Peace Research* 3, no. 3 (1993): 273; Aksel Kirch, "Russians as a Minority in Contemporary Baltic States," *Bulletin of Peace Proposals* 23, no. 2 (1992): 205–6.

136. "Year in Review 1998," *Russia Today,* January 26, 1999.

137. *Russia Today,* January 21, 1999.

138. Anthony Georgieff, "Estonia: Ethnic Russian Voters May Play Key Role," *RFE/RL Research Report,* March 5, 1999, p. 1.

139. Ibid., p. 2.

140. *Russia Today,* April 3, 1998.

141. See Laitin, "National Revival and Competitive Assimilation in Estonia," *Post-Soviet Affairs* 12, no. 1 (1996): 25–39; and Laitin, "Language and Nationalism in Post-Soviet Republics," p. 4.

142. Laitin, "Language and Nationalism in Post-Soviet Republics," pp. 4–38; and Vello Pettai, "The Gains of Ethnopolitics in Latvia," *Post-Soviet Affairs* 12, no. 1 (1996): 40–50.

143. *Russia Today,* April 3, 1998.

144. *Russia Today,* August 25, 1998.

145. *Russia Today,* August 26, 1998.

146. Ibid.

147. Radio Free Europe/Radio Liberty, November 30, 1998, www.rferl.org/nca/features/1998/10F.RU.98.html.

148. RFE/RL *Newsline,* November 30, 1998.

149. *Globe and Mail,* July 8, 10, 1999; *Russia Today,* July 8, 1999.

150. *Globe and Mail,* July 16, 1999; *Russia Today,* July 15, 1999.

151. *Globe and Mail,* July 10, 1999.

152. *Russia Today,* April 2, 1998.

153. *Russia Today,* April 10, 1998.

154. *Globe and Mail,* August 6, 1999.

155. *New Baltic Barometer III* (Glasgow: Centre for the Study of Public Policy, University of Strathclyde, 1997), pp. 11–13, 50.

156. Laitin, "Language and Nationalism in the Post-Soviet Republics," Table 1, p. 7. It should be pointed out though that even though ethnic Russians in Latvia seem to have bought into what Laitin calls the "tipping game" and are willing to integrate, they also had (somewhat cynically) the lowest estimation of any of the four cases that learning the titular language would be economically useful to them. Pettai, "Gains of Ethnopolitics," p. 48.

157. *New Baltic Barometer III*, pp. 50–52.

158. *Russia Today*, August 10, 1999.

159. *Russia Today*, November 25, 1998.

160. *Russia Today*, November 13, 1998; *Nezavisimaya gazeta*, November 13, 1998; *Canadian Jewish News*, January 7, 1999.

161. *Russia Today*, November 21, 1998.

162. *Russia Today*, November 29, 1998.

163. *Russia Today*, December 24, 1998.

164. See "Russia and America Try to Make Up," *Economist*, July 31, 1999, pp. 39–40.

165. *Globe and Mail*, July 30, 1999.

166. *Le Monde*, August 5, 1999.

167. *Economist*, July 31, 1999, p. 40.

168. See the interesting piece by Aileen Kelly, "When Russians Look Inward," *New York Times*, September 6, 1998.

169. Aurel Braun and Richard Day, "Gorbachevian Contradictions," *Problems of Communism* (May–June 1990): 36–50; "Political Development in Central and Eastern Europe," in *U.S. Relations with Central and Eastern Europe*, Aspen Institute Congressional Program 9, no. 4 (August 1994): 8–12.

170. As Robert Sharlet, for instance, has written, genuine participation refers to "input" rather than "output," and value pluralism would need to be accepted by the political elite as a condition for the existence of the political pluralism that in turn is necessary for the protection of genuine political rights. R. S. Sharlet, "Systematic Political Science and Communist Systems," in F. J. Fleron Jr., ed., *Communist Studies and the Social Sciences: Essays on Methodology and Empirical Theory* (Chicago: R. McNally, 1969).

171. Fareed Zakaria, "The Rise of Illiberal Democracy," *Foreign Affairs* (November/December 1997): 22–42.

172. Juan Linz and Alfred Stepan, *Problems of Democratic Transformation and Consolidation: Southern Europe, South America, Post-Communist Europe* (Baltimore: Johns Hopkins University Press, 1996).

173. Ibid.

174. Andrew Arato, "Civil Society Transition and Consolidation of Democracy," in Braun and Barany, eds., *Dilemmas of Transition*, pp. 225–50.

175. See an excellent article by David Remnick in which he counters the worst "expectation" school of thought on Russia. "Can Russia Change?" *Foreign Affairs* (January/February 1997): 35–48.

176. Leonard Schapiro, *Russian Studies* (New York: Penguin, 1988), pp. 31–64.

177. Kelly, "When Russians Look Inward."

178. Michael McFaul, "Russia's 1996 Presidential Elections," *Post-Soviet Affairs* 12, no. 4 (1996): 319.

179. Michael McFaul and Nikolai Petrov, "Russian Electoral Politics After Transition: Regional and National Assessments," *Post-Geography and Economics* 38, no. 9 (1997): 507–49.

180. *Russia Today*, July 27, 1999.

181. Richard Rose and Evgeny Tikhomirov, "Russia's Forced-Choice Presidential Election," *Post-Soviet Affairs* 12, no. 4 (1996): 351–97.

182. Michel Camdessus, "Russia and the IMF: Meeting the Challenges of an Emerging Market and Transition Economy," Paper presented at the U.S.-Russia Business Council, Washington, D.C., April 1, 1998, www.imf.org/external/np/speeches/1998/040198.htm.

183. *Economist*, January 9, 1999, p. 98.

184. *Russia Today*, July 27, 1999; *Globe and Mail*, August 6, 1999.

185. Stephen Handelman, *Comrade Criminal: Russia's New Mafiya* (New Haven, Conn.: Yale University Press, 1995).

186. Timothy J. Colton, "Economics and Voting in Russia," *Post-Soviet Affairs* 12, no. 4 (1996): 289–317.

187. See also Zakaria, "The Rise of Illiberal Democracy," p. 37.

188. See particularly Christopher Layne, "Kant or Cant: The Myth of Democratic Peace," *International Security* 19 (Fall 1994): 5–49; David E. Spiro, "The Insignificance of Liberal Peace," *International Security* 19 (Fall 1994): 51–59.

189. Michael Doyle, "Liberalism and World Politics," *American Political Science Review* 80 (December 1996): 1151–69; Doyle, "Liberalism and World Politics Revisited," in Charles W. Kegley, ed., *Controversies in International Relations Theory: Realism and the Neo-Liberal Challenge* (New York: St. Martin's Press, 1995), esp. pp. 95–102; Doyle, *Ways of War and Peace* (New York: Norton, 1997); Jack S. Levy, "Domestic Politics and War," in Robert J. Roberg and Theodore K. Rabb, eds., *The Origin and Prevention of Major Wars* (Cambridge: Cambridge University Press, 1989), esp. p. 88; Zeev Maoz and Bruce Russett, "Normative and Structural Causes of Democratic Peace, 1946–1986," *American Political Science Review* 87 (September 1993): 624–38.

190. Edward Mansfield and Jack Snyder, "Democratization and War," *International Security* 20 (Summer 1995): 5–38.

191. See Michael Mandelbaum, *The Dawn of Peace in Europe* (New York: Twentieth Century Press, 1996).

192. Michael Mandelbaum, "The Post-Cold War Settlement in Europe: A Triumph of Arms Control," *Arms Control Today*, March 9, 1997, pp. 3–8.

193. Text of the Founding Act, *Globe and Mail*, May 16, 1997.

194. Ibid.

195. Zbigniew Brzezinksi and Anthony Lake, "For a New World, a New NATO," *New York Times*, June 30, 1997.

196. *Nezavisimaya gazeta*, December 24, 1997.

197. Klaus-Peter Klaiber, "The NATO-Russia Relationship a Year after Paris," *NATO Review* 46, no. 3 (Autumn 1998): 16–19.

198. Ibid., p. 5.

199. *New York Times*, July 5, 1997.

200. See Floriana Fossato, "Russia: Top Level IMF Talks Resuming in Moscow," *RFE/RL Research Report*, March 26, 1999, p. 1.

201. *Russia Today*, June 12, 1999; RFE/RL *Newsline*, March 25, 1999.

202. "An Alliance for the 21st Century," Clause 27, NAC-S(99)64, NATO Press Release, Washington, D.C., April 24, 1999.

203. Paul-Marie de la Gorce, "NATO on Russia's Doorstep," *Le Monde Diplomatique*, English edition (July 1997).

204. Even Mikhail Gorbachev used the harshest terms to condemn the attack. He declared, "NATO showed the world its madness and irresponsibility—Yugoslavia is a sovereign country and NATO does not have a right to attack it." *Russia Today*, April 22, 1999.

205. See K. P. Foley, "NATO: U.S. Says No Geographic Exclusions," RFE/RL, July 19, 1999, pp. 1–2.

206. RFE/RL *Newsline*, March 12, 1999.

207. Aurel Braun, "The Russian Factor," in Braun and Barany, eds., *Dilemmas of Transition*, pp. 273–300.

208. See Geza Jeszenszky, in *Magyar Nemzet*, September 2, 1996.

209. *Russia Today*, October 3, 1997.

210. Donald McConnell, "Charter with NATO Will Help Ukraine Regain Its Rightful Place in Europe," *NATO Review* 35, no. 4 (July/August 1997): 22–25; Ihor Kharchenko, "The New Ukraine-NATO Partnership," *NATO Review* 45, no. 5 (September/October 1997): 27–29.

211. *Russia Today*, February 27, 1998.

212. On occasion, though, statements by Ukrainian leaders on NATO have made Moscow nervous. Although Kuchma has repeatedly stated his

position that there were no reasons for Ukraine to seek NATO member-ship in the near future, in April 1999 in Washington he signed a declara-tion at NATO's fiftieth anniversary that the Alliance's enlargement to Eastern Europe made "a significant contribution to stability in Europe." See "Declaration of the Heads of State and Government participating in the NATO-Ukraine Commission Summit," Washington, D.C., April 24, 1999, NATO Press Release NUC-S(99)68.

213. Arel, "A Lurking Cascade of Assimilation in Kiev?" p. 74.

214. Angus Reid Poll, March 25–April 17, 1999, in *Economist,* April 24, 1999, p. 50.

215. *Economist,* June 5, 1999, p. 49.

216. Democracy, however, is currently under considerable threat in Ukraine. Three of the seven most serious candidates for Ukraine's presidential elec-tion in October 1999 favor reunification with Russia (and Belarus). None of them, though, is in favor of democracy. In fact, Kuchma's own tactics for reelection have been so authoritarian that even the usually accommo-dating Council of Europe has expressed concern about the prospective election. See "Grim Choices," *Economist,* July 10, 1999.

217. *Russia Today,* January 28, 1999; *Izvestiya,* January 29, 1999.

218. *Izvestiya,* January 29, 1999.

219. Zbigniew Brzezinski, for instance, has stated that "without Ukraine, Russia ceases to be an empire, but with Ukraine suborned and then sub-ordinated, Russia automatically becomes an empire"; quoted by Sherman Garnett, *Keystone in the Arch: Ukraine in the Emerging Security Environ-ment of Central and Eastern Europe* (Washington, D.C.: Carnegie Endow-ment, 1997).

220. Opinion polls in 1999 have repeatedly shown Primakov not only to be the most trusted politician but according to the Vtsion polling organization he would dramatically increase support for the Fatherland Party or a coalition if he joined it. *Russia Today,* May 14, 1999, and August 6, 1999.

221. Quoted by Floriana Fossato, "Top-Level IMF Talks Resuming in Moscow," RFE/RL, March 26, 1999.

222. *Russia Today,* August 4, 1999; *Segodnya,* August 4, 1999.

223. *Segodnya,* August 14, 1999.

224. Y. Primakov, "Novaya filosofiya vneshnei politiki" (A new philosophy of foreign policy), *Pravda,* July 10, 1987.

225. *Moskovskie novosti,* no. 2, January 14–21, 1996, p. 13.

226. Ibid.

227. Yevgeny Primakov, "Russia in World Politics: A Lecture in Honor of Chan-cellor Gorchakov," *International Affairs* (Moscow) 44, no. 3 (1998): 7–13.

228. Ibid., pp. 9–11.

229. Ibid., p. 10.

230. Ibid., pp. 11–12.

231. *Moskovskie novosti,* no. 25, June 23–30, 1996, p. 10.

232. Ibid.

233. *Nezavisimaya gazeta,* December 24, 1997.

234. See "Russia and Kosovo: A Toothless Growl," *Economist,* May 1, 1999.

235. Most of the studies on inadvertent war have tended to focus on the dangers of nuclear conflict and the risks of misperception; see, for instance, Marc Trachtenberg, "The Meaning of Mobilization in 1914," *International Security* 15 (Winter 1990–91): 120–50. Historically, though, there have been conventional conflicts that occurred as a result of miscalculation and misperception.

236. Zevelev, "Russia and the Russian Diasporas," pp. 270–84; Gail Lapidus's reply in "A Comment on 'Russia and Russian Diasporas,'" *Post-Soviet Affairs* 12, no. 3 (1996), pp. 285–87; and Jack Snyder, *Myths of Empire: Domestic Politics and International Ambition* (Ithaca, N.Y.: Cornell University Press, 1991).

237. Aurel Braun, "The Incomplete Revolutions: The Rise of Extremism in East-Central Europe and the Former Soviet Union," and "Russia: The Land in Between," in Aurel Braun and Stephen Scheinberg, *The Extreme Right: Freedom and Security at Risk* (Boulder, Colo.: Westview Press, 1997), pp. 138–60, 162–84.

238. *Russia Today,* November 29, 1998.

239. *Russia Today,* August 10, 1999.

240. For a good treatise on "consociation," see Arend Lijphart, *Democracy in Plural Societies* (New Haven, Conn.: Yale University Press, 1977); Laitin, "National Revival," pp. 22–23.

3

Diaspora, or the Dangers of Disunification? Putting the "Serbian Model" into Perspective

SUSAN L. WOODWARD

T HE CONTEMPORARY view that diasporas can be dangerous owes
much to the case of the Serbs. According to conventional wisdom,
their desire to live in one state—a Greater Serbia—rather than
accept their fate as minorities in republics bordering the republic of Serbia caused the collapse of Yugoslavia. The president of Serbia, Slobodan
Milošević, is said to have planned the breakup and the creation of a
Greater Serbia after his goal of becoming the new dictator of Yugoslavia
was foiled by political leaders in the republics of Slovenia, Croatia, and
Bosnia and Herzegovina. His instrument was the transborder Serbs. By
reviving and manipulating their memories from World War II, when
Serbs in Croatia and Bosnia and Herzegovina were, along with Jews
and Gypsies, the victims of a genocidal campaign by fascist governments, and by then persuading the Yugloslav People's Army, which
was formed in the antifascist struggle of World War II, to aid the Serbs'
rebellion against the legitimate governments of these two republics,
Milošević unleashed an avalanche of aggression and genocide in both
republics that lasted from 1991 to 1995.

The persuasiveness of this argument, and the essential role in the
violence of diaspora Serbs, was confirmed early on in the Yugoslav collapse by the brevity of the Slovene war for independence. Lasting only
ten days, at the cost of no more than 68 dead, the Slovene secession did

not provoke significant violence, it is said, because there were few Serbs in Slovenia to give Milošević both the claim to land and the excuse to intervene. In contrast, substantial numbers of Serbs in areas of Croatia and Bosnia and Herzegovina bordering Serbia took up arms and received Belgrade's support in order to "unify Serb lands" and avoid becoming part of a diaspora outside Serbia. Beginning in 1985, moreover, the demand from the Serb minority in the southern Serbian province of Kosovo for protection from Belgrade against alleged discrimination by the Albanian-majority provincial government had propelled Milošević to power as the head of the Serbian League of Communists in 1987 and was said to be the grounds for a new campaign of violence in 1998–99 against the majority Albanian population there.

As early as late summer–fall of 1991, during the war in Croatia, predictions based on the Serb case sounded alarms throughout the entire region of dissolving communist regimes. The parallel was particularly strong with the collapse of the Soviet Union. Would Russians who suddenly found themselves living outside the Russian Federation in new, neighboring states, supported by Moscow, repeat the "Serb model"?[1] What of the reach for domestic legitimacy through nationalism by postcommunist governments in Eastern Europe? Was there a harbinger of more Miloševićes in statements like that, for example, of Hungarian Prime Minister Jószef Ántall, when he greeted the Brioni Accord of July 1991, which marked the end of the conflict in Slovenia, with a veiled, revisionist allusion to the 1920 Treaty of Trianon frontiers: "We gave Vojvodina to Yugoslavia. If there is no more Yugoslavia, then we should get it back"?[2] Although the population of Vojvodina, an autonomous province in Serbia on Hungary's southern border, was only 16.9 percent Hungarian in 1991, that figure was greater than the 12.2 percent of the Croatian population in that year who were Serbs.[3] Such rhetoric from Budapest alerted many to the large Hungarian populations living outside Hungary in neighboring Serbia, Croatia, Slovakia, and Romania and the potential for the Serb example to move northward, provoking more efforts to change borders—if necessary, through war.[4]

Although the Serb population of Macedonia—the federal republic of Yugoslavia located to the south of Serbia—was only 2 percent in the 1991 census, the model had become sufficiently implanted in policymakers' minds by December 1992 that international troops were deployed, under United Nations Security Council mandate, to the Macedonian-Serbian border to prevent these Serbs from becoming another source of war. Like the economic sanctions first imposed on Serbia and Montenegro in May 1992 (when the two created a new state called the Federal Republic of Yugoslavia) to weaken Belgrade's ability to aid Serbs in eastern Bosnia, the troops remained in Macedonia into 1999 to prevent a Serbian campaign in Kosovo from provoking spillover into Macedonia. The link in this case would be Albanian diasporas in both Serbia and northwestern Macedonia that might go to war, like Serbs, for a Greater Albania.[5]

The fears about Russians and Hungarians did not, for the most part, materialize. Most of the states emerging from communist rule in Eastern Europe adopted legislation early on that claimed their right to protect their conationals living in other states, but violence did not follow. Worry over the repeat of the Serb model among Albanians outside Albania (in Montenegro, Macedonia, and Greece as well as Kosovo) took a backseat to the focus on Slobodan Milošević, and the cause of the Albanian armed rebellion against Serbia, led by an inchoate Kosovo Liberation Army in 1996–98, came to be seen widely as a predictable and legitimate response to Serbian repression in the province. The analogy drawn between Milošević and Adolf Hitler, who used protection of transborder Germans in Sudetenland and Silesia as the excuse to invade Czechoslovakia and Poland but did not stop there, redirected attention away from the Serb diaspora and toward Milošević's guilt.

The German parallel, in fact, underlay most public debate about the Serb national question from 1991 to 1999 and motivated policy toward Yugoslavia. For example, an international criminal tribunal was established during the war in Bosnia and Herzegovina modeled after the one established at Nuremberg, Germany, after 1945 to try Nazis, and Serbia was treated as a pariah state in order to expunge the region of Milošević, until 1999, an unindicted but widely recognized "war criminal." U.S. Secretary of State Madeleine Albright referred frequently to the Hitler analogy, drawing emotional force from her own origins as a child in wartime Czechoslovakia, and the Jewish community was particularly prominent in the campaign to defend Bosnian Muslims, based on the argument that the case fit its own commitment to prevent a repetition of the Nazi Holocaust, a commitment denoted by the slogan "never again."[6] For all in this camp, there was no choice but the use of force—preferably bombing so that American troops were not at risk, but massive bombing nonetheless. Even those who criticized the unsympathetic view of Serbs in this conventional wisdom and in policy used the analogy to Nazi Germany. Contrasting the effects on Germany of sharply differing postwar settlements in 1918 and 1945, they argued that an international policy aimed at peace that punished Serbia with economic disaster would only give rise to a new Milošević and more violence in the future, similar to the effect of the punitive Versailles settlement on Germany in the 1920s and 1930s.

By March 24, 1999, the Hitler parallel had won. So rooted had the conventional wisdom become that all 19 NATO powers agreed to inter- rupt negotiations at Rambouillet, France, aimed at stopping the vio- lence between Yugoslav security forces and the Kosovo Liberation Army and to begin an aerial bombing campaign of Yugoslavia that lasted 78 days. Having "taken a stand," they also began to succumb to the view that Serbs, after all, were collectively responsible for Slobodan Milošević and the four wars in the Balkans in the 1990s. The only solu- tion to peace in the region was said by summer 1999 to be a thorough program of "de-Nazification" and the continued denial of aid until Serbs began openly to acknowledge that guilt.

Is There a Model?

The unexpected and horrific violence of the Yugoslav wars so shattered the optimism that first accompanied the end of the Cold War in Europe that they had unusually great influence on policy thinking and expecta- tions for the future. It is therefore particularly important to get the story of the Serb case right. Anomalies that contradict the conventional wis- dom should not be swept aside as inconsequential but made more promi- nent, as a necessary check against the costs, and the possibility, of error.

The first such check is to ask what a diaspora population is. In the more classic sense of far-flung émigrés, the striking characteristic of the Yugoslav story is the contrast between Croat and Serb diasporas. The Croatian diaspora—members of whom live in the United States, Canada, Australia, Germany (originating as foreign workers in the 1960s), and elsewhere, and were conscious of their status as a dias- pora—was unusually active and influential in promoting and winning Croatian independence from Yugoslavia. Although for many of these Croats the campaign began immediately after (and in response to) the communist takeover in 1944, and included a period of intense activity in the second half of the 1960s and early 1970s, in the early to mid-1980s it included efforts to promote Franjo Tudjman and Croatian national rights. Tudjman became president of the Croatian federal republic in the first multiparty elections of April 1990, but his nationalist, indepen- dence platform won only 41.5 percent of the local vote—not an over- whelming mandate. This translated into a parliamentary majority only as a result of the election law written in 1989 by an overconfident League of Communists of Croatia. The role of the Croatian diaspora was critical, however, for it is difficult to imagine that electoral "vic- tory" without the $8 million sent to Tudjman and his party, the Croat- ian Democratic Union (HDZ, or "party of all Croats in the world"), by

Croatian émigrés when no other party in Croatia had any funds.[7] Albanians in the United States and in Switzerland and Germany (again as foreign workers originally) also contributed substantial monies and volunteers to the independence struggle of Albanians in Kosovo, particularly its armed phase.

In contrast, the Serb diaspora community—largely in the United States but also in Australia and Canada, and as foreign workers, like Croats, in Germany and Austria—played a negligible role in the Yugoslav collapse and the Serbian cause therein. Few émigrés returned and little money was sent either to the nationalist effort at home or the public relations campaigns abroad. In a brief period *after* the Yugoslav dissolution, several prominent émigré Serbs, including the crown prince, Alexander Karadjordjevich, a businessman in London with little knowledge of the Serbian language, and Milan Panić, a wealthy pharmaceuticals émigré in California, did become significantly involved in attempting to influence politics within Serbia, but they were far more circumspect in relations with Serbs outside Serbia in the new neighboring states.

If, however, by diaspora is meant transborder minorities *in the area*, and in the Yugoslav case, those living within the same state but in different federal units from those identified with their nation (Slovenes outside Slovenia, Croats outside Croatia, and so forth), then the role of diaspora Serbs historically "in Serbian and Yugoslav politics [has been] disproportionate to their numbers."[8] Proto-political activity of Serbs outside Serbia, as Serbs, became quite substantial during the 1980s, in the form of cultural and educational activities to revive a sense of what it was to be a Serb. Many of these activities were organized by Serbian intellectuals from Belgrade who were also promoting a national renaissance, in many instances (like Tudjman) as anticommunism. But, if one compares Serbs outside of Serbia to other "internal diasporas" within Yugoslavia (people living outside the republic of their nation), they were relative latecomers.

This was particularly evident once the political ferment of the 1980s moved toward the creation of political parties independent of the communist party. Of those that formed along ethnonational lines, for example, Franjo Tudjman did initial organizing for his nationalist party among Croat residents of the Serbian province of Vojvodina and of western Herzegovina in Bosnia and Herzegovina; Alija Izetbegović likewise began campaigning for his new Muslim party, the Party of Democratic Action (SDA), in an area of Serbia with a large Muslim population, the Sandžak. Muslims from the Sandžak (who preferred the label Bosniac by 1994) are prominent in Sarajevo politics and business, and many Bosniacs (Bosnian Muslims) speak hopefully of eventually uniting their new country with the Sandžak. Similarly, Croats from Herzegovina became increasingly dominant in Zagreb business and politics after Croatian independence, while Croats in Herzegovina and other parts of the western borderlands of Bosnia and Herzegovina were supported politically, financially, and militarily by Zagreb and Tudjman in their war against the Bosnian government and the SDA and even after the peace, and they still hoped in 1999 to unite with Croatia. Those who might be called "diaspora" Serbs, in Croatia and in Bosnia and Herzegovina, by contrast, formed their own political party, the Serb Democratic Party, not branches of a Belgrade party. It was the dominant Serbian party in these areas during the breakup of the country, but it was not the largest vote-getter. Serbs in Croatia voted overwhelmingly not for Serb "ethnic" parties but for the re-formed communist party, called the Party for Democratic Change (SDP). In Bosnia and Herzegovina, where 90 percent of the population voted for a national party in 1990, Serbs voted for ethnic parties, but that vote was spread among many Bosnian Serb parties, reflecting differences of political opinion and ideology within the community, not a nationalist vote per se. Only after 1991 did Serbian parties become politically involved among Serbs in Croatia and especially in Bosnia and Herzegovina.

In sum, while there is no doubt about the political, military, and economic support for Serbs in Croatia and Bosnia and Herzegovina from political parties and authorities in Belgrade, that relationship between diaspora and homeland capital was late in coming, when compared to other national groups in the former Yugoslavia. And the reverse relationship, the role of diaspora Serbs in the homeland capital of Belgrade, was insignificant compared to that of diaspora Croats and Bosniacs, respectively, in Zagreb and Sarajevo.

These facts—that the only relevant Serb "diaspora" for the question of violence in the former Yugoslavia was the "internal" diaspora of a federal system, and that these Serbs were not the only ethnonational groups there to behave as diasporas of their future homelands once Yugoslavia broke apart—suggest a second crucial anomaly of this "model." When diaspora populations are transborder minorities, the real issue at stake is the location of a political border. They are diaspora not by choice of emigration but by virtue of a political decision, over which they had no influence, to draw a state border in a way that leaves them outside the state of their national group.

The creation of Yugoslavia after World War I by the great powers convened at Versailles in 1918 gathered into one state most of the people in the area of southeastern Europe who were south Slavs, with the exception of Bulgarians.[9] They had lived under different imperial regimes (Byzantine, Ottoman, Habsburg [Austria-Hungary after 1867], and Venetian) and had followed very different political trajectories toward common citizenship in Yugoslavia, but their distinct national histories and cultures were joined into one, unitary state. Some Slovenes and Croats were left outside the country, in Austria and Italy, while some Macedonians found themselves in Greece, Bulgaria, or Albania. The new Yugoslav border also created many non–south Slav diasporas within the country, such as Albanians, Italians, Hungarians, Turks, and Romanians. After World War II, the new Communist regime restructured the country into a federation that recognized the distinctness of these south Slav peoples and drew internal borders along "national" lines that, reflecting the motley pattern of settlement within the country if ethnicity is considered, added to the number of people living outside their home state although still within the same country. The largest such group was Serbs. By the census of 1991, when these internal borders were transformed into international borders, about 25 percent of the Serb population in Yugoslavia did not live in the Serbian republic: They numbered at least 2.5 million out of 8.5 million Serbs, not including those who chose the "Yugoslav" identity (700,400 in total in 1991) instead.[10] The constitutional order of federal Yugoslavia recognized the rights of national self-determination of all of its six constituent, south Slav nations, regardless of the divisions imposed by these internal borders; but once the country began to head toward dissolution into separate nation-states, the burning issues became the fact of these borders, where they had been drawn in 1945, and what it might mean to be a Serb in a non-Serb state.

Thus the second check on this model is that the Serb case is not an issue of Serbs per se but of the breakup of the country, the political decisions made about where the borders of the new states would be, and the nature of citizenship rights and national identity in these new states. International norms and actors play a significant part in this aspect of the story, for it is an international decision to recognize new states and their borders. Had the internal, federal borders been drawn differently in 1945, or redrawn in 1991, there would not have been a substantial Serb diaspora contiguous to Serbia or any violence contesting those borders. This is why the idea of a diaspora in Eastern Europe is better stated as one of transborder minorities—people trapped on the other side of a border that could have been drawn differently, and their status as an ethnic minority in a state claiming legitimacy on the basis of the majority nation.[11]

The third check on this conventional wisdom—that the Serbs are analogous to the Third Reich, where an aggressive, expansionist leader

in the homeland capital links up with, and is even propelled by, diaspora Serbs to break up a state and foment war to create a Greater
Serbia—is provided by the great variety of behavior among Serbs themselves in this internal Yugoslav diaspora. In both the Croatian and the
Bosnian wars, the violence was concentrated for the most part in border
areas and in ethnically mixed communities. More than two-thirds of the
Serb population of Croatia remained loyal to Croatia as it was becoming independent and remained in place to take out Croatian citizenship.
Of the third who lived in or fled to the contested border areas, many
fled to Serbia rather than remain a minority, yet even the majority of
those tried to stay but were expelled by Croatian military force in 1995.
The Serb population of Croatia had been reduced by death, emigration,
or expulsion from 12 percent in 1991 to 3 percent in 1995. How many
Serbs in Bosnia and Herzegovina out of the 33 percent of the prewar
population remained loyal to the new leadership of Bosnia and Herzegovina is difficult to assess. We do know that about 17 percent remained
in "non-Serb" areas (controlled by and contested between Bosnian
Muslims and Bosnian Croats) at the time of the Washington Agreement
of March 1994, even though this agreement created a federation
between these two Bosnian nations as an alliance against Bosnian Serbs
and denied Serbs their prewar status as a constituent nation in their
own country. This Serb minority in the federation was equal to the proportion of the entire prewar Bosnian population who identified themselves as Croats. And although during the war many Serbs fled these
areas for regions controlled by the Bosnian Serb army or to Serbia itself,
a very large percentage did not leave "federation" territory until the
Dayton peace agreement of November 1995 acknowledged the tripar-
tite division of Bosnia and Herzegovina according to "ethnonational
identity." Similarly in Macedonia, the Serb community was internally
split between a larger part that remained loyal to Macedonia and a
much smaller part, largely from an area bordering Serbia, that tried
repeatedly to gain attention from politicians in Serbia (including
Milošević) to come to their aid as an endangered diaspora, without success. Nearly all chose Macedonian citizenship, moreover.

A majority of Serbs outside Serbia, in other words, did not become
mobilized under the nationalist banner to commit violence. An individual or family decision to stay and become a minority in a non-Serb
state, to flee to Serbia or abroad, or to fight, moreover, was made in
response to an environment shaped by others—most important, shaped
by what the government of the new state signaled about the prospects
as a Serb in a non-Serb state. As Rogers Brubaker argues, the role of
diaspora is not dyadic, between the diaspora and its homeland state,

but triadic, between the diaspora and the nationalizing state in which its members unwittingly find themselves as new citizens, and between the diaspora and a homeland state with some interests (whether of state or nation is not foreseeable) in their fate.[12] Because the issue of minority rights has been a prominent feature of European security regimes throughout the twentieth century, beginning with the post–World War I settlements that created national states out of the dissolving multinational empires, this, like the issue of borders, is also subject to outside influence and policy.

More than 600,000 Serbs, furthermore, chose to flee instead to Serbia or Montenegro. There they were received in private homes rather than being housed in camps, as were Bosnian Croats in Croatia, for example. Nonetheless, they were classified as refugees (as citizens from Croatia or from Bosnia and Herzegovina),[13] and as economic hardship grew more severe in Serbia, their hosts increasingly treated them as a burden, considering them as distant kin, perhaps, but not Serbian Serbs.[14] The Serbian leaders who claimed the mantle of Serb protectors did little or nothing to provide for them or make them feel welcome in Serbia. Of the Serbs expelled from Croatia in 1995, the 150,000 to 200,000 who went across the river to Bosnia remain stateless, with no prospects of citizenship in the Serb Republic of Bosnia and Herzegovina. The reason is that international authorities support the wishes of the government in Sarajevo, against that of leaders in the Serb entity in Bosnia, to deny them the rights to Bosnian citizenship that might increase Serb numbers proportionally. International efforts instead aim (unsuccessfully by late 1999) at persuading Croatia to allow Serbs to return to their homes and minority status there. Moreover, many hundreds of thousands (the numbers remain imprecise) of Serbs from Serbia also fled their homeland during the wars to go abroad rather than be drafted to fight for Serbs in Croatia or Bosnia and Herzegovina. Most striking of all perhaps is the treatment of Serbs from Kosovo, who are alleged to have started the problem in the first place. When a NATO bombing campaign against Yugoslavia in March–June 1999, following through to the letter in policy and rhetoric on the conventional wisdom regarding Serbs and Milošević, and a subsequent international protectorate in Kosovo led to the flight, or expulsion, of nearly all of Kosovo's Serbs, these Serbs felt compelled at the start to hide their presence in Serbia proper. If discovered, they were refused any rights to a job, their pension, or residence as a government policy to force them to return to Kosovo.

The case of the Serbs, in sum, cannot be explained by simple and uncritical reference to an analogy with post–World War I Germany. Instead, the explanation must focus on the causes of the country's breakup, and the reasons why some Serbs outside of Serbia were willing to risk their lives and fight so as *not to become a diaspora* after the loss of Yugoslavia. These reasons include the mobilizing role of national ideology, the political struggle over the national question within and between the Yugoslav republics at issue, the characteristics of those who did fight, and, not least, the role of international actors and decisions.

The Breakup of Yugoslavia

In the course of the 1980s, the Yugoslav socialist political and economic system was heading toward collapse.[15] The primary cause was a balance-of-payments and foreign debt crisis that was in turn a result of dramatic external shocks to the country's current account and the conditions for financing the trade deficit. The fact that a foreign debt crisis was general in Eastern Europe and Latin America at the time confirms the existence of some external causes, but the consequences were domestic. Throughout Eastern Europe, the final result was the same—the end of the socialist system. But while elsewhere socialism in time was replaced by market economies and parliamentary democracy, its demise in Yugoslavia brought an end to the country itself. The violence that accompanied its dissolution—in contrast, for example, to the breakup of Czechoslovakia—is easily explained as a contest over where the new borders of the successor states would be; but why the country did dissolve, and why there was such a contest over borders, requires a much deeper understanding of the reform process, the constitutional system that required change, and the way that the opposing sides of the political contest over reform used cultural idioms in their fight and made the contest into a "national question."

The remedy proposed by domestic economists and required by the International Monetary Fund (IMF) in exchange for credits in 1982 was a harsh austerity program of domestic contraction and export promotion, accompanied by a decade-long series of economic and political reforms. While the critical reform was liberalization of foreign trade and domestic prices, the creation of institutions necessary to implement such a policy mandated a radical change in the locus of political power over domestic and foreign currency. This was not the first IMF-financed effort to reform the Yugoslav socialist economy, but in all previous programs, the advice had been to decentralize. In line with a Marxist ideological commitment to the withering away of the repressive and extractive state, the communist leadership had concurred and progressively decentralized—and socialized (moving from state to social ownership and parastatal associations)—decision-making on monetary, fiscal, developmental, and social policy. This entailed repeated constitutional amendment of the relationship between the federal government and the republics. The result, by the early 1980s when the debt crisis hit, was a central government with almost no authority over the economy and unable to act without the consent of all the republics. Decentralization had gone too far, the market promoters concluded. A true central bank had to be created; authority over monetary aggregates, debt repayment, and foreign exchange policy had to be reunified; barriers to the flow of capital and labor across republics had to be removed; and a state administration capable of performing the functions necessary to an open, market economy had to be restored.

The resulting reform program, beginning with the long-term stabilization program for debt repayment, restoring growth, and fighting inflation that was adopted by parliament in 1982, triggered three destabilizing political shocks to the Yugoslav system.

The first shock was the challenge to revise the 1974 constitution, the fourth constitution for Yugoslavia since 1945. Each new constitution was a type of way-station in which intervening amendments to the previous constitution were codified before a new process began. Each new constitution had been hotly contested because each one invariably raised the most neuralgic issue of the Yugoslav state since 1919: how to accommodate, through constitutional mechanisms, the rights and interests of the separate nations that had come together to form one country. The first Yugoslavia, created at the Versailles conference, had a unitary constitution. The legitimating ideology of this new state—Yugoslavism—was a Croatian idea (that the three south Slav peoples—Slovenes, Croats, and Serbs—were one, "triune" people). The union of these three was the choice not of Serbs but of Slovenes and Croats from the defeated Habsburg Empire who saw the new state as their means of national survival over absorption into Italy or Austria. (Serbs had been fighting for their own national state.) But the decision by the Versailles powers to institute a unitary constitution in 1919 under a Serbian king and army was opposed by the Slovene and Croatian political elite. Repeated administrative reforms to accommodate regional and cultural differences within a unitary constitution[16] only led Croatian leaders, in particular, to push harder for a federal constitution and to view the government in Belgrade as anti-Croat. The constitutional fight also dominated factional politics within the Yugoslav communist party, the League of Communists, which ousted a Serb leader in 1928 and committed its revolutionary platform, under Croat and Slovene leadership, to a federal constitution and a fight against "Great Serb hegemony."

Croats won an exception to the constitution in 1939, in a pact between a Serbian prime minister and the leading Croatian party politician, that gave them autonomy over territories they claimed historically, but the Axis invasions in 1941 splintered the country into separate territories and competing local armies. The Communist-led Partisan forces created a government by 1943, called the Anti-Fascist Council for National Liberation of Yugoslavia (AVNOJ, in Serbo-Croatian), and announced their commitment to a postwar republic and federal constitution. Although Serbs—particularly but not only from Croatian and Bosnian areas—were among the most numerous contingents of the Partisan forces, the majority of the population in Serbia tended to support the fighting units of the Royal Army, which called themselves Chetniks and which rebuffed, under their leader, Colonel Draža Mihailović, repeated offers by the Partisan leader, Josip Broz Tito, to form a wartime alliance. For these average Serbs who did not join the Partisans, the abolition of the monarchy in 1943, the execution of Mihailović in 1945, and the defeat of the Serbian political parties in communist-controlled elections in 1947 left a mark, to be exploited only 25 to 35 years later, that the bittersweet victory in 1918 had been overturned and that the purpose of the 1943 Communist ("AVNOJ") constitution and its federal boundaries was a form of revenge aimed at weakening the Serbs.

As a socialist system with a single ruling party, the effective political units of the second Yugoslavia were not political parties but the governmental units of this federation—the republics and the local organs of power called municipalities. The republics were said, moreover, to recognize the rights of national self-determination of the country's five constituent peoples—Croats, Macedonians, Montenegrins, Serbs, and Slovenes. A sixth nation—Muslims—was recognized in 1968. Therefore, by 1952 all matters of culture and education were assigned to the republics, and the first of the series of trade-oriented, decentralizing reforms in 1949 to 1952 made concrete the fiscal federalism written into the 1945 constitution.[17] By 1974 (after the adoption of a constitution that only codified the amendments to the 1963 constitution adopted during 1967 to 1971), the balance of power lay with the republics, and the federal government had responsibility only for the common defense, veterans, setting guidelines on foreign trade–oriented investment policy, legislating standards for wage and labor policies in the separate republics, and managing the federal fund for regional development, which taxed the wealthier northern republics for redistribution to the south.

The economic reform required to obtain IMF loans and restore foreign credibility in the Yugoslav economy (when 90 percent of industry depended on imports at some stage of production) went for the jugular of the Yugoslav political system. The reformers insisted that the country could not perform effectively in foreign markets if market relations did not also apply at home. Liberalization required the re-creation of a single market over the entire Yugoslav area, and this in turn required the reunification of monetary and foreign exchange policy, including the administrative apparatus necessary to such policy. The level of decentralization achieved by the mid-1970s, however, meant that the reform was a direct attack on the economic power of the republican governments—or fiefdoms, as they were called colloquially. Because the politics of the socialist system was a contest over money and economic assets among the republics (as party-governments), the reform could not avoid attacking the key bases of political power in the country as well. And in sharp contrast to the more centralized systems of Eastern Europe, or to the imperial basis of the Soviet state and Russia's role in it, the Yugoslav federal system was a delicate although frequently shifting balance among its politically equal nations. An attack on the power of the republics and their mutual relations at the federal level could not escape the "national question."

The particular reforms required in the 1980s were most threatening to the wealthier regions. Opposition was strongest from Slovenia but also from Vojvodina and Croatia, particularly where local industries had successful exports to hard-currency markets, earning the foreign exchange necessary to a heavily import-dependent economy and republic-based growth. Although their attack was on the market reform, their arguments were phrased in the neoliberalism then dominant in the West. The main obstacle to economic growth, they said, was not the chaos of the banking system but the federal policies of redistribution. Thus, a better reform would go the rest of the way toward dismantling the federal government. Those who believed in the re-creation of a single market were "unitarists" as well as "federalists," they said, reviving memories of interwar constitutional debates to signal that this was no economic reform but a campaign by those who would destroy the federal system, including parliamentary supremacy (where the republican factions dominated and were not required to form a common consensus as in the executive branch) and thus "national rights." By using the term "unitarism"—referring to the unitary constitution of the interwar kingdom—moreover, they cast the center-republic fight in ethnonational terms. They implied that this new threat from "Belgrade" was from Serbs. (Such obfuscation always was possible because Belgrade was the capital of both the federation and the Serbian republic.) Their alternatives were the decentralized status quo or confederation.

For the Serbian government and other "federalists" (including, e.g., many Slovene economists), the historical context of this emerging contest over economic reform was more immediate: the 1974 constitution, which to them had been disastrous for Yugoslavia. It was the culmination of a constitutional fight over an earlier market reform, introduced between 1958 and 1965 to meet the conditions of membership in the General Agreement on Tariffs and Trade (GATT), which also pitted proponents of decentralization and republican rights against proponents of a single market and liberal economy. In that reform, the decentralizers won and the market lost, for the 1974 constitution introduced a system of contractual bargaining among economic (public sector) actors in its place. Most significantly for Serbia, which was the only republic with autonomous provinces, this governmental decentralization applied to all federal units. Vojvodina and Kosovo were given all the powers of republics—separate legislatures, executives, and fiscal authority, and representation as equal partners in federal bodies—except in name. Serbia was thus, de facto, reduced to "inner Serbia," without its provinces and without even the same right to veto legislation in Vojvodina and Kosovo that provincial authorities had regarding legislation in Serbia and at the federal level. Second, the contest over market reform in the 1960s had given rise in Croatia to a nationalist movement. In it republican leaders demanded greater rights for the republic over the proportion of foreign currency earnings of "their enterprises" that they could retain in Croatia, using Croatian cultural associations and local party committees of Croatian nationalists in ethnically mixed communities to pressure federal authorities. In later stages of the movement, leaders went so far as to demand a separate foreign policy and representation in the United Nations, on the model of Ukraine. Slovene authorities, in fact, stopped short of pushing republican rights to the maximum in 1970–71 when they saw the effects in Croatia, but it was only the federal army and its repeated entreaties to President Tito about the serious threat of this Croatian populist "mass movement" (*Maspok*) of 1967 to 1971 to the very existence of Yugoslavia that brought an end to Croatian demands in December 1971. The standard Titoist solution was to require the Croatian republican leadership to resign, replacing them with antinationalist conservatives (including some Serbs), and then to balance this demand by purging the leadership of the Serbian party, who were highly regarded political liberals in Serbia, as threats to the communist system. For Serbs, this double loss—of the liberal reform and of their liberal leaders and managers—was adding insult to injury after a prominent feature of the Croatian events was explicit nationalist attacks, both rhetorical and physical, on Serbs and on the coexistence of

Serbs and Croats in mixed communities in Croatia. Within this political balancing act, Tito actually proceeded with economic reforms favoring the republics: granting Croatian demands for higher retention quotas of "its" foreign currency earnings and forcing the resignation of the market-oriented Serbian managerial elite, both in Serbia and in other republics (such as Croatian tourist areas) where market opportunities for investment had been followed.

The political legacy of the 1974 constitution and the constitutional amendments of 1967 to 1971 that it codified was resentment in both Croatia (including a political interpretation, which was factually incorrect, of republican investment and employment policy aimed at restoring the injured confidence of the Serb minority in Croatia) and Serbia (including a political interpretation of the 1974 constitution as an explicit continuation of the effort to weaken Serbs since 1943). In Croatian political life, resentment at the purge of nationalist liberals produced a "great silence," but in Serbia resentment at the purge of liberals and managers who had not been nationalists produced a core of writers, professors, and economists in Belgrade who increasingly saw federal policy in nationalist terms, as anti-Serb, and began to say so. Thus, when Slovene and Croat politicians began to use anti-Serbian rhetoric in their campaign against the 1980 reforms aimed at revising the 1974 constitution, Serb intellectuals already were engaged in a campaign to change the constitution for national reasons.

Two events at the time of the global debt crisis, which first hit Yugoslavia in 1979, were critical to the path of this emerging contest over economic and political reform in the 1980s. In May 1980 President Tito died. And in March 1981 a student riot against bad food in the cafeteria at the University of Pristina, the capital of the Albanian-majority Serbian province of Kosovo, escalated unexpectedly into street demonstrations demanding a separate republic, on the grounds that Albanians were a majority (77.5 percent in 1981) in the province and deserved full rights to national self-determination.

Tito's death opened the floodgates that had checked political criticism—violating taboos, reassessing history, challenging the system. By the mid-1980s substantial discontent with the economic crisis, severe unemployment, rising inflation, and political stagnation had given rise to explicitly anticommunist criticism from all quarters, from Slovene youth to Serbian intellectuals. Among the angry slogans of this intellectual ferment in Belgrade was the denunciation of "Tito's borders," the borders of AVNOJ, that had cut historical Serbia down into a small republic, internally divided with two autonomous provinces, and with 40 percent of the Serb population in other republics[18] but with no protection as minorities equivalent to the autonomy granted to minorities in Serbia. The long-held but unspoken belief that Tito's Yugoslavia had been created on the principle that "a weak Serbia means a strong Yugoslavia" began to be expressed openly. At the same time, the level of decentralization had gone so far that some arbiter for republican competition and disputes was needed. The decision-making rules at the federal level of equal representation and consensus were recipes for stalemate. The one unified federal institution—the armed forces—had a constitutional obligation to safeguard the integrity of the socialist system, but it reported to the collective presidency, which Tito had created to replace him and which was composed of representatives of each of the eight federal units plus the armed forces. Without Tito's authority, the army could no longer perform the protective role it had played in 1971 when its warnings about developments in Croatia prevented the independence aspirations of republican leaders from threatening the very integrity of the state.

This absence of authority committed to the country as a whole also made the second event—the demonstrations in Kosovo—far more threatening to the country's integrity than they seemed on the surface. The demand, in effect, to secede from Serbia—to be "masters in their own house"—raised the question of borders for the first time since the Croatian events of 1967 to 1971, provoking concern throughout the country over the status of the internal borders. The greatest reaction was in neighboring Macedonia, where one-third of a large Albanian minority was concentrated territorially and bordered Kosovo. But even in Slovenia, the demand for recognition of national rights on the basis of *numbers* (the Albanians were not south Slavs and none of the non–south Slav citizens of Yugoslavia had a constitutional right to self-determination) revived periodic concern about the fate of the smaller nations in Yugoslavia. Moreover, the League of Communists leadership reacted immediately to the demands as "counterrevolutionary" and imposed martial law. Although all republican leaderships voted to approve such a policy, the decision to impose martial law also had a more insidious effect by raising doubts about the use of the army to restore internal order and therefore about the powers of the federal government to order martial law. Finally, the protest in Kosovo fed directly into the debate within Serbia proper over the 1974 constitution, the place of Serbia in the federation, the fragmentation of Serbs by the federal borders, and the formidable problem of governance that the extensive provincial autonomy of Vojvodina and Kosovo presented to republican authorities. There were few issues more likely to act as a lightning rod of Serbian nationalism, moreover, than Kosovo because of its central role in the historical development of Serbian national consciousness and identity.[19]

The first political shock—that the relation between the federal and republican governments set out in the 1974 constitution be revised fundamentally in the interest of economic reform and debt repayment— pushed the system toward polarization between factions favoring a confederal and those a federal concept of the state, with ever more open innuendos drawn from history about it being a contest between federalist ("unitarist") Serbs seeking to dominate the country in the absence of Tito and confederalists standing up for their national rights. The second political shock made the contest even worse. The decade-long austerity program and deflationary approach to economic revival mandated by the IMF forced cuts in public expenditures that placed on the public agenda the question of what interests the people (and peoples) of Yugoslavia had in common and wanted to preserve through a common state. What should federal revenues (and the taxpayers in the republics) finance, and what should be cut or be handed to the republics?

In the past, major differences on economic policy among the republics had been overridden and consensus found by compensating financially those republics that did not agree with the winning decision. But the banking reform and restrictive policy required by the IMF conditionality program eliminated this mechanism of maintaining harmony among republican leaders. The huge new investments needed in each republic to reorient its industries toward exports in Western markets, moreover, put an additional burden on republican coffers. The economic differences among them—in what they produced, in the size of the population that needed budgetary assistance (e.g., pensioners, the unemployed, the farming population), and in their dependence on federal aid for development or budgetary transfers—became an increasingly powerful motor of political conflict. While the confederalist camp protested the drain on members' incomes for federal taxes by claiming that the poorer republics were "less productive" and should not be handed money they would only waste, the poorer republics pointed to the federal subsidies to exporters and communications with Western markets that favored the wealthier regions and that kept them wealthy. In time the rich simply stopped paying federal taxes, and in Slovenia a pacifist and then a nationalist campaign against the federal army added a political argument to the assertion of their economic interests and a focus for their larger, confederalist agenda, with its historical echoes of attacks on Serbs.

Serbian authorities, however, faced a particularly difficult situation in the 1980s. Tax rates for federal redistribution were assessed on economic indicators of a republic: Were they above or below countrywide averages? Serbia was classified, along with Slovenia and Croatia, as a wealthier republic that paid taxes accordingly, but by the 1980s its economic growth aggregates were all below average. Its investments in the 1970s had been oriented more toward Eastern markets and lower value-added goods (particularly textiles and agricultural products), so a fundamental restructuring of its productive activities was required to adjust to the new conditions. Unemployment in 1982 was at 17 percent and rising, and a new wave of immigration to Belgrade was predicted from the rural and poorer areas of Serbia proper and also from poorer Serb communities in Bosnia-Herzegovina and Montenegro; Serbia also had a disproportionately high number of citizens—pensioners, farmers, and unemployed with rights to welfare or income supplements—dependent for their subsistence on public transfers—the same government budgets (in this case, the republic's) that had to be cut under the new orthodoxy. The republic was taxed as a "northerner" but had the problems of a "southerner." It needed resources from a functioning federal government for investment and budgetary supplements, the benefits of a market economy, and a share of the developmental aid sent to the republic that went exclusively to the provincial authorities in Kosovo.

Despite the purge of the liberal faction of the Serbian party in 1972, 1980s party leadership was dominated by what would have been called liberals at the time: pro-federalist economic reformers, who gave priority to market reform and believed that economic growth would reduce political conflicts. This leadership also knew that if it confronted the Kosovo problem directly, it would be portrayed as anti-Albanian, a situation that would open it up to attack from the federal party for violating the constitutional prohibition (Article 170/3) against "incitement of national, racial, or religious hatred and intolerance." It also would feed the simmering nationalism of intellectuals' discontent in Serbia, which was ever more blatantly anticommunist. The leadership's choice was to try to toe a middle line and ignore the nationalist aspects of the Kosovo conflict, but the result was to provide, in the eyes of many Serbs, yet one more example of an indifferent ruling party that swept grievances under the rug and was responsive to no one.

By 1985–86, Serbs and Montenegrins in Kosovo, who had been trying to get attention for their complaints of discrimination against them and pressure to leave the province, under majority-Albanian rule since 1974, decided to take their grievances to higher authorities. In a series of petitions, local demonstrations, and delegations to the republican parliament in Belgrade, they set off a spiral of protest and reaction. Federal authorities first called their petition a provocation and ordered arrests; Serbs countered with new protests; and Albanian authorities in Kosovo, who imagined they were facing an insurgent minority rebellion, responded with repression which appeared to justify Serbs' complaints and provoked a new cycle of protest and reaction. For nationalist intellectuals in Serbia who believed that Serbs were victimized by the Titoist system, the plight of minority Serbs in Kosovo was too useful an instance of endangered Serb rights to ignore. Academicians—members elected to the Serbian Academy of Sciences and Arts (SANU)—had been meeting since early 1982 to analyze the causes of and remedies for the economic and political crisis in the country. By 1986 those critics of a nationalist persuasion had captured the group, and a draft memorandum on the crisis was leaked to newspapers in September, apparently by members of the communist party aiming to fight it through public exposure. Yet, in the context of rising nationalism in the other republics, the anti-Serb rhetoric of the western republics in the reform debate, the Kosovo turmoil, and growing economic troubles in Serbia, their strategy backfired by giving legitimacy to the strand of Serbian nationalism that included a concern with Serbs outside Serbia proper. The language of the memorandum is notable for its references to "Serbs at risk"—what a Serbian critic has called an "aggressive self-pity"—and the problem of borders.[20] The memorandum linked accusations of the damage caused by "Tito's borders" to Serbian economic and cultural development to claims of a "Serbian Holocaust" and "genocide against the Serbs." Its remedy for reversing the "injustice" of borders that had put Serbs at risk not only in Kosovo but also in Croatia and in Bosnia: Unite all Serbs in one state.

The academicians were locally influential but small in number, and they had no political vehicle; the mass media was, after all, controlled by the state.[21] Only through the conjunction of the protests of minority Serbs in Kosovo and a generational change in the Serbian party did their memorandum get any attention at all, and the resulting political link was created not by a concern for border revision but rather by the economic crisis and the agenda of market reform, beginning with the need to restore monetary control and governing capacity within the republic to Belgrade authorities. Quite by chance, the Serbian president, Ivan Stambolić, decided in April 1987 to send his protégé, party leader Slobodan Milošević, to Kosovo in his place, to listen once more to Serb demands for protection of their human rights. Instead of a delegation, a chanting crowd of 15,000 met Milošević; chaos ensued, the police responded with their batons, and the crowd reacted by pelting stones. Milošević succeeded in reimposing the normal political rite, having the protesting Serbs select representatives for a closed meeting in which he was regaled with grievances all night long. But he also sought to calm the crowd with an expression of outraged sympathy.[22] Saying "Nobody must ever again dare to beat this people!" he appeared to accept the obligation to protect Serb minority rights and their claim to the land, abandoning the technocratic language of the party leadership and its political silence at growing grievances:

> You should stay here. This is your land. These are your houses. Your meadows and gardens. Your memories. You shouldn't abandon your land just because it's difficult to live, because you are pressured by injustice and degradation. It was never part of the Serbian and Montenegrin character to give up in the face of obstacles, to demobilize when it's time to fight. You should stay here for the sake of your ancestors and descendants. Otherwise your ancestors would be defiled and descendants disappointed. But I don't suggest that you stay, endure, and tolerate a situation you're not satisfied with. On the contrary, you should change it with the rest of the progressive people here, in Serbia and in Yugoslavia.[23]

Laura Silber and Alan Little, journalists who have written one of the most widely read analyses of the Yugoslav collapse, shaping the conventional wisdom, argue that, with this speech, Milošević "donned the mantle of protector of all Serbs."[24] There is little evidence for what he thought about what the nationalists call "Serb lands." What is clear is the clarion call to defend Kosovo as part of Serbia and as an issue of borders—as he said in another infamous speech in April 1991, borders are "essential questions of state. And, borders, as you know, are always dictated by the strong, not by the weak"—and also his use of Serb cultural idioms for political purpose (witness his references to land, memory, injustice, struggle, and ancestors in the speech quoted above).

Apparently emboldened by the reaction to his speech to the Kosovo crowd, Milošević went on by September 1987 to engineer an inner-party coup against the old guard (including his mentor, Stambolić), then to purge the mass media in Serbia of his opponents. By December he was president of the Serbian party, and he began exploiting or mobilizing his own mass rallies as the means of breaking the political deadlock in the country. During 1988 weekly "meetings of truth" were organized by Kosovo Serbs in Belgrade and in Novi Sad, the capital of Vojvodina, to pressure for the resignation of the Vojvodina government, which had been so important a player in the antifederalist coalition and in vetoing policies preferred by the leadership in Belgrade. What Milošević came to call their "antibureaucratic revolution" used protests by steel workers and miners threatened with unemployment in neighboring Montenegro (where about 50 percent of the population identify as Serbs) to follow his example in 1989: force the resignation of the government and replace it with leaders more in line with Serbian positions at the federal level. The result was to reduce the perceived disparity between Serb numbers and their institutional power by creating a voting coalition of four (out of eight) in federal bodies. Then in March 1989, to obtain parliamentary approval of a new republican constitution, Milošević exploited a strike of Albanian miners in Kosovo, who were protesting the replacement of their provincial leadership, and a burst of Serb outrage at Slovene leaders' accusations at a huge rally in support of the miners that their strike was a defense of "AVNOJ Yugoslavia" and that Serbia was now the enemy of Slovene democracy. The Serbian parliament approved a new republican constitution, and the extensive autonomy of the two provinces granted by the reviled 1974 constitution came to an end.

While some saw Milošević's actions as a juggernaut of populist fever mobilized in support of Serbian domination of Yugoslavia or its destruction in favor of a Greater Serbia, the actual results were fully within the constitutional order. They were remarkably similar in many aspects to the way that Croatian authorities, in 1968 to 1971, had used mass support to pressure the federal authorities for republican interests, defined nationally. Moreover, in this traditional battle of republican politicians over federal policy, Milošević's goals faced a formidable obstacle on the other size of the polarized divide, in the form of Slovene intransigence in defense of its perceived republican rights, also increasingly defined nationally. Until 1987 this intransigence had amounted simply to Slovene noncompliance with federal rules and regulations it considered contrary to Slovene interests, such as the lifting of limits on landholding, the wage controls of the stabilization package, the educational reform aimed at facilitating labor mobility and a countrywide core curriculum, and changes in financing the defense budget. But in October 1987, when Milošević was beginning his purge of the Serbian party, Slovenia voted to reject the IMF program; and in November its delegates left the federal parliament in opposition to the 29 constitutional amendments for economic reform, stopped paying into the special fund for Kosovo, and used the veto to defeat the IMF proposal for majority rule in federal decisions and a strengthened executive branch, arguing instead for continuing the rule of consensus and for parliamentary supremacy. By November 1988 Slovene authorities also used the excuse of popular protests in Slovenia to veto a countrywide referendum on the new federal constitution. In response to a more radical IMF program in 1988, it adopted a new republican constitution that effectively made the republic fully sovereign. By May 1989 (when Milošević was becoming president of Serbia), the Slovene leadership made clear that its goal was independence. By October this was formulated in an interim proposal, which the Croats also joined, that the country should become a confederation of independent states, linked only by a customs union but without a common defense, until such time as Slovenia was a member of the European Community (EC). Equally, if not more, radical were the reforms required by a 1988 IMF loan and a new federal prime minister committed to market reform: to reorganize the federal administration on the functional rather than the territorial principle and to adopt enterprise and labor legislation ending the socialist system.

The third destabilizing political shock to the system was the effect of the austerity program and the banking reform on republican finances. On top of the challenge to revise the 1974 constitution and its particular balance between republican and federal powers—and to do so in the context of an economic policy (federal budget cuts and export orientation westward) that raised intense conflicts of economic interest among the republics about those federal powers—the economic reform also reduced the means available to republican governments to finance social welfare and new investment. During the 1970s republican authorities were allowed to borrow abroad in capital markets; they also resorted to enterprise and banking debt to finance what was in effect deficit spending. Under the 1982 stabilization reforms, the resulting economic recession, and severe fiscal pressures, republican and local governments had to achieve solvency in other ways. The primary alternative to inflation and debt was to cut public employment and reduce the number of beneficiaries of social welfare and public programs. This was not the first time in postwar Yugoslavia that "downsizing" of the socialist commitment had been required by the needs of foreign trade and balance-of-payments deficits and debt, as translated into the borrowing terms of IMF conditionality. In the past the federal government always had made this adjustment by decreasing the number of people who remained in the protected public sector of employment and increasing those who were shunted, even if temporarily, to the private sector (private agriculture, crafts, household economies and dependencies, and unemployment).[25] The economic reform program of 1982 repeated this approach, but during the 1980s republics also began to make their own specific rationalizing decisions.

The first, and for a long time the only, republic to confront the employment/incomes trade-off of the anti-inflationary cuts was Slovenia. As the only republic with full employment, it faced a political decision quite different from that facing all other five republics: The issue was how to maintain or increase public expenditures and Slovene incomes under austerity, not how to avoid more unemployment. Early on Slovene planners began to be concerned about the economic and social costs of the labor they had imported from other republics, particularly from Bosnia and Herzegovina and from Kosovo, and about the exodus abroad of Slovene professionals and skilled laborers, who were attracted by higher wages, particularly to Austria in factories set up along the border for the purpose. Their solution was to send the Bosnians and Kosovo Albanians home, on the grounds that Slovene cultural distinctiveness was at risk from non-Slovene speakers with high birth rates, and to ignore the federal wage controls so as to attract Slovenes back home. This "ethnicization" of the labor force in one republic never had a planned equivalent elsewhere, but the economic crisis triggered by the balance-of-payments deficit and foreign debt crisis did give rise in other republics to more spontaneous equivalents: for example, scapegoating and a growing sentiment, particularly among nationalist youth, that jobs should be reserved for certain groups, such as ethnically Croatian males in Croatia, where nationalist gangs were particularly vociferous against minorities and women. The fright caused by the Albanian demands in Kosovo led to restrictions on Albanian civil rights in Macedonia, and in Bosnia and Herzegovina political dissidents often were charged with nationalist tendencies, leading many to flee to other republics, particularly to Serbia.

The critical moment in this differentiation of citizens' rights according to national identity, in a system that had prided itself on formal guarantees of equality among citizens (including as members of national groups), came with the revisions of the republican constitutions in 1989, revisions that all republics were required to make to bring their constitutions into agreement with the proposed changes to the federal constitution. The changes in the Serbian and Slovene constitutions have been mentioned already. In Croatia and Macedonia the changes were also profound: Both changed their preambles, as did Slovenia, to declare that the sovereignty of their republics resided in the majority nation—the Croatian, Macedonian, or Slovene people. This implied second-class citizenship for residents from other constituent nations, no matter for how many generations they had been there; their national rights of self-determination were demoted to the status of cultural rights of minorities. What Croatia and Macedonia did was to establish the Slovene model where Slovene conditions of ethnic homogeneity did not exist. By implying that each republic was a national unit, when in fact the borders of the republics were not congruent with the national distribution of the population, the three parliaments were creating internal diasporas. And they were doing so in places where the diasporas formed a territorially concentrated minority and could make the same claim as the Slovene government, namely that human rights and political freedoms for a nation could be guaranteed only by territorial sovereignty. The reaction followed logically: A series of demands for territorial autonomy (by groups of towns, areas of cities, regions, provinces) within republics began to unfold during 1990 and early 1991, from Serbs in different parts of Croatia; Hungarians in Vojvodina; Serbs, Croats, and Muslims each in different areas of Bosnia and Herzegovina; Italians and others in Istria (Croatia); Albanians in Macedonia and Kosovo; and so on.

This shift occurred prior to the democratic (multiparty) elections that took place between April 1990 in Slovenia and Croatia and November–December 1990 in the other four republics. By then political parties had formed in every republic appealing for votes on the basis of national identity. The Yugoslav League of Communists, which had stood for the equality of citizens, regardless of national identity or republican residence, had dissolved, and the federal reform legislation abolishing the system of individual security and social insurance of the socialist regime had been introduced.

The trigger destabilizing an equilibrium based on individuals' expectations about the political system in which they live, its protections, and their own survival is strikingly illustrated by the shift of public opinion in Bosnia and Herzegovina during 1990. In mid-1990 the Bosnian population "pronounced itself 74 per cent in favour of a ban on nationally or confessionally based parties," but "six months later, vote[d] in the same proportion for precisely such parties."[26] Pan-Bosnian parties representing economic interests (e.g., social democrats or liberals) and the Yugoslav political system (e.g., as the reform party of the prime minister) received less than 20 percent of the vote and parliamentary seats. These election results were a shock to many in Bosnia, who saw their republic as the most pro-Yugoslav of all, in part because the only sure guarantee of its multinational composition was a multinational Yugoslavia. The vast majority of Bosnian voters had clearly chosen not only to express their national identity politically but to see the protection of that identity and access to goods and services in national leaders and parties, not nonnational, republican or Yugoslav ones.

For Serbs outside Serbia, the election campaign of Franjo Tudjman in Croatia was particularly influential, for he waged an anticommunist campaign using anti-Serb slogans. He asserted that a vote for him and his party was a vote for "decommunization," which he specified as the removal of Serbs from all official and political posts. The majority of Serbs in Croatia actually voted for the reformed communists, under the new name Party for Democratic Change, not for Serb national parties, as later assertions about Serb nationalism would have predicted. Such a party to represent Serbs as Serbs was formed in the areas of ethnically mixed population along the border, but its fortunes rose only after the elections as a direct result of President Tudjman's policies toward Serbs, such as his decision that all Serbs in Croatia had to prove their loyalty by signing loyalty oaths, could no longer serve as members of police forces in border areas, and had to pay special taxes on homes in Croatia if their primary residence was elsewhere. (The Adriatic coast was a favorite place for vacation homes of many, including Serbs.)

During the 1980s the three destabilizing political shocks that were triggered by the economic crisis and particular market reforms required by two IMF conditionality packages led to increasing polarization on the very fundamentals of the political system, in a system still formally ruled by consensus; increasing nationalism in the political conflicts among and within republics; and increasing ethnicization of labor policies, citizenship rights, and political and partisan identities. The outcome of these developments was interrupted by a preemptive move in Slovenia. The manner in which the country dissolved, including the violence, cannot be understood, however, outside of the particular context in which it occurred.

Violence

The Slovenes followed through on their nationalist objective, despite the late-hour misgivings of many, and declared independence on June 25, 1991. Croatia followed—indeed rushed its actual parliamentary declaration so as to be first. As argued earlier, the collapse of Yugoslavia that this represented, and its particular form of collapse—into nationalist states—was not solely the work of a Slobodan Milošević or a Greater Serbia agenda. The shift from socialism to nationalism is not unique to Yugoslavia in the east European transitions,[27] and the causes of the Yugoslav collapse are far more complex, begin earlier than 1987, and are more political, in the sense of an interactive dynamic among political players in a serious contest over economic reform and constitutional change, than could be produced by the actions of one man or one nation. Nonetheless, external mediators who rushed to the scene in May and June 1991, particularly those representing the EC, Council of Europe, and Conference on Security and Cooperation in Europe, knew little of these developments and assumed that the country could break apart without undue trauma along the seams of its internal borders into "national states." Until April 1992 the dominant external actor, Germany, actually believed that the country could survive the independence of these two republics, breaking into three independent states—Slovenia, Croatia, and a rump Yugoslavia of the remaining four republics. The American view, which took precedence after Germany won its campaign to recognize Croatian independence in December 1991 and was shared by many Europeans, was that the country should break into six states, divided along the borders of the federal republics. (The American view was embodied in a declaration of the European parliament in March 1991, the EC peace plan of October 1992 for a comprehensive settlement of the dissolution, and the invitation to the remaining four republics to request recognition in December.) In either view, there was no reason for violence.

Conventional wisdom therefore blames the violence on the Serbs in Croatia during 1991 and the Serbs in Bosnia and Herzegovina beginning in March or April 1992 who refused to accept this fait accompli. Like the Serbs who found themselves an ever smaller and harassed minority under Albanian majority rule in Kosovo during the 1980s, these truly diaspora Serbs sought and received protection from Milošević's regime in Belgrade. (The term "diaspora" only applies once the borders of Croatia and of Bosnia and Herzegovina were internationally recognized and Serbs found themselves minorities there rather than in one state with other Serbs.) In these two cases, it led to war.

A complete history of the violence requires a more complex picture. For example, Slovene and Croatian preparations for independence included preparations for war. Slovenes and Croats secretly built up independent armies with both domestic and foreign arms and developed a public relations campaign in foreign capitals to promote the legitimacy of their cause. The prime minister and parliament[28] ordered the Yugoslav army to retake control of border posts on the international border (including the Ljubljana airport) after the Slovene national guard had replaced Yugoslav signs and flags with those of an independent Slovene state; most states would consider deploying the army a legitimate move against a rebel region. From all accounts, moreover, Slovenes were the first to fire—shooting down a federal army helicopter carrying food supplies and killing its crew.[29] Likewise in Croatia, the incidents of violence in the border region, in the Dalmatian hinterland around and north of Knin and in eastern Slavonia near Croatia's border with Serbia, preceded independence. It can be attributed as easily to the initiative of marauding Croatian youth against Serb families and businesses, to Croatian authorities who demanded that all Serbs in police forces be fired and dispossessed of their weapons (and sent militia to enforce its demand), and to the actions of right-wing Croatian paramilitaries aiming to accelerate the momentum for independence as it can be to the Serb citizens and paramilitaries who took up arms.[30] During the war, even the horror of the battle over the town of Vukovar, which the federal army finally leveled with artillery, had its beginnings in a deliberate and violent instigation by the Croatian minister of defense.[31] Who first began to arm in Bosnia and Herzegovina will remain a matter of bitter dispute for generations. The decision of Bosnian Serb leaders to go to war against Bosnian independence and to join a struggle for "uniting all Serb lands" followed a genuine effort at negotiation, under European sponsorship, which was interrupted by an American decision that recognition should occur immediately, despite Serb opposition. The Serb cause célèbre in Bosnia, a murderous attack on a Serbian wedding party in the heart of Sarajevo by a still-unknown assailant, had, like events in Croatia, been preceded by serious local violence in the west, north, and east of the country by paramilitary gangs from Serbia and from Croatia, by Bosnian Croat and Bosnian Muslim militia, and by the federal army as well as by Bosnian Serbs.

The point of these examples is not to absolve Serbs of responsibility but to seek understanding that will support the design of better foreign policy toward such cases in the future. Three variables are crucial for explaining the role of diaspora Serbs in the violence surrounding the breakup of Yugoslavia: the role of ideology, the role of social origin and of politics, and the role of foreign powers. To act politically as a Serb diaspora required, as does any collective action, an ideology. A national ideology is an ideology of statehood and citizenship, identifying whom one would fight for, what state one would defend or send one's children to defend, and why. A Serbian national ideology, which explains to individuals who identify as Serbs why they should act as members of the Serb nation, does exist. But not all Serbs chose to follow leaders who sought to mobilize their support behind that ideology; instead they chose their citizenship and state on other principles. As mentioned earlier, fewer than one-third of all Serbs in Croatia were in the area where violence occurred; and no studies have been done on how many of those were simply trapped and how many chose to fight, as Serbs. Similarly, at least 20 percent of all Serbs in Bosnia and Herzegovina, and surely many, many more (again, studies remain to be done), chose to remain behind Bosnian government lines, to fight in the Bosnian government army, or were expelled by force by non-Serbs into Serb-held areas. And in both Croatia and in Bosnia and Herzegovina, the choice of citizenship; loyalty to region, nation, or state; and violence was rarely an individual choice alone but one made in a political context, frequently by others or by circumstances outside a person's control. At the same time this political dynamic was internal to the Serb nation, between different strands of national ideology and different factions of Serbs, between Serbs who found themselves without a country (Yugoslavia) in which they could live as one nation and the leaders of the new states being formed where they lived, it also was shaped by foreign powers, which made critical decisions on borders and rights to self-determination in the course of the Yugoslav breakup that limited the choices available to many Serbs.

SERBIAN NATIONAL IDEOLOGY

What did it mean for Serbs to have their state collapse such that, unlike most Russians after 1991 or Hungarians after 1920, and Czechs or Slovaks in 1992, for example, some would go to war? Those who did fight fought behind a nineteenth-century banner of four Ss ("Samo Sloga Srb Spašava [only unity can save the Serbs]," usually appearing as four Cs, in the Cyrillic alphabet) and to create a state that would "unite all Serb lands." This nationalist goal had found one solution in Yugoslavism after 1918: that all Serbs and Serb lands could be united in one state called Yugoslavia. The end of Yugoslavia raised the question anew: What would replace it?

Historians trace the formation of a modern Serbian nation to the defeat of the medieval Serbian state by Turkish armies, over a series of battles between 1389 and 1459. Without a state to preserve Serbian culture and religion, and living as subjects (*raja*) under the millet system of Ottoman rule, which defined social status and political rights according to religion (each forming one millet) and granted substantial autonomy to these subject, non-Muslim millets, the leadership of the Serbian community passed to the church. The governance structure of the Orthodox Church, in contrast to Roman Catholicism, was national, and Serbs already had won recognition of an independent patriarchate in Constantinople by 1219. After the Ottoman conquest, church leaders began to promote a national ideology that sought redemption—national liberation from the occupying Turks, preservation of the Christian faith, and status reversal (back to ruler from *raja*)—through the reestablishment of an independent Serbian state. Memory of the lost glories of medieval statehood was propagated by the church hierarchy and by an oral tradition of epic poetry and its traveling (secular) practitioners (*guslari*, named after the one-stringed musical instrument, the *gusle*, with which they accompanied their poems) who glorified Serbian battles and heroes and remained active into the 1930s.[32]

Political independence became possible again when the Ottoman empire began to weaken in the late eighteenth century. The increasing repression of a declining imperial center, which imposed limits on local traders and higher taxes that were enforced by the garrisoned Janissary troops who had asserted increasing autonomy from Istanbul over their commands, led to a series of revolts by wealthy pig traders and peasants in central Serbia in 1804 to 1813 and in 1815 to 1829. Ideological leadership for these insurrections, however, came from the educated middle class across the imperial border in Habsburg Vojvodina. These diaspora Serbs had migrated in many great waves, fleeing Ottoman rule throughout the sixteenth, seventeenth, and eighteenth centuries, above all in the Great Migration of 1690 when the Serbian patriarch led his entire community north into southern Hungary, fleeing reprisals for Habsburg-instigated Christian uprisings. There he received, in compensation, church autonomy, privileges, and authority over Serbs.[33]

This difference between state-building rebels and nation-building ideologists created a significant tension between state and national interests that lasts to this day. The borders of the Serbian state that emerged in the course of the nineteenth century were drawn by successive rulers, with advice and aid from Polish and Czech nationalists who hoped that Serbia would lead the liberation of all Slavs, to maximize security against renewed invasion, and to make Serbia as large and militarily defensible as possible in the vise between Turkey and Austria-Hungary. The revolutionary ideology provided by these Habsburg Serbs (called *prečani*, meaning those on the other side of the border), however, was based on ethnicity—defined by religion (according to the church-based autonomy granted by the emperor) and language (the "national awakening" of Serbs occurred here, in southern Hungary, and included linguistic reformers such as Vuk Karadžić and Dositej Obradović in Novi Sad and Vienna)—to defend rights to religious and cultural autonomy that were losing out to official Hungarian and German expansion. The goal of these Habsburg Serbs, and the state boundaries that goal implied, was the unification of all Serbs, as defined by Orthodoxy and the Serbian language, into one state.

The Serbian rulers won full recognition of sovereignty in 1878 from the Congress of Berlin, but they lost Bosnia and Herzegovina, including access to Bosnia's substantial mineral wealth, which they claimed on demographic as well as historical grounds. The great powers made it a protectorate of Austria, which was intent on preventing Serbia from becoming a serious rival and Balkan power and on countering its ability to aid emancipation movements of south Slavs in the empire (primarily Croats and Slovenes). The failure of nationalists throughout the Balkan peninsula to complete the revolutions of the mid-nineteenth century led to a new stage in the relation between the new states and the people and territories that remained within imperial control (whether Habsburg or Ottoman). In the case of Serbia, the two strands of Serbian national ideology merged into a program for a Greater Serbia, transposed to Belgrade.

At the same time, however, the Serbian national movement was part of a larger arena of liberation movements, such as not only other Balkan peoples (Bulgarians, Greeks, Macedonians, Albanians, Croats, Slovenes) but also imperial peoples, such as the Young Turks and a Hungarian independence movement. While the consolidation of Serbian statehood shifted the balance of revolutionary leadership away from the Habsburg "diaspora" to Belgrade, therefore, a new division emerged within the ideology—between those who favored a Greater Serbia and those who aimed at broader south Slav liberation and some political arrangement unifying Serbs, Croats, Slovenes, and Bulgarians. These anti-imperial activities also interacted with broader European politics, in which the ambitions and alliances of the great powers in the Balkans were undergoing major shifts—with the exception of Austria, which remained consistently anti-Serbian.[34] Initiating a customs war with Serbia in 1906, which it lost, and then railway construction that provoked the opposition of the great powers, Austria responded to the growing revolutionary activity of youth in Bosnia and Herzegovina by annexing the province in 1908 and setting the stage for a truly bloody contest by 1914.

The complex revolutionary activities in the Balkans in the first decades of the twentieth century demonstrate the danger of any simple reading of national ideology. For example, the young revolutionaries in Bosnia and Herzegovina, who switched tactics in this period from uprisings to assassinations and terror, came from all national groups in the province, not just Serbs. They gained support from a secret military society in Belgrade, Union or Death, whose goals included the union of all Serbs, but official Belgrade was ambivalent about these Bosnian groups and played no hand (despite Austrian accusations) in the conspiratorial activities of the Black Hand (formally, Union or Death).[35] A national ideology is, instead, a repository of many themes, weighted by historical events but available for selection. Nevertheless, although the assassination in Sarajevo of the visiting Habsburg archduke, Franz Ferdinand, by a Serb rebel youth, Gavrilo Princip, was merely the spark of a great power war, it did much to implant in the minds of Europeans an image of dangerous and violent Serbs. Only one year after the relatively successful but bloody Balkan wars of 1912–13 over the statehood and boundaries of the Ottoman succession in the Balkans—Albania, Bulgaria, Greece, Montenegro, Serbia[36]—Serbs joined the world war on the side of the Allies and suffered casualties—from exposure, disease, or battle—among nearly half their male population.

The wars reinforced the dominant element of the church's ideology of nearly 500 years, which had been commemorated in 1889, when the 500th anniversary of the battle of Kosovo Plain on June 28 was declared an official day of remembrance,[37] and contributed to what sociologist Veljko Vujačić calls a "special psychology" of the nation: a "sense of historical mission, the emphasis on military valor and their special role in the state-building process, as well as in any situation of grave state crisis . . . [and a] sense of martyrdom at the hands of empires." The "costly road to independence" in the wars of 1912 to 1913 and 1914 to 1918, in which every Serbian family lost someone, made the "cult of strong statehood," the sense of a "common political destiny," and the martyrdom won by a "righteous struggle against tyranny" essential elements in Serbian political culture.[38]

The creation of the Yugoslav state at the end of World War I was the culmination of this state-creating and liberating national ideology and experience. It was a solution to the many conflicts over territory with other national movements in the area, which also were trying to create independent states, and the victory of the south Slav movement and the ideology of Yugoslavism—first developed by Croats in Austria-Hungary but championed as well by Serbs in Austria-Hungary—in the struggle against the Habsburgs. The creation of a south Slav state was also the preferred choice of the great powers at Versailles, who were thinking not of national liberation but of regional stability on the basis of balance of power, when they decided the borders of the new state.[39] The new state was also, however, the denial of more than 500 years of political struggle to realize (by reestablishing) a Serbian state. It gathered into one state all Serbs, as was the goal of nineteenth-century nationalists, but it did so only on the condition that they unite in a multinational state, not a Serbian state. This created, some argue, a 70-year "national identity crisis" for Serbs.[40]

The interwar state—the Kingdom of the Serbs, Croats, and Slovenes, renamed the Kingdom of Yugoslavia in 1929—for example, was governed by one of the two Serbian royal houses, the Karadjordjević dynasty, and by the Serbian political elite, in a series of shifting alliances with elites in other areas, particularly, at different times, Slovenes and Bosnian Muslims. It faced a wide range of social and economic issues related to the integration of very different legal, economic, transport, and political systems and the prolonged global crisis: the agrarian depression and foreign debt crisis in the 1920s, the financial and industrial depression of the 1930s, and the rearmament and war in Europe after 1937. Nonetheless, it could never escape the constitutional issue: the disputed legitimacy of the 1919 unitary constitution among Slovenes and Croats, who wanted a federal state, and the continuing and some-times violent challenge to the state from Croatian (and later Macedon-ian) nationalists, aided by Benito Mussolini (including the assassination of Yugoslav King Alexander in Marseilles in 1934). The label "uni-tarism," applied to this state by its critics, also hides a reality of disunity among Serbs. Now joined in one state, they nonetheless brought to it different political experiences and interests, formed a variety of politi-cal parties, and had ongoing disagreements, particularly between Serbs from the former Habsburg territories and those from the independent Serbian state. When Prince Regent Paul signed a pact with Hitler in 1941, it was Serbian air force officers who staged a coup d'état against him, provoking German occupation. The Germans set up a puppet gov-ernment in Belgrade under Aleksandar Nedić. The government itself set up an all-Yugoslav government-in-exile in London, while a colonel in the royal army, Draža Mihailović, took to the hills to organize a resis-tance force—called the Chetniks—with the goal of restoring not Yugo-slav but Serbian state institutions: the army, the king, and the ruling party. At the same time, a large proportion of the Serb popula-tion played "an important role in the reintegration of Yugoslavia"—particularly "'Western' Serbs from Croatia and Bosnia and Herzegov-ina [who] participated *en masse* in Tito's partisan movement."[41] Among the leadership of this "antifascist struggle for national liberation" orga-nized by the Yugoslav communist party and other patriotic forces were prominent figures from Serbia and Montenegro.

Outsiders captured by the idea that the 1991 to 1999 wars in Yugo-slavia reflect "ancient ethnic hatreds" read back to the elements of civil war during World War II and wrongly see an ethnic struggle, in part because of the racist elements of fascist ideology and practice. No bet-ter evidence against this proposition can be found than the divisions among Serbs, many of whom fought each other in the civil war that the Axis invasions provoked between the nationalist Chetniks and the antifascist Partisans. These Serbs thus also fought together with Croats, Muslims, and many other Partisans against the Croatian fascist forces (Ustashe) and Muslim fascist units (Handžar units) in Croatia and in Bosnia-Herzegovina. The platform of the Yugoslav communist party, which emerged victorious from those wars, however, had been set instead in the interwar period, in part by Comintern policy on the nationality question and in part by an inner party struggle over the con-stitutional question. As early as 1928, it defined its struggle as the over-throw of "Great Serbian hegemony" and the creation of a federal republic that would protect the smaller nations of Yugoslavia from Ser-bian domination and "unitarism." Not long after the Partisans' founding assembly for a postwar state in 1943, Winston Churchill shifted Allied support from the Chetniks to the Partisans.

The Serb population in the new federal Yugoslavia was still the largest national group (41.5 percent of the population in the first postwar census of 1948, when the second largest group, Croats, was 24 percent[42]), but the internal borders of this federation cut across Serb settlements, scattering them among different federal units. The new Serbian republic also was subdivided by the creation of two autonomous units—Vojvodina and Kosovo-Metohija[43]—while Serb requests for an autonomous province in border areas of Croatia, where Serbs were either the majority or half of most communities, were rejected. The creation of a separate republic of Bosnia and Herzegovina, where 44.4 percent were Serbs in 1953, instead of the long-sought division between Croatia and Serbia, was also interpreted by some Serbs as a further effort to punish Serbs. Nearly 40 percent of the Serb population would be citizens of non-Serb republics or share power with minorities in autonomous regions. At the same time, one of the primary reasons that many Serbs joined the communist party during or after the war was its fight against nationalist extremists and its program of national equality. For many, Yugoslavism was, before World War I and even more so after World War II, a solution to the Serbian national question—a state Serbs could embrace "as the Serbian homeland."[44]

It is for this reason that the economic reforms and constitutional conflict in the 1980s created a national problem for Serbs. The Yugoslav communist party leadership had rejected the idea of a Yugoslav nation in 1928; occasional efforts to implant Yugoslavism as a national ideology and identity in the federal era were all fought successfully, particularly by Croats, as "unitarist" violations of national freedom. It was as if "Great Serbianism" (and, by implication, Serbs) remained the primary threat to the country rather than an insufficiently developed common Yugoslav identity. One could choose to identify individually as a Yugoslav on census and other official forms, but the identity was not institutionalized in the sense that the six constituent nations were—in the rights of the republics and the official quota requiring representation of each national group. The more decentralized the federation became, along the territorial lines of the republics, the more citizenship became effectively a matter of one's republic, despite the Yugoslav identity one had abroad. The greater the decentralization, the more the inherent contradiction in the structure of the federation, between its organization into republics and its legitimation by the principle of national self-determination when the borders of the nations were not congruent with those of the republics, created a serious problem for Serbs.

It is not surprising that the major intellectual debates over decentralization were between Slovenes and Serbs, not between Croats and Serbs, whom many see as the primary source of conflict in Yugoslavia because they shared a language[45] and a territorial border. As historian Audrey Helfant Bunting nicely shows in the debate between Slovene literary critic Dušan Pirjevec and Serbian novelist Dobrica Ćosić in 1961–62—which had a disastrous Slovene-Serbian reprise in 1989[46]—there was a "structurally-determined difference of perspective between Slovenes (the only Yugoslav nation whose republic approximated a homogeneous nation-state) and Serbs (who were furthest from that ideal of modern nationalism)."[47] For Slovenes, the republics were "clearly formed national organisms . . . decentralisation and increased republican powers [were] the logical expression of national self-determination," while for Serbs, republican centrism was a constant reminder that their nation was divided. As Bunting writes, "Ultimately, the Slovene assumption that national and republican rights were identical would provide a 'simple' model of secession that was workable for Slovenia, but disastrous for the rest of Yugoslavia."[48]

At the same time, the communist party's idea that socialism and its commitment to national equality would, over time, make particularistic (usually called "chauvinist") nationalism obsolete gave an ideological content to Yugoslav identity that had its own internal time bomb. What did Yugoslav identity mean independent of socialism? If the contest was between socialism and particularistic nationalism, what identity would bind people to Yugoslavia and protect the option of Yugoslav identity for non-nationalists if the West won the Cold War and socialism went? Alternatively, would pressures for democratization be resisted as a threat to the very idea of Yugoslavia? Intellectual debates raised the issue already by the early 1960s, when market reforms were leading to similar debates on economic policy, decentralization, and the role of the party similar to those in the 1980s. If socialism was internationalism, as some claimed, it could not give a national content to Yugoslavism. Even before the end of the socialist regime itself in 1989–90, the Serbs faced an unresolved dilemma—a turning point, in Budding's view—with the way that the purge in 1966 of Vice President Aleksandar Ranković from the party leadership was justified. Although this purge sealed a critical political victory for the proponents of decentralization in a complex factional fight over foreign policy, the organization of internal security services, defense policy, and economic reform, Ranković was charged—by the Serbian party leadership[49]—with "Great-Serbian chauvinism" and "unitarism, nationalism, and centralism." As Budding writes, "When the [Serbian] Party denounced Ranković as both a Serbian chauvinist and Yugoslav unitarist, it made the 'Yugoslav option' all but unusable for Serbs."[50] The 1918 alternative to a Greater Serbia looked ever less like an alternative, and the result, Budding argues, was the emergence of two competing Serbian programs to fill the vacuum.

Serbian liberals supported the radical decentralization to the republics but gave priority to economic modernization and political liberalization. They focused Serbian national interests on the republic of Serbia, arguing that the "location of state borders mattered far less than the nature of the state they enclosed" and rejecting "the idea that Serbia could or should act as the protector of Serbs in other republics." Given the structure of Yugoslav federalism, they even argued that "identifying Serbia with Yugoslavia" had led to economic neglect ("because Serbia's economic interests were wrongly assumed to be identical with the federation's") and to political interference ("because the federation assumed in Serbia, and especially in Belgrade, the right to intervene in affairs that in all other republics were considered internal"). "The premise that political centralism worked to Serbia's advantage was false."[51]

On the other side were Serbian cultural nationalists, who defined the nation as Serbdom rather than the republic of Serbia. Focusing more on cultural and literary aspects of national identity, they responded in kind to the Croatian language declaration in 1967 by accepting its premises. Each nation had the right to develop its own cultural associations, use its own language and alphabet (Cyrillic in the case of Serbs, in contrast to the preference for Latin by the liberals who were modernizers and Westernizers), and protect its historical heritage. Opposed to decentralization because of its further fragmentation of the Serb nation into separate political universes, this historicist program focused increasingly after 1971, when the decentralizing amendments were adopted, on the problematic role of Serbia in the federation, attacking the internal borders as then drawn and adopting a stance of *ressentiment*—the idea that the Serbian national community was an "endangered species" and its national identity was formed on "the enmity of other Yugoslav peoples."[52]

The similarities between these two programs and those of the nineteenth century reveal the extent to which decentralization had focused politics on the republics and diminished a common Yugoslav space; not only in Croatia and Slovenia but also in Serbia, the amendments of 1967 to 1971 and the 1974 constitution ended the achievements of unification and revived a pre-1918 state-building process. Tito's 1972 purge of the liberal leadership in Serbia also deprived the first program not only of leaders but of legitimacy, giving far greater weight by default to the ethnic elements of Serb national ideology. But most serious of all was the silencing of any political debate on the costs and benefits of decentralization independent of the national question and the historical baggage and emotion it evoked. The serious problem of governance created for Serbia by the extensive autonomy granted its two provinces by 1974 could not be discussed without inviting charges of unitarist nationalism, Serbian hegemony, and the threat posed by Serbs to other Yugoslav nations, as the persistent but unsuccessful efforts by Serbia's leadership from 1974 until 1987 to find a way around this trap demonstrate so tragically. When the core issues of economic and political reform in the 1980s, as in the 1960s, polarized into a debate between federalists and antifederalists, the liberal leadership in Serbia was deprived of acceptable language to argue in support of either reform, restoration of federal powers, or republican nationalism. The result was an intellectual renaissance of Serbian cultural and ethnic nationalism—the second program—and its critical reassessment of postwar history, including Titoism.

Vesna Pešić identifies seven key themes of Serbian nationalist intellectuals' *ressentiment*, as portrayed in the media in the late 1980s and in the infamous 1986 draft Memorandum of the Serbian Academy of Sciences and Arts:

1. Yugoslavia is a Serbian delusion, into which Serbs were duped while other Yugoslav nations continued to build their national states.

2. There is a conspiracy against the Serbs by outsiders, from the Comintern in interwar Yugoslavia, to the League of Communists and Tito.[53]

3. Serbian economic backwardness is due to economic exploitation by Croatia and Slovenia.

4. Serbs are the losers because they "are the only ones who do not have a proper state. They win at war, but lose in peace."[54]

5. Serbs are exposed to hatred from all other Yugoslavs.

6. Serbs are exposed to genocide.

7. The goal of a national state for all Serbs is to be rid of these hatreds from others and of Serbophobia.[55]

In contrast to the period of Serbian state-building and liberation, ideological debate and leadership on these questions now were centered in the Serbian republic, not among Serbs outside Serbia or between them and Belgrade. Many liberal commentators tried to protect the alternative legacy by emphasizing that the origins of this new Serbian political and intellectual leadership still appeared to be disproportionately from diaspora Serbs who had moved from Croatia, Montenegro, Herzegovina, or Bosnia *to* Belgrade. The legacy of migration—in reverse direction after 1945 from that of the Ottoman period—still haunted an unresolved debate: Who was a proper Serb, who would become the leader of Serbia, or Serbs, and with what platform and borders?

The deadlock in the Serbian political system was broken as a result of Serbs and Montenegrins not within Serbia, but in the province of Kosovo. Their appeals for protection—as if they had already become a diaspora—gave an opportunity to party leader Slobodan Milošević to kill two birds with one rhetorical stone: to end the imposed silence on the constitutional order of the Serbian republic and to preempt, for the ruling party, the growing challenge to the socialist system from nationalist anticommunists in the Serbian Academy, writers' and cultural associations, and universities. His innovation was not his challenge to the federal system or to the communist party, as his opponents allege, but his skillful combination of elements of socialist and Serbian nationalist ideology to channel growing social discontent toward his rivals, both within the party and outside it. The theme, as Jasminka Udovički (a member of the true Serbian diaspora, in the United States) has analyzed so well, was an appeal not to Serbs as an ethnonational group, as his critics charge, but to the theme of injustice:

> Rather than addressing ethnicity directly, Milošević addressed something much less abstract and closer to heart: his people's sense of fairness. He drew on their real grievances and then conjured up others that began to appear real only after endless repetition. His focus, however, had never been on ethnicity, but on national injury and injustice. The point was to awaken among the Serbs a sense of being, through no fault of their own, massively wronged by others, endangered wherever they lived as a minority outside of Serbia itself—in Kosova, Croatia, or Bosnia. The voice was shrill, warning of the possibility of physical peril and drawing parallels to the genocide of World War II. The appeal was not to ethnic hatred and revenge but to the innate need for elementary fairness: the Serbs have not deserved this. The appeal was also for righting the painful wrongs by claiming back the inalienable rights of the Serbs as a people—no more. Milošević portrayed himself as their only true friend: of all Serbian politicians, he alone was committed to assisting the Serbs in regaining their pride and fighting for fairness. This approach worked infinitely better than the appeal to square some fictitious ancient accounts would have done, particularly because Milošević was talking to the Serbs in Serbia not about their own experiences and grievances but about someone else's: those with whom most of his audience had little contact—the Serbs

in Kosova, Croatia, and Bosnia. Their grievances were not verifiable through direct personal perceptions of the Serbian Serbs; the truth of Milošević's claims could not be challenged without an uncomfortable sense of betrayal of one's own kin.[56]

The purpose of this appeal mirrored precisely that of its primary rival within Yugoslavia—the leadership of Slovenia—namely, the development of a mass-based ideology to maximize support for a political contest increasingly defined in terms of national rights, within Yugoslavia. But the actors in this contest were still governmental—the republican and federal government and party leaders—and Milošević's synthesis was to exploit Serbian ethnic themes for a republican agenda. Its transformation during 1990[57] cannot be explained apart from its context: the interaction between republican leaders, each using national arguments in the constitutional and reform contests; emerging anticommunist politicians who had no reason to remain confined by republican borders and who used national arguments against the regime itself; and the emerging collapse of Yugoslavia.

In the case of Serbia, the contest for leadership ratcheted up by January 6, 1990, when the oppositional nationalist activities of writers, clergy, and historians emerged from their camouflage in cultural associations, both in Serbia and outside it (and therefore in response in part to the nationalist politics of other republics) and took on partisan form.[58] The program of the Serbian National Renewal Party, the first radically anticommunist Serbian political party, was, in the words of its chief ideologist, writer Vuk Drašković, "to create a democratic and multiparty Serbian state within her historical and ethnic borders, according to the ethnic map dated April 6, 1941, thereby preventing contemporary or any future Croatian state from benefitting from the genocide committed under Croatian banners during World War II."[59] In the party's printed program, it was more specific: incorporation into Serbia "of our people in Bosnia, Hercegovina, Lika, Kordun, Baranja and Kninska Krajina."[60] Prohibited one week later for being too "pro-Chetnik," it split into three nationalist parties, whose leaders remain prominent today. Within a month the Serbian liberal tradition also found partisan form, in the Democratic Party, which emphasized that "the national problem is a problem of democracy." But their "Letter of Intentions" revealed how far the pendulum had swung from the liberals of 1971, for it added that "the future independent ex-Yugoslav states cannot claim their right over territories populated mainly by members of another Yugoslav nation."[61] Only a few associations of liberal or social democratic, antinationalist intellectuals refused to take a position on the national question; among them were the Association for a Yugoslav Democratic Initiative, formed in February 1989 and operating throughout the country, and the Civic Alliance.

On January 23, 1990, the Slovene party walked out of the extraordinary party congress called, at the urging of the army, to confront the political crisis and disunity. Although Milošević called for continuation, the party committees from Croatia, Macedonia, Bosnia and Herzegovina, and the army voted to adjourn, thus ending the Yugoslav League of Communists. By April the first of six multiparty elections for new republican parliaments and governments was held in Slovenia. Fifteen months earlier, in January 1989, the federal prime minister, Ante Marković, had introduced legislation that ended the property rights of the socialist system, including job security, local solidarity wage funds, limits on landholdings, managers' rights to hire and fire without consulting the workers' council, and party supervision of managerial appointments. The time bomb that had equated Yugoslavism with socialism by the 1960s exploded, and now it is clear that the days of Yugoslavia itself were numbered. The 70-year-long "national identity crisis" for Serbs no longer had a solution in Yugoslavism, socialism, or antifascism. Thus Serbs had no choice but to begin a search for a new ruling myth, choosing one or another strand of nationalism and its concept of the Serb nation and its borders.

POLITICS AND SOCIOLOGY

While Serbian national ideology contained sufficient elements to justify going to war to create a national state out of the collapsing Yugoslavia—the "righteous struggle" to recapture lost statehood, "regaining with the sword what was lost with the sword," the glorification and martyrdom of those who avenge the "traitors of the land," "a people chosen by God"[62]—they were not sufficient to make these particular ideological appeals, as opposed to alternative elements in the national tradition, credible to individual Serbs. A second element—the factors of politics within and between the republics and of social origin that influences individual choice—is necessary to explain the violence. No study has been done on the relative numbers of Serbs in Serbia who refused conscription, hiding from the police with support from their families or leaving the country; of those who joined paramilitary gangs organized by criminals such as Željko Raznatović[63] interested as much in looting as in national goals or who became "weekend warriors" on a youthful jag; and of those who fought as members of the Yugoslav People's Army out of the conviction they were fighting to prevent the destruction of their country, in hopes of keeping as much of it together as possible, because they were paid in necessities such as heating fuel they could no longer afford for their families, or felt duty-bound as professional soldiers. The smallest numbers of all were those who joined paramilitary gangs formed by right-wing nationalist political parties claiming to be heirs of the Chetniks (e.g., the Serbian Radical Party of Vojislav Šešelj or the Serbian Renewal Movement of Vuk Drašković) and committed to uniting all Serbs into one state. Much of the brutal campaign of terror against civilians in eastern Bosnia, across the Drina River from Serbia, in the spring and summer of 1992 appears to have been the work of "outsiders"—not Serbs threatened with becoming a diaspora but Serbs from Serbia—as was some of the fighting in eastern Croatia, across the Danube River from Serbia. But Serbs outside Serbia, particularly in Croatia or in Bosnia and Herzegovina, had to make a choice—to become a minority in a new state, finding some accommodation with the new rulers, or to fight to unify with Serbia.

The central question, in other words, was one of citizenship. It was therefore a choice determined in no small part by others—the signals sent by non-Serbs and by the authorities of the nationalizing state in which they lived about their status, rights, and welcome as citizens. As Rogers Brubaker attempts to explain in his emphasis on a triadic field of struggle—among national minorities, nationalizing states, and national homelands—the claims that Serbs outside Serbia were endangered and in need of protection by Belgrade were credible because they "resonated" with experience in the recent past—the genocidal policies against Serbs in Croatia and the parts of Bosnia and Herzegovina incorporated into the "murderous wartime Independent State of Croatia" in 1941 to 1945. In addition, the policies and rhetoric of the Croatian president, Tudjman, in his campaign after the election of April 1990 to create a Croatian national state and gain independence generated genuine "grievances and fears" of a "repeat performance" that had "their own destabilizing logic; they were not orchestrated from Belgrade."[64]

Serbs in Croatia already had been victims of physical attacks by nationalist gangs before the election campaign of April 1990, but Tudjman's campaign was run on a theme of "decommunization," which he defined as "de-Serbianization" and that he proceeded to execute after being elected. In addition to losing their jobs because they were Serbs, Serbs in Croatia found they had no choice but to identify ethnically because they were labeled as Serbs by their fellow citizens, were required to sign loyalty oaths by the new government as if their loyalty were in question, and had to endure a Croatian nationalist euphoria that included the restoration of key national symbols (e.g., the flag, shield, and currency) that had last been used during the wartime fascist state. Serbs also had to tolerate neofascist gangs, uniforms, and songs, which like the symbols struck visible terror into those who had lost family in the World War II pogrom. The signals being sent about Serb rights and safety as citizens of Croatia were worrisome, to say the least.

The concept of citizenship also influences what a member of a national minority can expect. The difference between Slovenia and Croatia, for example, was less the size of the Serb minority and imputed interest or disinterest of Belgrade politicians in its fate than it was the different concepts of a nation and definition of citizens between the two republics. The concept of a nation can vary, from ethnic and exclusionary definitions to civic and inclusionary ones. Before the founding of Yugoslavia, Slovenia belonged to the Austrian crownlands, which had a multiethnic, incorporative concept of citizenship that did not require one to abandon one's ethnic identity to serve in state office or be viewed as loyal; similarly, in border areas of Croatia (Krajina) where Serbs settled at the invitation of the Habsburg rulers in the fifteenth and sixteenth centuries, and that also were under direct Austrian rule (by the war ministry), Serbs were allowed to retain their religious and linguistic identity while serving as border guards and members of the army. As a result, Serbs in Krajina were among the most loyal subjects of the empire. Slovene nationalists jealously guarded what they considered their cultural distinctiveness, above all the language that differentiated them from other south Slav nations. In the first years after independence, Slovenia was sufficiently inhospitable to non-Slovenes that persons with Serbian or Croatian surnames who could find another family name, such as that of a German relative, sought safety against discrimination in a name change. Nonetheless, Slovene citizenship was available to all those who met the residence requirements. The recognized status of a minority, with cultural rights, was granted only to so-called autochthonous populations, specifically Italians and Hungarians whose governments had agreed to reciprocal guarantees for the rights of Slovenes living in Italy and Hungary. By contrast, the core area of Croatia before the founding of Yugoslavia, that is, "civil Croatia-Slavonia," had been under Hungarian rule. There an organic, integralist concept of the nation had defined entrance into the political elite. Serving in state office and the top ranks of the military was possible only if one rejected one's national background and adopted the official language and political nationality of the Hungarian state.[65] Whereas in 1989 both the Croatian and the Macedonian parliaments amended their constitutions to declare their republics the state of their majority nation (Croats and Macedonians, respectively), the two governments elected in 1990 did not adopt the same policies because their concepts of citizenship were not the same. In contemporary Croatia, Tudjman's regime institutionalized an exclusionary, *jus sanguinis*, ethnic concept of the Croatian nation, and made it clear that Serbs, in particular, were no longer welcome, even in their ancestral homes. The government coalition formed under President Kiro Gligorov after the elections in Macedonia in December 1990 chose instead to work toward a civic concept of Macedonian nationality and to make welcome all those with citizenship in the republic.[66]

In addition to the political decisions made by new nationalizing governments about whether Serbs were welcome, the choice to accept minority status or to fight to join Serbia was influenced by social background and community context. A second difference between Slovenia and Croatia, and between Serbs in different areas of Croatia and of Bosnia and Herzegovina, is that Serbs faced different kinds of choices depending on where they lived. Where populations are territorially concentrated, they can more easily imagine succeeding at autonomy or even secession, whereas populations that are in urban areas and disbursed as individuals or households in multiethnic environments must think in terms of minority or individual rights rather than sovereignty. The latter focus on the right to equal treatment before the law and against discrimination as well as social rights and cultural rights of freedom of expression, including in protecting one's language, religious practices, and traditions. Nowhere in Slovenia were Serbs, and for that matter other south Slav nationalities such as Croats and Montenegrins, in territorial concentrations. The choice in Croatia between Croatian citizenship and fighting to unify with Serbia differentiated those tellingly called "urban Serbs" from the landowning or land-serving rural population of the border areas. The exceptions were those urban Serbs whose anger or fear at losing their jobs and other forms of mistreatment because they were Serbs led them to move from Croatian cities to the Krajina area, or those who found themselves literally trapped in that area when the fighting began, had no way to cross the confrontation lines, and were refused Croatian documents and their pensions if they did. Similarly in Bosnia and Herzegovina, where the circumstances of Serbs differ substantially in many respects from the situation in Croatia, fighting was most intense in border areas—along the border with Serbia, Croatia, and Montenegro, and near the new, internal borders being drawn by the three constituent nations of Bosnia and Herzegovina—where a military reality had some hope of being recognized eventually with border changes. But even within these areas, there was a difference in the kind of violence—between military operations of armies in strategic areas and the atrocities against neighbors and individualized expulsions of people by their ethnicity, which came to be called "ethnic cleansing" by foreign observers. In both Croatia and Bosnia-Herzegovina, ethnic cleansing occurred primarily in communities that were ethnically mixed in more or less even proportion[67] so that the political fate of that community was uncertain, the national stake in the land had to be established demographically in order to affect external decisions about whose territory it was, and conditions existed that are necessary to make credible a nationalist argument—that one's community is at risk from another.

In fact, what had been an urban intellectual and political movement for republican or national sovereignty within Yugoslavia became, once war began, a conflict among rural populations—not because they are more inclined to violence, but because the wars were about territory, which, in concrete terms, meant people's homes and farms.[68] Rural populations in the Balkans have a tradition of territorial defense and gun ownership, tend to retain a patriarchal culture of male heroism, are the bearers of national memory and consciousness, tend to be more religious and elderly, and as a rule are less educated and more vulnerable to the media terror and propaganda that were emanating from both the nationalizing states and the Serbian capital. Primarily individual householders in the private sector, they were second-class citizens in the socialist system, while they also suffered more than any group, other than pensioners, in the collapse of the protective policies that had included domestic agriculture. Although this was true of all groups who fought, Serbs in border areas of Croatia and in Bosnia and Herzegovina—the new diaspora—were disproportionately farmers and rural dwellers.[69]

Finally, the fact that violence occurred more in ethnically mixed areas points to another characteristic of the Yugoslav wars: The violence intensified over time. In other words, violence was not an automatic response or a universal one. Serbs who found themselves minorities in the new nationalizing states attempted at first to negotiate political rights, including territorial autonomy; only upon being repeatedly rebuffed did they pick up the gun. This was particularly graphic in Croatia, where the Croatian leadership refused the many efforts in the border areas by Serb leaders, particularly Jovan Rašković, beginning in May 1990, to find a political solution for Serbs within Croatia.[70] The Bosnian Serb leaders negotiated the future of the republic throughout 1991 and into the spring of 1992. Second, violence was not natural. Once Bosnian Serb wartime leader Radovan Karadžić led his party to war, on the grounds—to justify separate statehood—that the peoples of Bosnia could no longer live together, he faced a defiant reality. Violence would not have been necessary, had people already lived in relatively homogeneous national communities, as in Slovenia, or if people had wanted to separate voluntarily. To separate people with generations of common life, violence was necessary. And then, as was true of all communities at war, the more tired populations became of war and thus the more willing they were to criticize their leaders and question the purpose of the destruction and fear, the more loyalties had to be renewed and reinforced with violence.

THE ROLE OF FOREIGN POWERS

Violence in the former Yugoslavia, from whatever party, was aimed at changing borders. Because the borders of states are a matter of international recognition, any explanation of that violence must include the decisions taken by the major powers. External commitment to the territorial integrity of Yugoslavia would have preempted early attempts at creating new states and the serious violence that followed in Croatia, Bosnia and Herzegovina, and Kosovo. Diplomatic management of the breakup and recognition of new borders for the successor states could have aimed at minimizing violence. Assertive support for the rights of people who found themselves in a minority in new nationalizing states, including enforcement of those rights, would have provided these new minorities a necessary measure of protection and reduced the credibility of the nationalist argument that only in a state of their own nation would they be safe and fully citizens. None of these policies was followed. Foreign involvement in the breakup of Yugoslavia was extensive, competitive, and decisive, as it was in previous moments of critical political definition in the Balkans, such as 1878, 1908, 1918, 1941, and 1943 to 1945.

The lack of support for Yugoslavia completed the domestic process of decentralization and political purge that delegitimized the two strands of Serbian national ideology that could have prevented violence—the liberal strand that accepted Serbia's republican borders and emphasized political democracy and a market economy and the Yugoslav strand that viewed a south Slav state as an alternative, even a preferable alternative, to a Greater Serbia for uniting all Serbs in one state. Only with the end of the Yugoslav state did Serbs have to seek a new state and an ideology that would legitimize it.

The European decision to recognize Slovenia and Croatia as independent states, and in some cases such as Austria and Germany even to encourage secession, was based on the Slovene and Croat claims to the right of national self-determination. Not only did the EC members thereby violate the territorial integrity of Yugoslavia, they also declared the internal borders of the republics as inviolable. Referendums for independence in Slovenia and Croatia, and then by Croats and Muslims in Bosnia and Herzegovina, were recognized as legitimate; as with the Serb boycott of the Bosnian referendum of February 28–March 1, 1992, the referendums among Serbs within those two states for their own autonomy or statehood were declared illegitimate. Yet because the national populations were not contiguous with republican borders, the recognition of national states out of multinational Yugoslavia on the basis of the right to self-determination would seem to have required a willingness to redraw borders. The Dutch proposed just that to EC member states in July 1991 when the Netherlands took over the EC presidency but were refused.

Moreover, as a result of skillful public relations campaigns for independence and of historical preferences among Western states, international actors differentiated among good nationalist assertiveness and bad, putting the Serbs and their leaders in the latter category, even before there was violence. With each new condemnation and punishment, making Serbia into a pariah state, the Serbs who wanted to argue for a liberal nationalist position or against all nationalisms had a more difficult task of persuasion. Thus the decision on the location of borders not only ignored Serb rights, but the rhetoric justifying decisions on the location of borders gave credibility to the arguments made by Slobodan Milošević and nationalists to his right: that Serbs needed a Serbian state, leaders, and army to defend them. Providing no international support or protection to Serbs, the major powers did not oppose but strengthened those elements of the third, historicist strand of Serbian national ideology that was becoming dominant in the 1980s, such as Serbs' historical willingness to fight against injustice to their people at the hands of outsiders and to fight for their land.

In areas of the world historically subject to imperial contest, border areas will be nationally mixed. When a state is allowed or even encouraged to disintegrate and new states are formed, the defense of those new borders will be a priority for new leaders. Nationalizing states are likely to view the national loyalty of those border populations as a strategic imperative. Had the international community allowed negotiation about the ex-Yugoslav borders, or had it insisted that each republic seeking independence "give demonstrable proof of minority rights" to its Serbs, the claim that Serbs were vulnerable and victims of injustice could not have been sustained. Given his tendency to favor state interests over national interests, Milošević might even have claimed a political victory within the republican borders of an independent Serbian state. Instead, the decisions of the Arbitration (Badinter) Commission in January 1992 that Croatia did not yet meet this condition for recognition were ignored by Germany, the Vatican, Ukraine, and, as a result, the rest of the European Union (EU) and the United States. Similarly, the EU decision that recognition of Bosnia and Herzegovina must follow an internal agreement among the three national communities on its constitutional order was overruled by American insistence on (and EU acceptance of) immediate recognition.

The role of foreign powers in the Yugoslav tragedy says as much or more about the inadequacy of international regimes for borders and for international supervision of minority rights than about any "Serb model" or the role of diaspora in the postcommunist era of Eastern Europe. Inflexibility on borders without a willingness to go to war to defend international decisions or to be zealously assertive about protections for minorities within new states, as the Croatian case particularly illustrates, is a simple recipe for violence and forced migration.

Conclusion

To apply the model of the Third Reich and Hitler to Serbia and Milošević is to assume that national states already existed in the space of the former Yugoslavia. The violence of its breakup must direct attention to the process of creating new national states in a multinational and supranational environment. To fight for a particular set of borders requires an ideology that takes a position on borders and evokes an obligation to take up arms. The fact that a minority of Serbs did fight demonstrates that decisions on the location of borders did matter and that the historical, ethnic strand of Serbian national ideology had to be credible to those individuals, who had to choose between the uncertain fate of citizenship in the new states or resistance against becoming an "endangered" member of a diaspora so close to their homeland. The Brubaker triad is useful in the Serb case as it calls attention to the fact that fears and choices are not historically given but occur in a political context, one in which leaders and their interactions send, reinforce, or counteract signals about security and citizenship. The Serb model cannot be understood without reference to the actions of leaders in the other republics of the former Yugoslavia, particularly of Croatia, which set the tone for diaspora Serbs, and the poisonous interaction among three distinct groups: the "homeland state," the national minority, and the "nationalizing state." But the Brubaker triad also takes much for granted that should not be: that there were multiple possible outcomes in the 1980s, that the borders were not given, and that each Yugoslav nation has an ideology with many elements that also got selected in a complex political inter-action, among Serbs and between some Serbs and non-Serbs in the country. The Brubaker triad also ignores the influence of foreign pow-ers, which in the case of the Serbs tended to reinforce repeatedly the strand of Serb history and ideology that would lead some to fight, view-ing themselves victims of injustice and forces outside their control that only they could right.

Afterword

This chapter was written before the NATO bombing campaign against Yugoslavia in March–June 1999, which was based on and publicly jus-tified by the model it intended to refute. For the first time in the Yugoslav conflicts, one part of the international community did go to war, although no declaration of war occurred. The cause was said to be the defense of Albanian human rights in Kosovo and of universal humanitarian principles, although the issue between Kosovo Albanians and the Serbian government was one of borders. And although the sub-sequent exodus of most of the Serb minority from Kosovo, in the sum-mer of 1999, appears at this writing to have created, de facto, a new border, the international military and civilian presence deployed after the withdrawal of Yugoslav security forces from Kosovo—the inter-national security force called KFOR and the U.N. transitional adminis-tration called UNMIK—were authorized by a U.N. Security Council Resolution declaring the continuing territorial integrity of Yugoslavia, including Kosovo. The exodus of this new Serb diaspora, although its creation as a diaspora was not yet recognized, occurred largely through violent means or threats from the Albanian majority. Whatever the final political status of Kosovo and resolution of the Albanian national ques-tion, the role of foreign powers thus had not changed. They had not yet found an adequate regime to determine borders or to supervise minor-ity rights, and they continued to reinforce the strand of Serb history and ideology which stood accused. Whether this would be the last in a series of historical reversals for Kosovo and for Serbs or that strand would find new defenders, it was too soon to say.

Notes

1. Anatol Lieven, *Chechnya: Tombstone of Russian Power* (New Haven: Yale University Press, 1998), analyzes Russian policy toward Chechnya as the failure of what he calls the "Serbian option": "the move by major sections

of the Communist ruling elite to radical nationalist positions in an effort to preserve their own power, with resulting attempts by state forces to whip up national fear and terror, especially among members of a given nationality living beyond the state borders; the mobilisation of local ethnic groups, above all from such diasporas, partly as a result of 'manipulation' and partly on the basis of real historically based fears and hatreds and local fighting traditions; and the exploitation of the resulting conflicts by criminal gangs and warlords posing more or less sincerely as nationalist militias" (p. 219). See chapters 6 and 7, pages 219–68.

2. "It Could Do the Most Harm to Vojvodina Hungarians," *Népszabadság*, July 9, 1991, cited in Foreign Broadcast Information Service (FBIS), *Daily Report: East Europe*, July 11, 1991, p. 40.

3. That is, who registered as Serbs in the 1991 census. National identity in socialist Yugoslavia was an individual choice, expressed in the decennial censuses, which also included the choice "Yugoslav" and "nationally undetermined." The census figures themselves do not give much clue about the salience of that chosen identity for an individual nor the extent to which it reflects a nationally mixed background, which in many areas of the country could be as high as half the population, if several generations are taken into account.

4. For the Hungarian story, see chapter 1.

5. For the Albanian story, see chapter 4.

6. For the ironic position this created for Serbian Jews, see the illuminating essay by Marko Živković, "The Wish to Be a Jew: Or the Struggle Over Appropriating the Symbolic Power of 'Being a Jew' in the Yugoslav Conflict," ms., March 1994.

7. For more on the relationship during the election campaign, see Laura Silber and Alan Little, *Yugoslavia: Death of a Nation* (New York: Penguin, 1997, rev. and updated), pp. 85–87.

8. Veljko Vujačić, "Historical Legacies, Nationalist Mobilization, and Political Outcomes in Russia and Serbia: A Weberian View," *Theory and Society* 25, no. 6 (1996): 780.

9. See Ivo J. Lederer, *Yugoslavia at the Paris Peace Conference: A Study in Frontiermaking* (New Haven, Conn.: Yale University Press, 1963).

10. In the 1991 census, 6.8 percent of the Serb population in Yugoslavia lived in Croatia; another 16 percent lived in Bosnia and Herzegovina; 13.4 percent (about 1,200,000) lived in Vojvodina (an autonomous province within Serbia), 2.3 percent (around 200,000) in Kosovo (the other autonomous province in Serbia), and 0.5 percent (about 12,000) in Macedonia— totaling 39 percent of Serbs outside Serbia proper. This does not include the proportion of the population in Montenegro, generally considered about 50 percent who identify ethnonationally as Serbs.

11. Vladimir Gligorov, a Belgrade political scientist of Macedonian origin, summed up the conflicts that led to violence with the collapse of Yugoslavia into "national states" with the aphorism, now widely quoted, that represents this contingent character of borders, subject to a different outcome: "Why should I be a minority in your state when you could be a minority in mine?"

12. Rogers Brubaker, "National Minorities, Nationalizing States, and External National Homelands in the New Europe," in Brubaker, ed., *Nationalism Reframed: Nationhood and the National Question in the New Europe* (New York: Cambridge University Press, 1996), pp. 55–76.

13. According to the Office of the United Nations High Commissioner for Refugees (UNHCR) register in September 1997, there were 617,728 refugees and other victims of the Bosnian war who had found haven in Yugoslavia, of which 60 percent said they wished to remain in Yugoslavia and only 10 percent said they wished to return home. "Federal Republic of Yugoslavia: BETA Views Status of Refugees," BETA, September 4, 1997, transcribed by the Foreign Broadcast Information Service (FBIS-EEU-97-247).

14. By late 1998, UNHCR officials were speaking openly of these Serb refugees in Yugoslavia as "the forgotten group of refugees." See, for example, the statement of Nicholas Morris, regional director for UNHCR, in the transcript of the biweekly press conference in Sarajevo, November 24, 1998, Coalition Press Information Center, Tito Barracks: "one of the things that has been highlighted, perhaps paradoxically, by the Kosovo crisis, is the fact that the largest number of refugees, by far, remain those in the Federal Republic of Yugoslavia—over half a million—and they have tended to be neglected, between the focus, this year, on Kosovo on the one hand, and all the emphasis on Dayton implementation that's Bosnia-centric on the other. But, some of these people are starting their seventh year in collective centers . . . a breakthrough in minority return would be key, but not just that; many of them may decide to stay in the FRY . . . this forgotten group of refugees."

15. The following analysis draws heavily on the author's *Balkan Tragedy: Chaos and Dissolution after the Cold War* (Washington, D.C.: Brookings Institution Press, 1995), particularly chapters 2–5.

16. See Lenard Cohen and Paul Warwick, *Political Cohesion in a Fragile Mosaic: The Yugoslav Experience* (Boulder, Colo.: Westview Press, 1983).

17. Despite the consensus that this was a Stalinist constitution, which it was not, the parallel between this aspect and the Union Treaty adopted in the Soviet Union in August 1991 and that provoked an attempted putsch is clear.

18. At the time of the new state, in 1945; this number outside Serbia had declined as a result of migration to Serbia and national differences in demographic rates of increase (Serbs having nearly zero reproduction rates for a long time) to about 25 percent by 1991.

19. See Thomas A. Emmert, *Serbian Golgotha: Kosovo, 1389* (New York: East European Monographs, distributed by Columbia University Press, 1990), and Robert Elsie, comp. and ed., *Kosovo: In the Heart of the Powder Keg* (Boulder, Colo.: East European Monographs, distributed by Columbia University Press, 1997).

20. Vesna Pešić, *Serbian Nationalism and the Origins of the Yugoslav Crisis* (Washington, D.C.: United States Institute of Peace, Peaceworks no. 8, April 1996).

21. This phenomenon, whereby intellectuals' arguments precede political change and provide the rhetoric and argumentation for politicians when the moment is ripe, is not limited to former Yugoslavia. Many who lived through the 1980s in Yugoslavia are surprised that the draft memorandum has received so much attention—one might say vituperative accusation—as the source of the collapse of Yugoslavia and Serbian violence after 1990; at the time, it passed almost unnoticed.

22. A fascinating eyewitness account is in Slavko Ćuruvija and Ivan Torov, "The March to War (1980–1990)," in Jasminka Udovički and James Ridgeway, eds., *Yugoslavia's Ethnic Nightmare: The Inside Story of Europe's Unfolding Ordeal* (New York: Lawrence Hill Books, 1995), pp. 81–83; see pp. 75–90 for an excellent short analysis of the Kosovo issue. Videotapes of the public face of these events are part of the five-part BBC documentary *The Death of Yugoslavia* (Brian Lapping Associates) and are discussed in Silber and Little, *Yugoslavia,* pp. 37–40, and in Branka Magaš, *The Destruction of Yugoslavia: Tracking the Break-Up 1980–92* (London: Verso, 1993), pp. 179–217.

23. Silber and Little, *Yugoslavia,* p. 38.

24. Ibid., p. 37.

25. See Susan L. Woodward, *Socialist Unemployment: The Political Economy of Yugoslavia, 1945–1990* (Princeton, N.J.: Princeton University Press, 1995).

26. Xavier Bougarel, "Bosnia and Hercegovina—State and Communitarianism," in David A. Dyker and Ivan Vejvoda, eds., *Yugoslavia and After: A Study in Fragmentation, Despair and Rebirth* (London: Longman, 1996), p. 99.

27. An excellent example is the analysis of Katherine Verdery, based on the Romanian case but generalizable beyond it. See *What Was Socialism? And What Comes Next?* (Princeton, N.J.: Princeton University Press, 1997), especially Part II, "Identities: Gender, Nation, Civil Society," pp. 59–130. On the powerful dynamic pulling toward nationalist forms of expression, see Pamela Ballinger's analysis of the failure of the Istrian movement to avoid nationalism through a focus on region-

alism, in "'Authentic' Hybrids in the Balkan Borderlands: The Istrian Regionalist Movement,'" ms.

28. Their legal authority to do so was questionable, since the constitutional authority lay with the state presidency, but it was temporarily without a chair because of a Serb refusal to accept the Croatian candidate, Stipe Mesić, by normal order the next in line, because he had declared that his task as Yugoslav president was to ensure the independence of Croatia and the end of Yugoslavia.

29. See Silber and Little, *Yugoslavia*, p. 158, and the video footage in the BBC documentary *The Death of Yugoslavia*.

30. See, especially, Misha Glenny, *The Fall of Yugoslavia: The Third Balkan War* (London: Penguin, 1994).

31. See Silber and Little, *Yugoslavia*, pp. 140–44, particularly on the murder of the regional police chief, Josip Reihl-Kir, who tried to stop it.

32. The centerpiece of this tradition and of the oral poetry was the legend of the battle of Kosovo in 1389; see Emmert, *Serbian Golgotha*. The *gusle* and oral poetry were studied by Harvard linguists Milman Parry and Albert Bates Lord; see, for example, Lord's *The Singer of Tales* (Cambridge, Mass.: Harvard University Press, 1960).

33. As Ivo Banac writes, "Serbian homesteads in the Sandžak of Novi Pazar, Metohia, and Kosovo, which the subsequent generations of Serbs named Old Serbia, as well as in northern Macedonia and Serbia proper, were literally uprooted. . . . Srijemski Karlovci in the Slavonian Military Frontier became the see of Serbian Orthodox metropolitans; and Novi Sad, the principal Serb cultural center." Banac, *The National Question in Yugoslavia: Origins, History, Politics* (Ithaca, N.Y.: Cornell University Press, 1983), p. 38.

34. Dimitrije Djordjević and Stephen Fischer-Galati discuss the interaction among the changing Balkan policies of European powers, the decline of the empires, and the national liberation movements in this period in *The Balkan Revolutionary Tradition* (New York: Columbia University Press, 1981), chapter 6, especially pp. 182–89, 194–99, and 210–14.

35. A secret society of Serbian military officers operating from 1911 to 1917, Black Hand (formally, Union or Death) was led by men from the rural interior who had achieved their status through the military reforms of 1897–1900, had conspired to assassinate the Serbian king in 1903, and sought the creation of a Great Serbian state from western Bosnia to southern Macedonia.

36. The tragic parallels with the 1990s led the president of the Carnegie Endowment for International Peace, Morton Abramowitz, to decide to reissue the endowment's 1913 inquiry into those wars 80 years later. See *The Other Balkan Wars: A 1913 Carnegie Endowment Inquiry in Retro-*

spect with a New Introduction and Reflections on the Present Conflict by George F. Kennan (Washington, D.C.: Carnegie Endowment for International Peace, 1993).

37. See Emmert, *Serbian Golgotha,* pp. 126–31, and on the efforts by Austrian and Hungarian authorities to prevent the celebrations from spilling over Serbian borders, such as in neighboring Croatia. This "invention of tradition," as Eric Hobsbawm and Terence Ranger record, in which national myths are "modified, institutionalized, and ritualized" for new purposes, was taking place at the same time—the 1870s and 1880s—throughout Europe and North America. See Hobsbawm and Ranger, eds., *The Invention of Tradition* (New York: Cambridge University Press, 1983).

38. Vujačić, "Historical Legacies," pp. 774, 781.

39. See Lederer, *Yugoslavia at the Paris Peace Conference.*

40. A "national identity crisis is a crisis of self-understanding by the members of a nation . . . in the case of the Serbian nation, . . . based on a degree of confusion of Serbian identity with a broader Yugoslav identity." Vojin Rakić, "Politics, Culture and Hegemony: The Failure of Democratic Transition in Serbia," Ph.D. diss., Rutgers University, Department of Political Science, April 1998, p. 40.

41. Vujačić, "Historical Legacies," p. 780. On the role of Serbs in the partisan movement, see Ivo Banac, *With Stalin Against Tito: Cominformist Splits in Yugoslav Communism* (Ithaca, N.Y.: Cornell University Press, 1988).

42. George W. Hoffman and Fred W. Neal, *Yugoslavia and the New Communism* (New York: Twentieth Century Fund, 1962), p. 29. The numbers in 1921, when the first Yugoslav census occurred, according to Banac's reanalysis, were 38.83 percent for Serbs; see *The National Question,* pp. 49–58.

43. Between 1945 and 1965 this area of mixed Serb, Albanian, Turkish, Gypsy (Roma), and other population had the status of an autonomous region, not a full province, and was called Kosovo-Metohija, after the battlefield of Ottoman fame—Kosovo—and the church territories—Metohija—where most of the Byzantine Orthodox churches and monasteries were to be found; when its status was promoted to a province, it was renamed Kosovo; Serbs restored the name Kosovo-Metohija when they denuded its autonomy in 1990; Albanians call it Kosova.

44. Pešić, *Serbian Nationalism,* p. 7.

45. For most of the Yugoslav period, Serbo-Croatian was considered two variants of the same language. Croatian nationalist revivals always began, therefore, with fights against this assumption, such as the 1967 declaration on the Croatian language by politically interested linguists

that the Novi Sad declaration of 1954 was wrong. The statement in the text is not intended as a political position but only to indicate that the two variants, or languages, are so similar as to make communication nearly effortless. In contrast, Slovene and Macedonian are distinct languages, although part of the south Slav family, and Albanian and Hungarian are not even Slavic.

46. See the discussion of the Slovene-Serb exchange emanating from Taras Kermanauer's "Letters to a Serbian Friend," in Ivo Banac, "The Fearful Asymmetry of War: The Causes and Consequences of Yugoslavia's Demise," *Daedalus* 121 (Spring 1992): 160.

47. Audrey Helfant Budding, "Yugoslavs into Serbs: Serbian National Identity, 1961–1971," *Nationalities Papers* 25, no. 3 (1997): 405.

48. Ibid., p. 409.

49. One aspect of Yugoslav federalism is that the party was also federal, and chains of responsibility and accountability required that republican parties enforce democratic centralism and execute disciplinary actions. Hence the Serbian party had to remove Ranković, even though it was a federal level decision.

50. Budding, "Yugoslavs into Serbs," p. 410.

51. Ibid., p. 412.

52. Pešić, *Serbian Nationalism*, p. 18.

53. And by the 1990s, pride of place in this conspiracy was held by Germany.

54. This slogan, revived from Serbian historians of the early twentieth century by Dobrica Ćosić in the 1970s, reemerged during the wars of Yugoslav succession after 1991.

55. Pešić, *Serbian Nationalism*, pp. 18–20.

56. James Ridgeway and Jasminka Udovički, "Introduction," in Udovički and Ridgeway, eds.,*Yugoslavia's Ethnic Nightmare*, pp. 12–13.

57. In terms of the elements of Serbian national ideology regarding borders, the transformation begins in 1990 when Milošević warns Slovene and Croatian leaders that if they choose secession, he will insist on a redrawing of republican borders to give Serbs a nation-state as well; but as for the elements in support of his policies in the 1990s, one cannot speak definitively of a transformation from state interests to national interests; if that had occurred, Milošević would not have survived the loss of what nationalists call "Serb lands" in Croatia and in Bosnia and Herzegovina (and eventually Kosovo) if he had become a true follower of this second strand of the ideology.

58. The political role of cultural associations in authoritarian environments has a legacy on which to draw in the region, beginning under the Habs-

burgs, and not only among Serbs. Like the repetition of experiences that reinforced elements in Serb national ideology, organizations such as Zadruga, Matica Srpska, Zora, and Prosveta helped to keep alive a national consciousness during periods of statelessness or political repression. For that reason, the organizations were treated with suspicion by overlords, including most recently their abolition in the immediate post–World War II period in Croatia and the Croatian government's views toward their revival in the 1980s.

59. April 6, 1941, was the day that Germany began the bombing of Belgrade and the start of occupation and dismemberment of Yugoslavia by Axis forces. In response to the Serbian officers' coup against Prince Paul, which also restored political party government to Yugoslavia in a cabinet representative of all regions and replaced Paul with the young King Peter, the attack destroyed the first Yugoslavia. See Robert Lee Wolff, *The Balkans in Our Time* (New York: Norton, 1967), pp. 198–201.

60. Rakić, "Politics, Culture, and Hegemony," p. 154.

61. Ibid., p. 158.

62. See Emmert, *Serbian Golgotha*.

63. Wanted by Interpol for the assassination of a Yugoslav diplomat in Sweden in the 1980s, Raznatović, under the *nom de guerre* Arkan, formed the Serbian Volunteer Guard (also known as the Tigers) to fight in eastern Croatia and eastern Bosnia, using terror to force non-Serbs to leave and rewarding his men with permission to loot. How much Slobodan Milošević explicitly used Arkan, simply allowed him to act, or had influence on him is the subject of much debate, including that on the factual grounds for Milošević's indictment for war crimes at the International Criminal Tribunal for the Former Yugoslavia. The fact that the indictment in May 1999 was for actions in Kosovo and not in Croatia or in Bosnia and Herzegovina was due to the difficulty of proving chains of command in the latter two cases. Arkan's accumulated wealth, local popularity, engagement in criminal economic underlife, and elected representation in the Serbian parliament heading a political party of Serbs in Kosovo are also the subject of much journalistic attention.

64. Brubaker, "National Minorities, Nationalizing States, and External National Homelands in the New Europe," pp. 69–73. For a particularly parsimonious and elegant construction of the argument that Serbs in Croatia acted as they did out of fear, that the nationalist appeal by Milošević to provide them protection had to be credible in order to succeed, and that this credibility came from the rhetoric and actions of Tudjman in his electoral campaign for president and his subsequent actions once in power, see Rui deFigueiredo and Barry R. Weingast, "The Rationality of Fear: Political Opportunism and Ethnic Conflict," in Barbara F. Walter and Jack Snyder, eds., *Civil Wars, Insecurity, and Intervention* (New York: Columbia University Press, 1999), pp. 261–302.

65. See Robert W. Seton-Watson, *The Southern Slav Question and the Habsburg Monarchy* (New York: H. Fertig, 1969, reprint of 1911 ed.).

66. In his fascinating analysis of the 1994 internationally financed and monitored census in Macedonia, "Observing the Observers: Language, Ethnicity, and Power in the 1994 Macedonian Census and Beyond," in Barnett R. Rubin, ed., *Toward Comprehensive Peace in Southeast Europe: Conflict Prevention in the South Balkans*, Report of the South Balkans Working Group of the Council on Foreign Relations Center for Preventive Action (New York: Twentieth Century Fund, 1996), pp. 81–105, Victor Friedman shows how far this ideal had deteriorated in only three years and how much of the difficulty came from outsiders, despite their apparent preference for the same ideal. He writes, "By attempting to impose a Western European construct equating language with nationality (and nationality with statehood), ICOM [the International Census Observation Mission] helped force on people the kind of choices that have led to the current conflict" (pp. 97–99).

67. Paul Shoup provides an analysis of the fighting in Croatia according to the ethnic composition of border communities, in "The Future of Croatia's Border Regions," *RFE/RL Report on Eastern Europe*, November 29, 1991, p. 32, and Xavier Bougarel offers an explanation, by data on the ethnic composition of communities in Bosnia-Herzegovina, for why Muslims were victims far more frequently of ethnic cleansing than Serbs or Croats, in *Bosnie: Anatomie d'un Conflit* (Paris: La Découverte, 1996), p. 144.

68. See Woodward, *Balkan Tragedy*, pp. 236–46.

69. The overrepresentation of Serbs in farming activities in Croatia and in Bosnia and Herzegovina has historical origins in the policies of the imperial regimes, both Habsburg and Ottoman, which were reinforced by the policies of economic development in socialist Yugoslavia and by patterns of internal migration, in which the more educated and ambitious members of declining communities left for urban areas and those with fewer opportunities outside subsistence farming remained. On Croatia, see Drago Roksandić, *Srbi u Hrvatskoj* (Serbs in Croatia) (Zagreb: Vjesnik, 1991).

70. See, for example, Silber and Little, *Yugoslavia*, pp. 94–104. On the tendency toward radicalization in general, see Woodward, *Balkan Tragedy*, pp. 352–63.

4

The Albanian National Question: The Challenges of Autonomy, Independence, and Separatism

Elez Biberaj

A LMOST a century after the great powers redrew the map of southeastern Europe in 1913, recognizing the independence of a truncated Albania and forcibly placing nearly half of the Albanian nation under the jurisdiction of neighboring states, the Albanian question has come back to haunt the international community and has emerged as an issue of paramount importance to peace and stability in the Balkans. The long simmering clash over Kosova (Kosovo, in Serbian) between the Serbs, who claim the province on historical grounds, and ethnic Albanians, who base their claims on the democratic, majoritarian principle—they make up more than 90 percent of Kosova's population—and on the fact that they inhabited the region long before the Serbs, led to an armed conflict and large-scale violence in 1998–99. While long recognized as one of the most critical flashpoints in postcommunist Eastern Europe, Kosova had been ignored by the international community and excluded from international peace talks on the former Yugoslavia. Although numerically the third-largest ethnic group in the former Yugoslavia, after the Serbs and the Croats, the Albanians were denied the right to self-determination when the federation dissolved in 1991. Moreover, to use Rogers Brubaker's terminology, ethnic Albanians found themselves living in two "nationalizing states,"[1] Yugoslavia and Macedonia, as a new international border separated the

Albanians in Kosova from their kin in the newly independent Macedonia. The two nationalizing states differ significantly in the tactics they have employed to deal with the Albanians. Serbia's strongman, Slobodan Milošević, who in the late 1980s arbitrarily abolished Kosova's autonomy and used the issue of ethnic Albanians to whip up nationalist feelings and thus consolidate his power, pursued a policy of severe repression against Albanians, marginalizing them politically and economically. Under the leadership of Ibrahim Rugova, a Sorbonne-educated literary critic committed to nonviolence, the Albanians responded by unilaterally declaring independence in 1991 and establishing a shadow government. But Milošević's harsh military rule and the ineffectiveness of Rugova's peaceful resistance caused widespread disenchantment and radicalization. The mid-1990s witnessed the emergence of an underground organization, the Kosova Liberation Army (KLA, or Ushtria Çlirimtare e Kosovës [UÇK] in Albanian), which vowed to wage an armed struggle for Kosova's independence. In February–March 1998, three years after the Dayton agreements brought a truce to Bosnia, Kosova rapidly spiraled into violence when Milošević unleashed his military, police, and paramilitary forces against the Albanians in an attempt to suppress their drive for independence. Yugoslav government forces engaged in massive and dramatic ethnic cleansing and horrendous human rights violations that the West had pledged would never be permitted to be repeated after Bosnia.

After months of idle threats and in the wake of Milošević's failure to accept an internationally drafted accord for an interim political solution, on March 24, 1999, the United States and its allies in the North Atlantic Treaty Organization (NATO) launched air strikes against Yugoslavia with the aim of halting the campaign of ethnic cleansing and preventing the conflict from spilling over into Albania and Macedonia. Milošević responded by implementing a meticulously planned campaign of ethnic cleansing. Nearly one million ethnic Albanians were forcibly deported to Albania, Macedonia, and Montenegro, and an additional half a million internally displaced; an estimated 10,000 were slaughtered by Serb army, police, and paramilitary forces; and countless villages and towns were leveled, and physical, economic, and social infrastructure destroyed. But after 78 days of air strikes, in early June 1999 Milošević acceded to NATO's demands. The accord provided for the effective end of Serbian control over Kosova: The withdrawal of all Yugoslav troops and special forces; the return of refugees; the introduction of a peacekeeping force led by NATO; the creation of a United Nations–led interim administration for Kosova; and the demilitarization of the KLA. It also reaffirmed Yugoslavia's territorial integrity.

Despite the war with Yugoslavia, NATO policy continues to be based on the assumption that Kosova must remain within Serbia. Western leaders fear that the secession of Kosova would undermine the idea of a multi-ethnic Bosnia and have a domino effect on Macedonia, where ethnic Albanians, accounting for a quarter of its population, might then demand unification with an independent Kosova state or with Albania. This policy is untenable and is likely to lead to renewed conflict. After all the suffering that they have endured, it is difficult to imagine Albanians in Kosova acquiescing to renewed Serbian rule and accepting the sovereignty of a state that expelled them en masse from their native land.

The war in Kosova had an immediate and profound impact on Albanians in Albania and Macedonia. It led to the emergence of a pan-Albanian movement, reigniting the old dream of Albanian national unification. While this movement is still in its formative stage and there are differences between the diasporas and the national state over the ultimate goals, the longing for Kosova's separation from Serbia, but not necessarily unification with Albania, appears to be virtually universal among the Albanians. The overwhelming majority considers current borders, which were imposed by the great powers in 1913 without consideration for ethnolinguistic divisions, unjust. Most Albanians in Kosova and an increasing minority in the national state see a chance to set right what they consider a great historical injustice.

This chapter focuses on the internal and external dynamics of the Albanian problem, assessing the relative weight of political, ideological, ethnic, and regional factors. It describes and analyzes the Albanian question in terms of what Brubaker calls a "nationalizing triad"[2]—a pattern of interaction linking the two Albanian diasporas in Yugoslavia and Macedonia, the homeland state, Albania, to which ethnic Albanians feel attached and that reciprocates the sense of attachment, and the governments of the two nationalizing states—Yugoslavia and Macedonia. It analyzes the main strands of thinking and the principal players in the triad. What follows also examines the impact on the Albanian question of the international environment, in particular the policies of the United States, its European allies, and Russia.

Historical Background

The Albanian question and the violence surrounding it long predated the dissolution of Yugoslavia in 1991. With the exception of the Jews, Albanians represent, proportionally, the world's largest diaspora. Roughly 40 percent of Albanians live outside the borders of the current Albanian state—the result of the arbitrary drawing of borders and the mismatch between their national state and nation. Of the more than six million Albanians in the Balkans, only 3.5 million live in Albania proper. Almost as many live in Kosova and Macedonia, inhabiting compact areas contiguous to their national state (see Map 4.1). The exact number of the Albanian diasporas in the two nationalizing states is a source of considerable controversy. Albanians have consistently challenged official censuses, charging that their numbers have been deliberately underreported for political reasons. Nevertheless, it was estimated that before the war there were about 2 million Albanians in Kosova, accounting for 92 percent of the total population. An additional 100,000 are to be found outside the current administrative borders of Kosova but within Serbia: mainly in three southern communes on the Serbia-Kosova border—Presheva, Bujanovc, and Medvegja. Tiny Montenegro, with a population of 630,000, also has a sizable Albanian minority: about 50,000. According to official statistics, in 1994 Albanians in Macedonia numbered 442,000, or 23 percent of the total population. But Albanians dispute these figures, insisting that they represent between 30 and 40 percent. Albanian activists in Macedonia maintain that several hundred thousand Albanians were not counted in the 1994 census. In 1992 the Macedonian parliament had passed a law establishing a 15-year residency requirement for citizenship. Large numbers of Albanians who did not have appropriate documents or who had lived for extended periods in Kosova or other Yugoslav republics were not counted in the official censuses. Thus the total number of Albanians is probably higher than the official figures indicate.

Although in recent decades their population growth rates have declined steadily, Albanians have an exceptionally high birthrate and are among the youngest populations in Europe. In the mid-1990s Albania registered 22.46 live births annually per 1,000 people; the figure for Albanians in Kosova and Macedonia was close to 25 per 1,000—among the highest in the world. The average age in Albania is 26 years; more than one-third of the population is under 15. More than half of the Albanians in Kosova and Macedonia are under 27 years old. In contrast, the Serbs and Macedonians have significantly lower birthrates and aging populations. Since the early 1990s an estimated 600,000 Albanians have left Albania, Yugoslavia, and Macedonia in search of a better and more peaceful life in the West; still, based on current projections, within a generation there will be as many Albanians as Serbs in the Balkans and several times more Albanians than Montenegrins and Macedonians. The exceptionally high birthrates, a function of the Albanians' overall socioeconomic conditions and cultural and religious traditions, have had a direct, adverse impact on their relations with their neighbors, causing the latter to

Map 4.1   Ethnic Albanians in Southern Balkans
Source: State Department.

charge that the Albanians have deliberately pursued a policy of "breeding" themselves into a majority population.[3]

Albanians are distinguishable from other Balkan nations by history, language, and a strong sense of ethnic distinctiveness rooted in their traditional social and cultural beliefs. Religion is another important distinguishing factor. Serbs and Macedonians are predominantly Christian Orthodox, and their national churches have played a vital role in fostering national unity. The Albanians, on the other hand, do not have a single, official religion, being divided among three faiths: Muslim,

Orthodox, and Roman Catholic. Roughly 70 percent of the population in Albania is Muslim, 20 percent Orthodox, and 10 percent Roman Catholic. The overwhelming majority of Albanians in Kosova and Macedonia are Muslim. While at times the three religions tended to divide them, Albanians traditionally have displayed a high degree of religious tolerance among themselves and in relations with their neighbors. Some Yugoslav officials and scholars have attempted to interject religion into the debate on Kosova, claiming that the Serbs are defending Christendom against Albanian Islamic fundamentalists. The Albanian-Serbian conflict, however, is not a religious but a territorial one. The revival of fundamentalist organizations and groups in the Islamic world has had little if any impact on the Albanians, who identify with the West rather than the East.[4]

Albanians are the direct descendants of the Illyrians, who settled the western part of the Balkan peninsula during the first millennium B.C. Although at various times in their troubled history Albanians occupied wider territory, they were driven by more powerful neighbors and foreign invaders into the areas they currently inhabit. A battleground between eastern and western influences, Albania witnessed conquests by Celts, Romans, Goths, Slavs, and Turks. But despite waves of successive foreign invasions, the Albanians were able to preserve their separate identity and language. They were the last Balkan peoples to free themselves from the close to five-century-long Turkish occupation. The Albanians, most of whom had embraced Islam by the end of the seventeenth century, lacked ethnic or religious affinity with any of the great powers and, unlike their Christian neighbors, could not expect the assistance of any "big brothers" against the Turks. In addition, their liberation struggle was adversely affected by territorial designs of their neighbors, particularly the Serbs, who laid claim to Kosova and other predominantly Albanian-inhabited areas that had been part of the Serbian medieval empire. The first signs of an organized national movement appeared in 1878 with the founding of an Albanian League in the Kosovar town of Prizren. The league advocated administrative autonomy from Turkey and vowed to fight against the cession of Albanian-inhabited regions to Serbia and Montenegro. Although the league, which was violently crushed in 1881, was a pan-Albanian movement, most of its activities were centered in Kosova, western Macedonia, and parts of today's Montenegro.[5] Similarly, subsequent movements as well as the main struggle that led to the proclamation of Albania's independence on November 28, 1912, were centered in Kosova and the surrounding areas, thus making Kosova, not Albania, the center of Albanian nationalism.[6] The Albanians' dream of including all predominantly Albanian-inhabited territories in one state was shattered by the 1912 Balkan war. Serbia, Montenegro, and Greece defeated Turkey and occupied large parts of Albania, including Kosova and, in the south, Çamëria. Despite strong opposition by the Albanians, a special commission appointed by the great powers assigned more than half of Albania's territory and about 40 percent of its population as war spoils to Serbia, Montenegro, and Greece. This decision was made without regard to the ethnic composition of the territories in question or the will of the local population.

The Serbs, who received the largest part of Albanian territories, based their claims on historical arguments. Kosova had been part of the Serbian medieval kingdom in the fourteenth century and the Serbian Patriarchate had moved its seat to Pejë (Peć), a town on the border between Kosova and Albania. Serbs claimed that at the time they were defeated by the Turks in 1389, the Serbs accounted for the majority of Kosova's population. The Albanians, so the Serb argument went, emigrated in massive numbers to Kosova during the seventeenth and eighteenth centuries, under direct Turkish encouragement.[7] The Kosova battle was mythologized to such an extent that generation after generation of Serbs were taught that the region was the cradle of Serbia. But as Noel Malcolm points out,

> Kosovo was not, as Serbs claim, the "birthplace" or "cradle" of the Serb nation, and it came under Serb rule for only the last part of the medieval period. Since then it has been excluded from any Serb or Yugoslav state for more than 400 out of the last 500 years. It was conquered (but not legally annexed) by Serbia in 1912, against the wishes of the local Albanian majority population, and it became part of a Yugoslav kingdom (not a Serbian one) after 1918. In other words, out of the entire span of modern history, Kosovo has been ruled from Belgrade for less than a single lifetime.[8]

If the issue were to be decided on historical grounds, the Albanians could make as strong a case as the Serbs. They had inhabited the territory long before the Serbs. Kosova was also the cradle of Albanian nationalism, and the Kosovars had played the decisive role in the national struggle that led to Albania's independence.

The Albanian Question, 1912–45

The amputation of Albania had a devastating impact on the political, economic, and social development of the Albanian nation. For the new

Albanian diasporas, the Turkish occupation was replaced by an even harsher foreign rule bent on denationalizing or expelling them from their homes. Rump Albania, on the other hand, could never become a truly viable state.

The Albanian diasporas have had a largely unhappy experience. Albanians' history under Yugoslav rule has been marked by a succession of unsuccessful attempts to break off Yugoslavia. While Yugoslav approaches in dealing with the Albanians have alternated between deliberate attempts of forced assimilation and denationalization to granting them a degree of autonomy, Belgrade always regarded their well-developed national consciousness as a potential threat to the consolidation of the Serb-dominated Yugoslav state. Having "liberated" Kosova in 1912, the Serbs moved swiftly to pacify the region and dismantle the very fabric of Albanian society and culture, in the process committing large-scale atrocities and forcing thousands of Albanians to flee the region. Temporarily interrupted by the outbreak of the war in 1914, these efforts were resumed at the end of the war by the Kingdom of Serbs, Croats, and Slovenes, renamed Yugoslavia in 1928. Albanians were subjected to forced assimilation and denationalization, which devastated the Albanian political elite and cultural heritage. Belgrade depicted this process as being aimed at "modernizing" the underdeveloped Albanian society, which was based on the traditional clan structure characterized by blood feuds and fierce clan and tribal loyalties.[9] As the historian Ivo Banac has observed, "Serbian propaganda simultaneously dehumanized Albanians, presenting them as utterly incapable of governing themselves and as the sort of element that ought to be exterminated, and elevated them to the standing that warranted their assimilation."[10] The government closed down all Albanian schools and foreclosed Albanian access to Serbian-language schools, prohibited the use of the Albanian language, and refused to recognize Albanians as a distinct ethnic group. In addition, a program of massive colonization was launched aimed at changing the ethnic structure of the region and diluting the predominantly Albanian character of Kosova. About 40,000 Serb and Montenegrin colonists were settled in Kosova; most were given land forcibly taken away from Albanian farmers. By 1941 more than half a million Albanians were pressured into emigrating; most of them ended up in Turkey. Belgrade's drive to dilute the political impact of the Albanian population by settling Slavs into their area and pressuring Albanians to leave intensified Albanians' resentment.

The loss of Kosova and other Albanian-inhabited areas had a profound impact on Albania and, until the mid-1920s, dominated its political discourse. During this period Kosovar leaders who had found refuge in Tirana played a critical role in Albania's policymaking, which was reflected in Tirana's official demand that the borders be changed. But after Ahmet Zogu (later King Zog) came to power in 1925, Kosova gradually ceased being a salient issue. Zog turned his attention to the consolidation of the Albanian state. In conformity with his emphasis on state interests over national ones, the Albanian monarch severely limited the activity of Kosovar separatists and only occasionally protested at the League of Nations the harsh treatment of ethnic Albanians by the Belgrade regime.[11]

Despite the use of brute force by Yugoslavia, an organized and powerful state, ethnic Albanians, who had distinct political identities before the Serb occupation, demonstrated a remarkable cultural resilience and refused to be assimilated into what the Serbs regarded as their higher culture. Yugoslav efforts to nationalize them, and the accompanying harsh persecution and denial of their basic rights, only strengthened the Albanians' ethnic consciousness and aspirations for unification with Albania. Thus it came as no surprise when Albanians, like Hungarians, supported the Axis powers for revisionist reasons and welcomed the 1941 German invasion of Yugoslavia. The Germans decided to attach most of Kosova and parts of Macedonia and Montenegro to the Italian-occupied Albania. This was the first time since 1912 that the overwhelming majority of Albanians in the Balkans were included in a single, unified state. That Albania was ruled by a puppet government was less important for the Kosovars than the fact that they were finally free from Serbian rule and reunited with their brethren.

As the partisan movement gained momentum during World War II, the Yugoslav League of Communists took measures to mobilize the Albanians in the struggle against the Germans. They hoped that two factors would make their task easier. First, Yugoslav communists had played a critical role in the creation of the Albanian Communist Party in 1941 and came to exercise almost complete control over its decisions. Until the end of the war, two senior Yugoslav communist officials were attached to the staff of the Albanian communist leader, Enver Hoxha. Second, before the war Yugoslav communists had been the harshest critics of government repression of ethnic Albanians. Moreover, on two occasions—at its Fourth Congress in 1928, and at its Fifth Conference in 1940—the Yugoslav communist party had endorsed Kosova's return to Albania.[12] Still, the Yugoslavs encountered serious difficulties in enlisting the support of Albanians, who had fresh memories of their persecution in the prewar Yugoslavia and feared that a communist victory would lead to their reincorporation into Yugoslavia. Nevertheless, Yugoslav communists improved their prospects by promising to respect the Albanians' right to self-determination. In line with this policy, the Kosovar branch of the Yugoslav communist party and the partisan movement were independent of the party and movement in Serbia.[13] In January 1944 the Kosovar partisan movement openly endorsed Kosova's unification with Albania.[14] But with their approaching victory, Yugoslav communists switched their position, insisting that Albanians would be granted equal rights with other ethnic groups but that Kosova would remain part of the new emerging federation. Having defeated the nationalist movement, the communists were not about to alienate further the Serbs, the country's largest and most important ethnic group, by giving up Kosova. In March 1944 the Yugoslav party leadership publicly ruled out Kosova's return to Albania.

Albanians under Communist Yugoslavia, 1945–91

The reincorporation in 1945 of Kosova and other predominantly Albanian-inhabited areas into Yugoslavia was a major blow to Albanian national aspirations and ushered in an era of renewed persecution and nationalizing pressures that would last until the end of the 1960s. One of the first actions of the Yugoslav communist government was the declaration of martial law in Kosova in February 1945. The army launched a major offensive against ethnic Albanian nationalist forces, committing widespread atrocities. The Albanians opposed renewed Yugoslav rule and were the only ethnic group to put up armed resistance to Josip Broz Tito's government.

As was the case in the interwar Yugoslavia, the new Belgrade regime considered the Albanians, the country's largest non-Slav ethnic group, to be politically unreliable and a threat to the stability and territorial integrity of the federal state. Belgrade never made a serious attempt, as it did, for example, in the case of the Macedonians, to accommodate Albanian nationalism and grant ethnic Albanians genuine home rule. Without consulting the Albanians and contrary to the officially proclaimed policy of equality of ethnic groups, the regime designed new territorial arrangements aimed at ensuring easier control over Albanians and checking the rise of nationalism and separatism. Albanian compact territories were subjected to a process of gerrymandering:

Kosova was attached to Serbia, one of the country's six constituent republics, while southeastern and southwestern areas bordering on Albania were incorporated, respectively, into Macedonia and Montenegro. While they were recognized as a distinct ethnic group and permitted to open schools in their mother language, only in Kosova did the Albanians enjoy a degree of autonomy. Kosova was granted a special status within Serbia, being proclaimed an autonomous region (oblast). But Kosova enjoyed a lesser status and fewer rights than Vojvodina, Serbia's other autonomous unit. Vojvodina was proclaimed an autonomous province (*pokrajina*) and its governmental structure was similar to that of a republic, with its own supreme court and People's Assembly (parliament). In contrast, Kosova did not have its own supreme court or parliament, and its government structure resembled that of local administrative units. The region's autonomy was limited primarily to the execution of decisions made in Belgrade. But compared with their pre-1941 treatment, ethnic Albanians experienced considerable improvement in their status, economic lot, and educational opportunities.

Throughout this period, Albania proper played an insignificant role with respect to Kosova. Nationalist forces that had advocated the preservation of ethnic Albania's borders were defeated by Hoxha's communists. Indeed, one of the major factors that contributed to Albania's civil war in 1943–44 was disagreement over the fate of Kosova, with Hoxha insisting that the issue would be solved after the war in a "brotherly" fashion. The new elites that took power in 1945 were naive communists who believed in subordinating national interests to communist internationalism; in addition, their primary objective was to consolidate power in Albania itself. Between 1945 and 1948 Enver Hoxha's government blindly copied Belgrade's policies and displayed little independence in its foreign and domestic policies. Moscow had given Belgrade a free hand and Albania for all practical purposes had become a Yugoslav satellite. Having ruled out Kosova's return to Albania, the Yugoslavs now hoped to solve their Albanian problem by incorporating Albania itself into the Yugoslav federation. A series of treaties were signed closely binding Albania's political, economic, and military systems with those of Yugoslavia. Albania came close to losing its independence and sovereignty in early 1948, when its parliament approved plans for "union" with Yugoslavia. These plans, however, were thwarted by the break between Tito and Joseph Stalin and Yugoslavia's expulsion from the Soviet bloc. Hoxha allied himself with Stalin and embarked on a vociferous anti-Yugoslav policy. While Albania came to play a major role in the Soviet strategy of pressuring Tito, Moscow never expressed any support for Albanian claims to Kosova. Albania's own propaganda machine focused its criticism on what it termed the Yugoslav "un-Marxist" way of dealing with the Albanians, but Tirana never encouraged or sponsored the creation of a separatist movement in Kosova. In fact, Kosovar activists who fled Yugoslavia after the 1948 break usually ended up in Albania's prisons. In the official media as well as in school curricula, little attention was devoted to Kosova. Ironically, people in Hoxha's Albania came to know more about developments in the Soviet Union and other faraway places than in Kosova. But even though Tirana did little for Albanians in Yugoslavia, the very existence of an independent Albanian state stiffened the Kosovars' resolve to resist Serbian domination.

Albania's break with Yugoslavia and alliance with the Soviet Union impacted adversely on the position of Albanians in Yugoslavia. Contacts between the two parts of the Albanian nation were abruptly severed. Under the pretext of fighting Albanian nationalism and separatism, Yugoslav authorities implemented a well-coordinated policy of terror and intimidation. The secret police committed serious transgressions of the law, including the murder of many Albanians ostensibly suspected of nationalist activities. With very few exceptions, Albanians were denied positions of high responsibility, and the training of Albanian experts was severely curtailed. Belgrade also deliberately neglected Albanians' economic and cultural development. Kosova and other areas bordering on Albania were considered politically and militarily too vulnerable to be the sites of any significant economic projects. Although these were among the poorest parts of the country, they were not eligible for special federal development funds. Between 1947 and 1956, for example, per capita investments in Kosova amounted to only 36 percent of Yugoslavia's average, and between 1956 and 1965, to 59.1 percent.[15] And even the limited investments that were made in Kosova were exclusively concentrated in extractive industries. With its large reserves of minerals, such as coal, lead, zinc, silver, and chrome, the province served as a raw material supplier for the rest of Yugoslavia. The government also resorted to the prewar policy of pressuring Albanians to flee the country. More than 200,000 Albanians are estimated to have emigrated between 1953 and 1966 as a result of government-sanctioned pressures.

Belgrade attempted to supplant the national identity of the various ethnic groups comprising the federation with communist ideological identity. In the case of the ethnic Albanians, however, the government went much further than with the others. There were no doubts in policymaking circles that, given their size as well as their linguistic and cultural differences with the Slavs, Albanians could ever be molded into Serbs or Yugoslavs. The authorities, therefore, embarked on a policy of shaping the ethnic Albanians into a nation separate and distinct from their conationals in Albania. Although the Kosovars were linked with the Albanians in Albania by family, language, and historical, cultural, and sentimental ties, Belgrade refused to consider them a single nation. Albanians in Yugoslavia were referred to as *šiptari*, while those in Albania as *albanci*. The teaching of Albanian history, traditions, literature, and even folklore was considered as "a nationalist deviation," and drastic measures were taken against the Albanian intelligentsia. In Kosova, this misguided nationalization policy was largely a failure, breeding resentment among Albanians and deterring their integration into the Yugoslav mainstream. However, in Montenegro and Macedonia, where most Albanian-language schools were closed down in the wake of the break with Albania in 1948, it had a devastating impact on the cultural development of Albanians. Many Albanians in those areas were Slavicized; they were offered greater opportunities and a more stable future.

FROM COLONY TO AUTONOMY

The dismissal in 1966 of Aleksandar Ranković, the vice president and secret police chief, was a watershed event in the history of Albanians in Yugoslavia. It ushered in a period of unprecedented autonomy and cultural revival. Ranković was blamed for what officially was acknowledged as a policy of systematic persecution of ethnic Albanians.[16] Taking advantage of the post-Ranković liberalization, the Albanians, who until then had made very few demands on the system, began to assert themselves culturally and politically and to challenge the primacy of Serbs in Kosova's affairs. Albanian-language media launched a campaign aimed at stimulating greater awareness among ethnic Albanians of their past and current situation, thus sowing dissatisfaction with their current position. The intelligentsia, which had been terrorized under Ranković, played a major role in the Albanians' cultural revival, rejecting what until then had been the Serbian-inspired official interpretation of Kosova's and Albanians' history. In a highly significant move intended to send Belgrade a clear message that they considered themselves part and parcel of the Albanian nation, Albanians throughout Yugoslavia adopted the standard literary language officially used in Albania, which was based primarily on the southern dialect and which differed from the northern dialect used in Kosova and Macedonia.

The Albanian movement for greater autonomy was led by a rising young elite, loyal to socialist Yugoslavia. Skillfully employing the ruling Yugoslav League of Communists' pronouncements on "brotherhood and equality," intellectuals and some party officials publicly demanded that the Albanians be recognized as having the right to self-determination and that Kosova be elevated to a republic within Yugoslavia. The Serbs bitterly opposed such demands. As a republic Kosova would have enjoyed the formal constitutional right to self-determination and, by extension, secession, and so could have done what Slovenia and Croatia, not to mention Bosnia, did in the early 1990s. While advocating new political arrangements that would better promote ethnic Albanians' interests, Kosovar elites saw their future in Yugoslavia and did not consider Hoxha's Albania as an attractive alternative. After 1948 Albania and Yugoslavia had embarked on entirely different political and economic paths. Hoxha pursued a rigidly Stalinist internal policy. As other members of the Soviet bloc experimented with limited political and economic reforms, Albania became more and more repressive, with the ruling party dominating all aspects of life. In 1961 Albania broke with the Soviet Union and aligned itself with China, further isolating itself from reformist trends. In the mid-1960s Hoxha, emulating the Chinese, launched his own "cultural revolution." However, he went further than the Chinese, outlawing religion, declaring Albania an atheist state, and totally abolishing private property.[17] Yugoslavia, on the other hand, developed the reputation of being the most liberal communist country by opening up to the outside world, tolerating religious freedoms, and developing a market-type economy. Despite the repression that they had endured in the post-1945 period, Albanians in Yugoslavia enjoyed greater rights and freedoms and had a significantly higher standard of living than their conationals under Hoxha's dictatorship. While Yugoslav officials were eager to offer favorable comparisons of the situation of Albanians in Kosova with that of Albanians in Albania, for most Kosovars Albania was not the reference point. They were eager to achieve full equality with Yugoslavia's other ethnic groups, which meant being recognized as a constituent nation.

In the wake of Ranković's dismissal, the mainstream faction of the Yugoslav leadership, particularly Tito, seemed intent on addressing Albanian grievances. However, the leadership could not muster the necessary political will to overcome opposition from leaders of Serbia and grant Kosova republic status. By failing to cut Serbia's ties with Kosova, socialist Yugoslavia lost perhaps its best chance to defuse Albanian nationalism. With Ranković's political demise, Serbia's nationalists and extremists had suffered a major defeat and probably could not have mounted a serious challenge to Tito. Shocked by revelations of widespread human rights transgressions in Kosova, the general Yugoslav public was more disposed to accept an Albanian republic than at any time before or after. Had Kosova's status been elevated to that of a republic, most likely the international community would have approved Kosova's secession in 1991, and the subsequent bloodshed would have perhaps been avoided.

In November 1968 massive demonstrations broke out throughout the province. The demonstrators called for the establishment of a Kosova republic on a par with Serbia and the other five republics. Other demands included the establishment of a university in Pristina, a status for the Albanian equal to that of Serbo-Croatian, and immediate measures to improve Kosova's dire economic situation. Within a month the protests spread to Macedonia, where demonstrators demanded the incorporation of the predominantly Albanian-inhabited western Macedonia into a Kosova republic. These events alarmed the Serbian and Macedonian leaderships, which convinced the federal authorities to crush the demonstrations by force. Albanian calls for a republic were rejected but other demands were met. An Albanian-language university was opened in Pristina, Albanian was recognized as an official language in Kosova, the Albanians were permitted to display their national flag, and federal economic assistance was increased. The authorities introduced a national key form of representation, giving Albanians greater representation in local, republic, and federal government institutions. Gradually the provincial party and government leadership was replaced, with the Albanians gaining leading positions. But the most profound changes came with the adoption of Yugoslavia's new constitution in 1974. Kosova, as well as Vojvodina, was recognized as "a constituent element" of the federation and granted wide cultural and administrative autonomy. Serbia's powers were reduced significantly and decision-making transferred to the provincial level. The provinces now had their own constitutions and supreme courts, were directly represented in the country's top government and party institutions, and enjoyed veto power on major issues.[18] But while the provinces came to have de facto equal status in federal decision-making, they were still formally subordinated to Serbia constitutionally. Nonetheless, Tito hoped that these constitutional innovations would reduce the Albanians' sense of grievance and prevent the rise of Albanian nationalism and separatism.

The improvement of the status of Albanians in Kosova coincided with a lessening of tensions with Albania. Following the invasion of

Czechoslovakia in 1968, both Belgrade and Tirana were concerned that the Soviets might attempt to reassert control over their two former Balkan allies. Albania formally withdrew from the Warsaw Pact and, after decades of violent polemics and occasional border incidents, curtailed its propaganda attacks against Belgrade and publicly declared that it would come to Yugoslavia's assistance in the event of Soviet aggression. While Tirana viewed Kosovar demands for greater autonomy with sympathy, it showed unusual moderation when Yugoslav authorities used force to quell Albanian demonstrations in November–December 1968. Following the normalization of bilateral relations in early 1971, Albanian-Yugoslav economic ties expanded rapidly. But more important, Belgrade assigned Kosova the role of "bridge-building" with Albania. For the first time since 1948, Albania and Kosova developed direct contacts. Pristina University signed agreements with its Tirana counterpart, which provided for the exchange of lecturers, textbooks, publications, exhibitions, and sports teams as well as sponsoring joint projects in the fields of archaeology, ethnography, and linguistics. Contacts with the national state and exposure to an ever-growing number of Albanian-language publications, radio, and television reinforced ethnic Albanians' national consciousness and traditional bonds with Albanians on the other side of the border and thus intensified their ethnic assertion against the Serbs and Macedonians.

Belgrade had an important stake in developments in Albania. Traditionally, a weak and unstable Albania had presented a threat to Yugoslavia by providing opportunities for its potential adversaries, such as Italy and Germany before 1945 and the Soviet Union after 1948. With growing signs of the disintegration of the Tirana-Beijing alliance in the mid-1970s, and with Albania's deteriorating economy, Belgrade was concerned about Albania's foreign policy orientation and the possibility of a realignment, including a rapprochement with Moscow. By encouraging cooperation between Tirana and Pristina, the Yugoslav government hoped to develop an interdependent relationship with Albania and thus discourage Tirana from inciting nationalism in Kosova. Belgrade also wanted to be in a better position to influence developments in Albania after Hoxha's departure from the political scene.

Given their superior political and economic systems, the Yugoslavs displayed little concern about the possibility of nationalist or ideological "contamination" from Stalinist Albania. Indeed, Belgrade was prepared to develop much closer ties, but Tirana hesitated. Yugoslavia's relatively liberal domestic policies and its unique economic system of self-management, which ostensibly gave workers rather than the state bureaucracy the power to manage enterprises, were anathema to

Hoxha, who feared the potential influence of Yugoslav "revisionism" on Albania's domestic politics. After the initial euphoria in the early 1970s, Hoxha put the brakes on the improvement of relations with Yugoslavia, dismissed several senior officials on charges of having attempted to introduce Yugoslav-style economic reforms, and resumed ideological attacks on the Yugoslav model of socialism. But as far as Kosova was concerned, Yugoslavia's courtship paid off, at least in the short term. Tirana subordinated its ethnic ties with the diaspora to its overall political, security, and economic interests vis-à-vis Yugoslavia. Throughout the 1970s Tirana did not comment on the imprisonment of many Kosovars, nor did it incite ethnic Albanians against Yugoslav authorities. Albania was concerned that political instability in Yugoslavia could give the Soviets an opportunity to intervene. But if the Yugoslavs believed that by appeasing Albania that they would ensure interethnic harmony in Kosova, they were mistaken.

Whereas the 1974 constitutional arrangements represented a significant step forward aimed at appeasing the Albanians, they did not represent a viable solution of the problem, as Tito had hoped. For the Albanians, these arrangements fell far short of the genuine home rule that a republic status for Kosova would have entailed. Their enhanced status was still not commensurate with their number or publicly voiced preferences. Belgrade's reasons for denying Kosova the status of a republic with attributes of statehood had lost whatever plausibility they might once have had and boiled down to the fact that, as a non-Slav ethnic group, the Albanians would not be permitted to attain full political equality in Yugoslavia, the homeland of the south Slavs. The 1974 compromise was even less acceptable to Serb public opinion. Albanians' national self-assertion and cultural revival was accompanied by a resurgence of Serbian nationalism. While Kosova formally remained part of the republic, Serbia's control over the provinces' affairs was sharply reduced. Serb party officials complained that Belgrade had granted too many concessions to the Albanians. They claimed that the decentralization and the devolution of power had jeopardized the integrity of the republic of Serbia and had encouraged Albanian separatism.[19] Indeed, Albanian pressure, reverse discrimination, and the general lack of economic prospects were forcing many Serbs and Montenegrins to leave Kosova. The Serb presence in the province had been diluted gradually, while that of the Albanians had steadily grown. In 1948 the Serbs accounted for 23.6 percent of Kosova's population and Albanians, 68.4 percent. According to the 1971 census, Kosova had a population of 1.2 million; 18.3 percent were Serbs and 73.6 percent were Albanian. By 1981 Albanians accounted for 77.5 percent of the total population; Serbs and Montenegrins, 15 percent.[20] But Serbs were still over-represented in the administration, party, and governmental bodies and usually held better-paid jobs and enjoyed a higher standard of living than Albanians.

Stiff competition for scarce resources also aggravated interethnic relations. Despite increased federal assistance, Kosova remained Yugoslavia's poorest region. The inequality between the Albanians and other ethnic groups was stark. By the end of the 1970s, per capita annual income in Kosova was less than one-third of the average of the country. The primary reasons for the province's chronic problems were past backwardness, ongoing neglect and misrule, and inadequate investments. Albanians resented the fact that Kosova's considerable mineral resources were used for the manufacturing and processing industries in Serbia and other republics. In 1979 it was estimated that Kosova had over 20 percent of the country's coal deposits, over 60 percent of lead and zinc reserves, over 20 million tons of ferronickel ore, and 10.5 billion tons of lignite deposits, representing about one-third of Yugoslavia's total energy potential.[21] During the 1970s Kosova received the greatest share of the fund for the underdeveloped areas. But still investments continued to be concentrated in the extractive industries. Moreover, the rapid expansion of higher education produced thousands of graduates who could not find jobs. Albanian politicians, who had come to dominate decision-making in Kosova, explained the region's dire economic situation as the result of a premeditated state policy of internal colonialism. The implication was that only by becoming a republic could Kosova realize its economic and social potential and end its relative deprivation.

As the economy continued to deteriorate and with growing discontent and unrest among the Albanians, in the mid-1970s Kosova witnessed the emergence of a movement that sought to break Serbia's grip on the province. Pan-Albanian sentiments also resurfaced in Macedonia and Montenegro, where Albanian students began to propagate a union of Albanian-inhabited areas with Kosova. The authorities continued to insist that the 1974 constitution finally had resolved the Albanian problem in Yugoslavia and responded by cracking down on suspected nationalists and separatists.

THE END OF AUTONOMY: SERBS STRIKE BACK

Kosova of the 1980s is a good example of what Rogers Brubaker describes as a conflict between an assertive national minority and an insensitive, repressive nationalizing state.[22] The drive for an Albanian republic, motivated by a mix of Albanian nationalism, resentment at and humiliation by continued Serbian rule, and ambitions to maximize Kosova's autonomy, reached its climax in spring 1981, one year after Tito's death, when demonstrations broke out throughout the region. The protests touched raw nerves of anti-Albanian sentiments among the Serbs and spurred an immediate Serb nationalist mobilization in both Kosova and Serbia proper. Describing the demonstrations as a serious threat to the country's independence and territorial integrity, the Serbs pressured the weakened post-Tito national leadership to reassess the post-1974 policy that had granted Albanians a great deal of autonomy. The federal authorities reacted swiftly and with brute force: A state of emergency was proclaimed, and tanks and troops were used to suppress what essentially had been peaceful demonstrations. Ethnic Albanians became the subject of renewed harsh repression and persecution. Thousands were arrested and about 2,000 sentenced in summary proceedings. More than 400 Albanians, most of them students and intellectuals, received sentences of from 1 to 15 years of hard labor. The entire provincial leadership, including the chairman of the provincial League of Communists, Mahmut Bakalli, as well as most Albanian officials at all levels of the society were replaced. A Serbian-sponsored media campaign was launched against Albanian history, culture, and heritage, while a free rein was given to Serbian and Macedonian nationalism. Education in the Albanian language, Albanian textbooks, development of cultural programs, and the display of Albanian national symbols, including the flag, became subjects of dispute. As in the past, the Albanian intelligentsia became the main target of Serbian attacks. In an attempt to stem the growing migration of Serbs from the region, the authorities gave them priority in employment, housing, and allotment of plots for private houses. The sale of real estate involving Albanians and Serbs was prohibited by law. And following Tirana's public criticism of the Yugoslav actions and the endorsement of demands for a Kosova republic, all contacts between Kosova and Albania were severed, throwing Tirana-Belgrade relations into a deep freeze thereafter.

Albanians outside Kosova, particularly in the republic of Macedonia, also experienced renewed repression. Indeed, before the rise to power of Slobodan Milošević, the repression of Albanians in Macedonia was harsher than in Kosova. In an attempt to stamp out Albanian nationalism and separatism, the Macedonian government declared that Albanian names could no longer be used for places, and Albanians were prohibited from giving what the authorities described as "nationalist" names to newborn children. The Albanians also were denied the right to display their national flag. Albanian-language education was severely restricted. In a clear violation of the constitutional provision guaranteeing Albanians the right to education in their mother tongue, in 1987 the Macedonian government announced that instruction in secondary schools would be carried out solely in the Macedonian language. The authorities also introduced harsh administrative measures aimed at stemming the rising birthrate among Albanians. Couples with more than two children were denied all social and medical benefits. The Albanians interpreted this as a racist policy.

In the mid-1980s Serbian intellectuals began to articulate grievances on matters that the regime had long maintained were solved. They complained that Kosova was carved out of Serbia—a view that challenged the official Yugoslav communist claim that Albanians had voluntarily requested to join the republic of Serbia after World War II. Blaming Tito for Serbia's "downturn" in the post-1945 period, Serbian nationalists insisted that the two provinces, Kosova and Vojvodina, be brought under direct Serbian control. Eventually they went much further, raising the issue of the status of Serb populations in Croatia and Bosnia. Serb activists advocated new arrangements whereby Serbia would be recognized in what they termed its proper place in the federation. Serb nationalist grievances were articulated most succinctly in a memorandum prepared by Serbia's Academy of Sciences and published in 1986.

Tensions continued to rise throughout the 1980s as the government relied almost exclusively on police and military repression to stabilize the situation. While Albanians accounted for only 8 percent of the country's population, 70 percent of Yugoslavia's political prisoners were Albanians. By the end of 1988, some 485,000 Albanians "had passed through the hands of the police."[23] Continued repression and erosion of Albanians' rights had the effect of sharpening antagonisms in Kosova, producing explosive resentment among the Albanians and dealing a severe blow to the already strained relations between the two ethnic groups. The crackdown also failed to improve the situation of the Serb minority, which continued to leave in large numbers.

The conflict assumed a new and dangerous dimension in the second half of the 1980s. The advent of Slobodan Milošević to power in Serbia in 1986 established what was, in a sense, a textbook example of Brubaker's triadic nexus: Serbia became a "nationalizing state," with its legitimacy resting on nationalist assaults on the resident "minority" in Kosova. It was not a full-scale example of the triad, however, because Serbia was still formally part of the Yugoslav federation and because— and this is characteristic throughout—the "homeland state," Albania, played an insignificant role. Milošević's policy blended elements of Serbian ultranationalism; the widespread use of coercion, fear, and intimidation; general disenfranchisement; and the use of propaganda to demonize the Albanians. He exploited widespread Serb feelings that they had not received their share in the post-1945 Yugoslavia and used the Kosova issue to consolidate his power and pave the way for a Greater Serbia by stripping Kosova of its autonomy. Portraying himself as the protector of the Serbs in Kosova, Milošević purged the moderate elements within Serbia's and Kosova's leaderships, accusing them of being soft on Albanian nationalism. He whipped the Serbs into a delirium of nationalist indignation against the Albanians, using the state-controlled media to launch hate propaganda openly promoting anti-Albanianism, accusing Albanians of carrying out "genocide" against the Serbs, and identifying them as Serbia's and Yugoslavia's national enemies. A lingering perception was created both at home and abroad of Albanians bent on the destruction of Yugoslavia and horrendous mistreatment of local Serbs. This led to a dramatic increase in anti-Albanian sentiment in Serbia and some other parts of the country, particularly Macedonia. Having monopolized Yugoslavia's decision-making process regarding the Albanian issue, Milošević engineered the replacement of provincial leaders Azem Vllasi and Kaçusha Jashari and turned his attention to changing Serbia's constitution to bring Kosova under Belgrade's full control. This also offered Milošević a way of gaining and holding power.

Albanians bitterly opposed these measures. In February 1989 a protest by miners in Mitrovica led to an unprecedented general strike, paralyzing the province's economy. Belgrade imposed a state of emergency and dispatched thousands of troops and special federal police units to Kosova. Milošević ordered the arrest of Vllasi and dozens of other prominent Albanian leaders, blaming them for the demonstrations and strikes. On March 23, 1989, with Kosova under a state of emergency, the parliament building surrounded by tanks, and MiG-21 fighters flying low over Pristina, the Kosova parliament approved constitutional changes reducing the province's autonomy within Serbia. Albanians maintained that the vote was unconstitutional, arguing that many of those who voted in favor of the changes were not even members of the parliament and that many Albanian deputies had been interrogated by the secret police before casting their votes. While tens of thousands of Albanians battled security forces throughout Kosova, Serbs celebrated in Belgrade, claiming that Serbia had finally regained its national and spiritual integrity.[24]

The forced abolition of Kosova's autonomy plunged the province into a deep political, economic, and social crisis. The local League of Communists, which had at best made only half-hearted efforts to preserve the province's autonomy, disintegrated overnight, sparking a dramatic change in the Kosovar political scene. The League of Communists' demise had serious repercussions for Serbia's long-term aims toward the region. For the first time since 1945, Belgrade could not rely on local Albanian officials to implement its policies. At the end of 1989 and the beginning of 1990, Kosova witnessed the emergence of independent, noncommunist political groups and parties. A group of intellectuals, led by literary critic Ibrahim Rugova, formed the Democratic League of Kosova. In its initial platform, the Democratic League called for the preservation of Kosova's autonomy but did not demand republic status. During this period other parties also were created, the most important of which were the Peasants, the Social Democratic, the Parliamentarian, and the Christian Democratic parties. Albanians in Macedonia and Montenegro also formed their own political parties, which closely coordinated their activities with the Democratic League, Kosova's largest political force.

Disenchanted with Milošević's policy and rapidly losing popular support, Albanian members of the provincial parliament met on July 2, 1990, and proclaimed Kosova an "independent unit" within the Yugoslav federation. Three days later Belgrade responded by taking over full control of the province, suspending Kosova's parliament and government, and shutting down Albanian-language radio and television and the daily *Rilindja*. Albanian members of the suspended parliament responded by proclaiming Kosova a republic in a clandestine meeting on September 7 in the city of Kaçanik. They approved a constitution, which declared that "the republic of Kosova is a democratic state of the Albanian people and of the members of other nations and national minorities who are its citizens: Serbs, Muslims, Montenegrins, Croats, Turks, Romanies, and others living in Kosova." While the document denied Serbia's sovereignty, it stated that "the Republic of Kosova as a state is part of the Yugoslav community,"[25] thus accepting the inviolability of Yugoslavia's external borders. Belgrade interpreted the Kaçanik declaration as an unconstitutional act and a direct attack on the country's territorial integrity.

The authorities embarked on a policy of Serbianizing the province through a campaign of deliberate political, economic, and social marginalization of Albanians. In a swift and dramatic shift of control from Albanians to Serbs, Albanian civil servants were dismissed en masse, the police force was cleansed of almost all Albanians, and Serbs were appointed to all important government posts. More than 130,000 Albanian workers were fired from their state jobs. The authorities also initiated a policy of cultural disenfranchisement. In the wake of Albanians' rejection of Serbian educational programs, Belgrade withheld funding from Albanian educational institutions and closed down the Albanian-language university in Pristina. In an effort to change the population makeup of the province, Serb authorities openly pressured Albanians to emigrate while offering Serbs willing to resettle in Kosova various advantages, including higher wages and free housing.[26] Although many Albanians were traumatized by Serb repression and psychological terror, Milošević's policy of blatant colonialism sparked unprecedented political activism. Albanians throughout the country underwent a rapid process of homogenization.

By mid-1990 the Yugoslav government had been severely weakened and, even had it wished to, was in no position to play the role of an honest broker in the Albanian-Serb conflict. However, not only had the federal government failed to take any concrete action to block Milošević's actions but indeed it had endorsed Serbia's rollback of self-government in Kosova. By giving Milošević a free hand in Kosova, the leaders of Yugoslavia's other ethnic groups shared responsibility for the loss of the province's autonomy and the subsequent turmoil there. Had Slovene and Croat leaders maintained a more principled stand and resisted Milošević in 1989–90, they would have been in a better position to check his wider aims of national power for himself and Serbia. However, the crackdown in Kosova played into their hands by hastening Slovenia's and Croatia's independence.

Developments in Kosova received little attention abroad. The international community was sympathetic to Yugoslavia's geopolitical position and delicate internal situation. With the exception of international human rights groups, the repression of Albanians and the abolition of Kosova's autonomy were largely ignored by the West. U.S. and West European governments rejected calls to impose sanctions to persuade the Yugoslav authorities to comply with international human rights standards.

During this period Kosova became a serious concern for Albania. After the 1981 demonstrations, Tirana had publicly endorsed demands for a Kosova republic but repeatedly stated that it was not interested in border changes. While the substance of Albania's policy toward Yugoslavia had not changed, Tirana fiercely denounced the abolition of Kosova's autonomy, drawing charges from Belgrade that Albania was inciting the Kosovars. But the emergence of noncommunist political parties in Kosova had a direct and immediate bearing on Tirana's domestic developments: It stimulated demands for political pluralism in Albania. Although Tirana had provided only rhetorical support to Kosova, ethnic Albanians had been overwhelmingly sympathetic to

Hoxha and his successor, Ramiz Alia, maintaining a conspicuous silence on reports of widespread human rights violations and the disastrous failure of Albania's isolation and self-reliance policies. But by mid-1990, disappointed with the lack of any meaningful support from Tirana and realizing that the poor international image of Tirana's regime was hurting their own cause, ethnic Albanians began to call for the democratization of Albania. Once Alia was forced to accept demands of student demonstrators for political pluralism in December 1990, Albanians in Yugoslavia expressed overwhelming support for Albania's fledgling opposition, particularly the Democratic Party. In contrast to the communists, the Democrats from the outset focused on the plight of Kosova's Albanians. In its initial political platform, the Democratic Party vowed to fight for "the realization of centuries-long aspirations of the Albanian nation for independence, union and progress in accordance with the spirit of international documents."[27] Thus postcommunist Albania's legitimacy was bound up with the Kosova question.

Albanians and the Disintegration of Yugoslavia

With the dissolution of Yugoslavia, ethnic Albanians were in a precarious position. Not only had Milošević stripped them of their political autonomy, in clear violation of Yugoslavia's 1974 constitution, but the Serbian leader had imposed virtual military rule in Kosova and marginalized the Albanians politically, socially, and economically. While Albanians were not permitted to take part in the negotiations held by republic leaders during 1990–91 on the future of the country before the outbreak of Yugoslav wars of secession, representatives of Albanian political parties from Kosova, Macedonia, and Montenegro met on October 11, 1991, in Pristina and adopted a unified stand. A statement issued at the end of the meeting asserted that if agreement was reached to preserve the Yugoslav federation, Kosova had to be recognized as a republic and Albanian minorities in Macedonia and Montenegro guaranteed their national rights. In the event that Yugoslavia was preserved but internal borders changed, Albanian representatives insisted on the establishment of an Albanian republic encompassing Kosova and the predominantly Albanian-inhabited territories in Macedonia, Montenegro, and southern Serbia. Finally, if Yugoslavia disintegrated, Albanians insisted that they would exercise their right to self-determination and unite with Albania.[28]

These declarations, however, had no practical impact since the Albanians, unarmed and severely battered by years of police and military crackdown, were in no position to make their voices heard or organize an armed movement. Moreover, they did not have the backing of other ethnic groups in Yugoslavia or the international community. Ethnic Albanians also could not expect assistance from Albania, which was undergoing political and social upheaval in the wake of the downfall of its communist regime. Thus, while Slovenia, Croatia, Bosnia-Herzegovina, and Macedonia became independent, Kosova remained within Serbia.

THE KOSOVA SHADOW STATE

Before 1990 few ethnic Albanian activists had seriously advocated secession from Yugoslavia or unification with Albania. Indeed, even as late as 1991 the Albanians were hoping to find a solution within the framework of a Yugoslav federation or confederation. Belgrade's intransigence and increased repression, and the disintegration of Yugoslavia, contributed to a shift in Albanian demands from greater autonomy to outright secession. Stressing the legal and factual similarity between constituent provinces and republics in former Yugoslavia, Albanians insisted that Kosova had the right to independent statehood. They also argued that Kosova had never been incorporated legally into Serbia but rather into Yugoslavia. In September 1991 Albanian deputies of the suspended provincial parliament met clandestinely and declared Kosova a "sovereign and independent state." Following the example of Yugoslavia's secessionist republics, the Kosova parliament called for a national referendum to legitimize its decision. Despite Belgrade's attempt to prevent the referendum, Albanians overwhelmingly cast their votes for independence. Predictably, Belgrade responded by saying that the referendum was invalid because, as a minority and not a "nation," the ethnic Albanians did not have the right to self-determination. Nevertheless, in October 1991 the Albanians formed a provisional, shadow government. Rugova's associate Dr. Bujar Bukoshi was appointed prime minister. Bukoshi's government, based in Bonn, appealed to the European Community (now, the European Union) to recognize Kosova's independence. However, Albanians were accorded differential treatment and the European Community rejected their request, arguing that as a former province of Yugoslavia Kosova was not entitled to statehood.[29]

By the beginning of 1992, a system of effective apartheid had been created in Kosova, with Serbs maintaining all levers of power and Albanians totally excluded. In order to deter the Albanians from staging a violent uprising, the government maintained a heavy police and military presence.[30] The two communities came to see themselves as permanently divided and having diametrically opposed interests. Despite increased Serbian repression, the Albanians pushed ahead with their drive for independence, organizing, in May 1992, parliamentary and presidential elections for their self-proclaimed republic. Rugova was elected president and his Democratic League won 96 seats in the 140-seat parliament. The Parliamentary Party won 13 seats; the Peasants and Christian Democratic parties, 7 each; the Party of Democratic Action, 1; and independent candidates, 2 seats. Fourteen seats were reserved for the region's Serbs and Montenegrins, who boycotted the elections. Serb authorities used force to prevent the convening of the parliament in June 1992. Although the parliament never met in plenary session, it continued to function through its commissions, which met irregularly in Pristina. Albanians boycotted all political institutions in Serbia and Yugoslavia and proceeded to establish parallel institutions that included a separate government and education, health care, social services, and taxation systems. They also refused to serve in the Yugoslav armed forces or take part in Serbian or Yugoslav elections.

Recognizing the preponderant power Serbia enjoyed in relations with Kosova, Rugova exhorted Albanians to pursue their objectives through nonviolent methods. Despite Serb control, Rugova's movement adorned itself with the various attributes of statehood. A separate educational system from the elementary to the university levels and health services were funded through a Solidarity Fund, which was financed both locally and by the large Albanian diaspora in Western Europe and the United States. Kosova also saw the development of an impressive civil society. Cognizant of Serbia's and the international community's opposition to Greater Albania, Rugova indicated that the Kosovars would indefinitely postpone unification with their mother country. Instead, he proposed the creation of an independent state of Kosova, which would be demilitarized and would develop close links with both Serbia and Albania. In the proposed state, the Serb minority would enjoy the same status as a nation as the Albanian majority.

Rugova held out the hope that the conflict with Serbs could be resolved peacefully. He urged his fellow Albanians not to give Belgrade a pretext to carry out a campaign of ethnic cleansing, maintaining that Milošević's policy was doomed to failure and that time was on the side of the Albanians. But as his peaceful resistance failed to produce tangible results or moderate Serb behavior, Rugova became the subject of increased criticism. In contrast to Rugova's pacifist policy, prominent personalities such as academician Rexhep Qosja, former political prisoner and human rights activist Adem Demaçi, and journalist Veton Surroi called for active forms of resistance and civil disobedience, including massive street demonstrations. None, however, supported armed resistance. With his opponents unable to offer a credible plan of action, during the first half of the 1990s Rugova continued to enjoy great popularity. The brutal war in Bosnia, where Serbs fought fellow Slavs, had accentuated Albanian fears that if war broke out in Kosova, Serbian atrocities would be even more gruesome than those committed in Bosnia. While he insisted that full independence was imperative, Rugova advocated a gradual dissociation from Serbia. The Albanian leader repeatedly called for unconditional talks with Belgrade aimed at achieving initial agreement on less controversial issues and said that the thorny problem of the status of Kosova should be dealt with at an unspecified later date. Belgrade, however, showed no interest in negotiations with Pristina. There was no significant pressure from the international community or Albanians themselves to force a change in Belgrade's stand. Nevertheless, preoccupied with successive wars in Croatia and Bosnia and careful not to overextend itself by opening a second front in Kosova, the Yugoslav government tolerated the development and existence of the Albanian parallel system along the official Serbian one.

While Rugova was forced to operate under extremely difficult circumstances, he did not prove to be a particularly effective or dynamic leader. His failure to take any action to counter Serbia's harsh repression led to widespread feelings of humiliation, defeatism, and loss of national dignity. Between 1992 and 1997 there were no public demonstrations or any other kind of organized resistance against the Yugoslav government. Rugova, whose leadership was characterized by obsessive secrecy, had become the symbol of a status quo that, for the majority of Albanians, was becoming increasingly intolerable. He gradually lost contact with the masses and came to rely on a small group of trusted aides who had little political experience. He concentrated decision-making powers in his own hands and increasingly marginalized opponents within his party as well as leaders of other political parties. By the mid-1990s Rugova, according to his critics, appeared to have become too comfortable with his position as the dominant ethnic Albanian leader and largely oblivious to the daily sufferings of his people and the steady deterioration of the situation in Kosova. He was unable to lay down the cornerstone of Kosova's statehood or convince other countries to embrace the self-determination goals of the ethnic Albanians. Rugova's decision not to convene the parliament, the postponement of parliamentary and presidential elections, and failure to create a functioning administrative machinery seriously undermined his position and led to a steady radicalization of the Kosovar Albanians.

The international community was well aware of the dangers of a Kosova explosion.[31] In December 1992, amid reports of rising tensions, President George Bush warned Milošević that in the event of Serb-inspired violence in Kosova, the United States would "be prepared to employ military force against the Serbs in Kosovo and in Serbia proper."[32] What came to be known as the Christmas warning was repeated on several occasions by President Bill Clinton during his first term in office. The United States and its allies expressed strong support for Rugova's peaceful approach and counseled him not to engage in actions, including convening the parliament elected in 1992 or holding new elections in spring 1996, that could provoke Serbian crackdown. In a move clearly aimed at enhancing his standing at home, Western contacts with Pristina were almost exclusively with Rugova, and his opponents were deliberately sidelined. The Kosovar leader was invited often to Washington and West European capitals, and senior Western officials traveled to Pristina. The pro-Rugova media in Kosova portrayed Western support for Rugova as endorsement of Kosova's independence, although this was not the case. The United States and its European allies consistently expressed support for Yugoslavia's territorial integrity, demanding only the restoration of Kosova's autonomy. They continued to treat Kosova merely as a human rights issue and failed to take any meaningful steps to mediate the conflict. The prevailing view of Western governments was that raising the Kosova issue with Milošević would only complicate efforts to end the war in Bosnia. Thus Kosova was sacrificed to obtain Milošević's cooperation for the Dayton peace agreements. But this was a huge mistake. Had Kosova been addressed at the Dayton conference and granted the same status as Bosnia's Serb entity, Srpska Republika, the subsequent war might have been avoided. Dayton conveyed to Albanians the message that only those willing to fight for their cause would get a seat at the negotiating table.

The exclusion of Kosova from Dayton shattered illusions among Albanians that Rugova's pacifist policies could produce tangible results. The widespread perception that the international community was oblivious to the plight of the ethnic Albanians was further reinforced by the lifting of sanctions against Belgrade and the European Union's decision in 1996 to recognize the Yugoslav government. Washington's decision to maintain an outer wall of sanctions—refusing to send an American ambassador to Belgrade and blocking Yugoslavia's membership in the United Nations, Organization for Security and Cooperation in Europe (OSCE), and international financial institutions until "significant" progress had been made in Kosova—was insufficient to pressure

Milošević to open a dialogue with Pristina. Dayton deepened the frustration of ethnic Albanians and contributed to their progressive radicalization. Under Western pressure, Rugova was forced to postpone parliamentary and presidential elections scheduled to be held in 1996 and 1997, which seriously diminished his legitimacy in the eyes of Albanians. Other political forces began to challenge the Democratic League's dominant position in Kosova's politics. Adem Demaçi, an outspoken Rugova critic, who had spent almost 30 years in Yugoslav prisons on charges of nationalistic activities, resigned as chairman of a human rights organization and became leader of the Parliamentary Party. In the clearest sign of the breakdown of the cohesion that had characterized the Kosovar leadership, exiled Prime Minister Bukoshi publicly chastised Rugova for his "utopian" belief that his pacific resistance and reliance on the international community would "deliver" independence to Kosova. The prime minister insisted that Albanians had to back up with actions their demands for independence.[33]

However, the greatest challenge to Rugova came with the emergence of the underground Kosova Liberation Army (KLA). Founded by former political prisoners and activists disillusioned with Rugova's path of nonviolence, the KLA was funded by the large Albanian diaspora in Western Europe and the United States. Its leaders remained mysterious, but some were believed to be former Marxist-Leninists who had close ties to Hoxha's regime. However, the rank and file seemed largely devoid of any particular ideology; their main, indeed only, objective was to get rid of Serbian occupation. Beginning in 1996 the KLA carried out a series of synchronized attacks against Serb officials and policemen and individual Albanians it regarded as Serb collaborators. The shadowy group rejected Rugova's policies and vowed to wage an armed struggle for the liberation of Kosova. The KLA chose a highly symbolic date to make its first public appearance: the anniversary of the proclamation of Albania's independence (1912), which is observed by Albanians everywhere as Flag Day. On November 28, 1997, three armed, uniformed, and masked KLA fighters appeared at the funeral of Halit Geci, a teacher killed when Serb police forces fired at random into farmhouses, a shop, and the school in his village in Drenica. One of them addressed the 20,000 mourners, saying that the KLA had embarked on a national war for Kosova's independence.[34] With political leaders in Pristina unable to formulate a clear strategy and with increased Serbian repression, KLA actions resonated with many young Albanians, who saw the use of force as the only alternative to their dire situation. Rugova, however, continued to reject active resistance as dangerously irresponsible and an excuse for a devastating Serb military crackdown.[35] But the failure of the pacific policy to weaken the grip of Serbian rule over Albanians had left him with a paucity of creative political thinking, thus feeding the frustrations, fears, and desperation of ethnic Albanians. Concerned with the deteriorating situation, the Contact Group, which was created in 1994 with the aim of ending the war in Bosnia and composed of Britain, France, Germany, Italy, Russia, and the United States, for the first time issued a statement on Kosova. In a significant policy change, it called for "an enhanced status for Kosovo within the FRY [Federal Republic of Yugoslavia]," thus challenging Serbia's claims of sovereignty over Kosova. But the group ruled out Kosova's independence.[36]

ALBANIANS IN MACEDONIA

The dissolution of Yugoslavia abruptly interrupted the coordination of activities between Albanian political forces in Kosova and those in Macedonia. Albanians in the two regions had never before been separated by an international border, had very close ties, and considered themselves a unified community. Macedonia's Albanian political and cultural elite had been educated in Pristina; there were no Albanian-language universities in Macedonia. While Albanians welcomed the disintegration of Yugoslavia, once it became apparent that Kosova would remain part of rump Yugoslavia, many Albanians in Macedonia preferred that Macedonia too remain part of Yugoslavia in order to prevent further Albanian fragmentation. In the wake of Macedonia's independence, the two Albanian communities, facing different challenges, gradually adopted contrasting strategies in the pursuit of their goals. Whereas the Kosovars boycotted official state institutions, Albanians in Macedonia chose to work within the system to advance their interests. Government repression, which had reached disturbing levels in the mid- and late 1980s, abated significantly after independence. The ethnic Albanian Party for Democratic Prosperity, which was founded in August 1990 and rapidly developed into a mass movement with widespread popular support, joined Macedonia's coalition government in the hope of convincing the authorities to meet Albanian demands for greater political, cultural, and economic rights. Albanians demanded that the constitution, which had been adopted in 1991 and referred to the Albanians as a minority, be changed to grant them equal "nation" status with the Macedonians. They also called for proportional representation in government, economic, and cultural administration; the recognition of Albanian as an official language; and the free use of the Albanian national flag.

The issue of Albanian-language education, and particularly the lack of an Albanian-language university, became contentious, with ethnic Albanians insisting that failure to institutionalize Albanian as an official language infringed on their rights. Despite repeated government promises, the opening of an Albanian-language Pedagogical Academy in Skopje was postponed. In 1995 Albanians set up a private university in Tetova, Macedonia's largest Albanian city. Although its founders stressed that instruction at the university would be based on Macedonia's educational system, the government refused to recognize the university, insisting that as a minority the Albanians did not have the right to higher education in their mother language. The authorities expressed concern that Tetova University could become a hotbed of Albanian nationalism. Some Macedonians interpreted the Albanian move as the first step toward secession. After an initial government attempt to close down the university, which resulted in violent riots, the university was permitted to operate, although Skopje continued to consider it illegal.

While Skopje apparently recognized the importance of accommodating Albanians, it moved slowly in meeting their demands for fear of alienating Macedonian nationalists, who accused Albanians of engaging in deliberate actions to obstruct Macedonia's nation-building efforts. This caused cracks within Albanian political ranks as differences emerged regarding the best strategy and tactics to promote their political agenda. In 1994 the Party for Democratic Prosperity suffered a major split, which significantly undermined the Albanians' bargaining position. A radical faction led by the respected intellectual Arben Xhaferri, which argued that participation in the coalition government had been ineffective, set up a separate party, which later joined with another party to form the Democratic Party of Albanians in Macedonia.

Compared to the preindependence period, the position of ethnic Albanians in Macedonia improved significantly after 1991. However, they remained essentially second-class citizens.[37] As Human Rights Watch/Helsinki has noted, "Ethnic Albanians have been denied many of the basic rights guaranteed them in both Macedonian and international law."[38] Albanians continue to claim discrimination in all fields. In 1994 Macedonians accounted for 80.6 percent of those employed in the state sector, while Albanians accounted for only 10.4 percent.[39] In the same year, Albanians made up only 5.2 percent of students attending Macedonian universities, while Macedonians accounted for 90 percent.[40] By 1997 the Albanian proportion had increased to only 7.3 percent.[41] The Albanians were also heavily underrepresented in government institutions. In 1995, in the Ministry of the Interior, the Albanians made up only 4.19 percent, compared to 91 percent for the

Macedonians. In the Defense Ministry the picture was even bleaker: Albanians accounted for 3 percent, Macedonians for 85 percent. The state administration continued to be dominated by Macedonians, who made up 90 percent of it, with Albanians accounting for only 4.39 percent.[42]

While Albanians and Macedonians continued to coexist without significant interethnic conflict, they did not intermix and their relations were characterized by increased tensions. By the mid-1990s the gulf between the two groups had widened significantly as the government had failed to devise a formula to reconcile Albanians' demands for greater rights with Macedonians' desire for a unified state.

POSTCOMMUNIST ALBANIA AND THE ALBANIAN DIASPORAS

Before the collapse of the communist order in Albania in 1991, there were virtually no contacts between Albanians in Albania proper and those in the former Yugoslavia. Apart from a tiny and privileged group of intellectuals who taught at Pristina University between 1974 and 1981, few Albanian citizens visited Kosova. Likewise, only a small number of Kosovars had visited Tirana. With Albania's opening up in 1990–91, suddenly many ethnic Albanians were able to visit their mother country. First contacts were disappointing. After almost five decades of one of the worst dictatorial rules in the world, Albania was a wasteland. Most local Albanians were too preoccupied with their own problems to give much thought to Kosova's plight. Moreover, Ramiz Alia's government was engaged in a well-coordinated campaign to discredit visiting ethnic Albanians and drive a wedge between them and local Albanians. Kosovar leaders had publicly expressed support for the opposition Democratic Party, drawing communist accusations of "interfering" in Albania's internal affairs. The communists largely blamed the Kosovars for "exporting" political pluralism to Tirana and were disconcerted with Pristina's support for Albania's fledgling opposition parties. Rumors were spread that the more prosperous ethnic Albanians were engaged in various illegal activities and had embarked on a buying spree of recently privatized shops and small enterprises in Tirana.

The ethnic Albanians welcomed the Democratic Party's victory in March 1992 and the election of Sali Berisha as president. They believed that Berisha, who comes from the northern district of Tropoja on the border with Kosova, would be more supportive of their cause. Indeed, even before the legalization of opposition in Albania in late 1990, Berisha had attempted to justify calls for his country's democratization as also "a valuable contribution to the struggle of our brothers in Kosova."[43] The question of Kosova figured prominently in Berisha's first public speech, on the occasion of the establishment of the Democratic Party in December 1990. He denounced Milošević's repression of ethnic Albanians, adding that "The Democratic Party of Albania cannot accept the division of the Albanian nation as eternal; therefore, it will struggle by peaceful means and within the context of the processes of integration in Europe to realize their rights for progress and national unity."[44]

Once in power, however, Berisha toned down his fiery nationalist rhetoric. While insisting that Kosova's Albanians were entitled to self-determination, he tried to allay Western concerns about Albania's territorial claims, insisting that Tirana opposed border changes.[45] Berisha urged Rugova to strike a deal with Belgrade and give up hopes of establishing an independent state or unification with Albania. He insisted that the Albanians do everything within their power to prevent the outbreak of conflict with the vastly more powerful Yugoslavs. But he repeatedly warned that in the event of a war in Kosova, Albania would not stand idly by.[46] The Tirana government provided strong political and diplomatic support for the Kosovars. Rugova and his close advisers regularly visited Tirana for consultations and coordination of activities.

In the case of Macedonia, Berisha subordinated Tirana's ties with ethnic Albanians to bilateral relations with Skopje. He saw the existence of an independent Macedonia, separating Serbia and Greece, as crucial to Albania's vital national interests. Concerned that ethnic unrest could invite Serbian intervention or drive Skopje toward Belgrade, he urged Albanians to become a force for stability for the Macedonian state. Despite tension and continued snags in resolving thorny political issues, Tirana-Skopje relations evolved positively after 1992. However, Berisha's view that the possible destabilization of Macedonia could have serious repercussions for Albania was not widely shared in Albania or western Macedonia. Indeed, not a few nationalists insisted that in order for the Albanians to achieve their ultimate national goal, unification, Macedonia would have to be destroyed.

Concerned that an outbreak of armed conflict in Kosova not only would have serious consequences for the Albanian diaspora but also would entangle Albania, Berisha pursued a steady course of promoting regional stability by expanding cooperation with neighboring countries. Albania developed very close political and military ties with the United States, offered its air and sea facilities to NATO, and played a key role in the American strategy of containing the Yugoslav conflict. Washington offered Albania political and economic inducements and the possibility of protection in the event of Yugoslav aggression through increased bilateral military cooperation and in the framework of NATO's program of Partnership for Peace. Berisha was widely praised in the West for his responsible and constructive policy toward Kosova and Macedonia. During a meeting with Berisha at the White House in September 1995, President Clinton expressed appreciation for "Albania's responsible role in regions of the former Yugoslavia with large ethnic Albanian populations."[47] However, Berisha's appeals for the inclusion of Kosova in international peace talks on the former Yugoslavia and for international preventive action went unheeded. Tirana was deeply disappointed that the Albanian question was not part of the Dayton Accords and expressed concern about the implications of the agreement on Bosnia for Kosova's future and Albania's regional role.

While Tirana was not in a position to provide much assistance or influence positively events in Kosova, during the period from 1992 to 1996 Albanians witnessed profound psychological transformations. Albania made steady progress in its transition from the harshly authoritarian state of the past. The Albanians in Kosova and Macedonia saw a strong Albania as key to the solution of the national question. Interaction between ethnic Albanians and their national state increased significantly. While Albanians recognized the fact that their territorial union was not imminent, a process of "spiritual" unification was already under way. They no longer considered insurmountable the differences in mentality, political culture, and economic and social development, the result of having lived for so long in separate states with different social and political systems.

For a few years it appeared that Albania's long curse of repression and suffering might finally be over. For most of his first three to four years in office, Berisha had a virtual free ride from an admiring West as his country made steady gains and the former communists looked largely like a spent force. But the wind shifted markedly following flawed elections in 1996. The elections were followed by a progressive falling out between Berisha and the United States, which had been his key foreign backer. The political crisis was confounded by rising economic problems, caused by the mushrooming of bogus investment schemes. Taking advantage of the Albanians' poor understanding of how a market economy and financial institutions work, dubious businessmen set up fraudulent pyramid schemes. Tens of thousands of people put their life savings in get-rich-quick schemes, which offered interest rates of up to 50 percent a month. The government tolerated the schemes, insisting that it had no role to play in regulating such companies. In early 1997 the collapse of several pyramid schemes sparked an armed revolt, plunging the country into months of anarchy. Albania's police and armed forces disintegrated, military depots were raided, and on the order of a million weapons fell into civilian hands. In the hastily organized early elections in June 1997, the Socialist Party, formerly the Communist Party, won a landslide victory and its chairman, Fatos Nano, became the new prime minister. Berisha resigned as president and was replaced by the Socialist Party's Rexhep Meidani.

The sudden implosion and the power grab by former communists seriously derailed Albania's quest to remake itself after half a century of communist rule. These events also had a profound impact on Kosova's Albanians, who had overwhelmingly sided with the Democrats and against the Socialist-inspired revolt. While Albania's implosion did not force ethnic Albanians to rethink their goal of secession from Serbia, it was clear that Kosova could not expect meaningful political and diplomatic support from Albania. The turmoil in Albania also gave a new impetus to nationalists in Serbia and Macedonia, who saw it as an opportunity to crack down on the ethnic Albanians.

That Nano's government was less inclined than Berisha's to support the Kosovars' cause became evident immediately after it came to power. Nano redefined Tirana's relations with Belgrade and changed the nature of Albania's relationships in the region by forging unusually close relations with Greece at the expense of those with Italy, Albania's traditional patron. In a clear departure from the previous government's stand and without consultations with the Rugova leadership, in October 1997 Albanian Foreign Minister Paskal Milo met at the United Nations with his Yugoslav counterpart, Milan Milutinović, who in December 1997 was elected president of Serbia. But more important, Nano met Milošević during a Balkan summit in Crete in November 1997. Nano reportedly accepted that Kosova was Serbia's internal affair and agreed with Milošević that Belgrade should grant Albanians "basic human rights but not autonomy."[48] In a subsequent comment that caused great consternation in Pristina, Nano sharply criticized Kosova's parallel institutions and urged Albanians to give up their "ghettoization" and focus on "cohabitation" with their neighbors. He said that "Albanians in and outside Albania should understand that parallel institutions are no solution; on the contrary, they only radicalize the societies that have created them."[49] In an election speech in December 1997, Serbian presidential candidate Milutinović said that Nano's government "has made it clear through its representatives that [Kosova] is our affair, that these are our citizens, and that we should solve the problem ourselves."[50] While the OSCE and foreign governments criticized Belgrade authorities for the conduct of Serbia's presidential elections, Albanian Foreign Minister Milo welcomed Milutinović's victory, saying Serbia had distanced itself from its "warmongering policies of the past."[51] In an interview with a Greek newspaper in February 1998, Nano asserted that Kosova was "an internal affair of Yugoslavia" and added that his government expected the situation in Kosova to improve as Yugoslavia becomes "more democratic and more integrated into European institutions."[52]

Nano's attempt to bring a new dimension to the Albanian-Yugoslav relationship without any benefits to Pristina prompted across-the-board denunciation in Kosova and a serious deterioration in Tirana-Pristina relations.[53] Nano's policy also drew strong criticism from the Democrats and right-wing political forces in Albania. They also criticized Nano for urging Greece to mediate the Kosova conflict, saying that given Athens's close relations with Belgrade Greece could not be an impartial go-between. Most Albanians tended to view Athens less as an honest broker than as a public relations agent for Serbia.

Nano and Milo justified Tirana's shifts in its policy toward Belgrade and the departure from Berisha's more assertive stance on Kosova as part of the Socialist government's philosophy. The governing elite claimed that patriotism and nationalism were synonymous with chauvinism. For them, the consolidation of power and marginalization of the Democrats was paramount. Despite the often-repeated, ritualistic invocations of Albanian solidarity, Nano's government displayed an extraordinary indifference to Milošević's repression of Albanians—echoes of communist-era policy. This led to an almost total breakdown in communications between Pristina and Tirana. Concerned that Nano might attempt to reach a deal with Milošević at Kosova's expense, some Kosovar leaders branded Nano "a national traitor." Disenchanted with Tirana's new policy, Rugova rejected several invitations to visit Tirana for talks with Nano.

The Yugoslav Campaign of 1998: Prelude to War

The international community responded weakly to the Yugoslav government's use of violence against Albanians and the egregious violation of international human rights norms in Kosova. Preoccupied with the implementation of the Dayton peace agreements in Bosnia, the West was not particularly disturbed by what it came to regard as low-intensity ethnic conflict in Kosova. But with the Serbs committed to use force to retain control of Kosova and the Albanians determined to free themselves of Serbian control, it was obvious that the two sides would not be able to reach a settlement by themselves. But even as the situation on the ground was deteriorating rapidly, the United States and its NATO allies failed to take decisive action and attempt to manage a peaceful

Albanian-Serb divorce and minimize the cost of separation for both sides. The Albanian-Serb conflict simply was left to fester.[54]

The crisis in Kosova entered a new and dangerous phase in February–March 1998, as Serbia's decade-old repression, Rugova's fruitless Gandhism, and the international community's neglect finally triggered a widespread popular revolt, spearheaded by the Kosova Liberation Army. Yugoslav security forces went on a rampage in Drenica, a traditional stronghold of Albanian resistance, slaughtering more than 80 people, including women and children. In the village of Prekaz, 39 members of the extended family of Adem Jashari, a local KLA leader, were killed. The authorities claimed that security forces were responding to a KLA attack against a police patrol in which two policemen were killed. However, months before the massacre there had been signs that Milošević was preparing a crackdown. By the fall of 1997, with the non-violent strategy having reached a dead end, Albanians had become increasingly restive and it was clear that the status quo could not last much longer. Rugova's position as leader of the ethnic Albanians was under challenge by other political forces and prominent personalities as well as from a leftist faction within his own Democratic League, led by Hydajet Hyseni, a former political prisoner who had played a leading role in organizing the 1981 demonstrations. His opponents demanded that elections, originally scheduled for May 1996, be held as soon as possible, the parliament be convened, and a government be formed in Pristina. In defiance of Rugova's request, the Albanian student movement organized a series of demonstrations, beginning in October 1997, demanding the implementation of a 1996 agreement between Milošević and Rugova that would have permitted Albanian students to return to state educational facilities. These were the first organized protests since 1992 and coincided with several widely publicized KLA actions. In an apparent move to arrest his declining authority, Rugova announced that elections would be held on March 22, 1998.

Determined to frustrate Albanian aims and also to keep a lid on popular manifestations, Milošević responded by ordering, at the end of 1997 and the beginning of 1998, a significant army and police buildup. From his perspective, the time was ripe to strike the Albanians, prevent the emergence of a powerful armed resistance movement, and coerce Kosovar leaders to give up their goal of independence and accept a subordinate status within Serbia. A crackdown against the Kosovars also would rally the Serb public, deflect attention from Serbia's catastrophic economic situation, and help Milošević consolidate his weakening hold on power. In the post-Dayton period, Milošević's international position had improved significantly as the West had come to rely on him for the implementation of peace agreements in Bosnia. In mid-February 1998 the United States had eased sanctions against Belgrade as a reward for its support of the new Bosnian Serb government. The announcement was made in Belgrade by U.S. special envoy Robert Gelbard. The American diplomat may have inadvertently given Milošević the green light for a crackdown in Kosova by denouncing the KLA as a terrorist organization.[55] Only a week after Gelbard made his comments, Serbian forces carried out the massacre in Drenica.[56]

The international community strongly denounced Serbia's actions. U.S. Secretary of State Madeleine Albright called for swift action, insisting that Serbia had to "pay" a price for its crackdown against ethnic Albanians. Albright issued a stern warning to Belgrade: "We are not going to stand by and watch the Serbian authorities do in Kosovo what they can no longer get away with doing in Bosnia."[57] At an urgent meeting of the foreign ministers of the six-member Contact Group on March 9 in London, Albright, warning the international community against "being paralyzed by the kind of artificial even-handedness that equates aggressors with their victims," declared that Belgrade was responsible for the violence in Kosova.[58] But as with the Western failure to stop the war in Bosnia six years earlier, the tough rhetoric was not backed by tough action. Because of disagreements over the viability of using force, and pulled in different directions by conflicting national interests, the Contact Group was unable to muster a clear and unified response to prevent Milošević from unleashing a new round of ethnic killings in the Balkans. The meeting agreed to impose travel restrictions on top Yugoslav officials, seek a United Nations arms embargo, and ban immediately all government-financed credits, and it threatened to freeze all Yugoslav government assets abroad. However, Russia, Serbia's traditional ally, rejected the travel restrictions and the financial sanctions.[59] The second Contact Group meeting on Kosova, held in Bonn on March 25, revealed deep divisions within the group. In addition to Russia, Italy, Germany, and France also adopted a softer position, leaving the United States and Britain alone in advocating greater firmness. Italy had developed strong economic and political relations with Serbia and was hesitant to take any action that would weaken Yugoslavia, which it considered as the linchpin of stability in the Balkans.[60] Germany was primarily concerned about the deleterious effect that military intervention would have on relations with Russia, while France was constrained by strong "pro-Serbian" sentiments going as far back as World War I.[61] Moreover, Western countries were concerned that intervention would effectively aid Kosova's secession, which they opposed. Thus, instead of being punished, Milošević was rewarded with a four-week reprieve from the imposition of additional sanctions. At the end of March, the U.N. Security Council imposed an arms embargo on Yugoslavia. But the embargo had no impact on Yugoslavia's ability to wage war in Kosova since it was not directed against the Yugoslav power apparatus but was aimed at deterring the Albanians from arming themselves. Indeed, the Security Council measure amounted to a unilateral intervention in favor of Belgrade, giving the government forces carte blanche for actions against the Albanians.

Serb actions in Drenica were a clear test of the resolve of the international community. Although Milošević's track record clearly demonstrated that only the sustained threat of military force would secure his compliance, the Clinton administration could not convince America's allies to take effective measures against Belgrade. Moreover, the United States failed to muster the political will to go it alone and retreated from the Christmas warning. Forceful reaction in March, even the use of limited air strikes, might well have prevented the subsequent disaster. But the failure to enforce the Christmas warning and the tepid international response emboldened Milošević, further radicalized the Albanians, and squandered American and NATO credibility. Because of Russia's strong opposition and the reluctance of other group members, such as Italy and France, the Contact Group sent Milošević only weak diplomatic warnings. While Kosovar leaders pleaded for forceful and swift action,[62] condemnation of Serbia remained purely verbal. Many Albanians felt the West had let them down by first threatening Milošević with dire consequences if he attacked the Kosovars and then doing nothing when he did.

The Drenica massacres caused widespread outrage. Rugova responded by urging Albanians to refrain from violence, adding that "We must chose nonviolence, not only because it is the proper choice, but because it is the necessary choice."[63] He dismissed the KLA as a Serb invention: "I am still convinced that the Serbian intelligence service is behind [the KLA]: it is creating an alibi for the murders of the Albanian population."[64] He also decided to go ahead with the March 22 elections despite opposition from the KLA and several political parties, including Demaçi's Parliamentary Party. In response to the Contact Group's call at its March 9 meeting for Serb-Albanian negotiations, on March 24 Rugova announced the formation of a negotiating team. The 15-member group included Democratic League politicians Fehmi Agani and Hydajet Hyseni, former communist leader Mahmut Bakalli, journalist Veton Surroi, and student leader Bujar Dugolli. Adem Demaçi refused to join the group, saying he could not work with Rugova.

The crackdown sparked widespread support for the KLA. Throughout Drenica and other rural regions of Kosova, particularly in areas bordering Albania, people joined the KLA. The majority of the new recruits were simple villagers who saw no other choice but to take up arms. But many were officials or simply members of Rugova's Democratic League. The rapid rise of the KLA, from an estimated several hundred armed members in February 1998 to several thousand by May, changed dramatically Kosova's political and military scene and rendered Rugova an increasingly peripheral figure.[65] With an infusion of weapons smuggled from its staging area in Albania's northeastern district of Tropoja and sustained by a sympathetic rural population, the guerrilla force built roadblocks on Kosova's main highways and by May was in nominal control of 30 percent of the region. Buoyed by its success, the KLA switched from its original hit-and-run strategy of attacking soft targets and engaged in frontal battles with Serbian forces. But lacking experienced career military officers, equipped with little more than AK-47 assault rifles and rocket-propelled grenades, and with only rudimentary training, the KLA paid a heavy price for attempting to confront the Yugoslav army and security forces with conventional tactics. Whereas its ranks grew rapidly, it was unable to develop an effective command structure and a strategy integrating its military and political policy. The KLA's organizational deficiencies became clearly evident when it launched an aborted attempt to take over Rahovec (Orahovac) city on July 18. The attack provoked a heavy Serb retaliation. Using artillery, mortars, and helicopter gunships, Serbian forces literally destroyed Rahovec.[66] Government forces used long-range firepower to clear major roads, demolishing in the process villages along the way.[67] At the end of July Serbian forces recaptured Malisheva, the most important KLA stronghold. Although the guerrillas withdrew from the town without a fight and 35,000 Albanians fled, the city was burned down. As the Yugoslavs continued with their military offensive, the KLA was in no position to offer any meaningful resistance. By mid-August the outmanned and outgunned KLA was forced to resort to the more traditional guerrilla tactics of hit-and-run attacks.

While the conflict in Kosova continued to expand, the international community remained divided. Different historical, political, and economic interests prevented members of the Contact Group from agreeing on tougher actions. At a meeting in Rome on April 29, the Contact Group adopted a U.S.-crafted "dialogue and stabilization package" that ignored several prior demands and watered down others.[68] But the compromise mix of "sticks and carrots" made little impression on Milošević and there was no discernible change in his actions in Kosova.[69]

In early May the United States dispatched to Belgrade veteran diplomat and architect of the Dayton peace agreement Richard Holbrooke, who was known for his strong relationship with Milošević. After shuttling for days between Belgrade and Pristina, Holbrooke brokered a meeting between Milošević and Rugova. While originally the Contact Group had demanded the removal of Serb forces and the immediate beginning of Serb-Albanian talks with an international mediator, Holbrooke convinced Rugova to meet with Milošević without the presence of an international mediator and without Belgrade's meeting any of the Contact Group demands. This, as well as the U.S. suspension of a ban on investments in Serbia,[70] marked a major shift in American policy. Although Rugova's talks with Milošević on May 15 were characterized by Holbrooke as "an important procedural breakthrough," the meeting, which was described by an American observer as an encounter of "Bambi with Godzilla," yielded no positive results.[71] By brokering a meeting between the two leaders without the presence of an outside mediator, Holbrooke showed consideration for Milošević's position that Kosova was "an internal matter." In a move to bolster Rugova's standing at home, Holbrooke arranged for Rugova to meet Clinton on May 29. Clinton reportedly assured the Albanian leader that Bosnia "will not be repeated."[72] But the U.S. president's statement was obscured by the White House's failure to reiterate the Christmas warning. While Rugova was being received at the White House, Milošević launched a massive offensive in the western part of Kosova. Several thousand heavily armed special police and soldiers, backed by artillery batteries, moved to wipe out KLA enclaves along the border with Albania and in the Drenica region. Serb forces reduced the city of Deçan to rubble, destroyed almost all the villages, and created a free-fire zone along the border with Albania. Approximately 20,000 people were forced to seek refuge in northern Albania.

The offensive was clear proof that Milošević considered Western threats to be empty rhetoric. Holbrooke had been manipulated by Milošević, who had no intention of conducting talks with Albanians in good faith. The United States expressed its displeasure with Milošević's latest challenge by raising the possibility of military intervention. Meeting in London on the sidelines of the summit of key industrial countries, Albright and her counterparts from Russia and six other major industrial democracies gave Milošević an ultimatum to call off the offensive in Kosova, allow international monitors unimpeded and continuous access, let refugees return, and resume talks with Rugova. The foreign ministers warned that if these demands were not met by June 16, there would be "moves to further measures to halt the violence and protect the civilian population, including those that may require the authorization of a United Nations Security Council resolution." In a calculated move to pressure Milošević, who could count on a Russian veto of a Security Council resolution, American officials publicly declared that the United States believed that existing U.N. resolutions regarding the former Yugoslavia provided sufficient authority for any possible NATO action.[73] In an attempt to forestall NATO air attacks, Milošević traveled to Moscow for a meeting with President Boris Yeltsin. The Yugoslav leader pledged to give access to relief groups and international monitors, permit refugees to return, and begin talks with the Albanians. Although Milošević failed to meet the key demand to withdraw security forces from Kosova, the Contact Group agreed that he had made sufficient concessions.[74]

With the military option essentially ruled out, the United States focused its diplomatic efforts at convincing Belgrade and Pristina to begin direct talks aimed at reaching a political accord. Rugova had agreed to meet with Milošević without consulting his closest advisers. The meeting deepened the split within the Albanian political scene. Two members of Rugova's 15-member negotiating team, Hydajet Hyseni and Bujar Dugolli, resigned in protest. At the end of June Hyseni and another former Rugova ally, Mehmet Hajrizi, joined forces with Rexhep Qosja to form a new party, the Albanian Democratic Union. Together with Demaçi's Parliamentary Party, the new group called for the formation of a National Salvation Council, with representatives from all political forces and the KLA. Rugova rejected the idea, although Demaçi and Qosja had agreed that Rugova would head the council.

Recognizing that Rugova's position had been significantly weakened, Holbrooke sought to help the Albanians create an inclusive negotiating team. There was widespread agreement that the KLA held the key to any agreement with Belgrade. The United States engaged the KLA in an effort to convince it to join forces with political leaders in Pristina to develop a common position. Holbrooke met with KLA fighters in Junik, a village under Serbian siege on the Albanian border,[75] while Gelbard held talks with KLA representatives in Western Europe.[76] The KLA, however, refused to join Rugova's team.[77] Moreover, the KLA alienated Western governments with its statements that its ultimate goal was the creation of a Greater Albania. In an interview with a German newspaper, KLA spokesman Jakup Krasniqi declared: "We want more than independence. Our goal is the unification of all Albanians in the Balkans."[78]

Such statements led to widespread perceptions abroad that the KLA was a serious threat to peace in the region and further intensified the already existing uneasiness in the West over the Albanian cause. As the KLA gained ground, Western officials signaled that plans for possible military action were on hold because intervention would help Kosova win independence. The international community seemed more interested in preventing the establishment of such an entity than in dealing with the real causes of the Kosova conflict. Some diplomats privately advanced the claim that the Serbs and the KLA were morally equivalent. These sentiments also were reflected in a statement issued after a Contact Group meeting on July 8, 1998. The meeting signaled a major shift: While in the past Milošević had been viewed as the "sole villain," the Contact Group now drew a moral equivalence between Milošević and the KLA. The statement called for an immediate cease-fire but backed off demands that Belgrade withdraw security forces and cease attacks on civilians. The Contact Group specifically threatened sanctions against the Albanian insurgency, stating that the KLA had a responsibility "to avoid violence and all armed activities." It condemned outside support for the KLA and urged all countries to prevent Albanian exiles from financing arms for the insurgents.[79] But by drawing a parallel between Yugoslav forces and the KLA and by making gratuitous statements in favor of the preservation of Yugoslavia's territorial integrity, the United States and its allies in effect gave Milošević the green light to launch an all-out offensive to stamp out the insurgency. A Western official involved in Kosova policymaking was quoted as saying that "the KLA was getting too big for its boots and needed to be taken down a peg or two before there can be negotiations."[80]

Some Western officials evidently hoped that the Serbs would destroy the KLA as a significant force, which in turn would strengthen Rugova and open the door for negotiations between Pristina and Belgrade. Indeed, with the KLA on the run Rugova's position had improved and he backed off from an earlier agreement to create a broad-based government led by an opposition figure, Mehmet Hajrizi. A former political prisoner, Hajrizi was a member of the radical faction within the Democratic League. After Rugova's meeting with Milošević, he resigned from the Democratic League and played a leading role in the formation of the Albanian Democratic Union. He enjoyed the support of Rugova's political opponents, including Demaçi, as well as the KLA. But with the KLA routed on the battlefield and under Western pressure, Rugova suddenly dropped plans to name Hajrizi as prime minister and, on August 13, announced the formation of a new negotiating team. Unlike the first team, which had enjoyed broad support, the second team excluded Rugova's political opponents as well as the KLA.[81] Rugova's actions led to the further fragmentation of Albanian political forces.[82]

The KLA denounced Rugova's decision and announced that it had accepted Adem Demaçi's offer to serve as its political representative.

With Western policy mired in doublespeak and inaction, Milošević continued his campaign, which was directed primarily against the civilian population. Government forces engaged in massive ethnic cleansing, horrendous human rights violations, including the killing and torture of civilians, systematic burning and destruction of homes of Albanians forced to flee, and the manipulation of food and relief supplies for refugees. Western governments and NATO stood by idly as hundreds of thousands of innocent civilians were uprooted and entire areas depopulated. By October approximately 500,000 Albanians, 20 percent of Kosova's prewar population, had been forced to flee their homes; 50,000 Albanians were living in the open in mountains and forests, without any shelter; more than 2,000 were dead and thousands were missing. Between March and October 1998 some 150,000 ethnic Albanians had left the region.[83] Following indiscriminate shelling army and security forces leveled one-third of all villages, destroyed crops, killed livestock, blocked convoys, and imposed a food embargo aimed at the economic strangulation of Kosova.[84] Tens of thousands of civilian dwellings were made uninhabitable.[85]

Milošević was careful to hold his campaign below the threshold of violence and atrocities that would have forced NATO intervention. Borders with both Albania and Macedonia were mined, thus preventing large numbers of refugees from crossing, destabilizing those two fragile countries, and raising the possibility of Greek and Turkish involvement. But whereas Greek and Turkish positions on Kosova reflected their countries' respective interests in the region, with Athens showing sympathy for the Serbs and Ankara for the Albanians, both were careful not to add fuel to the fire. Greece continued to oppose military action against Serbia and the independence of Kosova. At the same time, it urged Milošević to restore autonomy to Kosova. Turkey, on the other hand, was careful not to raise Albanians' hopes that Ankara would support their drive for independence. Ankara also was concerned about the parallel between Kosova and its own conflict with Kurds and the precedent for Kurdish autonomy or even independence. The Turkish army has been accused of waging a scorched-earth policy toward the Kurds similar to that pursued by the Yugoslav army and security forces in Kosova.[86]

THE VIEW FROM ALBANIA AND MACEDONIA

The outbreak of conflict in Kosova found Albania in a precarious position. Albania's meltdown in 1997 and the subsequent change of government had seriously undermined Albanians' "spiritual unification." Ethnic Albanians, who had overwhelmingly supported Berisha, considered the former communists' return to power to be harmful to the interests of both Albania and the Albanian diaspora. The north-south divide, which had become clearly evident during the 1997 turmoil, was further intensified by Prime Minister Nano's failure to reach out to the north, which traditionally had been more supportive of the Kosova cause. Nano's government was composed exclusively of representatives from the south. The change of regime in Tirana had also led to a loss of discipline in the ranks of ethnic Albanian leaders. During his reign, Berisha was recognized as the predominant Albanian leader and enjoyed considerable influence over Pristina and Tetova. Nano, on the other hand, was widely distrusted and viewed as being heavily influenced by Greece, which had strongly supported the Socialist Party's drive to return to power.

The massacres in Drenica and the rapid extension of the conflict in March 1998 had a profound impact on Albania. With the motto "one nation, one stand," the country's main political parties pledged to rise above their narrow party interests and adopt a unified position on Kosova. The KLA encountered little difficulty in establishing a staging area in the northern district of Tropoja. In addition to acquiring light weapons on Albania's market, ethnic Albanians were able to import arms from other countries through the port city of Durrës and the Rinas airport in Tirana. While Nano's government publicly denied involvement, it was clear that top officials, some acting out of patriotic convictions and others taking huge bribes from the Kosovars, were instrumental in allowing arms shipments through.

Nano did not articulate a clear vision, oscillating between calls for the Kosovars to accept autonomy within Serbia to demands that Kosova be granted the status of a republic on a par with Serbia and Montenegro. During a visit to Lisbon in September 1998, Nano made comments supportive of continued Serbian sovereignty over Kosova. In a departure from his earlier statements advocating that Kosova be recognized as a third republic of Yugoslavia, Nano said Kosova should remain part of Serbia. The prime minister was sharply criticized even by members of his own party for abandoning Kosova's Albanians.[87] Even with the continued deterioration of the situation in Kosova, there was little, if any, political consultation between Tirana and Pristina. On several occasions and without public explanations, Tirana shifted its support from Rugova to the KLA and vice versa. This vacillation left the Kosovars wondering about the coherence of Tirana's policy.

Despite numerous provocations and incidents on the border, the Albanian government took no measures to strengthen the country's defense.[88] Instead, Nano demanded that NATO troops be stationed on Albania's borders with Kosova. The opposition Democratic Party questioned the wisdom of the move while blood was still being shed inside Kosova. It criticized Nano's proposal as intending to build a firewall around Kosova. The Democrats feared that a firewall would not only fail to protect the civilian population in Kosova but would trap refugees and also cut off Kosovars' access to fresh supplies of weapons. Rightwing parties accused Nano of national nihilism and cosmopolitanism. Advocating total support for the Kosovars, the right insisted that Albania's commitment to the Kosovars ought to transcend all other obligations. But rhetoric aside, Albania's two major political forces—the ruling Socialist Party and the opposition Democratic Party—displayed a substantial convergence of attitudes: Both paid lip service to nonviability of borders, did not advocate Kosova's unification with Albania, and called for international intervention.[89]

Whereas Tirana was deeply affected by the war, in Albania's domestic politics Kosova was not a salient issue. Albanians continued to be preoccupied with their own problems. Despite some success at normalizing life in what had become a largely anarchic and chaotic state, Nano presided over an ineffective government. He did not turn out to be the leader the international community had hoped would bring reconciliation to Albania. He also was accused of nepotism and corruption, favoring his clan and relatives in appointments to high-level posts. Largely as a result of Nano's inability to provide real leadership, government control of the country remained fragile and the security situation tenuous. Meanwhile, the Democratic Party, which had not accepted the results of the 1997 election, engaged in disruptive activities and took every opportunity to undermine the government. Thus, while Serbian forces were carrying out indiscriminate killings in a reign of terror in Kosova, Albanian politicians in Tirana were mired in internecine quarrels.

Continued political instability in Tirana not only denied the Kosovars any meaningful political or military support but also reinforced Western objections to Kosova's independence and possible unification with Albania. The *New York Times* columnist Thomas L. Friedman reflected the widespread view in the West when he wrote: "the Kosovo Liberation Army is now talking about uniting all the Albanian communities in the Balkans into a 'Greater Albania.' That is a frightening thought—not because Albanians aren't entitled to unification, but because they haven't proved they can properly run one Albania, let alone five put together."[90]

In August–September 1998, the conflict in Kosova was overshadowed by renewed unrest in Albania. The authorities arrested six former senior officials of the Berisha government and charged them with "crimes against humanity" for their role in the 1997 events. The arrests, which were denounced by the international community as politically motivated, infuriated the opposition, which staged daily demonstrations in Tirana calling for Nano's resignation and the establishment of a broadly based, technical government. Then on September 12 the popular Democratic Party figure and Berisha's right-hand man, Azem Hajdari, was assassinated in front of his party's headquarters in Tirana, touching off rioting. The Democrats accused Nano of being directly responsible for Hajdari's assassination. On September 14 Hajdari's supporters attacked the prime minister's offices and temporarily seized government buildings and state radio and television. Nano abandoned his post and vanished for two days, fleeing to Macedonia. After his return to Tirana, the prime minister vowed not to resign and accused Berisha of a coup attempt. On September 18 the Socialist-controlled parliament voted overwhelmingly to lift Berisha's immunity, clearing the way for his arrest. Amid fears that Albania was on the verge of reverting to the political and civil chaos that engulfed the country in 1997, the international community warned Nano against arresting Berisha. Nano's decision to flee Tirana and seek refuge in neighboring Macedonia had seriously undermined his already diminished authority. With his plans to arrest Berisha thwarted and facing increased opposition from within his own party, Nano resigned on September 28. He was succeeded by Pandeli Majko, the 31-year-old general secretary of the Socialist Party. Majko appeared to be more sensitive to the ethnic Albanians than his predecessor. He indicated that Tirana would no longer give ethnic Albanians "recipes" regarding the final status of Kosova, but instead it would support their inherent right to self-determination.

Meanwhile, Macedonia was rattled by the war in Kosova. Between March and November 1998 some 20,000 Albanians from Kosova had crossed into Macedonia. Concerned about the impact of the influx of such a large number of refugees on Macedonia's interethnic relations, the authorities did not even acknowledge their presence. Skopje was also very concerned about the possible spillover of the Kosova conflict. In September 1998 Vlado Popovski, head of Macedonia's intelligence agency, claimed that the KLA had established an organizational network in Macedonia.[91] While Macedonia and Yugoslavia had divergent national and state interests, on the Albanian issue the Macedonians and Serbs were potential allies. Skopje strongly opposed Albanian aspirations for an independent Kosova, insisting that the region had to remain under Serbia's jurisdiction, and welcomed the Yugoslav army's rooting out of the KLA.

Albanians in Macedonia watched the war in Kosova with great apprehension and criticized what they perceived as Skopje's pro-Serb stand. The two main Albanian parties—the Party for Democratic Prosperity and the Democratic Party of the Albanians—organized joint demonstrations and, for the first time, began to coordinate their activities. But contrary to government reports, Albanians from Macedonia provided little active support to those in Kosova. Moreover, leaders of the Albanians in Macedonia attempted to allay Western concerns by emphasizing that they were not interested in destabilizing Macedonia. Even leaders of the more nationalistic Democratic Party of the Albanians tempered their rhetoric and expressed support for Macedonia's territorial integrity and democratic transition.

While there were continued human rights violations and interethnic relations in Macedonia remained problematic,[92] the campaign for the October–November 1998 parliamentary elections, won by the center-right coalition of the Internal Macedonian Revolutionary Organization (VMRO-DPMNE) and the Democratic Alternative, was unusually peaceful and devoid of the extreme nationalistic rhetoric. The Party for Democratic Prosperity and the Democratic Party of the Albanians formed an electoral pact to field joint candidates in some districts. The center-right coalition won 62 out of 120 seats; the outgoing Social Democrats, former communists, obtained only 27 seats[93]; while the two Albanian parties won 25 seats. Although the center-right coalition had an absolute majority in the parliament, it invited the Democratic Party of the Albanians to join the government. The inclusion of the more radical Albanian party in Prime Minister Ljubco Georgievski's government was a positive development for stability and democracy in Macedonia.

THE OCTOBER 1998 AGREEMENT

With Serb nationalist rhetoric at fever pitch, Milošević had continued to scoff at threats of outside intervention. By September 1998, however, Western governments adopted a more assertive stand. An estimated 50,000 Albanians living in the open were threatened by starvation, hypothermia, and disease. Working against the de facto deadline of the oncoming winter, the West decided not to run the political risk of having tens of thousands of Albanians freeze to death in the forests of Kosova.

On September 23, 1998, the U.N. Security Council, asserting that the situation in Kosova constituted "a threat to peace and security in the region," approved a resolution calling for an immediate cessation of hostilities, the withdrawal of special Serb forces responsible for the repression, allowing the delivery of humanitarian aid, permitting the return of displaced persons, and the start of a "credible" political dialogue between Belgrade and Pristina. It also demanded that Albanian leaders condemn terrorism and renounce violence and requested that member states take steps to halt the flow of funds to guerrillas in Kosova. Resolution 1199 was passed under Chapter 7 authority of the U.N. Charter, which makes compliance mandatory.[94] But the resolution did not explicitly authorize an intervention to stop the ferocious Serb offensive nor did it set a deadline. Despite the Security Council's resolution, Milošević launched a new offensive, which displaced 20,000 people from their homes. On September 26 Serbian forces massacred more than 60 Albanians in the Drenica region, most of them women, children, and the elderly.[95] Although these were not the first reported massacres of civilians there, the widely publicized atrocities propelled Kosova onto the front pages of world papers and television screens and galvanized into action Western countries that had resisted using the threat of force against Yugoslavia.[96]

After all its saber rattling, NATO finally decided to act, sending Milošević an ultimatum: Unless Security Council demands were met military intervention would ensue.[97] Richard Holbrooke was dispatched to Belgrade to convey personally to Milošević the fact that military action was imminent. The United States and its allies insisted that NATO air strikes would be legitimate without a corresponding U.N. Security Council resolution. A master at exploiting the differences among members of the Contact Group, Milošević tested Western resolve right up to the brink, holding more than 50 hours of talks with Holbrooke. On October 13 Holbrooke announced that Milošević had accepted key international demands, thus averting the threat of NATO air strikes. Nevertheless, NATO voted to authorize air strikes against Yugoslavia if Milošević did not meet key Western demands within 96 hours. The activation order gave U.S. Army General Wesley Clark, the supreme commander of allied forces in Europe, authority to launch air strikes if Belgrade reneged on these commitments. On October 15 NATO gave Belgrade a ten-day extension of its deadline. At the end of the second deadline, NATO decided against launching air strikes, claiming that Belgrade was in substantial, but not full, compliance. However, the alliance issued an open-ended extension of the threat, with no fixed deadline. The activation order set an important precedent: NATO expressed willingness to intervene in the internal affairs of a European country without an explicit Security Council resolution. Russia criticized the NATO decision and underscored its unhappiness by recalling its representative to NATO headquarters. However, with Russia's economy in shambles, Moscow's leverage was limited.

As part of the agreement, the Yugoslav leader pledged a partial withdrawal of troops and police from Kosova, accepted 2,000 unarmed foreign inspectors from the OSCE, and allowed NATO surveillance planes to fly over Kosova and monitor compliance.[98] Milošević temporarily halted his offensive, many internally displaced persons living outside in the hills and mountains moved indoors, and international humanitarian relief organizations increased their presence, providing desperately needed food, clothing, and medicine to thousands of refugees.

While the Holbrooke-Milošević deal no doubt offered a breather and eased the humanitarian crisis, it was deeply flawed. The implementation of the agreement, which lacked provisions for enforcing compliance since the OSCE observers had no enforcement capability, depended more on Milošević's goodwill than on NATO pressure. Milošević also refused to allow the Hague-based International War Crimes Tribunal for the Former Yugoslavia to have jurisdiction in Kosovo. Despite the U.N. Security Council's explicit authorization of the tribunal to investigate war crimes in the former Yugoslavia, Belgrade barred Louise Arbour, the tribunal's chief prosecutor, and the body's president, Gabrielle Kirk McDonald, from traveling to Kosova to investigate allegations of war crimes committed by Yugoslav forces and the KLA. By failing to address the core problem—the political status of the region—the agreement was more a face-saving deal than an attempt to find a solution to the conflict. It still left Serbia effectively in control of Kosova and the Albanians essentially unprotected from future attacks by the Yugoslav army and police. Given the astonishing military and diplomatic firepower trained on forcing Milošević to comply with the Security Council resolution, the accord was modest at best and fell far short of NATO's original goals. From demanding a pullback of all Serb forces involved in repression in Kosova, Holbrooke settled for a return to the level of some 20,000 military and police forces.

The continued presence of such large numbers of Yugoslav forces sustained a climate of fear among the local population and gave Milošević the opportunity to resort to his brutal methods at any time. Indeed within weeks of the signing of the October agreement, it became clear that Milošević had no intention of respecting the deal. Not only did Belgrade fail to draw its forces down to the levels stipulated in the accord, but the Yugoslavs began building up their army and police forces in and around Kosova. Milošević replaced the army chief general, Momčilo Perišić, who apparently opposed using army forces in

Kosova and had expressed concern about Yugoslavia's having become a pariah state. He also removed the head of the air force, and the chief and several senior officials of the security service. Loyal officers were placed in key positions. After a lull in fighting, large-scale violence flared up again in late December 1998 when Yugoslav forces launched a major crackdown against KLA bases in the northern Drenica region. On January 15, 1999, in an act of revenge for the killing of four policemen by the KLA, Serbian security forces massacred 45 unarmed Albanians in the village of Reçak (Račak, in Serbian). The head of the OSCE verification mission in Kosova, U.S. Ambassador William Walker, called the killings "an unspeakable atrocity" and "a crime very much against humanity."[99]

The War of 1999

With Milošević having reneged on the October accord and clearly poised for renewed conflict, Washington and its allies intensified efforts to forge a political settlement and prevent an all-out war. U.S. Ambassador to Macedonia Chris Hill, a career diplomat with extensive experience in Balkan affairs who in July 1998 had been appointed as special envoy on Kosova, had worked for months with both sides in an unsuccessful attempt to broker an interim peace accord. The Hill plan called for wide self-rule for the Albanians but stipulated that Kosova would remain within Serbia. It deferred any decision on the question of the final status of Kosova for three years but did not define the procedure that would enable the reaching of a final agreement.

THE RAMBOUILLET PEACE PLAN

The Reçak massacre put Kosova back to the top of the international agenda, prompting the United States and its allies to launch a new effort to halt the violence and impose an interim political solution. The main factor driving the West's new assertiveness was not only the hope of forcing Milošević to accept a political settlement but the need to prevent a major humanitarian catastrophe. An additional reason was the need to restore NATO's badly tarnished image. For nearly a year NATO had failed to carry out its own threats to use force, looking the other way while Serb forces engaged in brutal attacks on ethnic Albanians and widespread ethnic cleansing. On January 29, 1999, the United States, Britain, France, Germany, Italy, and Russia summoned the two sides to a peace conference in Rambouillet, France, co-chaired by British Foreign Secretary Robin Cook and French Foreign Minister Hubert Vedrine. The two sides were given two weeks to accept a Contact Group–drafted peace accord or face grave consequences. The Serbs were threatened with NATO air strikes if they rejected, but the Albanians accepted, the accord. The Albanians, on the other hand, were informed that they could not expect NATO intervention or assistance if they did not accept the interim peace settlement.

Based largely on Hill's plan, the Rambouillet document stipulated that Kosova would remain a province of Serbia but would have a high degree of self-governance with free elections, its own legislative, executive, and judicial branches, and a local police force reflecting the ethnic makeup of the population. The plan called for the withdrawal of all but 2,500 Yugoslav security forces and 1,500 army troops, which would patrol Kosova's external borders, and the deployment of a NATO peacekeeping force to ensure implementation of the accord. Milošević refused to attend the conference, sending instead a low-level delegation that clearly was not empowered to make a deal. The Serbs indicated from the very beginning that the accord was unacceptable. They strenuously objected to the provisions that called for the withdrawal of Yugoslav troops and the deployment of a NATO peacekeeping force.

The Albanians put together an all-inclusive delegation: Rugova, Bujar Bukoshi, Fehmi Agani, and Edita Tahiri representing the Democratic League; Rexhep Qosja, Mehmet Hajrizi, Bajram Kosumi, and Hydajet Hyseni of the United Democratic Movement, an umbrella organization grouping half a dozen parties that was founded in spring 1998; and two independents: prominent journalists Veton Surroi, publisher of Kosova's most important newspaper, *Koha Ditore*, and Blerim Shala, chief editor of the popular magazine *Zëri*. Representing the KLA were Hashim Thaçi, the head of the KLA's political directorate; Jakup Krasniqi, spokesman of the guerrilla movement; and Azem Syla, Ramë Buja, and Xhavit Haliti. In a significant development with far-reaching ramifications for Kosovar Albanian politics, Qosja's group, Surroi, and Shala joined forces with the KLA against Rugova, selecting Thaçi as head of the delegation. They apparently believed they could control the inexperienced, 29-year-old KLA leader. But this decision helped Thaçi consolidate his position as the nominal head of the KLA and thrust him to the forefront of Kosovar politics. In an apparent effort to placate the KLA, the organizers of the conference went along with this decision, thus further weakening Rugova's position and by extension that of other moderates in the delegation. Rugova, who was clearly intimidated by the KLA, resigned himself to a subordinate position and apparently played a minor role in the negotiations.[100] Thus Thaçi eclipsed not only Rugova but also Qosja and Surroi.

The Albanian delegation sought guarantees that a referendum on independence would be held after the three-year interim period. The mediators pledged that the Albanians would be allowed to hold a referendum but made it clear that it would not be legally binding. Contrary to subsequent press reports, the Rambouillet document did not contain specific wording on a referendum on independence, stipulating only that at the end of the three-year interim period an international conference would be convened to determine a mechanism for a final settlement, which would take into account "the will of the people, opinions of relevant authorities, each Party's efforts regarding the implementation of this Agreement, and the Helsinki Final Act."[101] Thaçi was reluctant to sign the agreement without a clear stipulation for a referendum on independence. He also raised strenuous objections to calls to disarm the KLA and almost derailed the whole process. Finally, on February 23 the Albanian delegation accepted in principle the agreement, but said it would only sign it after a period of two weeks of consultations with the people of Kosova. The delay was an extraordinarily reckless mistake for which Kosova paid a heavy price. It eased NATO's pressure on Yugoslavia. Milošević took maximum advantage of this delay by ordering a substantial buildup of his troops around and in Kosova. Using artillery, tanks, and antiaircraft guns, Yugoslav troops drove thousands of civilians from their homes in the Drenica region. The peace conference reconvened on March 15 in Paris. Three days later, at a low-key ceremony, four Albanian representatives—Thaçi, Rugova, Qosja, and Surroi—signed the accord. Although the plan would have kept Kosova within Serbia, the Yugoslavs rejected the deal. On March 19, the Contact Group adjourned the Paris talks. In a joint statement, British and French foreign ministers, cochairmen of the conference, warned Belgrade that any new military offensives on the ground would have "the gravest consequences." On March 19, the OSCE ordered its monitors to leave Kosova despite concerns that the Serbs would take advantage of this to launch an all-out offensive against the Albanians. The withdrawal of international monitors removed the last restraint on Yugoslav forces. In a last-ditch effort to convince Milošević to accept the accord, the United States dispatched Holbrooke to Belgrade. The Serbian leader refused to budge.

NATO AIR STRIKES AGAINST YUGOSLAVIA

Only a day after Milošević rebuffed a final peace plea from Holbrooke, on March 24, 1999, NATO launched air strikes against Yugoslavia in the hope of forcing Belgrade to accept the Rambouillet peace plan. In a nationwide address, President Clinton said that the NATO action was aimed at averting a humanitarian disaster and preventing the spillover of the conflict into neighboring countries.

> Our mission is clear: to demonstrate the seriousness of NATO's purpose so that the Serbian leaders understand the imperative of reversing course; to deter an even bloodier offensive against innocent civilians in Kosovo; and, if necessary, to seriously damage the Serbian military's capacity to harm the people of Kosovo. In short, if President Milošević will not make peace, we will limit his ability to make war.[102]

From the beginning, NATO leaders made it clear that this would be a limited campaign and that the use of ground troops was not an option. Western decision makers evidently expected Milošević to capitulate after the first few days of air strikes and were not prepared for a prolonged period of bombing. Milošević, however, responded by launching a systematic campaign of ethnic cleansing. There is credible evidence that the campaign was meticulously planned. Months earlier, senior Yugoslav officials in Belgrade had hatched Operation Horseshoe (*Operacija Potkovica*) to cleanse Kosova of its Albanian majority. In a meeting in early March 1999, Milošević admitted as much to visiting German Foreign Minister Joschka Fischer, insisting that Serbian forces could empty Kosova "within a week."[103] As early as January 1999 there were indications that the Serbs were preparing for a major spring offensive aimed at eliminating the KLA and crushing the Albanian uprising. As the first NATO bombs fell over Yugoslavia and with OSCE monitors, international aid workers, and journalists having left Kosova, Serb army, security, and paramilitary forces lashed out against the Albanians, rounding up and force-marching hundreds of thousands of civilians to the borders with Albania and Macedonia, and looting, pillaging, burning, and killing at will. Many cities and hundreds of villages were torched by masked and armed bands of Serbs. In scenes reminiscent of Nazi Germany, in Pristina thousands of citizens were rounded up, marched to the main station, and forced at gunpoint to board trains bound for Macedonia. Within a period of two months, an estimated 10,000 Albanian men, women, and children were slaughtered, 850,000 deported, and some 600,000 internally displaced. Albania absorbed more than 450,000 refugees, and Macedonia nearly 250,000. Montenegro, which had distanced itself from Serbia's Kosova policy and did not recognize the state of war declared by the federal government, hosted 70,000 Kosovars. Others went to Bosnia, Germany, Turkey, Italy, and the United States.

Not only did Milošević cause the worst refugee crisis that Europe had seen since the end of the Second World War, but he also attempted to destabilize Albania and Macedonia, seriously taxing their already limited resources. Poverty-stricken and plagued by a lack of law and order, rampant corruption, and failing state institutions, Albania pulled itself together. Although not in a position to take military measures to stop the ethnic cleansing in Kosova, Albania welcomed the refugees and allowed the KLA to establish and maintain bases in the northern part of the country. The crisis provided an unprecedented opportunity for Albania to appear on center stage and improve its image, which had been badly tarnished in the wake of the 1997 unrest. The government and the opposition largely put aside their differences and maintained a common stand. Albania placed all its naval and air facilities at NATO's disposal.

The impact of Milošević's tactics had far more serious implications for Macedonia, threatening to plunge the former Yugoslav republic into political and social turmoil. By driving hundreds of thousands of Kosovars across the border, Milošević fomented resentment among local Albanians and Macedonians, who are overwhelmingly sympathetic to the Serbs. Unlike in Albania where they were welcomed with open arms, refugees in Macedonia were treated harshly, particularly in the first weeks of the NATO bombing campaign. Thousands were stranded in the open for days in Blace on the border. Macedonian authorities forcibly deported refugees to Albania and other countries; hundreds of families were separated in the chaos. Albanian members of the Macedonian cabinet were deliberately excluded from the decision-making process, seriously undermining the cohesion of the coalition government. While the authorities had legitimate concerns about the presence of huge numbers of radicalized Albanian refugees, their treatment of the refugees may have inflicted long-term damage on an already troubled relationship between local Albanians and Macedonians.

The Serbs conducted their campaign against the Albanians with virtual impunity. The NATO campaign was conducted in a halfhearted manner. Instead of launching massive air attacks inflicting substantial damage to Yugoslavia's armed forces and its national infrastructure, and strategic centers of gravity that supported the regime, in the first weeks of the campaign NATO attacked a limited range of targets. Despite clear evidence of the ineffectiveness of its constrained air attacks, NATO was slow to widen its campaign and, in order to minimize the risk to allied pilots, avoided low-level bombing. Moreover, NATO, which already had stationed more than 12,000 troops in Macedonia, refused to deploy special operations forces to attack Serbian troops and forestall the massacres and the massive ethnic cleansing. NATO's timid air campaign and the exclusion of the option to use ground troops emboldened Milošević, extended the suffering of Albanians, and thus prolonged the war.

Milošević's brutal campaign caught the Albanians totally unprepared to deal with it. Plagued by deep-seated friction, Rugova and other Kosovar leaders failed to rise to the occasion. Rugova was held under house arrest until May 5, when he was allowed to go to Italy. Most other prominent politicians, intellectuals, journalists, and activists, who were considered "leaders" and enjoyed considerable popularity, fled the country or went into hiding. With its elites essentially out of commission, the population at large, already severely traumatized by Serbian brutality, remained leaderless and disoriented. The Belgrade regime made maximum efforts to create confusion and divisions in Albanian ranks, and to this end it tried to use Rugova. Yugoslav state television showed a smiling Rugova meeting with Milošević. He was reported to have criticized NATO's bombing campaign and signed a statement calling for the solution of the Kosova question through "political means."[104] On April 28, the Serbian media reported that the Albanian leader had signed an agreement with Serbia's President Milan Milutinović to form "a new, temporary government for the province, resume negotiations on a form of self-rule for Kosovo, and invite some foreigners as 'guests' to attend the talks."[105] Rugova's meeting with Milošević and a subsequent meeting with other senior Serbian officials sent shockwaves through the ethnic Albanian population, with his rivals calling him a "traitor" to the national cause. Without any explanation, on May 5 Rugova with his family were given permission to go to Italy. Rugova claimed that he had met with Milošević under duress. While many Albanians accepted Rugova's explanation, his credibility dropped considerably. His stature suffered further when he refused to travel to Tirana and meet with other Kosovar leaders and plan a joint strategy. Rugova's failure to seek a united front with other political forces and the KLA was a major blow to ethnic Albanian aspirations and a shirking of leadership responsibilities during a most critical period.

The KLA attempted to fill the vacuum left by the debilitated civilian leadership. While Rugova was still under house arrest in Pristina and without consulting the Democratic League, Kosova's largest political party, Hashim Thaçi announced in Tirana the formation of a provisional government. He said he was acting according to an agreement that the Albanian delegation had reached at Rambouillet to replace Bukoshi's government in exile with a provisional government, with a KLA representative serving as prime minister until new elections could be held.

Thaçi's self-declared government was made up largely of representatives from the KLA and its close allies from the United Democratic Movement, although Rexhep Qosja, the leader of the umbrella organization, was excluded. Not only did Thaçi fail to form an all-inclusive government but he appointed to the cabinet people without experience and close friends and relatives, including his own uncle Azem Syla as minister of defense. Rugova's Democratic League refused to join, arguing that the Rambouillet understanding had been overtaken by subsequent developments and insisting that Bukoshi's Bonn-based government was still the legitimate one. Thaçi did not announce a political program nor did he give any indication what his government's main objectives would be except for the widely shared desire to see Kosova free of Serbian rule. Tirana's socialist government promptly recognized Thaçi's government.

Meanwhile, the KLA continued its resistance against Serbian forces. But overwhelmed by tens of thousands of internally displaced persons, it was unable to protect the population or stop ethnic cleansing. Short of ammunition and food supplies, guerrilla fighters were swept from most of their strongholds and forced to retreat into the hills. NATO repeatedly rebuffed the KLA's requests for arms. Western governments remained suspicious of the KLA leadership because of its uncertain commitment to democracy and reputed ties to criminal and drug-trafficking groups. Although the KLA was unable to mount a significant campaign against the Yugoslav forces, it still survived intact. In mid-May the KLA top command was reshuffled. Agim Çeku, a former brigadier general in the Croatian army, was named chief of staff. The 39-year-old Çeku received his military training in Belgrade and Zadar, Croatia, and served in the Yugoslav army until summer 1991, when he joined the Croatian military. He distinguished himself in Croatia's war of independence, and was rapidly promoted to the rank of brigadier general. He resigned his commission in January 1999 and returned to Kosova to fight with the KLA. According to his official biography, Çeku is said to have had contacts and worked closely with the KLA since its very inception.[106] Çeku appointed more experienced commanders to leading posts and attempted to transform the KLA from a loose amalgamation into a unified military organization. Its ranks were swelled with new recruits from camps in Albania and from abroad. By the end of May, helped by NATO's attacks against the Yugoslav military, the KLA rebounded, its membership swelling to more than 15,000 fighters. But still it remained an ineffective military force. In May, the KLA launched an offensive from northern Albania, but the assault was foiled by Yugoslav forces.

The systematic, forced eviction of Albanians, the summary executions of men, women, and children, and large-scale destruction of property only strengthened NATO's resolve. Despite the fact that some alliance members, notably Greece and Italy, were uneasy over the air attacks, NATO persisted with the campaign, now insisting that Milošević had to withdraw all his troops from Kosova, agree to the return of all refugees, and accept the deployment of an international peacekeeping force. Gradually, NATO escalated its attacks, inflicting considerable damage on Yugoslavia's infrastructure. NATO hit Yugoslavia's oil refineries, factories, electrical power systems, rail lines, and television transmitters. With increasing signs that the air campaign was not giving the desired results, Western leaders raised the possibility of a ground invasion. President Clinton publicly declared that he would consider sending ground troops if it became clear that the air campaign was failing.[107] In a related development, the International War Crimes Tribunal indicted Milošević and four other senior officials, including Serbia's President Milan Milutinović, with crimes against humanity, including the murder, forced deportation, and persecution of ethnic Albanians.[108]

Concomitantly with its military campaign, the United States and its allies continued to search for a diplomatic solution. At a meeting in early May 1999 in Bonn, the foreign ministers of the seven most industrialized nations plus Russia agreed to a draft plan to end the conflict. The accord called for the withdrawal of Yugoslav troops and forces according to a NATO-approved timetable; the return of all refugees; the deployment of an international peacekeeping force; the creation of a U.N.-led interim administration for Kosova; and the demilitarization of the KLA. At a later, unspecified date, Yugoslavia will be permitted to deploy fewer than 1,000 uniformed Serbs to guard key border posts and Serb holy places. But while it provides for substantial self-government for Kosova, it takes account of the "principles of sovereignty and territorial integrity" of Yugoslavia and contains no provision on holding a referendum after the interim period.

Milošević had held out in the hope that NATO cohesion would crumble under the pressure of public opinion. But his barbaric assault on the Albanians bolstered NATO's determination. The Serbian leader also had strong hopes of continued support from Russia, which had suspended its cooperation with NATO and recalled its chief military representative to the alliance to protest the attacks. But Russia's decision to support key elements of the NATO peace plan increased pressure on Milošević and further isolated Yugoslavia. Finally, on June 3 Milošević accepted the plan presented to him by President Martti Ahtisaari of Finland and Viktor Chernomyrdin, the Russian envoy for the Balkans and former premier.

Postwar Kosova

The U.N. Security Council passed a resolution authorizing the deployment of a nearly 50,000-strong NATO-led international peace force, KFOR, and the establishment of a U.N. Interim Administration Mission in Kosova (UNMIK), thus in effect making Kosova an international protectorate. KFOR entered Kosova on June 12 and established five separate sectors: American, British, French, German, and Italian. Russia insisted on having its separate zone, in the north on the border with Serbia, but NATO refused. On June 11–12, some 200 Russian troops, who had been stationed in Bosnia, entered Kosova only hours before NATO troops and unexpectedly seized the Pristina airport, causing a momentary crisis in Russia's relations with the West. After intense negotiations, the United States and Russia reached an agreement: Russian troops will not get a separate sector but will operate at the Pristina airport and within the American, French, and German sectors. They will serve under Russian commanders, who in turn will report to the top NATO commanders of their sectors. Nevertheless, the Albanians, who see the Russians as protectors of Serbs, expressed deep disappointment. Albanians allege that during the war Russian mercenaries fought alongside Serbian paramilitary forces.

Bernard Kouchner, French health minister and cofounder of Doctors Without Borders, was named U.N. Special Representative with overall responsibility for civil administration, humanitarian affairs, institution building, and reconstruction. The interim civil administration will run Kosova and oversee the establishment of democratic institutions and the holding of elections, after which the administration will gradually be handed over to the Albanians. UNMIK established a Transitional Council, comprised of representatives from different political forces and ethnic groups, which will serve as Kosova's highest political forum. The U.N. administration faced formidable challenges in rebuilding civil service structures, establishing the rule of law, and creating a mechanism for the democratization of Kosova's society. The international community announced an ambitious multibillion-dollar program for the rehabilitation of Kosova's society through economic regeneration and institution building, and a stability pact for the region.

The repatriation of refugees, which had become NATO's most important objective, was seen as the most staggering problem for postconflict Kosova. However, the entry of international peace troops was followed by an immediate, massive surge of refugees back into Kosova. In one of the most spectacular reverse population movements ever, by the end of August 1999 more than 90 percent of the 850,000 refugees returned to Kosova, most of them without any assistance from humanitarian organizations. Around 715,000 returned from Albania, Macedonia, and Montenegro. An additional 50,000 returned from third countries. Ironically, while Milošević intended to rid Kosova of the Albanians and completely change the ethnic structure of the population, his ethnic cleansing policy could end up achieving the opposite: an ethnically pure Albanian Kosova. Milošević's submission to NATO and the campaign of terror, harassment, and intimidation by returning Albanian refugees sparked a massive exodus of ethnic Serbs, most of whom, if not directly involved in crimes, had supported Milošević's policy. KFOR was unable to ensure a secure environment or prevent revenge attacks by Albanians seeking retribution for the repression and atrocities committed by Serbian forces. By the end of October 1999 the Serb population was estimated at about 100,000 from a prewar figure of some 200,000. The exodus of Serbs, as well as tens of thousands of Roma, accused by the Albanians of having collaborated with Yugoslav forces, made NATO's goal of preserving a multiethnic society in Kosova look increasingly elusive.

The war radically changed Kosova's political landscape, seriously undermining the moderate civilian leadership and catapulting to the top a new breed of leaders. The KLA is the only force to emerge from the war with a considerable degree of credibility. While some blame the KLA for having provoked with its hit-and-run tactics indiscriminate Serbian reprisals against the civilian population, the guerrilla movement seems to enjoy widespread popularity since it was the only force that fought against the Serbs. As KFOR deployed into Kosova, KLA troops swept triumphantly into and seized control of cities and areas throughout the province. Although the KLA signed an agreement to demilitarize within a 90-day period, it is not about to go out of business. The international interim administration has pledged to give special consideration to the hiring of KLA members for the new civilian police force. Moreover, Hashim Thaçi's self-declared government, taking advantage of the vacuum left by the departure of Yugoslav authorities and UNMIK's slow progress in establishing its own administrative mechanism, set up a network of ministries, and established regional civil administrations, clearly challenging the primacy of the international interim administration as the only legitimate authority in Kosova. But the KLA is riven by personal and ideological differences, petty rivalries, and a struggle for power. Thaçi's position has been

challenged by regional commanders, who believe that he is more interested in consolidating his political position than in supporting the
movement's interests. He has attempted to marginalize his rivals,
appointing close friends and relatives to key positions in his government. In July one faction of the KLA formed a new political party, the
Party of Democratic Union, headed by Bardhyl Mahmuti, a former
political prisoner who from his base in Switzerland had played a key
role in collecting funds for the KLA from Albanian communities in
Western Europe. Thaçi refused to join the party, but many prominent
KLA officials, including four regional commanders, joined it.[109]

Thaçi and other KLA leaders have shown little tolerance toward dissent, and their commitment to democratic processes remains to be
proven. Originating largely from the rural areas that bore the brunt of
the Serbian onslaught, they harbor a deep sense of resentment toward
the urban intellectuals of Pristina, whom they blame for having stood
on the sidelines during the war. They are determined to establish a new
order and do not seem very mindful of the rule of law and democratic
procedures. For them, the consolidation of Kosova's de facto independence from Serbia has priority over the establishment of a democratic
society, a view not necessarily shared by the urban intelligentsia. Thaçi
claims that he is committed to building a modern, democratic society,
and has pledged to cooperate with other political forces and support the
development of a free and independent media. He has also denounced
reprisal attacks by the Albanians against Serbs, emphasized the need
for ethnic harmony, and called on Serbs to return to Kosova. However,
he and people around him were believed to be behind the campaign to
intimidate Rugova's followers, journalists not willing to toe the KLA line,
and attacks against Serbs and KFOR troops, particularly the Russians and
French, who are perceived as being pro-Serb. Thaçi's image also has been
tarnished by allegations that he ordered the elimination of his rivals. He
is accused of having directed a campaign that resulted in the assassination of as many as half a dozen top KLA commanders, a journalist who
had criticized the guerrilla movement, and several persons close to
Rugova and Bukoshi. Thaçi is said to have carried out the campaign of
assassination in close cooperation with Tirana's Socialist government.[110]

Rugova's Democratic League and other political parties have lost so
much ground that if elections were to be held soon they would not be
in a position to compete on an equal footing with the KLA. Rugova's
stature has suffered not only because he met with Milošević—most
Albanians assumed he did this under duress—but because of his subsequent ineffectiveness and reclusive behavior. He was the last prominent politician to return to Pristina, on July 15—a month after Thaçi and

others had come back. He was welcomed warmly, but left within hours and without explanation. He finally returned to Pristina on July 30 following persistent pressure from senior Western officials. But by delaying his return from his self-imposed exile, he did significant damage to his party and made it easier for the KLA to consolidate its new predominant position. Despite his uninspiring leadership, Rugova and his Democratic League still seem to enjoy considerable support, particularly in urban areas, where the more traditional elites fear being replaced by radicals from the regions. But even if the Democratic League does not split among different factions, it will face an uphill battle to regain the limelight from the KLA.

Other political forces and personalities that had played an important role in the prewar period have likewise lost credibility. Political parties grouped in the United Democratic Movement do not appear to enjoy much popular support. Thaçi has successfully co-opted many of their leaders, while skillfully marginalizing Rexhep Qosja, who before the war was recognized as Kosova's most important figure after Rugova. Qosja is not likely to go along indefinitely with such a situation. Of Kosova's most important personalities, only Adem Demaçi and Veton Surroi stayed in Kosova during the war. Demaçi decided to withdraw from public life after his falling out with the KLA because of his rejection of the Rambouillet accord. Surroi, very popular with the younger generation but lacking a political structure, says that he has no political ambitions and that he will concentrate on reviving his daily, *Koha Ditore.* But should he chose to, Surroi, who enjoys widespread international support, is well positioned and capable of playing a leading role in Kosovar politics. There are also other, younger activists poised to take an active role in politics.

If Kosova is to develop a truly democratic society, the international community will need to maintain an active dialogue with a range of political forces and figures, assist in the revival of political parties, and foster democratic principles and institution building. While the challenges ahead are formidable, the international community will not have to start from scratch. Before the war, Albanians had nurtured their own democratic institutions and managed to forge significant rudiments of a pluralist democracy and a civil society, with a wide range of independent grassroots associations and groups engaged in the broad sphere of a social interaction aimed at advancing the public interest.

While Kosovar politics continues to be factional, almost without exception all forces have welcomed the establishment of an international interim administration. There appears to be widespread recognition among Albanians that Kosova will remain an international protectorate for many years. Likewise, there is complete unanimity that at the end of the interim period Kosova should become an independent state. The option of Kosova remaining within Serbia or Yugoslavia as a province, even with a substantial degree of autonomy, is today simply unthinkable for the overwhelming majority of ethnic Albanians. Any attempt to revert Kosova to Yugoslav rule will likely lead to a dangerous confrontation with the Albanians.

The United States and its Western allies have lacked a practical strategy of dealing with the Albanian-Serb conflict: first ignoring Kosova at Dayton, then issuing declarations leading the Albanians to believe that NATO would intervene on their behalf, but failing to carry out the threat even after considerable violence had taken place. Finally, the United States and its NATO allies launched a noble war against Serbia over its genocidal attacks against Albanians and succeeded in reversing one of the largest ethnic cleansing campaigns that Europe has witnessed in the last half century. Yet Western policy continues to be based on the assumption that Kosova must remain within Serbia, albeit with substantial autonomy. To the chagrin of most Albanians, the accord that NATO forced Milošević to accept before halting its bombing campaign papers over the difference between affirming Serbia's sovereignty and Albanian insistence on Kosova's independence. Kosova's long-term political status is left vague. In one clause, the U.N. Security Council resolution reaffirms the "sovereignty and territorial integrity" of Yugoslavia. In another clause, however, the resolution pledges that the U.N. interim administration will facilitate "a political process designed to determine Kosovo's future status, taking into account the Rambouillet accords."[111] But despite the agreement's reaffirmation of Yugoslavia's territorial integrity, the reality on the ground today reflects little substance to Serbia's assertion of sovereignty.

In view of Serbia's utter disregard for the norms of the international community and its attempt at a final solution to the Albanian question, the Serbs have forfeited their right to rule Kosova. The Albanians have been so radicalized that they will not agree to any deal that would leave them under Serb rule. Therefore conditioning a final settlement on denying Kosovar Albanians the right to self-determination will only postpone the day of reckoning and will lead to renewed armed conflict. Albanian efforts at self-determination have been legitimized by Serbia's ruthless policies and lack of responsiveness to concrete Albanian grievances. Kosova represents a clear instance in which self-determination must be viewed as a higher good than support for the sovereignty and the preservation of the territorial integrity of a country whose actions have been compared by Western leaders to those of Adolf Hitler. Serbia remains a rogue state and it is doubtful that it will be able to develop a truly democratic polity anytime soon. But even if there were a regime change and democratic forces came to power in Belgrade, there is little chance that Albanians and Serbs could live peacefully in the same state. Serbs in general have displayed no meaningful opposition to Milošević's policy of ethnic cleansing. There are only a few courageous Serbs, such as Sonja Biserko, director of the Serbian branch of the Helsinki Committee, and Nataša Kandić, head of the Humanitarian Law Fund, who have publicly denounced this policy. Serbs in general have yet to acknowledge the commission of crimes in Kosova and accept a measure of guilt.

The United States and its allies have a historic opportunity to set the stage for a permanent solution of the Albanian-Serb conflict by endorsing Kosova's phased independence. During the interim administration, Kosova will be assisted in the development and nourishing of democratic institutions and processes of governance, the training and establishment of a professional police force, and ensuring the respect of the rights of Kosova's Serbs and the protection of their cultural and religious sites. After the interim period of international administration, Kosovar Albanians must have the right to collectively determine their political destiny through a binding referendum. The establishment of a democratic society in Kosova is likely to be less formidable than in Bosnia. Since the early 1990s, practically under an apartheid system, Albanians established their own democratic institutions and managed to forge significant rudiments of a civil society. Kosova already enjoys some attributes of a statelike entity: It has a defined territory, an overwhelmingly Albanian demographic majority population, and institutions whose authority to govern is based on the will of the majority of the population. The case for Kosova's independence is also clear in legal and constitutional terms. The West interprets the 1991–92 breakup of Yugoslavia as an example of a complete dissolution of a federal system and does not consider the current Yugoslavia (Serbia and Montenegro) as a continuation of the old one. Kosova is a former constituent unit of Yugoslavia, although it had a double status—it was defined also as part of Serbia. Its borders were guaranteed at the federal level. Before Milošević arbitrarily abolished its autonomy in 1989, Kosova in all practical ways functioned as a federal unit. Its independence, therefore, would be analogous to that of former Yugoslav republics and, strictly speaking, would not involve changes in international borders. The international community would simply follow the precedent set by the recognition of Slovenia, Croatia, Bosnia, and Macedonia, that is, upgrade the status of existing borders. As Noel Malcolm points out, this will not set any dangerous precedents for other parts of the world since "other countries would become liable to the application of this precedent only if they were federal states in a process of complete dissolution."[112]

The basic factor that has determined Western rejections of Albanian self-determination claims is not whether this would promote democracy and human rights in Kosova but concern that recognition of Kosova's independence would lead to runaway disintegration and instability in the region. But the argument that Kosova's secession would have an adverse impact on Bosnia and Macedonia does not hold. Bosnia has no functioning central government, and in reality it is already partitioned into antagonistic ethnic enclaves. As Gale Stokes writes, "the multi-ethnic light at the end of the Bosnian tunnel is very dim."[113] The existence of an independent Macedonia is now accepted by all its neighbors, including Albania, Greece, and Bulgaria, and its borders are guaranteed by the international presence there. What Macedonia needs is the firm establishment of the rule of law and the adoption of more flexible policies to accommodate Albanian desires for greater local government and meaningful cultural and educational advancement. The future of interethnic relations there will depend on the government's willingness to take measures to recognize Tetova University, increase Albanians' representation in state institutions, and work on changing the country's constitution to recognize Albanians as equal citizens with the Macedonians. Given the fact that Albanians account for at least a quarter of the population, Slav Macedonians cannot insist that Macedonia is only "the national state of the Macedonian people." Albanian leaders, on the other hand, seem to recognize that they have to do more to reassure their Macedonian neighbors. As Arben Xhaferri, chairman of the Democratic Party of Albanians, puts it, "We have to overcome the psychological presumption among Macedonians that if you offer Albanians a finger, they will take your whole hand."[114]

The war in Kosova fueled enormous sympathy among Albanians throughout the region and reawakened dreams of Albanian unification. Yet Kosova's unification with Albania does not appear to be a realistic option in the near future. In terms of Rogers Brubaker's triadic nexus, which links the diaspora, the nationalizing state, and the national homeland,[115] the conflict in Kosova has remained dyadic. The mother country, Albania, has been largely a bystander rather than an active participant. Because of its preoccupation with internal problems and the failure of the main political actors to join forces in the reconstruction and healing process following the 1997 revolt and the subsequent collapse of state authority, Albania probably will not be able, in the midterm, to play the role of a spiritual and political "mother country." Albania faces formidable challenges, as the government and the opposition are divided by deep enmity. Its primary challenge remains the establishment of an effective government able to perform the elementary tasks of governance, notably providing a minimum degree of order, enforcing the laws of the land, collecting taxes, and policing its external borders. Moreover, nationalism in postcommunist Albania appears to be less deeply rooted and a less powerful force than, for example, the Serb variety. One important consequence of this is that the Albanian diaspora does not look to the national homeland as the primary actor working for unification. The impetus for changing the status quo, therefore, will likely not come from Albania but from Kosova. However, unless there is a renewed threat from Serbia, the Kosovars are in no hurry to push for unification with Albania. What is important for the Kosovars is that what they refer to as the Albanian "Berlin Wall" is finally down and borders with Albania are open. Veton Surroi probably reflected the view of many of his Albanian compatriots when he declared:

> The war is over. We must strive for a level of communication where borders no longer play any role. Albanians have to be able to communicate in their own language and travel freely. Then it will no longer matter whether you live in Albania, Kosova, Macedonia, or wherever else. Then "Greater Albania" will be where you live.[116]

But while immediate unification is not considered a viable proposition in either Tirana or Pristina, the entire political spectrum in Albania has become more nationalistic. The war has ushered in a qualitative transformation of the relationship between Tirana and Pristina, and Albanians have never been closer together than they are now. An increasing number of Albanians have come to believe that their nation can never play its rightful role in the region if Kosova is not separated from Serbia and eventually united with Albania. While all recognize that the road to Albanian reunification is likely to be complex and protracted, for most Albanians, in and outside the national state, the ultimate goal remains a unitary state of all Albanians.[117] An independent Kosova state naturally would gravitate to and eventually unite with Albania. Despite the current Western aversion to such an outcome, the unification of Kosova and Albania, if achieved peacefully and gradually, would represent a permanent solution to the Albanian question and would be consistent with self-determination and the creation of nation-states elsewhere in Europe. A unitary Albanian state would not be in a position to present a serious threat to any of its neighbors, including Macedonia.

Notes

1. Rogers Brubaker, *Nationalism Reframed: Nationhood and the National Questions in the New Europe* (New York: Cambridge University Press, 1996).

2. Ibid., p. 4.

3. See Miranda Vickers, *Between Serb and Albanian: A History of Kosovo* (New York: Columbia University Press, 1998), p. 219.

4. A public opinion poll conducted in 1996 revealed that 88 percent of Albanians in Albania consider themselves part of the European community of nations and only 8 percent of the "Muslim community." See U.S. Information Agency, Office of Research and Media Reaction, "On Security Matters, Albanian Public Looks to the West," *Opinion Analysis*, M-73-96, April 2, 1996, p. 2. See also H. T. Norris, *Islam in the Balkans* (Columbia: University of South Carolina Press, 1993).

5. Kristo Frashëri, *Lidhja Shqiptare e Prizrenit 1878–1881* (Tirana: Toena, 1997).

6. Stavro Skendi, *The Albanian National Awakening 1878–1912* (Princeton, N.J.: Princeton University Press, 1967).

7. For background see Dimitrije Bogdanović, *Knjiga o Kosovu* (Belgrade: Serbian Academy of Sciences and Arts, 1986); Alex N. Dragnich and Slavko Todorovich, *The Saga of Kosovo: Focus on Serbian-Albanian Relations* (Boulder, Colo.: East European Monographs, distributed by Columbia University Press, 1984); Arshi Pipa and Sami Repishti, eds., *Studies on Kosova* (Boulder, Colo.: East European Monographs, distributed by Columbia University Press, 1984); H. T. Norris, "Kosova and the Kosovans: Past, Present and Future as Seen Through Serb, Albanian and Muslim Eyes," in F. W. Carter and H. T. Norris, eds., *The Changing Shape of the Balkans* (Boulder, Colo.: Westview Press, 1996), pp. 9–24; Tim Judah, *The Serbs: History, Myth and the Destruction of Yugoslavia* (New Haven, Conn.: Yale University Press, 1997); and Lenard J. Cohen, *Broken Bonds: The Disintegration of Yugoslavia* (Boulder, Colo.: Westview Press, 1993).

8. Noel Malcolm, "Kosovo: Only Independence Will Work," *National Interest* 54 (Winter 1998–99): 25. See also Malcolm's *Kosovo: A Short History* (New York: New York University Press, 1998), pp. 58–80.

9. The tribal pattern of social life survived well into the second half of the twentieth century in Kosova and parts of northern Albania. Clans composed of extended families were grouped into tribes, led by chiefs who exercised patriarchal powers. See Margaret Hasluck, *The Unwritten Law in Albania* (Cambridge: Cambridge University Press, 1954).

10. Ivo Banac, *The National Question in Yugoslavia: Origins, History, Politics* (Ithaca, N.Y.: Cornell University Press, 1984), p. 293.

11. Bernd Jürgen Fischer, *King Zog and the Struggle for Stability in Albania* (Boulder, Colo.: East European Monographs, distributed by Columbia University Press, 1984), p. 203.

12. See Paul Lendvai, *Eagles in Cobwebs: Nationalism and Communism in the Balkans* (New York: Doubleday, 1969), p. 225.

13. Asllan Fazlija, *Autonomija e Kosovës e Metohisë në Jugosllavinë Socialiste* (Pristina: Rilindja, 1966), pp. 38–39.

14. Ibid., p. 39, and Stanoje Aksić, *Položajautonomnih pokrajina u ustavnom sistemu SFR Jugoslavije* (Belgrade: Naučna Knjiga, 1967), p. 56.

15. Ali Hadri, "Nacionalni i politički razvoj albanaca u Jugoslaviji," in *Klasno i nacionalno u svremenom socijalizmu* 1 (Zagreb: Naše Teme, 1970), pp. 540–41.

16. See Malcolm, *Kosovo: A Short History*, pp. 314–33; Vickers, *Between Serb and Albanian*, pp. 154–65; and Ramadan Marmullaku, *Albania and the Albanians* (Hamden, Conn.: Archon Books, 1975), pp. 148–49.

17. For background information on Albania under communism, see Nicholas C. Pano, *The People's Republic of Albania* (Baltimore: Johns Hopkins University Press, 1968); Anton Logoreci, *The Albanians: Europe's Forgotten Survivors* (London: Victor Gollancz, 1977); Peter R. Prifti, *Socialist Albania Since 1944: Domestic and Foreign Developments* (Cambridge, Mass.: MIT Press, 1978); Arshi Pipa, *Albanian Stalinism: Ideo-Political Aspects* (Boulder, Colo.: East European Monographs, distributed by Columbia University Press, 1990); and Elez Biberaj, *Albania: A Socialist Maverick* (Boulder, Colo.: Westview Press, 1990).

18. See Sabrina P. Ramet, *Nationalism and Federalism in Yugoslavia, 1962–1991*, 2d ed. (Bloomington: Indiana University Press, 1992), pp. 70–78; and Radošin Rajović, *Autonomija Kosova: Istorijsko-pravna studija* (Belgrade: Ekonomika, 1985), pp. 306–10.

19. See Ilija Vuković, *Autonomaštvo i Separatizam na Kosovu* (Belgrade: Nova Knjiga, 1985).

20. Between 1966 and 1981, 52,000 Serbs and Montenegrins moved out of Kosova. See Hivzi Islami, *Dimensioni Demografik i Çështjes së Kosovës* (Prishtinë, 1997), p. 187. See also Spasoje Djajković, *Sukobi na Kosovu* (Belgrade: Prosveta, 1984); Vuksan Cerović, *Kontrarevolucija Koja Teče* (Belgrade: Nova Knjiga, 1989); and Miloš Mišović, *Ko Je Tražio Republiku Kosovo 1945–1985* (Belgrade: Narodna Knjiga, 1987).

21. *Borba* (Belgrade), October 14, 1979.

22. Brubaker, *Nationalism Reframed*, p. 57.

23. Interview with the chief of Kosova's police, Rrahman Morina, in *Rilindja*, October 26, 1988.

24. Laura Silber and Allan Little, *Yugoslavia: Death of a Nation* (New York: TV Books/Penguin USA, 1995), pp. 37–47 and 58–73; and Mark Thompson, *A Paper House: The Ending of Yugoslavia* (New York: Pantheon Books, 1992), pp. 125–47. See also Borisav Jović, *Poslednji Dani SFRJ: Izvodi iz Dnevnika* (Belgrade: Politika, 1995).

25. Zenun Çelaj, "Kosova Proclaimed a Republic Within the Framework of Yugoslavia," *Zëri i Rinisë* (Pristina), September 14, 1990.

26. Henry Huttenbach, "Serbian Ethnic Cleansing: The Kosova Variant," *Association for the Study of Nationalities (Eurasia and Eastern Europe)* 4, no. 9 (July 1993): 2.

27. *Rilindja Demokratike* (Tirana), January 5, 1991.

28. See Elez Biberaj, "Kosova: The Balkan Powder Keg," *Conflict Studies*, no. 258 (February 1993): 12–13; and Vickers, *Between Serb and Albanian*, p. 253.

29. Richard Caplan, "International Diplomacy and the Crisis in Kosovo," *International Affairs* 74, no. 4 (October 1998): 747–50; and Susan L. Woodward, *Balkan Tragedy: Chaos and Dissolution After the Cold War* (Washington, D.C.: Brookings Institution, 1995), p. 214.

30. The systematic violation of human rights and the establishment of a police state in Kosova have been thoroughly documented by human rights organizations. See the Committee on International Human Rights of the Association of the Bar of the City of New York, *The Kosovo Crisis and Human Rights in Yugoslavia* (New York, February 1991); Helsinki Watch, *Yugoslavia: Human Rights Abuses in Kosovo 1990–1992* (New York, October 1992); Human Rights Watch/Helsinki, *Open Wounds: Human Rights Abuses in Kosovo* (New York, 1993); and Alush A. Gashi, ed., *The Denial of Human and National Rights of Albanians in Kosova* (New York: Illyria Publishing Co., 1991).

31. See Barnett R. Rubin, ed., *Toward Comprehensive Peace in Southeast Europe: Conflict Prevention in the South Balkans* (New York: Twentieth Century Fund Press, 1996); International Commission on the Balkans, *Unfinished Peace: Report of the International Commission on the Balkans* (Washington, D.C.: Carnegie Endowment for International Peace, 1996); Sophia Clément, *Conflict Prevention in the Balkans: Case Studies of Kosovo and the FYR of Macedonia* (Paris: Institute for Security Studies, Western European Union, 1997); Thanos Veremis and Evangelos Kofos, eds., *Kosovo: Avoiding Another Balkan War* (Athens: University of Athens Press, 1998); and Stefan Troebst, *Conflict in Kosovo: Failure of Prevention? An Analytical Documentation, 1992–1998* (Flensburg, Germany: European Center for Minority Issues, 1998).

32. David Binder, "Bush Warns Serbs Not to Widen War," *New York Times*, December 28, 1992; and John M. Goshko, "Bush Threatens 'Military Force' If Serbs Attack Ethnic Albanians," *Washington Post*, December 29, 1992.

33. Bujar Bukoshi, "The Kosova Leadership Must Come Down to Earth and Stop Dreaming," *Zëri,* December 1997.

34. *Financial Times,* December 20–21, 1997.

35. Belgrade BETA in Serbo-Croatian 1603 GMT, January 17, 1998, translated by the Foreign Broadcast Information Service, FBIS-EEU 98-017, January 21, 1998.

36. Statement of the Contact Group Foreign Ministers on Kosovo, New York, September 24, 1997.

37. Hugh Poulton, *Who Are the Macedonians?* (Bloomington: Indiana University Press, 1995), pp. 125–36; Robert W. Mickey and Adam Smith Albion, "Success in the Balkans? A Case Study of Ethnic Relations in the Republic of Macedonia," in Ian M. Cuthbertson and Jane Leibowitz, eds., *Minorities: The New Europe's Old Issue* (New York: Institute for East-West Studies, 1993), pp. 53–98; and Thomas Buck, "Fear and Loathing in Macedonia: Ethnic Nationalism and the Albanian Problem," *International Affairs Review* 5, no. 1 (Winter 1996): 1–23.

38. Human Rights Watch/Helsinki, *A Threat to "Stability": Human Rights Violations in Macedonia* (New York, 1996), p. 27.

39. *Flaka e Vëllazërimit* (Skopje), March 2, 1994.

40. International Research and Exchanges Board Roundtable Report, *Macedonia: Ethnic and International Issues* (Washington, D.C., April 27, 1995), p. 13.

41. Skopje MIC in English, February 19, 1997, translated in FBIS-EEU 97-035, February 24, 1997.

42. *Flaka e Vëlazërimit,* October 27, 1995, p. 3. See also Predrag Dimitrovski, "Radical Song Echoes over Border," Vecer (Skopje), May 25–26, 1996, pp. 4–5, translated in FBIS-EEU 96-104, May 29, 1996, pp. 44–45.

43. Sali Berisha, "Democracy and Humanism: An Inseparable Pair," *Bashkimi* (Tirana), September 17, 1990.

44. *Rilindja Demokratike,* January 5, 1991.

45. Constantine P. Danopoulos and Adem Chopani [Çopani], "Albanian Nationalism and Prospects for Greater Albania," in Constantine P. Danopoulos and Kostas G. Messas, eds., *Crises in the Balkans: Views from the Participants* (Boulder, Colo.: Westview Press, 1997), pp. 186–87.

46. In August 1996 Berisha told a Western reporter that "Albania is doing everything to prevent a conflict. However, Albania will not tolerate a partition [of Kosova] and accept ethnic cleansing because the Albanians have lived [in Kosova] since time immemorial." See *Die Presse,* August 16, 1996, translated in FBIS-EEU 96-163, August 21, 1996, p. 1.

47. The White House, Office of the Press Secretary, "President Clinton Meets with Albanian President Berisha," September 12, 1995.

48. RFE/RL *Newsline,* vol. 1, no. 153, part 2, November 5, 1997.

49. *Kosova Daily Report* (Pristina), no. 1342, February 10, 1998.

50. Belgrade Radio Beograd Network in Serbo-Croatian, December 2, 1997, translated in FBIS-EEU 97-336, December 7, 1997.

51. RFE/RL *Newsline*, vol. 1, no. 185, part 2, December 23, 1997.

52. Quoted in RFE/RL *Newsline*, vol. 2, no. 26, part 2, February 9, 1998.

53. *Kosova Daily Report*, no. 1342, February 10, 1998; and interview with Nano, *Nova Makedonija*, January 20, 1998, p. 2, translated in FBIS-EEU 98-022, January 27, 1998.

54. See Misha Glenny, "Bosnia II?" *New York Times*, December 9, 1997; and International Crisis Group, *Kosovo Spring* (Brussels, 1998), pp. 90–104.

55. *Kosova Daily Report*, no. 1352, February 23, 1998.

56. Gelbard rejected these charges, insisting that in his meeting with Milošević he had warned the Yugoslav leader against cracking down in Kosova. See Jonathan S. Landay, "Kosovo: Next Balkan Boilover?" *Christian Science Monitor*, March 6, 1998.

57. Steven Erlanger, "Albright Warns Serbs on Kosovo Violence," *New York Times*, March 8, 1998.

58. Office of the Spokesman, Department of State, "Statement by Secretary of State Madeleine K. Albright at the Contact Group Ministerial on Kosovo," March 9, 1998.

59. Steven Erlanger, "U.S. and Allies Set Sanctions on Yugoslavia," *New York Times*, March 10, 1998.

60. See Serpicus, "Why Italy Helps Serbia," in *Italy and the Balkans* (Washington, D.C.: CSIS Press, 1998), pp. 31–39. Serpicus is a pseudonym for a "high-ranking Italian diplomat."

61. During the war in Bosnia, the late French President François Mitterrand reportedly said, "As long as I live, France will never make war against Serbia." Quoted in Craig R. Whitney, "France Offers to Lead Force Sent to Kosovo with Monitors," *New York Times*, November 6, 1998.

62. See Veton Surroi, "Token Sanctions Won't Help Kosovo," *New York Times*, March 14, 1998.

63. Chris Hedges, "Kosovo Leader Urges Resistance, But to Violence," *New York Times*, March 13, 1998.

64. See *Der Spiegel*, March 9, 1998.

65. Chris Hedges, "Kosovo's Next Masters?" *Foreign Affairs* 78, no. 3 (May/June 1999): 24–42.

66. An American journalist thus described the Serbian retaliation in Rahovec: "The scale of destruction was so great that years of repair work and an enormous sum of money will be needed to overcome what machine guns, mortars, grenades and tank cannons wrought in just a few

days." See R. Jeffrey Smith, "Kosovo Town Is Destroyed So the Serbs Could Save It," *Washington Post,* July 23, 1998.

67. Justin Brown, "NATO: Going Easy on Serbs?" *Christian Science Monitor,* August 5, 1998.

68. The Contact Group said it would ban foreign investments in Yugoslavia within ten days unless Belgrade agreed to withdraw its security police and begin unconditional talks with ethnic Albanian representatives. It offered to reward Yugoslavia with membership in international financial institutions if it took steps toward a peaceful settlement of the conflict. William Drozdiak, "New Sanctions Freeze Assets in Yugoslavia," *Washington Post,* April 30, 1998; Alessandra Stanley, "U.S. and Allies Put Pressure on Yugoslavia to Negotiate," *New York Times,* April 30, 1998; and Open Society Institute, *Serbia/Kosovo Watch,* no. 77, April 30, 1998.

69. In early May the Contact Group announced a ban on all investments in Yugoslavia and a freeze of Yugoslav assets abroad. Russia said it would not support these measures. See Steven Erlanger, "West Puts Pressure on Serbs with a Ban on Investment," *New York Times,* May 10, 1998.

70. Steven Erlanger, "Allies Upset as U.S. Eases Stance on Kosovo," *New York Times,* May 28, 1998.

71. United States Institute of Peace, *Kosovo Dialogue: Too Little, Too Late* (Washington, D.C., June 1998), p. 3.

72. Quoted in Steven Erlanger, "Clinton Meets Delegation from Kosovo Seeking Talks," *New York Times,* May 30, 1998. See also John F. Harris, "Kosovo Leaders Press for U.S. Intervention," *Washington Post,* May 30, 1998.

73. Craig R. Whitney, "Key Industrial Countries Demand Serbs Halt Offensive in Kosovo," *New York Times,* June 13, 1998.

74. Michael R. Gordon, "Milošević Pledges Steps to Hold Off Attack From NATO," *New York Times,* June 17, 1998.

75. Chris Hedges, "U.S. Envoy Meets Kosovo Rebels, Who Reject Truce Call," *New York Times,* June 25, 1998.

76. Steven Erlanger, "U.S. Meets With Kosovo Rebel Army Leaders," *New York Times,* June 28, 1998.

77. Frustrated by Albanians' inability to develop a common position for the negotiations, Holbrooke publicly complained that there was "no viable negotiating team" on the Albanian side. *Washington Post,* July 6, 1998.

78. *Der Spiegel,* July 6, 1998, pp. 122–23, translated in FBIS-EEU 98-187, July 7, 1998.

79. Craig R. Whitney, "Frustrated by Kosovo Stalemate, the West Criticizes All Sides," *New York Times,* July 9, 1998.

80. *New York Times,* July 29, 1998.

81. The team included Fehmi Agani, Fatmir Sejdiu, and Edita Tahiri of the Democratic League; Tadej Rodiqi of the Christian Democratic Party; and Iljaz Kurteshi of the Social Democratic Party.

82. Even Rugova's advisers acknowledged that the new team had little chance of succeeding and was put together under outside pressure. Alush Gashi, a close adviser to Rugova, publicly complained of Western pressure: Western "diplomats threaten us by saying, 'If you don't do this, you will be on your own, the West will go. Ambassador Hill is blaming us for not uniting. But we can't unite for anything less than independence; without that the war will continue." See Mike O'Connor, "Kosovo Separatist Chief Picks Delegation Without Rebels," *New York Times,* August 14, 1998.

83. *Informatori Ditor* (Pristina), no. 2233C, November 5, 1998.

84. Guy Dinmore, "No Hiding Place as Villagers Flee Serbian Advance," *Financial Times,* August 6, 1998.

85. See Mike O'Connor, "Serbian Soldiers Loot and Burn In Stepped-Up Kosovo Offensive," *New York Times,* August 16, 1998.

86. Turkey reportedly agreed in October 1998 to endorse NATO's activation order only after it was assured that the decision could never be applied to Ankara's treatment of Kurds. See William Drozdiak, "U.S., European Allies Divided Over NATO's Authority to Act," *Washington Post,* November 8, 1998.

87. See A. Ikonomi, "Nano 'Seals' Kosova's Future," *Koha Jonë,* September 12, 1998.

88. Former Defense Minister Alfred Moisiu denounced Albania's passivity toward developments in Kosova and urged the government to take "immediate" measures to prepare the country for a possible war with Serbia. Alfred Moisiu, "Mistake or Betrayal," *Gazeta Shqiptare,* July 21, 1998.

89. Berisha was viewed abroad as an extremist on the Kosova issue. However, he did not advocate independence for Kosova. Instead, Berisha called for a Kosova republic "within the internationally recognized borders" of Yugoslavia. See Berisha's interview in *Dnevni Avaz* (Sarajevo), June 27, 1998, translated in FBIS-EEU 98-182, July 6, 1998.

90. Thomas L. Friedman, "Desperado Democracies," *New York Times,* July 14, 1998.

91. *Nova Makedonija,* September 22, 1998.

92. See Human Rights Watch, *Police Violence in Macedonia* (New York, April 1998).

93. Patrick Moore, "Macedonians Choose Change," RFE/RL *Newsline,* endnote, November 6, 1998.

94. Barbara Crossette, "Security Council Tells Serbs to Stop Kosovo Offensive," *New York Times,* September 24, 1998.

95. In one village, Obrinje, 19 members of the extended Deliaj family were shot at close range and in some cases mutilated. Among those killed was Luljeta Deliaj, who was eight months pregnant. See Peter Finn, "Massacre Haunts Child Survivors," *Washington Post*, October 17, 1998. In the nearby village of Golubovac, 13 Albanian men were executed. Holbrooke secured Milošević's agreement to evacuate from Kosova Selman Morina, the sole survivor of the mass execution in Golubovac. Morina could testify before the War Crimes Tribunal. See Jane Perlez, "Milošević Releases Villager Who Reportedly Saw Mass Execution," *New York Times*, October 8, 1998.

96. These were not the first reported massacres after those in Drenica in February–March. In June, there were reports of mass graves, containing more than 500 bodies, in Rahovec (Orahovac). See Human Rights Watch, *Humanitarian Law Violations in Kosovo* (New York, 1998); Mike O'Connor, "Kosovo Albanians Fear for Lost Kin," *New York Times*, August 6, 1998; R. Jeffrey Smith, "Freshly Dug Mass Graves Found in Kosovo," *Washington Post*, August 5, 1998; Philip Smucker, "Kosovar Bodies Bulldozed to Dump," *Washington Times*, August 6, 1998; and Guy Dinmore, "Survivors Tell of Massacre in Orahovac," *Financial Times*, August 10, 1998. In July, Serbian special forces allegedly abducted and executed about 100 Albanians. See Chris Hedges, "Serb Forces Said to Abduct and Kill Civilians in Kosovo," *New York Times*, July 17, 1998.

97. NATO's credibility was seriously undermined by its inaction as reflected in a statement by a cynical Serbian diplomat: "A village a day keeps NATO away," that is, as long as the Serbs were careful not to commit large-scale atrocities, NATO was not likely to intervene. Quoted in Georgie Anne Geyer, "Kosovo Countdown: Any Plans After Bombs?" *Washington Times*, October 5, 1998.

98. See *New York Times*, October 14, 1998; and *Washington Post*, October 14, 1998.

99. *New York Times*, January 17, 1999; and William Walker, "Improvisational Peace," *Newsweek*, February 1, 1999, p. 44.

100. Rugova's closest associate, Sabri Hamiti, was seriously wounded by unknown assailants in fall 1998, while another of his close aides, Enver Maloku, was assassinated in January 1998. The KLA is widely believed to have been behind both incidents.

101. *Interim Agreement for Peace and Self-Government in Kosovo*, February 23, 1999, p. 81.

102. *New York Times*, March 25, 1999.

103. RFE/RL *Newsline*, vol. 3, no. 67, part 2, April 7, 1999.

104. *New York Times*, April 6, 1999.

105. Ibid., May 6, 1999.

106. See the official KLA news agency *Kosovapress*, April 29, 1999.

107. John F. Harris, "Clinton Says He Might Send Ground Troops," *Washington Post*, May 19, 1999.

108. Roger Cohen, "Warrants Served for Serbs' Leader and 4 Assistants," *New York Times*, May 28, 1999.

109. R. Jeffrey Smith, "Kosovo Rebel Leaders Form Political Party," *Washington Post*, July 10, 1999.

110. Chris Hedges, "Kosovo's Rebels Accused of Executions in the Ranks," *New York Times*, June 25, 1999.

111. *New York Times*, June 9, 1999.

112. See Malcolm's updated version of *Kosovo: A Short History* (New York: HarperPerennial, 1999), preface, p. 16.

113. Gale Stokes, "Containing Nationalism: Solutions in the Balkans," *Problems of Post-Communism* 46, no. 4 (July–August 1999): 9.

114. See Xhaferri's interview in *Dnevnik* (Skopje), October 26, 1998.

115. Brubaker, *Nationalism Reframed*, p. 55.

116. Rotterdam NRC Handelsblad in Dutch, June 23, 1999.

117. Academy of Sciences of Albania, *Platformë për Zgjidhjen e Çështjes Kombëtare Shqiptare* (Tirana, 1998).

Conclusion

MICHAEL MANDELBAUM

T HE MESSAGE that emerges from the foregoing descriptions and analyses of the Hungarian, the Russian, the Serb, and the Albanian national triads is a mixed one. Two of these cases give cause for optimism that relations within a national triad created by the mismatch between state and nation can be peaceful. But all four also demonstrate that peace is by no means certain.

Two of the cases count as success stories. In the postcommunist period neither the Hungarian nor the Russian diasporas have occasioned violence on any significant scale; and this is so, in both cases, at least in part for reasons that are relevant elsewhere. Hungary has absorbed Western political values. It aspires to be part of the economic, political, and cultural community known as the West and understands that observing Western-endorsed international norms, above all the norms of nonaggression and nonviolence, is one of the conditions for admission (or, as many Hungarians would see it, readmission) to this community.

As for the Russians—with the conspicuous exception of the Chechen case—they have had some success in negotiating terms of coexistence with non-Russians in their own state, and this may have increased their willingness to accept similar arrangements for Russians living in newly independent countries in which they are in the minority.

Yet the relative tranquility in which the postcommunist politics of the Hungarian and the Russian triads have been played out can also be plausibly imputed to an attribute that cannot be replicated: size. It may be that while Hungary has been denied the possibility of changing its borders because it is small, Russia has been spared the need to do so because it is large.

Hungary, a country of only 10 million people, felt able to try to overturn the post–World War I settlement in alliance with a far greater power, Germany. In the absence of a powerful revisionist ally, Hungary concluded that it had no choice but to accept the internationally imposed division of the Hungarian nation.[1]

Russia, still the largest country in Europe, may assure respectful treatment for its conationals outside its borders by virtue of geography, demography, and the military potential they underwrite. During the Cold War nuclear weapons were so powerful that simply by possessing a very few, and regardless of the strategic doctrine adopted to govern their deployment and use, the possessor may have been able to deter any attack on its territory. Russia may protect its conationals in neighboring countries through a comparable pattern of "existential deterrence."[2]

Nor is the post–Cold War tranquillity necessarily destined to endure. In the case of the Russians, if not of the Hungarians, it is all too easy to imagine circumstances in which the status of one or more of the diaspora communities becomes the rationale for disruptive or aggressive policies on the part of a Russian minority, or Moscow, or both. Aspirants to the Russian presidency have tested this theme for its public appeal. Further discord over citizenship in the Baltic countries, or an effort to promote the Ukrainian language at the expense of Russian speakers in Ukraine, or a campaign to eliminate Russians from official positions in Kazakhstan—each of which was entirely possible as the twentieth century ended—could enhance that appeal. To the extent that the indifference of Moscow to the fate of ethnic Russians elsewhere has its roots in the relatively weak sense of Russian national identity, this could change over time, with the definition of what it means to be an ethnic Russian coming to include greater metropolitan interest in the diaspora and a correspondingly deeper loyalty to Moscow on the part of Russians living in other countries.[3] Finally, Russian acceptance of the political division of the Russian nation rests on the understanding that this occurred voluntarily. But it was not endorsed by all Russians when it occurred, and it is not beyond imagining that someone who does not accept the legitimacy, or the permanence, of the collapse of the Soviet Union in December 1991 will one day come to power in Moscow.

In contrast to the Hungarian and Russian national triads in the postcommunist period, neither of the two Balkan cases can be considered a success. With the end of Yugoslavia, the Serbs engaged in bitter fighting that, as the decade ended, was in abeyance in Bosnia but not necessarily finished. At the same time, the dissatisfaction of ethnic Albanians at being part of the new, smaller, Serb-dominated Yugoslavia produced, in Kosovo, turmoil, bloodshed, and ultimately a Serb assault that drove hundreds of thousands of Albanians out of the province and a war between the North Atlantic Treaty Organization (NATO) and the Belgrade regime. In each of the four cases there has been an ongoing struggle between forces promoting instability and disruption on one hand, and elements of stability and accommodation on the other. On the basis of the four chapters it is possible to identify these two sets of forces, if not to predict how the contest between them will tilt in any particular national triad at any particular time.

Source of Instability

Instability is built into the triad of diaspora, host country, and homeland state. The triad's founding circumstances create discontent in each of its three parts. Indeed, both in terms of their own needs and by the standards of international affairs, the national minority, the homeland country, and the host state all have reason to be discontented.[4]

Those circumstances predispose a national minority to view itself as a kind of kidnap victim, snatched from its own home and held captive in alien territory. The homeland state similarly has grounds for regarding itself as a victim—of a theft: Territory and people rightfully under its jurisdiction have been wrongly, often forcibly, seized by outsiders. The country within which the minority has been placed might seem to have reason for satisfaction, as the beneficiary of the loss that the national minority and homeland state have suffered. More often, however, it too nurtures a sense of grievance, for it is invariably a new state, created in the wake of an imperial collapse and thus afflicted with political insecurity. Lacking a well-established history of sovereignty, it is uncertain of its identity, its powers, and its prospects. It is, in Rogers Brubaker's term, a "nationalizing state"—that is, a state seeking to create a nation,[5] a newly and hastily erected structure trying, after the fact, to lay a solid foundation for itself. As such, it often sees a national minority as a threat to its own cohesion, a potential fifth column. Nor has that perception always been groundless. The host state will thus seek to impose on the minority not only its laws but also its customs and, especially, its language. This, in turn, provokes resentment and resistance in the other two parts of the triad. The efforts of the nationalizing state constitute, after all, an assault on their common national identity. During the communist period, the Romanian regime pursued such a policy toward the ethnic Hungarians it governed. Postcommunist Croatia adopted similar tactics in dealing with its Serb communities. Pressure by the government of the nationalizing state on the people of the national minority it governs to conform to what seem to the minority to be alien and arbitrary demands is perhaps the most common source of tension within the national triad, but it is not the only one.

What makes the triadic nexus potentially so explosive is that such violence can originate, and in the course of the twentieth century *has* originated, in each of its three parts. In the case of Weimar Germany and post-Trianon Hungary, it was the homeland state that was committed to overturning the national divisions imposed by others and that took the lead in trying to do so. In the post–Cold War era, national minorities have pressed for changes in their status without the active support— even, sometimes, against the opposition—of homeland states. It was the Slavic population of the Transdniestria region of Moldova and the Russians of the Crimean peninsula in Ukraine, for example, who took the initiative in trying to secede from the new post-Soviet states in which they suddenly found themselves. The central government in Moscow (although not the national parliament, the Duma) was unsympathetic to both. Albania neither initiated nor did it consistently or wholeheartedly support Kosovo's efforts to break free of Serb control.

Trouble beginning in any part of the triad can infect the other two; and it can spread as well from one national diaspora to another: The conflict in Kosovo had the potential to enhance secessionist sentiment among Albanians in neighboring Macedonia. The national minority, the homeland nation, and the nationalizing state are all repositories of politically flammable sentiment that, once ignited, can engulf the other two. Within this triad, political conflict and the violence it can trigger are difficult to isolate and to limit. Trouble spreads quickly. This is what happened in the case of the Serbs when Yugoslavia disintegrated. But it need not happen. The four chapters demonstrate that, within these triads, there are forces that promote stability as well.

Nationalism and Stability

The best insurance against the violence that a mismatch between the borders of nations and the borders of states can create is the alignment of the two. Homogeneous nation-states are, on the whole, more stable than multinational states, especially multinational states created in the manner common in Eastern Europe in the twentieth century. National homogeneity is, on the whole, a force for stability. The surest way to avoid conflict is to apply the national principle. This finding cannot be an altogether welcome one, for applying the national principle is arguably undesirable, often difficult, and sometimes quite impossible.[6]

As a formula for state creation, that principle is, in the first place, incoherent. No single definition of a nation can serve as the basis for determining where state borders should be drawn. Language is a rough but not a foolproof standard. Religion is often but not always germane. The twentieth-century history of South Asia illustrates the point. Muslims living in Punjab and Bengal in British India had more in common with their Hindu neighbors, including language, than with each other. But in 1947 the Muslims were divided from those neighbors and united with each other on the basis of their common Islamic faith in the state of Pakistan—even though Pakistan's two wings were separated by 1,100 miles of Indian territory. The union was a tense and fragile one, and in 1971 Bengali Pakistan seceded, amid considerable violence, to form the independent country of Bangladesh. Meanwhile, since 1947 India has been a single sovereign state containing more than 15 distinct linguistic groups. Most Indians cannot communicate directly with most of their fellow citizens; all the same, the country remains united and relatively peaceful.

Where nationalism is concerned, the most nearly viable definition turns out to be a tautology: Nations are groups that believe that they are nations and are willing and able to mobilize themselves to secure their own state. But even that definition can give an erroneous impression of how some contemporary states have become sovereign, especially in the postcommunist period. The successor states of the Soviet Union in Central Asia, for example, were not created by national movements that wrested power from the communist authorities. There was no Uzbek or Kyrgyz national movement, or even much nationalist sentiment worthy of the name, in either place. Uzbekistan and Kyrgyzstan came into existence by default. Like the man playing the tuba the day it rained silver dollars, these two now-sovereign states happened to be in the right place at the right time: When the Soviet Union collapsed they were, for a variety of reasons, union republics, and so had sovereignty thrust upon them.

Nationalism has also been condemned, again with some justice, as being objectionable in principle: By stressing a set of similarities within groups as the basis for political organization it automatically places equal and perverse emphasis on what divides these groups from others. Nationalism is narrow, exclusive, potentially chauvinistic. It is "an affirmation that men have the right to stand on their differences from others, be these differences what they may, fancied or real, important or not, and to make of these differences their first political principle."[7]

If nationalism is incoherent and objectionable in theory, its critics have said, it is dangerous in practice. Partly because it cannot be clearly defined, lines of political division that are intelligible and acceptable to all can never be drawn on the basis of the national principle. The effort to do so is bound to lead to conflict. The danger was recognized when the principle was first introduced. During the Paris Peace Conference after World War I, President Woodrow Wilson's secretary of state, Robert Lansing, wrote in his diary: "The phrase [self-determination] is simply loaded with dynamite. It will raise hopes which can never be realized. It will, I fear, cost thousands of lives."[8] The subsequent history of the twentieth century has, alas, borne out this fear.

Yet for all its shortcomings, the national principle has triumphed. As the basis for apportioning sovereignty, it is deeply embedded in international practice. In fact, whether or not there is any natural solidarity among conationals and no matter how nationality is defined, the national principle is self-reinforcing. While not every state is the only homeland of one particular nation, every group with a claim to being a nation now believes that that claim brings with it the right to its own state. Like the Microsoft Windows operating system for personal computers, once nationalism was established as the world standard for sovereignty, every group seeking the benefits associated with statehood acquired an interest in professing allegiance to and conformity with it.[9]

Individuals and groups in Eastern Europe may have been safer and happier in the past living under the benevolent domain of multinational states, but those states cannot be restored.[10] The Habsburgs and the communists have been relegated to the dustbin of history, and there, for better (certainly in the case of the communists) and for worse (arguably in the case of the Habsburgs) they will remain. Nor will groups with a common language or common descent cease to assert that they are nations and demand to be treated accordingly. Nationalism and the national principle as the basis for sovereignty at the end of the twentieth century are like winter in the northern latitudes: a pervasive fact of life. A lucky few can escape it by moving to warmer climes. But the vast majority who remain must adjust. How is this possible?

There are two ways: by moving borders or by moving people. Neither, however, is always feasible or ever attractive.

Perhaps the most vivid evidence in favor of the soothing effect of national homogeneity is to be found in the largest country of Central Europe, Poland. Its population is among the most uniform in all of Europe; virtually all of its citizens speak the same language and profess the same religion. And for all the burdens with which the four decades of life under communism left the Poles, with independence they did not face the danger of conflict that those living in one part or another of national triads confront. This happy prospect stands in contrast to the Polish experience in the interwar period, when—and because—one out of every three people living in the country was not a Polish-speaking Catholic ethnic Pole.

The method by which Poland was transformed from an unstable multinational country to a stable, ethnically uniform one is the odious process that has come, courtesy of the wars of the former Yugoslavia, to be known as "ethnic cleansing." Poland's Jews were murdered during World War II, its Germans evicted in the war's aftermath. Poland's was scarcely the only pre-Yugoslav case of twentieth-century ethnic cleansing. Forcible, large-scale exchanges of population took place between Greece and Turkey in the aftermath of World War I, the collapse of the Ottoman Empire, and the Greco-Turkish War of 1922, and between the newly created states of India and Pakistan after the 1947 partition of the Asian subcontinent. After World War II, Germans were expelled not only from Poland but also from other territories east of the new borders of Germany, where their ancestors had lived for centuries.

Ethnic cleansing may well have contributed to political stability in Poland. The post–World War I histories of Greece and Turkey, neither of them impeccably harmonious, might have been more turbulent but for the exchanges of population between them.[11] It is conceivable that the expulsion of many, although not all, of its Serbs will make the political path of independent Croatia smoother than it would otherwise have been. But the forced movement of populations cannot be justified even if it could be proven to reduce future conflict. The international community may not always muster the will and the resources to prevent it, but the world surely cannot accept the practice of forced population transfer as a legitimate tool of statecraft.

Population movement need not take place in sanguinary bursts of ethnic cleansing. More or less voluntary—or at least not murderously coerced—migrations have often followed the shift of borders, the creation of new states, and the division of previously united nations.[12] After World War I, Germans moved to Germany from territories that had long been German but that the postwar settlement had made part of Poland.[13] Similarly, Hungarians left what became diaspora communities for the new, shrunken Hungarian nation-state. In the post-Soviet period, Russian nationals have left Central Asia for Russia proper, and it is possible that the stream of Russian emigrants from Kazakhstan will become a large-scale "cascade."[14]

Such migrations can serve as safety valves for nationalist pressure that might otherwise explode in violence. They drain the diaspora communities of people who are dissatisfied with their new circumstances.

They reduce in size, and therefore in disruptive potential, the national minority. But peoples do not often move en masse voluntarily. It is, after all, normal for them to wish to remain in their homes, especially when these have been the homes of their forbears for centuries. Voluntary migration is at best slow, gradual, and partial; coerced migration is immoral. The mismatch between state and nation is not going to be solved by moving people.

Nor can it be readily solved by moving borders. While not impossible, by current international norms, which emphasize the inviolability of existing borders, border change is unusual, if not illegal. Even if it enjoyed more international legitimacy, moreover, changing borders could not solve all minority problems. In some places national groups are intermingled and cannot be cleanly divided merely by redrawing borders.[15] In the twenty-first century, as in the twentieth, sovereign states in Europe and elsewhere will contain more than one nation. A central question for the coming century will therefore be: What policies, what practices, and what institutions can mitigate conflict between and among different nations that inhabit the same state? Peaceful coexistence between and among sovereign states was the great task of the second half of the twentieth century. Peaceful coexistence within states seems likely to be the preoccupation of the first decade of the 21st century. What can contribute to it?

Techniques of Harmony

Perhaps the leading candidate for promoting stability where nations are divided is economic growth. It is one thing that programs for conflict resolution invariably emphasize.[16] Prosperity is presumed to be a powerful, all-purpose solvent of every kind of political stain and blight, a miracle drug for social and economic problems. Is this true? If a rising economic tide lifts all boats, does it soothe all bruises and repair all fractures in the body politic?

Economic growth certainly has some healing properties. All other things being equal, prosperous countries are no doubt more harmonious than those that are poverty-stricken. Economic failure did more to set the peoples of the former Yugoslavia against one another than is commonly recognized.[17] When the economic climate turns harsh, minorities, whether or not they have actually contributed to the economic distress, become targets of anger, discrimination, and persecution on the part of the majority. Ethnic Chinese learned this when the Asian fiscal crisis struck Indonesia in 1997 and 1998, and Jews in Europe have had painful, indeed disastrous, occasion to know it for centuries. From the standpoint of communal harmony, economic activity is beneficial in and of itself because it requires, and thus fosters, cooperation, including cooperation across national and ethnic divisions.

While prosperity may erode, however, it cannot eradicate the grievances, few of them economic in character, that cause conflict when nations are divided. Moreover, economic growth cannot be produced on demand, as the extensive but far from wholly successful twentieth-century history of efforts to do so demonstrates.

In the post–Cold War period democracy has come to be for politics what prosperity is for economics: something universally desirable if not quite universally desired, a source of all blessings, a necessary part of the public agenda of every sovereign state, new or old. The attitudes and institutions necessary for managing the conflicts that the national triad creates are common in Western democracies and almost nowhere else: tolerance, wide opportunities for effective political participation, and social space for the expression of cultural differences. But Western democracies are *liberal* democracies, which combine the rule of the majority with constitutional protections for minorities. Liberal, or constitutional, democracy is a system both for determining how a government is chosen and for limiting what that government can and cannot do with the power vested in it by the people. The first feature empowers the majority; the second protects the minority.[18]

It is possible to have the first without the second, and democracies that are illiberal can aggravate rather than reduce national tensions when they are new states without well-established political institutions or practices. In such states political competition is intense, as old elites try to maintain power and new groups seek to gain it. The rules governing political competition are weak, precedents are lacking, and debate over marginal changes in the government's role in the economy and the society and the distribution of economic output, the stuff of politics in Western liberal democracies, is not relevant. Instead, nationalism becomes the most promising material out of which to fashion a political appeal. Contenders for power find it advantageous to evoke—or provoke—fears among the majority that their patrimony is being diminished, or subverted, or is otherwise at risk from the minority.[19]

Unhappily, precisely such combustible conditions have been present in states that are part of the national triads of Eastern Europe. The homeland states and host countries in all four cases are new, fragile, uncertain of their legitmacy and even of their permanence.[20] In all of them the temptation to rally political support by posing as the defender of the majority against the minority is substantial. In some of them—Serbia,

Croatia, and Slovakia, for example—it is a temptation to which would-be leaders have succumbed. The Serb and Croat leaders responsible for the carnage that enveloped the former Yugoslavia—Slobodan Milošević, Radovan Karadžić, and Franjo Tudjman—all had popular mandates won through nationalist appeals.[21] So, for that matter, did history's most bloodthirsty crusader against imposed frontiers, Adolf Hitler. Even in postcommunist Russia and Hungary, where murderous demagogy has been absent, governments have asserted that a proprietary interest in their fellow nationals living in other jurisdictions is central to their foreign policies.

To put it in the starkest terms, one reason for the danger of violence in the national triad is that a requirement for legitimacy and success in the host country is precisely the opposite of what is required for peace within the triad.

Free elections without working liberal institutions are a part of the political landscape of many of the 27 postcommunist countries of Eastern Europe and the former Soviet Union. But while illiberal democracy became more prominent at the end of the twentieth century than it was in previous decades, it was hardly new. It was a preoccupation of the nineteenth century, one that was reflected in two of that century's best-known and most influential works of political inquiry: Alexis de Tocqueville's *Democracy in America* and John Stuart Mill's *On Liberty*. Thus one of the great postcommunist political projects, on the success of which the prospects for triadic peace will rest, is the establishment not simply of majoritarian but of fully liberal democracy. The prospects for its success in any particular postcommunist country will, in turn, be affected by which of the two types of nationalism that are common in Europe prevails on its territory.

There can be more than one type of nationalism because nationalism has no single definition: Each national group must choose how to define itself. It must select criteria for deciding who belongs to the nation and who does not. Ethnic nationalism defines the nation, as the name suggests, in ethnic terms. Historically, a German has been anyone who could prove German ancestry. Civic nationalism, by contrast, defines the nation in territorial terms: Anyone residing in France can be a French citizen.[22]

The two definitions have different implications for citizenship. Someone of German descent whose family has lived for centuries on the Volga River, in the heart of Russia, historically has been eligible to be a German citizen, while German speakers born in Germany but of Turkish descent have not. By contrast, someone born in West Africa but resident in Paris has been eligible for French citizenship. Of the two, civic nationalism is the more compatible with peace within national triads than ethnic nationalism. It is inclusive. It recognizes that minorities have rights, notably the right to full citizenship. It removes the stigma of alien status and the suspicion of disloyalty that the ethnic variety of nationalism imposes on national minorities.

Desirable as it may be, is civic nationalism feasible in postcommunist Europe? Is it within the power of a nation or a government to choose one or the other? After all, the German and French varieties of nationalism developed in different historical circumstances, which accounts for the differences between them that persist in the present.

The German nation-state was consolidated relatively late in European history, in 1871. When Prussia emerged as the core of that state, it included non-Germans, above all Poles, who had their own national identity and no interest in becoming German; at the same time, Prussia's borders excluded large ethnically German communities that did not wish to abandon their national identity. It was therefore logical to define German nationality, and ultimately citizenship, in ethnic rather than territorial terms.

By contrast, the French state is the oldest continuous one in Western Europe, dating back to the twelfth century. It had centuries to turn Bretons, Normans, and Provençals into Frenchmen,[23] a task made easier by the fact that none of the various local loyalties within France's borders turned into a full-fledged alternative national identity. Nor were there as many ethnic Frenchmen outside France as there were Germans outside Germany whom defining citizenship in territorial terms would exclude.[24]

In their founding circumstances, the postcommunist states among which Hungarians, Russians, Serbs, and Albanians are scattered more closely resemble Germany than France. The process of state formation occurred relatively late in historical terms, and different self-conscious nations inhabit the same political entity. Ethnic rather than civic nationalism seems the plausible choice for them.[25]

But it is not the inevitable choice.[26] The postcommunist states are not destined to define nationalism in ethnic rather than civic terms. The type of nationalism adopted, like nationalism itself, is not simply the immutable product of fixed circumstances. National identity and the impulse to achieve statehood are modern, and in most cases relatively recent, developments. Nations are not "as old as history,"[27] and nationalism is not a social force that has been present in the world from time immemorial.

To the contrary, the corpus of contemporary studies of nationalism has found that it is "constructed," not "primordial"—although it cannot be constructed, so to speak, out of thin air, without any preexisting sense of common history and destiny. The components of which nationalism is fashioned are not the same thing as nationalism itself.[28] National identity can be—indeed, it inevitably is—at least partly created and deliberately shaped. It follows that the adoption of the ethnic or the civic variety is at least in part open to purposeful choice. In the early years of postcommunist independence, both Ukraine and Russia seemed to be opting—in their laws, in governmental decrees, and in the ethos accepted and propagated by their political elites—provisionally and tentatively (and not irreversibly) for civic nationalism.

To the extent that civic nationalism is established, this bodes well for tolerance, harmony, and peace within national triads. But civic nationalism is not a *guarantee* of tranquillity. As practiced in the West, moreover, one of its central features is in fact incompatible with peaceful coexistence between and among national majorities and minorities. Everyone living in France can become a French citizen, but everyone who does so is expected also to become a Frenchman or woman: The cultural follows the political. A French citizen is expected not only to obey French laws and to be loyal to the French state but also to adopt French customs and above all the French language. In France—and in the United States and the United Kingdom—the civic definition of nationalism carries with it the presumption of assimilation.[29]

In this crucial way their version of civic nationalism is like rather than unlike the ethnic kind long characteristic of the Germans: Both insist on a single, full-fledged nationality within a given state. The difference between the two is one of means, not ends. Civic nationalism seeks to achieve the monopoly of a particular nationalism by inclusion, ethnic nationalism by exclusion. The first type seeks to change the identity of individuals; the second all too often has sought to achieve its goal by forcibly changing the location of groups. Assimilation is an effective response to classical diasporas, created when individuals move; it is usually counterproductive, indeed dangerous, when applied to the new diasporas.[30]

Most of the groups of the new diasporas of Eastern Europe insist on full rights of citizenship but not at the price of abandoning their distinctive national identities. Hungarians in Transylvania do not wish to be second-class citizens of Romania, but neither do they wish to become ethnically Romanian.[31] The new diasporas of Eastern Europe want civil rights in the sovereign states in which history has placed them; but they also want measures that go beyond civil rights. The late-twentieth-century international consensus holds that sovereign states should not have two classes of citizens. But the demands of the new diasporas amount precisely to a second—although not an inferior—kind of citizenship: They wish to be equal but also, in some important ways, separate.

Techniques of Accommodation

The mismatch between state and nation in post–Cold War Eastern Europe is a problem that requires for its solution not only democracy but constitutional democracy and a constitution that, unlike those in the West, treats individuals equally but groups differently, that protects both the common rights of citizens and the separate preferences of national groups. In the civic democracies of the West, the idea of group rights is an oxymoron; in the multinational states of Eastern Europe, it would seem almost to be a political necessity.

There is a historical precedent for the constitutional protection of group rights: the post–World War I minority treaties. These were drawn up at the peace conference in Paris and applied to sovereign states in Eastern Europe with substantial national minorities within their borders. By their terms, the signatory governments promised to accord the national minorities they governed the right of collective organization and to respect their distinctive religions and cultures.[32] Violations of the treaties could be appealed to the League of Nations, which in theory was the agent of enforcement. But the League did not enforce the treaties. Britain and France would have had to take responsibility for enforcement, but neither was willing to spend the necessary political capital or exert sufficient military leverage to do so.[33] One lesson of the interwar experience is that, for the protection of minorities, pressure from without is unlikely to suffice. The institutions and the practices of the states in which they reside must be designed for this purpose and the government must be willing to carry them out.

One principle of constitutional design, familiar in the western part of Europe and relevant to the special circumstances of the east, is federalism. In a federal system some powers are reserved for smaller units of government. Russia seems to be developing, in ad hoc fashion, a federal system, one that gives some non-Russian groups an enhanced measure of control over their lives.[34]

Federalism will not always be the solution to the problems created by mismatch between state and nation, however. Its rationale in the West has little to do with the accommodation of national differences. The rationale is, rather, that smaller units of government tend to be more efficient and responsive to popular wishes than are larger ones and that dispersing power among different levels of governments is a barrier to the exercise of oppressive authority by any one of them. Federalism is not necessarily a method of empowering national minorities because, while it divides power along territorial lines, minorities are not always concentrated in geographically compact clusters.[35]

Finally, the federal principle ordinarily divides governmental functions among different levels of government but does not, in and of itself, provide the specific cultural, political, and legal guarantees that new diasporas seek. The United States is a federal system par excellence, but one in which education is primarily a local responsibility; nonetheless, the issue of instruction in languages other than English is a controversial one.

For the multinational states of Eastern Europe, a more appropriate model than the federalism of the large countries of the West is the more elaborate form of power sharing devised in several of the smaller ones—Belgium, the Netherlands, and Austria—a system known as consociationalism.[36]

It has four defining features, all of them of potential applicability to the new diasporas: close collaboration among the elites of the different communities within the same state, often in a single governing "grand coalition" in the national parliament; provisions for any group to veto measures in certain areas of policy that it disfavors, even when such measures enjoy majority support; proportionality as the basis for parliamentary representation and for allocating government employment; and a high degree of autonomy over internal affairs for each national group.[37] The guiding principle of consociational democracy, the common denominator of its defining features, is a dilution of the principle of majority rule. This is constitutional democracy with a very heavy emphasis on the constitution—that is, on statutory limits on the powers of the majority—at the expense of pure majoritarian democracy.[38] Belgium and the Netherlands are relatively old states, steeped in liberal values and confident and tolerant enough to accord considerable power to minorities. The homeland and host states that belong to the postcommunist national triads in Eastern Europe are all poorer in both the relevant historical experience and the liberal outlook: For consociationalist democracy, indeed for constitutional democracy of any kind, the soil becomes steadily less fertile the farther east in Europe it is located.[39]

In two of the triads in this volume, the Serb and the Albanian, events may have overtaken the possibility for constitutional arrangements for the peaceful coexistence within the same state of different nations. Serbs in Bosnia and Albanians in Kosovo have fought and died to change their status. In each case, the war aim was secession. In neither case did the national minority appear to be reconciled to remaining in a multinational state in which it was outnumbered. What the West preferred and prescribed, in the 1995 Dayton Accords for Bosnia and in the plan tabled at a conference at Rambouillet, France, in 1999 but rejected by the Belgrade government for Kosovo, bore some resemblances to the Belgian and Dutch models, with considerable decentralization and national self-government. But only the presence of Western troops kept Bosnia together; and it was unclear on what basis, if any, Albanian Kosovars could be reconciled to remaining part of Serb-dominated Yugoslavia over the long term. Even the most generous, permissive form of consociationalism seems unlikely to override the powerful impulse for separation. The alternative to continuing conflict in these two cases seems to be the redrawing of borders.

The provisions for diluting majority rule that are on display in the smaller countries of Western Europe might, however, be relevant to the future of the Russian and Hungarian diasporas and to the Albanians of Macedonia. Consociationalism offers procedures and institutions that may, in some cases, make more tolerable life within borders that were thrust unexpectedly on them.

Such arrangements may be acceptable to each of the three parts of the national triad. But if they are accepted, they will not be accepted gladly. Whatever form they take, such arrangements will fulfill the highest aspirations of none of the three. They will represent, for each, a second-best solution, the institutional embodiment of a willingness to compromise that, in this case as with all other political conflicts, is the necessary condition for peace.

National minorities must give up the hope of independence or of reincorporation into the territory of the national homeland in favor of a special status within the borders of the state in which history has placed them. The homeland nation must abandon the claim of ownership in favor of the role of external protector, conceding that it may press for change in the status of its conationals who live elsewhere but not of the borders within which the minority lives. This requires giving up the dream of a restored pre–World War I Hungary, of a Russia of Soviet dimensions, of a Greater Serbia, or of a Greater Albania in favor of international recognition of a special relationship with fellow Hungarians, Russians, Serbs, and Albanians living as minorities elsewhere. As for the host state, it must relinquish its preferred policy of ignoring or even obliterating the national differences among its citizens. Instead, it must accord official recognition to and practice toleration of those differences.

Preventing deadly conflict on a large scale involves meeting, in Eastern Europe, what Senator Daniel Patrick Moynihan has identified as the chief challenge of the post–Cold War period: "to make the world safe for and from" national differences.[40] This, in turn, requires that each of the three parts of the triad created by the mismatch between state and nation do what is often most difficult in public affairs and what has proven particularly difficult in postcommunist Eastern Europe: find and hold the middle ground.

Notes

1. It is surely one of the more pointed ironies of the twentieth century that Nazi Germany waged the greatest war in the history of Europe in order, among other goals, to bring all Germans under a single political roof and failed miserably, leaving what had been the Third Reich divided for almost fifty years, while the Federal Republic of Germany lived more or less comfortably with that division yet saw it ended.

2. "[W]e can now explain why the Russian minorities in thirteen of the fourteen former union republics have not been engaged in ethnic war. This can be explained by Russia's power and its mixed signals to the nationalist leaders in the near abroad (both titular and Russian) about their probable reactions if ethnic war broke out in a former union republic. Within those new republics, neither titulars nor Russians had sufficient surety (about Russia's probable reaction) to aggress upon the other." David Laitin, *Identity in Formation: The Russian-Speaking Populations of the Near Abroad* (Ithaca, N.Y.: Cornell University Press, 1998), pp. 329–30. Diaspora Russians, that is, are deterred by uncertainty that Russia would intervene on their behalf and the nationalizing state by uncertainty that Russia would *not* intervene.

   It is not only the strength of postcommunist Russia that has helped keep the peace, however; Russian weakness has also been a factor. The new Russia has showed itself, in Chechnya, incapable of serious large-scale military operations. And the political costs in relations with the rest of the world of launching a campaign of irredentism would be high even if Russia were militarily more competent.

   Russia is not necessarily fated to be weak forever, however, and the story of the various Russian (and Russian-speaking) diasporas created by the collapse of the Soviet Union is far from complete. In some ways it is just beginning. The status of these diasporas—their social identities and political goals—is not settled. This is the theme of Laitin, ibid.

3. It is possible that a distinct Russian-*speaking* social and political identity will be formed in the non-Russian, non-Ukrainian former Soviet republics that have become independent countries. See Laitin, *Identity in Formation*, chapter 10.

4. More generally, nationalism can carry with it a predisposition to conflict. At its core often lies resentment. It is, in Isaiah Berlin's phrase, a "bent twig," which snaps back fiercely after release from the pressure that has

bent it. To change the idiom slightly, nationalism, especially the nationalism of newly independent states, often carries a chip on its shoulder. It is the faith of those who feel that the past has deprived them of their full communal rights and who fear that they will somehow be similarly cheated in the future. Isaiah Berlin, "The Bent Twig: On the Rise of Nationalism," in Berlin, *The Crooked Timber of Humanity* (New York: Vintage Books, 1992.

5. Rogers Brubaker, *Nationalism Reframed: Nationhood and the National Question in the New Europe* (New York: Cambridge University Press, 1996), esp. chapter 3.

6. For this reason nationalism has attracted criticism. Two notable examples of such criticism, among many, are Elie Kedourie, *Nationalism*, 4th ed. (Oxford: Blackwell, 1994), and Eric Hobsbawm, *Nations and Nationalism Since 1780: Programme, Myth, Reality* (Cambridge: Cambridge University Press, 1990).

7. Kedourie, *Nationalism*, p. 74.

8. Quoted in Daniel Patrick Moynihan, *Pandaemonium: Ethnicity in International Politics* (New York: Oxford University Press, 1993), p. 83.

9. And once nationalism was established as the basis of sovereignty, homogeneous states acquired an advantage over multinational ones because they had one fewer potential cause for strife. At the end of the twentieth century, the multinational state in North America, Canada, was the scene of acute although not violent political conflict. Its southern neighbor, the United States, was scarcely without difficulties, but conflict based on national differences was not among them.

10. See, for example, the idyllic account of life in Romania before World War I and the creation of a Romanian national state reprinted in Moynihan, *Pandaemonium*, p. 133. For a more jaundiced appraisal, see Lewis Namier, "The Downfall of the Habsburg Monarchy," in Namier, *Vanished Supremacies: Essays in European History, 1812–1918* (New York: Harper Torchbooks, 1958).

11. Provision for these population movements was included in the treaty between the two countries signed at Lausanne, Switzerland, in 1923.

12. Some are discussed in Brubaker, *Nationalism Reframed*, chapter 6.

13. After World War II even greater numbers were absorbed by the German Federal Republic. "Including the 4 million Germans who fled from East Germany to West Germany from 1949 to 1990, almost one-fourth of the 82 million inhabitants of present-day Germany are expelled people, refugees, and voluntary German migrants." Hans Smits, "Watch Out for the Neighbors," *Transition* 5, no. 11 (November 1998): 27.

14. Laitin, *Identity in Formation*, p. 174.

15. The Hungarians of Transylvania are an example. Even where new lines could create ethnic and national homogeneity, the resulting units would sometimes be too small to be viable sovereign states, as the Abkhaz in Georgia and the Chechens of Russia may discover.

16. See, for example, Carnegie Commission on Preventing Deadly Conflict, *Preventing Deadly Conflict* (New York: Carnegie Corporation of New York, 1997), pp. 82–89.

17. This is a theme of Susan Woodward, *Balkan Tragedy: Chaos and Dissolution after the Cold War* (Washington, D.C.: Brookings Institution, 1995).

18. Fareed Zakaria, "The Rise of Illiberal Democracy," *Foreign Affairs* (November–December 1997): 22–43. As Aurel Braun notes in his chapter in this book, liberal democracy provides a "double layer" of protection against nationalist violence: By definition it affords protection to national minorities within "nationalizing states"; and historically liberal democracies have not been prone to go to war with one another, reducing the chances of conflict between a host and a homeland state that are both constitutional democracies.

19. On the combustible potential of fledgling democracy, see Edward Mansfield and Jack Snyder, "Democratization and the Danger of War," *International Security* 20, no. 1 (Summer 1995): 5. The authors find that new democracies are more likely than established ones, or established nondemocratic regimes, to go to war. Their analysis also applies to nationalist tension, which can, of course, lead to war. The historian Lewis Namier went so far as to assert that nationalism and liberal democracy were incompatible: "In practice . . . there is an antithesis between self-government, which means constitutional development within an existing territorial framework, and self-determination, for which there is no occasion unless that framework is called in question and territorial changes are demanded; and acute disputes concerning the territorial framework naturally retard, or even preclude, constitutional development." "Basic Factors in 19th-Century European History," in Namier, *Vanished Supremacies*, p. 166.

20. An exception is Hungary, which has been effectively sovereign since 1867. But all five countries where the Hungarian diasporas are located fit this description.

21. The aim of enforcing the prerogatives of the majority at the expense of the minority is implicit in the term that Rogers Brubaker employs to refer to the country that is host to a national minority: "nationalizing state." "Nationalizing" connotes the enforcement of the national characteristics— language above all—and favoring the interests—government jobs, for example—of the majority at the expense of the minority. Brubaker, *Nationalism Reframed*, esp. chapter 3.

22. The distinction is recognized in the Russian language: *"Russkii"* refers to a person of Russian descent, *"rossisskii"* to someone living within the post-communist borders of Russia who may not be ethnically Russian, reli-

giously Orthodox, or linguistically Russophone. Fifteen percent of the new Russia's 150 million people belong to the second but not the first category.

23. Eugen Weber, *Peasants into Frenchmen* (Stanford, Calif.: Stanford University Press, 1976).

24. Still, substantial francophone communities outside the borders of the French state—in Belgium and Canada—have not coexisted entirely comfortably with the non-French nations with which they have had to share a state.

25. On the debate about the nature of post-Soviet Russian citizenship see Laitin, *Identity in Formation*, pp. 313–14.

26. Nor is the choice immutable once made. France and Germany moved closer to each other—or, perhaps more accurately, moved in opposite directions—on this subject. In 1998, the new federal coalition government of Social Democrats and Greens proclaimed the need to broaden and liberalize German citizenship laws. In France, meanwhile, the xenophobic program of Jean-Marie Le Pen, which emphasized excluding non-Christians and non-Europeans from the French nation, gained political ground for much of the 1990s.

27. Hobsbawm, *Nations and Nationalism*, p. 3.

28. Summaries of the literature on nationalism are in ibid., introduction; and Ronald Grigor Suny, *The Revenge of the Past: Nationalism, Revolution, and the Collapse of the Soviet Union* (Stanford, Calif.: Stanford University Press, 1993), chapter 1.

29. In the nineteenth century the presumption of assimilation was not controversial. Some nations and their cultures were considered superior to others: that was an accepted fact of life. The point was made vividly by John Stuart Mill, certainly not a chauvinist by the standards of the age: "Nobody can suppose that it is not more beneficial for a Breton or a Basque of French Navarre to be . . . a member of the French nationality, admitted on equal terms to all the privileges of French citizenship . . . than to sulk on his own rocks, the half-savage relic of past times, revolving in his own little mental orbit, without participation or interest in the general movement of the world. The same remark applies to the Welshman or the Scottish highlander as members of the British nation." Mill, *Utilitarianism, Liberty and Representative Government*, cited in Hobsbawm, *Nations and Nationalism*, p. 34. Marx and Engels shared this view (see Namier, "Nationality and Liberty," in Namier, *Vanished Supremacies*, p. 48). The nineteenth century believed in the equality of individuals but in a hierarchy of nations. The twentieth has come to believe in the equality, in principle, of all nations and national cultures.

30. A single dominant nationality within its borders is arguably conducive to, if not strictly necessary for, democracy. Mill believed this (see Namier, *Vanished Supremacies*, p. 38). To accept democracy is to be willing to be outvoted;

in a stable democracy everyone is willing to risk being in the minority. This is rational only when the price for being on the losing side of an electoral contest is low. It is likelier to seem low when everyone is a member of the same group—that is, the same nation—than when this is not the case.

31. In the civic nationalist democracies of the West, far more modest demands for group recognition—affirmative action in employment and official status for languages other than English in the United States, for example, and special dress codes for Islamic schoolchildren in Britain and France—have aroused heated political controversy.

32. The first country to sign a minority treaty was Poland. Among the other signatories were Hungary, Romania, Germany, and Yugoslavia. See Mark Mazower, "Minorities and the League of Nations in Interwar Europe," *Daedalus* (Spring 1997), 47–64; and Inis L. Claude, *National Minorities: An International Problem* (New York: Greenwood Press, 1969), chapters 1, 2. Polish assent to its minority treaty was a condition of diplomatic recognition. In the wake of the Cold War, the European Union (EU) attempted something similar for Yugoslavia. It established the Badinter Commission, which was to certify that a Yugoslav successor state had made adequate provision for, among other things, the protection of the rights of the national minority or minorities within its territory before it could receive official recognition by the EU. At German insistence, however, Croatia was recognized in 1992 without meeting these conditions. See Woodward, *Balkan Tragedy*, pp. 178–84. See also Steven L. Burg and Paul S. Shoup, *The War in Bosnia-Herzegovina: Ethnic Conflict and International Intervention* (Armonk, N.Y.: M. E. Sharpe, 1999), pp. 92–96.

33. Their concerns in Eastern Europe revolved around geopolitical considerations. They were more interested in solidarity with European governments against Germany than in protecting national minorities against the depredations of these same governments. Mazower, "Minorities in the League of Nations," pp. 51–52, and Claude, *National Minorities,* chapter 3. In their policies toward Yugoslavia in the wake of the Cold War the Western Europeans lacked this excuse.

34. The clearest example of accommodating non-Russians through the federal principle is the case of Tatarstan.

35. The Habsburg Empire, with its checkerboard pattern of national distribution, inspired at least one proposal for nonterritorial nationalism, which was put forward by Austrian Marxists. Arendt Lijphart, *Democracy in Plural Societies: A Comparative Exploration* (New Haven, Conn.: Yale University Press, 1977), p. 43. In the most important non-Western federal system, that of India, the relevant distinction, language, is territorially concentrated. States organized on linguistic lines are a necessary condition for Indian unity.

36. Europe, east and west, is also home to experiments in supranational sovereignty. Neither the European Union in the west, however, nor the Russia-

centered Commonwealth of Independent States in the east offers a practical solution to the difficulties associated with the mismatch between state and nation in Eastern Europe. The first involves the partial surrender of sovereignty to a larger unit by states that are ethnically homogeneous or have found ways to resolve their minority problems. The purpose is to promote economic efficiency through economies of scale as well as to prevent conflict between and among, rather than within, sovereign states. The second is seen by virtually all countries other than Russia as at best an institution for enhancing Russian influence on the territory of the former Soviet Union, at worst a device for reimposing Russian domination. In any event, it is even theoretically relevant only to the Russian national triad.

37. Lijphart, *Democracy in Plural Societies,* chapter 2.

38. The former Yugoslavia had some of the features of consociationalism although it was a one-party state, not a democracy. On paper, the Bosnian federation established by the Dayton Accords looked like a form of consociationalism. On predissolution Yugoslavia, see Woodward, *Balkan Tragedy,* chapter 2; on the constitutional details of Dayton, see Burg and Shoup, *War in Bosnia-Herzegovina,* pp. 367–73.

39. It is not particularly fertile outside Europe. Much of Arendt Lijphart's book on consociationalism, *Democracy in Plural Societies,* published in 1977, is devoted to assessing the prospects for applying it to plural societies in Africa and Asia. A quarter century later there was little evidence of success. Rwanda is more typical of the experience in those regions than Switzerland.

40. His full phrase is "to make the world safe for, and from, ethnicity." Moynihan, *Pandaemonium,* p. 173. But he uses the term "ethnicity" to include the groups and sentiments that in this volume are called national.

About the Authors

ELEZ BIBERAJ is Director of the Albanian Service at Voice of America in Washington, D.C. He has a Ph.D. in political science from Columbia University and is the author of three books on Albania. Biberaj's most recent book is *Albania in Transition: The Rocky Road to Democracy* (1998).

AUREL BRAUN is Professor of International Relations and Political Science at the University of Toronto and a member of its Centre for Russian and East European Studies. His publications include *Dilemmas of Transition: The Hungarian Experience* (1999); *The Extreme Right: Freedom and Security at Risk* (1997); and *The Soviet–East European Relationship in the Gorbachev Era* (1990).

BENNETT KOVRIG is Professor Emeritus of Political Science at the University of Toronto and is currently living in Paris. He is the author of numerous works on East-Central Europe, including *Of Walls and Bridges: The United States and Eastern Europe* (1991). He served in 1987–88 as Director of Research and Analysis at Radio Free Europe.

MICHAEL MANDELBAUM is Director of the Project on East-West Relations at the Council on Foreign Relations and is Christian A. Herter Professor of American Foreign Policy at The Johns Hopkins School of Advanced International Studies in Washington, D.C. He has also held teaching posts at Harvard and Columbia Universities and at the United States Naval Academy. He is the Whitney A. Shepardson Fellow of the Council on Foreign Relations for 1999–2000. A regular foreign affairs columnist for *Newsday*, Professor Mandelbaum is the Associate Director of the Aspen Institute's Congressional Project on American Relations with the Former Communist World. He is the editor or coeditor of nine books published by the Council on Foreign Relations, including *The New Russian Foreign Policy* (1998), *Sustaining the Transition: The Social Safety Net in Postcommunist Europe* (1997), and *Postcommunism: Four Perspectives* (1996).

SUSAN L. WOODWARD is Senior Research Fellow at the Centre for Defence Studies, King's College, University of London. Until July 1999, she was Senior Fellow in the Foreign Policy Studies Program at the Brookings Institution. During much of 1994, she was head of the Analysis and Assessment Unit in the Office of the Special Representative of the Secretary-General for the former Yugoslavia, in the headquarters of the United Nations Protection Force, Zagreb, Croatia, and served from August to September of 1998 as special adviser to the Head of Mission, Organization for Security and Cooperation in Europe, in Bosnia and Herzegovina. She is the author of *Balkan Tragedy: Chaos and Dissolution after the Cold War* (1995) and *Socialist Unemployment: The Political Economy of Yugoslavia, 1945–1990* (1995) as well as numerous articles. Prior to going to Brookings she was Associate Professor of Political Science at Yale University.

Index

A

Accommodation, techniques of, 301–4
Afghanistan, 93, 110
Africa, 12, 13, 298
Agani, Fehmi, 265
Agriculture, 29–30, 36, 53, 65
Ahtisaari, Martti, 272
Aksyonenko, Nikolai, 109
Albania, 4, 6, 8–9, 14–15, 214–91; and Serbia, 160, 165, 176, 181–82, 205; and political instability, 292; and techniques of accommodation, 302–3
Albanian Democratic Union, 255, 256
Albright, Madeleine, 134, 161, 251
Alia, Ramiz, 237, 245
Aliyev, Haidar, 93
Alliance of Hungarians in Vojvodina, 70
Anschluss, 37, 39
Ántall, Jószef, 160
Anti-Comintern Pact, 38
Anti-Fascist Council for National Liberation of Yugoslavia (AVNOJ), 170, 173, 179
Arato, Andrew, 128
Armenia, 93
Asia, 12, 293, 296
Association for a Yugoslav Democratic Initiative, 197
Assyrians, 2
Atlanticism, 88
Australia, 162–63
Austria, 22, 39, 165, 187, 189, 199, 202

Austria-Hungary, 187, 189
Azerbaijan, 93

B

Bakalli, Mahmut, 232, 252
Balladur, Edouard, 60
Banac, Ivo, 221
Banglasdesh, 293
Belarus, 93, 94, 107–10, 136
Belgium, 71, 74
Beneš, Edvard, 27, 40
Berisha, Sali, 245–47
Berlin, Isaiah, 304n4
Berlin Wall, 279
Bethlen, István, 26
Biserko, Sonja, 277
Black Sea Fleet, 100, 102–3, 106, 137, 150–69
Bosnia, 7, 9–11, 13, 69, 233, 238, 277; and Serbia, 159–60, 166, 167, 170, 176, 181–204; and techniques of accommodation, 302–3
Brezhnev Doctrine, 86–87
Brioni Accord, 160
Britain, 27, 74, 272
Brubaker, Rogers, 146n5, 166, 204–5, 214, 216, 231, 278
Brzezinski, Zbigniew, 133, 157n157
Buja, Ramë, 265
Bukoshi, Bujar, 238, 242, 265
Bulgaria, 165, 278
Bunting, Audrey Helfant, 192
Burgenland, 28
Bush, George, 241

C

Camdessus, Michel, 124
Canada, 71, 74, 127, 162–63
Capitalism, 85
Caspian Sea, 112
Çeku, Agim, 270
Ceauşescu, Nicolae, 34, 47, 49, 51, 55, 63, 114
Census data, 30, 112. *See also* Population data
Central Asian Union (CAU), 94
Central European Initiative, 57
Chechnya, 89, 122, 289, 304n2
Chernomyrdin, Viktor, 141, 272
Chetniks, 198
China, 227, 229
Churchill, Winston, 191
Civil Alliance, 197
Clark, Wesley, 262
Clausewitz, Karl von, 85
Clinton, Bill, 241, 247, 254, 267, 271
Cold War, 9–10, 14–15, 292, 297, 301, 304; attitudes, and Primakov, 141; development of a common security order after, 132; and Hungary, 291; and the norm of inviolability, 12–13; practice of orderly promotion after, 14; and Russian diasporas, 132, 141–42, 144; and Serbia, 162, 192; and Yugoslavia, 192
Collectivization, 65
Commonwealth of Independent States (CIS), 89–91, 93–94, 98, 102–3, 108, 140–42
Communism: and Albania, 222–37, 245; collapse of, 5, 68; and Hungarian minorities, 20, 24–25, 42–56, 68, 75; and Russian diasporas, 84, 87, 117
Compromise of 1867, 22

Conference on Security and Cooperation in Europe (CSCE): and Hungarian minorities, 45, 51, 54–55, 57, 59, 74; and Serbia, 183; and Slovakia, 59. *See also* Organization for Security and Cooperation in Europe (OSCE)
Congress of Berlin, 187
Consociationalism, 74
Constantinescu, Emil, 66
Contact Group, 251, 252–56, 262, 265–66, 285n68
Cook, Robin, 264
Ćosić, Dobrica, 192
Council of Europe, 59–60, 65, 74, 75, 183
Council of the Transcarpathian District, 62
Council of Workers of Hungarian Nationality, 48–49
Crimea, 91, 94, 100, 106, 137, 139, 292
Crimean War, 139
Croatia, 6–7, 9, 11, 291, 295; and Albania, 227, 233, 238, 277; and Hungarian minorities, 70–76; and Russian diasporas, 127; and Serbia, 159–60, 162–64, 166–76, 181, 183–204
Croatian Democratic Union (HDZ), 162–63
Cultural Association of Hungarian Workers of Czechoslovakia (CSEMADOK), 44
Czechoslovakia, 4, 29–31, 40, 43–46, 58, 168

D

Daily Mail, 27
Dayton Accords, 9, 241–42, 247, 250, 303

Decentralization, 98, 192
Declaration on the Rights of
National Minorities, 63
Decommunization, theme of, 198
Demaçi, Adem, 242, 275
Democracy: and Albania, 245–46;
general importance of, 297,
298; and Hungarian minori-
ties, 71, 74–76; and interna-
tional peace, 130–32; and polit-
ical legitimacy, 126–30; and
Russian diasporas, 82, 90,
109–10, 113, 120, 126–32, 144;
and Serbia, 196–97
Democracy in America (De Toc-
queville), 298
Democratic Alternative, 261
Democratic Community of
Vojvodina Hungarians
(DCVH), 69
Democratic League, 235, 250,
253, 256, 269, 275
Deterrence, existential, 290
Dnieper River, 100, 114
Dobos, László, 44
Doyle, Michael, 131
Drašković, Vuk, 196
Dugolli, Bujar, 252, 255
Duray, Miklós, 45, 55, 61
Dzurinda, Mikulas, 61

E

Education: and Albania, 232–33;
and Hungarian minorities,
33–34, 44, 46–48, 58, 65–70, 72,
75; and Russian diasporas, 104
Estonia, 91, 94, 118–25
European Community (EC), 180,
183, 184, 203–4, 238
European Union (EU), 6, 57; and
Hungarian minorities, 61, 73;

and Latvia, 120; and Russian
diasporas, 113, 120–21, 136;
and Serbia, 204

F

Fatherland and Freedom Party,
121
Federalism, 74, 301–2
Federal Security Service, 123
Federation Council, 137
Ferdinand, Franz, 188
Fischer, Joschka, 267
Fischer, Stanley, 124
Founding Act, 134
Framework Convention on the
Protection of Minorities, 67
France, 10, 20, 23, 25–27, 298–99
French Revolution, 10
Friedman, Thomas L., 259
Frunda, György, 74

G

Gaidar, Yegor, 108, 144
Gashi, Alush, 286n82
Geci, Halit, 242
Gelbard, Robert, 251, 255
General Agreement on Tariffs
and Trade (GATT), 172
Georgia, 93
Georgievski, Ljubco, 261
Germany, 37, 38, 50, 141; and Al-
bania, 229, 251, 272; and ethnic
nationalism, 298–99, 300; inva-
sion of Yugoslavia by, 222; and
Poland, 295; and Serbia,
161–62, 202, 204. *See also*
Weimar Germany
Glasnost, 86
Gligorov, Kiro, 200
Glinka, Mikhail, 82
Göncz, Árpád, 61

Gorbachev, Mikhail, 5, 55; and the breakup of the Soviet Union, 89–90; and Lenin, 86–87; and the Sovietization myth, 86

Gorchakov, Aleksandr, 139–40

Grand National Assembly, 49

Great Migration of 1690, 187

Great War, 28

Greco-Turkish War, 295

Greece, 165, 220, 271, 278, 295

Groza, Petru, 41, 42

Gustov, Vadim, 108–9

H

Habsburgs, 10, 22, 165, 187–88, 294

Hajdari, Azem, 260

Hajrizi, Mehmet, 255–56, 265

Haliti, Xhavit, 265

Harmony, techniques of, 296–301

Havel, Václav, 58

Helsinki Committee, 277

Helsinki Final Act, 266

Helsinki process, 54–55

Hermet, Guy, 83

Herzegovina, 13, 159–60, 166, 167, 176, 181–204

Hill, Chris, 264

Hill plan, 265, 264

Hitler, Adolf, 3, 8, 276, 298; and Hungary, 27, 28, 37; and peace treaties, 27; and Serbia, 161, 162, 204

Holbrooke, Richard, 254–55, 262–63, 266

Horn, Gyula, 57, 60, 63

Horthy, Miklós, 26

Hoxha, Enver, 222, 224, 227, 230

Human Rights Watch/Helsinki, 244

Hungarian Coalition, 61

Hungarian Cultural Association of Subcarpathia (HCAS), 62

Hungarian Democratic Federation of Romania (HDFR), 64–66, 74

Hungarian Democratic Forum, 51

Hungarian Revision League, 35

Hungarian Writers' Union, 45

Hungary, 4, 6–7, 9, 11, 14–15, 289–91, 298; and irredentism, 26–37; minorities from, in Central Europe, 19–80; and political instability, 291; and Serbia, 199

Huntington, Samuel, 99

Hyseni, Hydajet, 250, 255, 265

I

Iliescu, Ion, 114, 127

Illyés, Gyula, 53–54

Ilyukin, Viktor, 124

Independent Hungarian Initiative, 58

India, 293

Indonesia, 296

Inflation, 130

Instability, sources of, 291–92

Internal Macedonian Revolutionary Organization (VMRO-DPMNE), 261

International Monetary Fund (IMF), 108, 124, 138, 168, 170, 175, 179–80, 183

International War Crimes Tribunal, 263, 271

Iran, 92, 94

Ireland, 127

Iron Curtain, 12, 43. *See also* Cold War

Irredentism, 26–37
Israel, 50
Italy, 74, 165, 199, 229, 271, 272
Ivanov, Igor, 135
Izetbegović, Alija, 163

J

Japanese-Americans, 127
Jashari, Adem, 250
Jászi, Oszkár, 24
Jeszenszky, Géza, 66
Judea, 2

K

Kádár, János, 51, 53–56
Kandić, Nataša, 277
Kant, Immanuel, 131
Karadjordjevich, Alexander, 163
Karadžić, Radovan, 201, 298
Károlyi, Mihály, 24–25
Kazakhstan, 14, 290; and nationalism, 295; and Russian diasporas, 92, 94, 110–14, 125, 145
Kazakh Statistics Agency, 112
Kazhegeldin, Akezhan, 113
KFOR, 205, 272, 273, 274
KGB, 123, 144
Khrushchev, Nikita, 91, 101
Király, Károly, 49
Kiriyenko, Sergey, 144
Kissinger, Henry, 134
Koha Ditore, 265, 275
Kosovo, 4–10, 172–84, 217, 228, 238–43, 250–79; and Hungarian minorities, 70; Liberation Army (KLA), 8, 215, 242, 250–56, 258, 263–65, 267, 269–71, 273–75; Plain, battle of, 189; and political instability, 292; and techniques of accommodation, 302–3

Kossuth, Lajos, 23
Kosumi, Bajram, 265
Koucher, Bernard, 272
Kozyrev, Andrey V., 88, 91
Krasniqi, Jakup, 255, 265
Krasts, Guntars, 121
Kravchuk, Leonid, 102–3, 105
Kristopans, Vilis, 121
Kuchma, Leonid, 100, 102–6, 136–37
Kun, Béla, 24–25, 28
Kyrgyzstan, 92, 293

L

Laitin, David, 15n4, 112, 304n2
Lake, Anthony, 133
Land reform, 29–30
Lansing, Robert, 294
Latvia, 91, 94, 118–25, 145
Le Monde, 124
League of Communists, 162, 169, 174, 182, 222, 234–35
League of Nations, 27, 38, 301
Lebed, Aleksandr, 89, 92, 116
Lenin, Vladimir, 14, 44, 84–85, 87–88. *See also* Leninism
Leninism, 84–86, 143. *See also* Lenin, Vladimir; Marxism-Leninism
Lenin's Revenge, 87
Levy, Jack S., 131
Linz, Juan, 128
Lithuania, 91
Little, Alan, 178
Luchinschi, Petru, 116
Lukashenko, Aleksandr, 107–8, 144
Lukin, Vladimir P., 101
Luzhkov, Yury, 89, 97, 98, 106, 137–38

M

Macartney, C. A., 15*n*7
McDonald, Gabrielle Kirk, 263
Macedonia, 4, 9, 292; and Albania, 214–18, 226, 228, 237–38, 243–45, 257–61, 277; and Serbia, 160–61, 166, 170, 181, 199
Magyar minorities, 19–23, 26–76
Magyar National Party, 33
Mahmuti, Bardhyl, 274
Majko, Pandeli, 260
Makashov, Albert, 124
Malcolm, Noel, 220, 277
Manelis, B. L., 85
Mansfield, Edward, 132
Maoz, Zeev, 131
Martonyi, János, 76
Marxism-Leninism, 5, 84–85, 87, 129. *See also* Leninism
Masaryk, Tomáš, 24
Matthias Corvinus (king), 23
Mečiar, Vladimír, 58, 59, 60, 61, 74
Meidani, Rexhep, 248
Memorandum of the Serbian Academy of Sciences and Arts, 194
Meshkov, Yuri, 105–6
Mesopotamia, 2
Microsoft Windows operating system, 294
Mihailović, Draža, 170, 190
Mill, John Stuart, 298, 307*n*29
Milo, Paskal, 248, 249
Milošević, Slobodan, 8, 70, 159–62, 177–79, 183–84, 195–204, 298; and Albania, 215, 246, 233–34, 236, 239–42, 249–55, 261–73, 276–77; and Hitler, analogy drawn between, 161, 162, 204; and the International Monetary Fund, 124; political goals of, 159–60; and Russia diasporas, 124, 127

Milutinović, Milan, 248, 269, 271
Minority Treaty, 34
Modernism, 95
Moldova, 94, 114–18, 125
Montenegro, 4, 215, 217; and Albania, 219–20, 231, 237; and Serbia, 176, 195, 200
Morozov, Oleg, 138
Moynihan, Daniel Patrick, 303
Mussolini, Benito, 190

N

Namier, Lewis, 1, 2
Napoleon Bonaparte, 10
National Democratic Front, 47
National equality, principle of, 52–53
Nationalism, 1, 5–6, 9; and Albania, 219–20, 224, 227, 230, 232, 233; and Hungarian minorities, 20, 24–25, 32, 42–44, 47–54, 58–59, 67–76; in the "nationalizing states," 99–125; and Russian diasporas, 81–82, 84–89, 95–30, 132–38, 143–44; and Serbia, 177, 178, 185–99, 201–3; and stability, 292–96
National question, 84–89
National Salvation Front (NSF), 63
Nazarbayev, Nursultan, 94, 110, 112
Nazi Party, 39
Nazism, 39, 105, 161, 267
Nedić, Aleksandar, 190
Netherlands, 203, 302
New Baltic Barometer survey, 123
Newly Independent States (NIS), 81, 83
New Russian Barometer survey, 94, 99

Nigeria, 13
North Atlantic Treaty Organization (NATO), 6, 8–10, 291; and Albania, 215–16, 246–47, 249, 252, 255, 257, 259, 262–73, 276; enlargement of, 132–38; founding of, fiftieth anniversary celebration of, 134; and Latvia, 120–21; and Hungarian minorities, 57, 61, 66–67, 69, 70, 73; Partnership for Peace, 134, 246; and Romania, 66, 67; Russia Founding Act, 138; and Russian diasporas, 84, 116–18, 120–21, 125, 132–38, 140–44; and the Russian quest for special status, 138–42; and Serbia, 162, 167, 205; and Slovakia, 61; and Yugoslavia, 57, 69–70, 136, 138, 141, 167, 249, 266–72
Nuclear weapons, 290

O

On Liberty (Mill), 298
Operation Horseshoe, 267
Orbán, Viktor, 57
Organization for Security and Cooperation in Europe (OSCE), 57, 241; and Albania, 248, 263–64, 266, 267; and Hungarian minorities, 60, 66, 74, 75; and Romania, 66; and Russian diasporas, 108, 113, 116, 121; and Slovakia, 60. *See also* Conference on Security and Cooperation in Europe (CSCE)
Otechestvo (Fatherland) Party, 97
Ottoman Empire, 10, 22, 32, 165, 186–87, 295

P

Pakistan, 94, 293
Panić, Milan, 163
Paris Peace Conference, 10, 40, 294
Paris Peace Treaty (1946), 72
Partnership for Peace (NATO), 134, 246
Party for Democratic Prosperity, 243, 244, 261
Party of Romanian National Unity (PRNU), 64–65
Pedagogical Academy, 244
Perestroika, 86
Perišić, Momčilo, 263
Perpetual Peace (Kant), 131
Pešić, Vesna, 194
Pirjevec, Dušan, 192
Poland, 11, 294–95
Popovski, Vlado, 260
Population data, 48, 230–31, 244–45. *See also* Census data
Primakov, Yevgeny, 84, 98–99, 109, 125; and anti-Semitism, 124; and NATO, 133–34, 137; and the Russian quest for special status, 138–42; and Yeltsin, 123
Primordialism, 95
Princip, Gavrilo, 188
Pristina University, 245
Prosperity, 296–97
Prussia, 299
Putin, Vladimir, 123–24, 144

Q

Qosja, Rexhep, 239, 255, 265–66, 270, 275
Quebec, 127

R

Rambouillet peace plan, 264–66, 270, 275, 303
Ranković, Aleksandar, 192, 226–28
Rašković, Jovan, 201
Raznatović, Željko, 197
Ressentiment, stance of, 193, 194
Revisionism, 37, 42, 56
Rilindja, 235
Romania, 11, 291; and Hungarian minorities, 25, 27, 55, 62–68, 71–72; and Russian diasporas, 114
Rose, Richard, 129
Rothermere, Lord, 27
Rugova, Ibrahim, 235, 239–42, 250–57, 265–66, 269–70, 274–75
Rukh Party, 90, 101
Russett, Bruce, 131
Russia, 3–4, 7–9, 14–15, 81–158, 289–91, 298; and Albania, 272; quest of, for special status, 138–42; and the security environment, 132–38
Russification, 96
Ruthenia, 30–31, 37, 40, 62

S

Sajudis independence movement, 91
Schapiro, Leonard, 128–29
SDA (Party of Democratic Action), 163, 164
SDP (Party for Democratic Change), 164, 182
Serbia, 7–9, 11, 14–15, 159–213, 289–91, 298; and Albania, 214–16, 217, 219, 231–49; and Hungarian minorities, 69; and political instability, 291; and techniques of accommodation, 302–3

Serbian Academy of Sciences and Arts (SANU), 177, 194
Serbian National Renewal Party, 196
Shala, Blerim, 265
Sharlet, Robert, 154n170
Shevardnadze, Eduard, 93
Silber, Laura, 178
Slota, Ján, 61
Slovakia, 4, 298; and Albania, 277; and Hungarian minorities, 28–31, 37, 39, 55–61, 70–76; and Serbia, 171, 173, 182, 202–3
Slovak Public Against Violence movement, 58
Smirnov, Igor, 114, 116
Smith, Anthony D., 95
Snegur, Mircea, 116
Snyder, Jack, 132
Sobchak, Anatoly, 91, 123
Solidarity Fund, 239
Soviet Union: and Albania, 227, 229; breakup of, 4, 13, 81, 96; and the Brezhnev Doctrine, 86–87; expansion of, under Stalin, 11; and Hungarian minorities, 43–55; and nationalism, 5–6, 293; rivalry with, end of, 9; and Russification, 96. *See also* Cold War; Russia
Spain, 74
Stability Pact, 59–60
Stalin, Joseph, 11, 224; and local nationalism, 86, 96; and Russian diasporas, 86, 96, 106. *See also* Stalinism
Stalinism, 21, 43. *See also* Stalin, Joseph
Stambolić, Ivan, 177
Starovoitova, Galina, 124
Stepan, Alfred, 128
Stepashin, Sergey, 123, 129, 138
Stoel, Max van der, 74, 121

Stokes, Gale, 278
Supreme Council of Belarus, 108
Surroi, Veton, 265, 266, 275
Switzerland, 74
Syla, Azem, 265, 270

T

Tahiri, Edita, 265
Tajikistan, 92–93
Talbott, Strobe, 134
Tatarstan, 97, 107
Taxation, 175–76
Teleki, Pái, 38
Tetova University, 244
Thaçi, Hashim, 265, 269–70,
    273–74
Tirgu-Mures confrontation, 64
Tito, Josip Broz, 52, 68, 170,
    172–74; and Albania, 223–25,
    233; and Hungarian minori-
    ties, 42; purge of the liberal
    leadership in Serbia by, 193–94
Tocqueville, Alexis de, 298
Transcarpathian district, 46,
    61–62
Transdniestria, 114, 116, 117–18
Transitional Council, 272
Transitology, 83–84
Transylvania, 5, 31–35, 40–42,
    47–52, 54
Treaty of Conventional Armed
    Forces in Europe (CFE), 133
Treaty of Friendship, Coopera-
    tion and Partnership, 102
Treaty of Trianon, 21, 25, 30–33
Tudjman, Franjo, 162, 163, 183,
    200, 298
Turkey, 187, 220, 286n86, 295
Turkmenistan, 92

U

Udovički, Jasminka, 195

Új Symposion, 53
Ukraine, 13, 14, 290; and Hun-
    garian minorities, 46, 61–62;
    and political instability, 292;
    and Russian diasporas, 90–94,
    100–107, 136–37, 143, 145; and
    Serbia, 204
Ukrainian-Russian treaty (1997),
    107
Ulmanis, Guntis, 121
Unemployment, 176, 180
Union or Death (society), 188
United Democratic Movement,
    265, 270, 275
United Nations: and Albania,
    241, 251–52, 255, 261–62, 272,
    276; Charter, 262; founding of,
    12; Interim Administration
    Mission in Kosovo (UNMIK),
    205, 272, 273; Security Council,
    123, 160, 205, 252, 255, 261–62,
    272, 276; and Serbia, 160, 172,
    205; and Yugoslavia, 42, 172
University of Pristina, 173
U.S.-Baltic Charter of Partner-
    ship Commission, 135
Uzbekistan, 92, 106, 293

V

Vatra Romaneasca (Romanian
    Hearth) movement, 63
Vedrine, Hubert, 264
Vienna Award, 37–38, 41
Vike-Freiberga, Vaira, 121–22
Visegrad Group, 57
Vojvodina, 42–43, 171, 172, 174,
    178

W

Waffen-SS Legion, 118
Warsaw Pact, 46, 133, 229

Weimar Germany, 7, 11, 292. *See also* Germany
Wilson, Andrew, 100
Wilson, Woodrow, 24, 294
World Bank, 108
World War I, 4, 7, 8, 10–11, 294–95; and Albania, 251; creation of Yugoslavia after, 164–65; Germany after, 167; and Hungary, 290, 303; and Russian diasporas, 88; and Serbia, 164–65, 167, 191
World War II, 3–4, 6–7, 10, 12; and Albania, 222, 233, 268; Holocaust during, 295; mistreatment of Japanese-Americans during, 127; and Russian diasporas, 86, 106; and Serbia, 159, 165, 190–91, 196, 199; Stalin's regime after, 86; and Yugoslavia, 190

X

Xhaferri, Arben, 278

Y

Yavlinsky, Grigory, 134
Yeltsin, Boris, 81, 90; agreements signed by, 102–4; and Albania, 255; and Belarus, 108–9; and the breakup of the Soviet Union, 89–90; and demographic reali-ties, 97; election of, 129; firing of Stepashin by, 138; and Kuchma, 102–4; and Leninism, 88; and Lukashenko, 108; and Moldova, 116; national security "Concept" signed by, 97–98; and NATO, 135, 136, 141; and Primakov, 123; Rose on, 129; and Russian hard-liners, 93; and the Treaty of Friendship, Coopera-tion and Partnership, 102
Young Democrats-Hungarian Civic Party, 70
Yugoslavia, 4, 6, 9, 11, 14, 162–83; and Albania, 221–64; breakup of, 13, 168–83, 202–4, 237–49; creation of, after World War I, 164–65, 189; and economic failure, 296; and Hungarian minorities, 35–37, 39, 52–55, 68–70; invasion of, by Ger-many, 222; and NATO, 57, 69–70, 136, 138, 141, 167, 249, 266–72; and Russian diaspo-ras, 82–83; and techniques of accommodation, 303

Z

Zëri, 265
Zhirinovsky, Vladimir, 97
Zogu, Ahmet (King Zog), 222
Zyuganov, Gennadi, 97, 102, 124